Lecture Notes in Computer Science 2496

Edited by G. Goos, J. Hartmanis, and J. van Leeuwen

T0217160

Springer
Berlin
Heidelberg
New York
Barcelona
Hong Kong
London
Milan
Paris
Tokyo

Kevin C. Almeroth   Masum Hasan (Eds.)

Management
of Multimedia
on the Internet

5th IFIP/IEEE International Conference on Management
of Multimedia Networks and Services, MMNS 2002
Santa Barbara, CA, USA, October 6-9, 2002
Proceedings

 Springer

Series Editors

Gerhard Goos, Karlsruhe University, Germany
Juris Hartmanis, Cornell University, NY, USA
Jan van Leeuwen, Utrecht University, The Netherlands

Volume Editors

Kevin C. Almeroth
University of California at Santa Barbara
Department of Computer Science, Santa Barbara, CA 93106, USA
E-mail: almeroth@cs.ucsb.edu

Masum Hasan
Cisco Systems Inc.
170 West Tasman Drive, San Jose, CA 95134, USA
E-mail: masum@cisco.com

Cataloging-in-Publication Data applied for

Die Deutsche Bibliothek - CIP-Einheitsaufnahme

Management of multimedia on the Internet : proceedings / 5th IFIP/IEEE
International Conference on Management of Multimedia Networks and Services,
MMNS 2002, Santa Barbara, CA USA, October 6 - 9, 2002 / Kevin C. Almeroth ;
Masum Hasan (ed.). - Berlin ; Heidelberg ; New York ; Hong Kong ; London ;
Milan ; Paris ; Tokyo : Springer, 2002
  (Lecture notes in computer science ; Vol. 2496)
  ISBN 3-540-44271-5

CR Subject Classification (1998): C.2, H.5.1, H.3, H.5, K.3

ISSN 0302-9743
ISBN 3-540-44271-5 Springer-Verlag Berlin Heidelberg New York

Springer-Verlag Berlin Heidelberg New York
a member of BertelsmannSpringer Science+Business Media GmbH

http://www.springer.de

© Springer-Verlag Berlin Heidelberg 2002
Printed in Germany

Typesetting: Camera-ready by author, data conversion by Markus Richter, Heidelberg
Printed on acid-free paper   SPIN: 10870716   06/3142   5 4 3 2 1 0

Preface

The 5th *IFIP/IEEE International Conference on Management of Multimedia Networks and Services (MMNS)* was held in Santa Barbara, California. This was the fifth year that MMNS brought together researchers and developers to discuss the latest advances and explore future directions for managing multimedia in the Internet.

As in past years, MMNS continues to be a competitive conference, attracting excellent papers with some of the top new ideas. This year we received 76 papers, of which 27 were accepted for inclusion in the program. What was particularly impressive this year was the large percentage of very high quality papers. The submissions made the job of the program committee extremely difficult.

The span of topics this year ranged from network-layer traffic differentiation to application-layer consideration for multimedia traffic. At the network layer, a number of papers attempt to develop better solutions for differentiated services in the Internet. The issue of bandwidth sharing, particularly in wireless networks, is the focus of another set of papers. Next, by increasing the level of abstraction slightly, researchers are focusing on managing "services". In particular, these services include one-to-many communication and video distribution architectures. Finally, from the user perspective there are two problems. What can applications do to help achieve better quality from the Internet? And, how can technology be applied to enterprise management systems? Taking the papers in the MMNS program together, they offer a range of solutions to key problems in managing multimedia traffic in the Internet.

The success of MMNS can largely be attributed to high caliber committee members who worked hard to make the conference the best it could be. Each paper submitted was typically sent to four reviewers. After all the reviews were collected, papers with conflicting reviews were extensively discussed by committee members in an attempt to reach a consensus and fully examine the contributions of the work. The result is a program consisting of numerous outstanding papers. As conference chairs, it was a delight to work with such a dedicated and conscientious program committee.

Finally, this year sees the continued support of IFIP and IEEE. Once again they handled many of the administrative tasks to make the conference run as smoothly as possible. In addition, we would like to thank Cisco Systems, Inc. for their financial support of MMNS.

For those of you who attended the conference we hope you found this year's MMNS to be a truly valuable experience, making new friends, visiting with old colleagues, and developing new ideas for next year's MMNS.

October 2002

Kevin Almeroth, Masum Hasan
Conference Chairs

MMNS 2002 Organizing Committee

Steering Committee

Ehab Al-Shaer, DePaul University
Raouf Boutaba, University of Waterloo
Giovanni Pacifici, IBM Research
Guy Pujolle, University of Pierre & Marie Curie

Conference Co-chairs

Kevin Almeroth, University of California, Santa Barbara
Masum Hasan, Cisco Systems

Proceedings Chair

Srinivasan Jagannathan, University of California, Santa Barbara

Web Chairs

Robert Chalmers, University of California, Santa Barbara
Sami Rollins, University of California, Santa Barbara

Program Committee

Kevin Almeroth, University of California, Santa Barbara
Masum Hasan, Cisco Systems
Nazim Agoulmine, University of Evry
Ehab Al-Shaer, DePaul University
Nikos Anerousis, VoiceMate.com
Mohammed Atiquzzaman, University of Oklahoma
Supratik Bhattacharryya, Sprint ATL
Raouf Boutaba, University of Waterloo
Greg Brewster, DePaul University
Andrew Campbell, Columbia University
Russ Clark, Georgia Tech
Metin Feridun, IBM Research
Dominique Gaiti, University of Troyes
Mohsen Guizani, University of West Florida
Abdelhakim Hafid, Telcordia
Go Hasegawa, Osaka University
Ahmed Helmy, University of Southern California
David Hutchison, Lancaster University
Muhammad Jaseemuddin, Ryerson Polytechnic
Gautam Kar, IBM Research
Ahmed Karmouch, University of Ottawa
Lundy Lewis, APRISMA
Derong Liu, University of Illinois, Chicago
Songwu Lu, University of California, Los Angeles
Hanan Lutfiyya, University of Western Ontario
Allen Marshall, Queen's University, Belfast
Ahmed Mehaoua, University of Versailles
Jose Neuman de Souza, University Fed. do Ceara
Jose M. Nogueira, University Minas Gerais
Giovanni Pacifici, IBM Research
Guy Pujolle, University Pierre & Marie Curie
Ed Perry, HP Labs
Puneet Sharma, HP Labs
Chien-Chung Shen, University of Delaware
Rolf Stadler, Columbia University
Ralf Steinmetz, University of Darmstadt
Burkhard Stiller, UniBw Munich and ETH Zurich
John Vicente, Intel
Alaa Youssef, IBM Research

Additional Reviewers

Nadjib Achir, LIP6
Toufik Ahmed, University of Versailles
Chedley Aouriri, Intel Corporation
Hakima Chaouchi, LIP6
Louise Crawford, Queen's University, Belfast
John Cushnie, Lancaster University
Paulo-Andre Da-Silva-Goncalves, LIP6
Marcelo Dias de Amorim, LIP6
Martin Dunmore, Lancaster University
Christopher Edwards, Lancaster University
Idir Fodil, 6WIND
Anelise Munaretto Fonseca, LIP6
Dan Gavenda, DePaul University
Alberto Gonzales, CTR/Columbia University
Jan Gerke, ETH Zurich
Gerard Gross, Intel Corporation
Hazem Hamed, DePaul University
Hasan, ETH Zurich
Bassam Hashem, Nortel Networks
David Hausheer, ETH Zurich
Pascal Kurtansky, ETH Zurich
Rui Lopes, Lancaster University
Dimitris Pezaros, Lancaster University
Nicholas Race, Lancaster University
Priya Rajagopal, Intel Corporation
Govindan Ravindran, Soma Networks
Abdallah Rayhan, Ryerson University
Lopa Roychoudhuri, DePaul University
Stefan Schmid, Lancaster University
Nabil Seddigh, Tropic Networks
Sakir Sezer, Queen's University, Belfast
Paul Smith, Lancaster University
Steven Simpson, Lancaster University
Perry Tang, Intel Corporation
Yongning Tang, DePaul University
Nguyen Thi Mai Trang, LIP6
Jason Yoa, DePaul University
Bin Zhang, DePaul University

Table of Contents

Distributed Video Architectures

Management Systems

Differentiated Network Services

User Level Traffic Adaptation

Multicast Congestion Control

A QoS Network Management System for Robust and Reliable Multimedia Services

S. Das, K. Yamada, H. Yu, S. S. Lee, and M. Gerla

Computer Science Department
University of California, Los Angeles
Los Angeles, CA 90095-1596
{shanky, kenshin, heeyeoly, sslee, gerla}@cs.ucla.edu

Abstract. In this paper, we introduce a practical network management system with QoS for multimedia traffic. Today, multimedia applications have evolved significantly and have become an essential part of the Internet. In order to effectively support the newly emerging network traffic, the underlying network protocols need to be aware of the characteristics and demands of the traffic. The proposed network system is ready to address the varied characteristics of multimedia traffic and can assure a high degree of adherence to the quality of service demanded from it. Considering the need for reliable QoS services, the system is also equipped with fault tolerance capability by provisioning multiple QoS paths. Moreover, the system has been practically designed and implemented to provide "cost-effective" QoS support with respect to control overhead. It deploys measurement-based QoS path computation and call admission scheme which may be deemed ineffective for bursty multimedia traffic. However, results conclusively prove that provisioning multiple paths and utilizing them in parallel in our system not only provides high fault tolerance capability but also effectively accommodates multimedia traffic by relieving its burstiness with multiple paths. We present the architecture of the system and discuss the benefits gained for multimedia traffic.

1   Introduction

Recently, the Internet has become a significant medium for real-time data as demands for multimedia services become more and more pervasive. In order to accommodate such new types of traffic in the Internet, researchers have addressed various issues with respect to provisioning QoS. QoS provisioning issues consist of several building blocks such as *resource assurance, service differentiation*, and *routing strategies*. Among these, QoS routing as a routing strategy is essential since it executes computations to find QoS-feasible paths. [1,2] address a possible use of the Bellman-Ford algorithm in the link state (OSPF) routing environment for QoS routing. In addition, [3,4] showed specifications and feasibility of such QoS routing approaches. The development of the Multiprotocol Label Switching Protocol (MPLS) [5] and the increased acceptance of Traffic Engineering as an important component of routing protocols has accelerated the coming of age of QoS routing.

K.C. Almeroth and M. Hasan (Eds.): MMNS 2002, LNCS 2496, pp. 1–11, 2002.

In this paper, we present a practical QoS network management system based on the proposed OSPF-based QoS architecture. This consists of OSPF with traffic engineering extensions running as the routing protocol, MPLS for explicitly routing packets, and a QoS path provisioning algorithm that also serves as a fundamental call admission control (CAC). The proposed network system is equipped with fault tolerance capabilities for unreliable network environment. This fault tolerance issue in QoS provisioning is considered as a very important aspect especially when mission-critical applications are running. This issue has been highlighted in [6,7]. Accordingly, a novel approach was recently introduced in [8] which deploys an effective algorithm to produce multiple QoS paths. Multiple QoS path provisioning also showed various benefits such as even network resource utilization and cost-effective link state information acquisition [9]. In addition, our proposed system in this paper provides statistical QoS guarantees. That is, it deploys measurement-based path computations and call admissions without any resource reservations. This helps in reducing the system complexity and achieving relatively fast QoS provisioning. It is well known that multimedia applications are likely to produce highly bursty traffic with hardly predictable characteristics [10,11]. This high burstiness keeps measurement-based approaches from properly performing. This is because the severe traffic fluctuation misleads the approaches into producing non-feasible QoS paths and making incorrect call admission decisions. The system that we propose carries out rather reliable call admissions and performs well since it provisions multiple QoS paths and spreads network traffic over them. Thus, it diffuses traffic burstiness and attenuates its negative impact.

Targeting such a fault-tolerant and reliable QoS-service architecture, we have implemented a QoS testbed. In this paper, we present the system architecture with the QoS routing approach for multiple path and show the fault tolerance capability with reliable multimedia services. In Section 2, the routing algorithms are briefly reviewed. Section 3 depicts the entire network system architecture, and Section 4 presents experiment results obtained with the implemented network system and demonstrates its effectiveness in representative traffic scenarios.

2   QoS Algorithms

The network system presented in this paper has QoS routing mechanisms which are ready to serve QoS applications in both conventional and fault-tolerant ways. The mechanisms serve as a simple call admission control (CAC). When a QoS application comes in and looks for its corresponding QoS services, it consults the underlying QoS routing algorithm (i.e., Q-OSPF with the enhanced routing algorithms in our case) for feasible paths. If no feasible path is found, the connection is rejected and the application exits. Thus, the QoS routing path computation algorithm not only provides the capability of finding QoS paths but also plays an important role in CAC. As previously mentioned and discussed in [8], we adopted the two different QoS routing algorithms in our system; the conventional single path algorithm and the newly introduced multiple path algorithm.

The single QoS path computation algorithm with multiple QoS constraints derives from the conventional Bellman-Ford algorithm as a breadth-first search algorithm minimizing the hop count and yet satisfying multiple QoS constraints. Each node in the network builds the link state database which contains all the recent link state advertisements from other nodes. With Q-OSPF, the topological database captures dynamically changing QoS information. The link state database accommodates all the QoS conditions, and we define each condition as a QoS metric and each link in the network is assumed to be associated with multiple QoS metrics which are properly measured and flooded by each node. Each of these QoS metrics has its own properties when operated upon in the path computation. The principal purpose of the path computation algorithm is to find the shortest (i.e., min-hop) path among those which have enough resources to satisfy given multiple QoS constraints, rather than the shortest path with respect to another cost metric (e.g., maximizing available bandwidth or minimizing end-to-end delay).

The proposed multiple QoS path algorithm is a heuristic solution. We do not limit ourselves to strictly "path disjoint" solutions. Rather, the algorithm searches for multiple, maximally disjoint paths (i.e., with the least overlap among each other) such that the failure of a link in any of the paths will still leave (with high probability) one or more of the other paths operational. The multiple path computation algorithm can then be derived from the single path computation algorithm with simple modifications. This multiple path computation algorithm produces incrementally a single path at each iteration rather than multiple paths at once. All the previously generated paths are kept into account in the next path computation. The detailed descriptions of the single and the multiple path algorithms are in [8].

3 System Architecture

The testbed consists of PCs running Linux, and all the QoS-capable features are embedded in the Linux kernel. Each of the machines has several modules running on it, namely the *link emulator, metric collector, OSPF daemon, MPLS forwarding* and the *applications*, and the entire system architecture is depicted in Fig. 1. The following sections describe in more detail each of these modules individually, explaining their functions and their implementation issues.

3.1 Link Emulator

The testbed that we implement uses the wired Ethernet LAN in the lab, as the physical communication medium. Since we want to emulate several scenarios with widely varying link capacities and propagation delays, we require a network emulator to do the job for us. We emulate the characteristics of bandwidth and delay over a link using tc, the Linux kernel traffic shaper and controller. tc can emulate a wide variety of policies with hierarchies of filters and class based queues on the outgoing interfaces. We require simple bandwidth and delay emulation

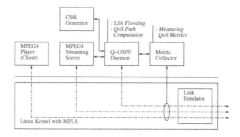

Fig. 1. The entire QoS system architecture for the experiment testbed.

which can be done quite easily. A simple "`tc qdisc add dev eth0 root tbf rate 10kbps latency 10ms`" emulates a 10 Kbps link with a latency of 10 ms on the `eth0` interface. Since we have bursty multimedia traffic, the buffer size is also an important factor, and after a few experiments, we settled on a value of 25 Kbits as a reasonable buffer to accommodate burstiness.

3.2   Metric Collector

To provide QoS, reserving bandwidth and bounding on delay for a connection, we require the knowledge of link characteristics at all times. This information is needed by the QoS allocation module which looks at the current usage of the network and figures out if the new request can be satisfied or not. The link metric collection module, therefore, is an integral part of any routing scheme implementation that provides QoS routing.

The OSPFD (OSPF daemon) implementation does not have any link characteristics measurement module. The metrics we are interested in are the available bandwidth in the link and the delay. One could think of other metrics also, such as queue length, loss probability, etc., but bandwidth and delay are the two most important metrics used in QoS routing. Thus, our design goal was to write a module to measure these two metrics and integrate this code with the existing OSPFD implementation.

For bandwidth metric collection, we opted to simply use the log file maintained in `/proc/net/dev/` which contains information about the number of packets and bytes received and transmitted on each interface. By examining this file at regular intervals, we calculate the bandwidth used on the each outgoing interface. Delay metric collection is done using the 'ping' utility to send ping probes to the other side of the link and collect the delay value. The metric collection code sends ping message and collects bandwidth values from the `/proc/net/dev` log file, every time interval (typically 10 ms). The values collected are exponentially averaged to smooth out the fluctuations.

3.3   Q-OSPF Daemon

To propagate QoS metrics among all routers in the domain, we need to use an Interior Gateway Protocol (IGP). OSPF is one of the major IGPs and significant researches have been recently made on OSPF with traffic engineering extensions. We selected the open source OSPF daemon (OSPFD) [12,13] to implement our QoS routing scheme. [14] defines Opaque LSA for OSPF nodes to distribute user-specific information. Likewise, we define our specific Opaque LSA entries by assigning new type values in the Opaque LSA format shown in Fig. 2.

When OSPFD runs at routers, it tries to find its neighbor nodes by sending HELLO messages. After establishing neighbor relationship, OSPFD asks the metric measurement module to calculate the QoS metrics of the established link. OSPFD gives as input the local interface address and the neighbor router interface address to the metric measurement module and generates the opaque LSA for each interface. The LSA contains the available bandwidth and queuing delay metric obtained from the metric measurement module. LSA update frequency is currently restricted to MinLSInterval (5 seconds). In our implementation, we followed this restriction, but we feel that the LSA update interval is an important parameter for the correctness of our algorithms because if there are too frequent changes to the generated LSA, there will be miscalculations during the QoS path computation due to the flooding delay.

In addition to LSA flooding, OSPFD exchanges router LSAs to build a full network topology. Router LSAs originate at each router and contain information about all router links such as interface addresses and neighbor addresses. We bind the link metrics that we are interested in, viz. bandwidth and delay to the opaque LSA specified by the link interface address. Thus, we introduce the pointer from each link of a router LSA to the corresponding opaque LSA as shown in Fig. 3. Whenever OSPFD receives router LSAs or opaque LSAs, it just updates the link pointer to point to the new traffic metrics reported by that link.

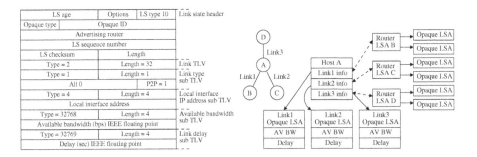

Fig. 2. Opaque LSA format.   **Fig. 3.** Router LSAs.

3.4   MPLS

One of the key assumptions for Q-OSPF to be effective is the capability of setting up explicit paths for all packets of a stream to use. Thus, we need to pin down the path that a connection uses. One of the main advantages of MPLS is its efficient support of explicit routing through the use of Label Switched Paths (LSPs). With destination-based forwarding as in the conventional datagram networks, explicit routing is usually provided by attaching to each packet the network-layer address of each node along the explicit path. This approach makes the overhead in the packet prohibitively expensive. This was the primary motivation behind deploying MPLS at the lower layer instead of using something like IP source-routing or application level forwarding.

3.5 Applications

An integral part to the whole process of making a testbed was the development of applications running on top of this architecture. These applications request QoS-constrained routes, generate traffic, and in turn change the QoS metrics of the network. We used the open source *Darwin Streaming Server* distributed by Apple [15] to stream MPEG-4 files using RTSP over RTP. The open source mp4player from the MPEG4IP project [16] was used to play these files over the network. Modifications to the source code involved extending the capabilities of the server and the player for streaming and playing over multiple paths, and designing an interface for the server to interact with Q-OSPF daemon and request paths to the client. For the experiments involving CBR traffic, we used a home-brewed traffic generator which generates UDP traffic at a given rate in either single path or multiple path mode.

4 Experiments

We performed two kinds of experiments for this paper. The first set of experiments involves comparing the performance of Q-OSPF with respect to the throughput of multimedia traffic using single paths and using multiple paths. The second set involves comparing the performance of Q-OSPF with respect to fault tolerance and robustness of multimedia connections using single path and using multiple path. Fig. 4 shows the network topology for the experiments. 9 nodes (i.e., routers) are connected directly to each other through 1.5 Mbps links.

We performed experiments in certain representative scenarios where multiple path is expected to give better results as well as in totally general scenarios.

1. The first experiment involved sending six streams of multimedia traffic from QOS6 to QOS5. There are three disjoint paths available that satisfy the bandwidth constraints, QOS6 - QOS2 - QOS1 - QOS5, QOS6 - QOS7 - QOS4 - QOS5, QOS6 - QOS9 - QOS8 - QOS5. Let us name them *QPath1*, *QPath2* and *QPath3* respectively. We run the experiment in both *Single Path* and *Multi Path* mode. In single path mode, each stream uses one of the three QPaths, while in multi path mode, each stream uses all the three QPaths. Results are in Fig. 5 and Fig. 6.

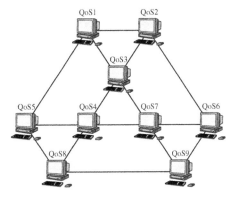

Fig. 4. The QoS testbed topology

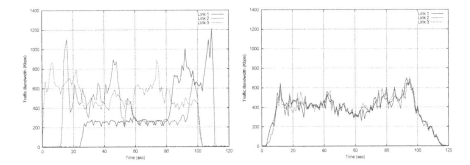

Fig. 5. Throughput profile on the three QPaths: single path

Fig. 6. Throughput profile on the three QPaths: multi path

2. The second experiment involved sending three CBR streams of 800 Kbps first on the three QPaths, and then introducing the six multimedia streams later. In the single path case, the calls get accepted and follow the same paths as before, two streams each sharing one QPath, but in this case due to burstiness, the total throughput on each path frequently goes above the 1.5 Mbps limit, and thus there are losses. One the other hand, with multi path mode, the traffic on all the paths is much smoother, and thus the total traffic never goes above 1.5 Mbps on any link and thus there are no losses. This scenario demonstrates the benefits on multi path with respect to smoothening the bursty traffic. Results are in Fig. 7 and Fig. 8.

3. The last experiment in this set was a totally general scenario, in which random connections were set up, and the traffic characteristics were measured. We first perform the experiment for well behaved CBR traffic in the single path mode and then perform it with bursty multimedia traffic first using single path mode and then multiple path.

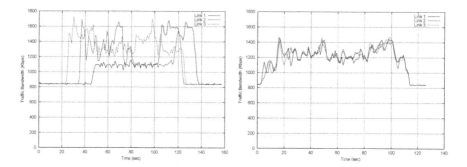

Fig. 7. Throughput profile on the three QPaths: single path

Fig. 8. Throughput profile on the three QPaths: multi path

Owing to performance bounds of the multimedia server and the CPUs of the nodes, we reduced the bandwidth emulated on each link to 1 Mbps. The total number of connections generated in both CBR and multimedia case was 28. These connections were generated using randomly chosen source and destination from the 9 QoS routers. The measured traffic characteristics are the usual throughput profile on the links. Fig. 9 shows the throughput characteristics on each link when CBR traffic is in the network and Q-OSPF is in single path mode. Fig. 10 shows the throughput characteristics when multimedia traffic (of the same average bandwidth as the CBR in the previous experiment) is in the network and Q-OSPF is in single path mode. We can see that with multimedia the performance of Q-OSPF is visibly worse and the traffic frequently goes above the threshold of 1 Mbps. Fig. 11 shows the throughput characteristics when multiple paths are provisioned. Here we see that on each link the burstiness is much less and the overall QoS constraints are being satisfied. The throughput is below the 1 Mbps limit. Thus, we clearly see the benefits of using multiple paths even in a completely random general scenario.

The second set of experiments examines the fault tolerance capability by provisioning multiple QoS paths between source and destination and spreading packets over the multiple paths. The network topology is the same as in Fig. 4. Here again we experiment with two extreme traffic scenarios, well behaved CBR traffic and bursty multimedia traffic. The pairs of source and destination nodes for the connections are randomly selected, and the link failures occur also randomly during the execution of the experiments. For the link failure model, we used a exponential distribution such that the average link down time is equal to 5 seconds. The number of multiple paths requested is kept at 3. The statistics which we collect during this experiment is the amount of time for which each connection is down. A connection is said to be down when none of its packets are reaching the destination for 2 seconds.

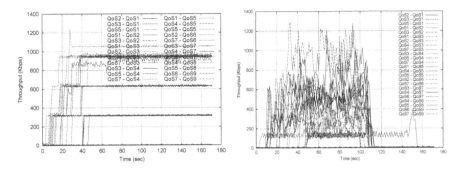

Fig. 9. Throughput profile on every link: CBR: Single Path

Fig. 10. Throughput profile on every link: Multimedia: Single Path

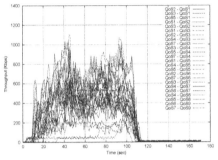

Fig. 11. Throughput profile on every link: Multimedia: Multi Path

The duration of the experiments was 10 minutes each. Fig. 12 and Fig. 13 show the connection down-time percentage when single path or multiple paths are provisioned for the connections for both the CBR traffic case and the multimedia case. The result shows that multiple path provisioning has lower connection down rate as expected. We can see that the benefits although almost equal are slightly lesser than in the CBR traffic case. The reason is that a lot of multimedia calls do not get 3 multiple paths due to the burstiness of existing connections which fill up the pipe. Thus, we show that we have greater fault tolerance for multimedia traffic when we provision multiple QoS paths compared to single QoS path. Note that the experiments are slightly different in spirit from the simulation experiments in [8]. In [8], the authors assume that a connection gets dropped when all its paths have one or more faults, and does not come up automatically when the fault gets repaired. However, the experiments have enough similarity to give similar results.

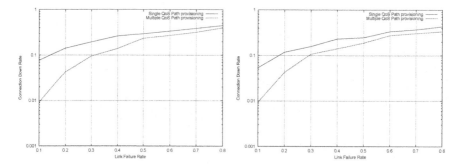

Fig. 12. Connection down rate as a function of link failure rates: CBR

Fig. 13. Connection down rate as a function of link failure rates: Multimedia

5   Conclusion

We proposed a QoS network management system in which QoS provisioning mechanisms are measurement-based and multiple QoS paths are computed. With the practical system implementation and experiments, we discussed the interaction of measurement-based call admission and bursty multimedia traffic. The experiment results verified that the bursty nature of multimedia traffic degrades the performance of measurement-based approaches. However, when multiple QoS paths are provisioned, the burstiness becomes diffused and its negative impact is lessened as the results showed. We also evaluated the fault tolerance capability of the network and found that the multiple paths provide a high degree of robustness in servicing QoS applications. In conclusion, provisioning multiple paths during call admission not only attenuates the impact of the burstiness but also provides highly robust QoS services.

References

1. R. Guerin, A. Orda, and D. Williams. QoS Routing Mechanisms and OSPF Extensions. In *Proc. of Global Internet (Globecom)*, Phoenix, Arizona, November 1997. 1
2. Dirceu Cavendish and Mario Gerla. Internet QoS Routing using the Bellman-Ford Algorithm. In *IFIP Conference on High Performance Networking*, 1998. 1
3. G. Apostolopoulos, S. Kama, D. Williams, R. Guerin, A. Orda, and T. Przygienda. QoS Routing Mechanisms and OSPF Extensions. Request for Comments 2676, Internet Engineering Task Force, August 1999. 1
4. Alex Dubrovsky, Mario Gerla, Scott Seongwook Lee, and Dirceu Cavendish. Internet QoS Routing with IP Telephony and TCP Traffic. In *Proc. of ICC*, June 2000. 1
5. E. Rosen, A. Viswanathan, and R. Callon. Multiprotocol Label Switching Architecture. Request for Comments 3031, Internet Engineering Task Force, January 2001. 1

6. Shigang Chen and Klara Nahrstedt. An Overview of Quality of Service Routing for Next-Generation High-Speed Networks: Problems and Solutions. 12(6):64–79, November 1998. 2
7. Henning Schulzrinne. Keynote: Quality of Service - 20 Years Old and Ready to Get a Job? *Lecture Notes in Computer Science*, 2092:1, June 2001. International Workshop on Quality of Service (IWQoS). 2
8. Scott Seongwook Lee and Mario Gerla. Fault Tolerance and Load Balancing in QoS Provisioning with Multiple MPLS Paths. *Lecture Notes in Computer Science*, 2092:155–, 2001. International Workshop on Quality of Service (IWQoS). 2, 2, 3, 9, 9
9. Scott Seongwook Lee and Giovanni Pau. Hierarchical Approach for Low Cost and Fast QoS Provisioning. In *Proc. of IEEE Global Communications Conference (GLOBECOM)*, November 2001. 2
10. S. Floyd. Comments on Measurement-based Admissions Control for Controlled-load Services, 1996. 2
11. Lee Breslau, Sugih Jamin, and Scott Shenker. Comments on the Performance of Measurement-Based Admission Control Algorithms. In *INFOCOM (3)*, pages 1233–1242, 2000. 2
12. J. Moy. OSPF Version 2. Request for Comments 2328, Internet Engineering Task Force, April 1998. 5
13. John T. Moy. OSPFD Routing Software Resources. http://www.ospf.org. 5
14. R. Coltun. The OSPF Opaque LSA Option. Technical report. 5
15. Apple Computer. The Darwin Streaming Server.
http://www.opensource.apple.com/projects/streaming. 6
16. Bill May David Mackie and Alix M. Franquet. The MPEG4-IP Project. http://mpeg4ip.sourceforge.net. 6

Federated Accounting Management System Architecture for Multimedia Service Usage Management

B. Bhushan[1], T. Gringel[1], C. Ryan[2],
E. Leray[2], E. de Leastar[2], and J. Cloney[2]

[1]Fraunhofer-FOKUS, Kaiserin-Augusta-Allee 31, D-10589 Berlin Germany
{bhushan, gringel}@fokus.fhg.de
[2]TSSG, Ground Floor Unit A, Waterford Business Park, Cork Road Waterford Ireland
{edeleastar,jcloney,cryan,eleray}@tssg.wit.ie

Abstract. Service consumers are increasingly becoming aware of QoS and service subscriptions. Service providers (SPs) are also recognizing the opportunity to generate revenue by bundling services in packages and providing them to customers. Standardization bodies have begun to address requirements of charging and usage accounting management as SPs are increasingly relying on them. Federated accounting management concept stems from these developments. It specifically supports the requirement of SPs to co-operate in a federated manner and share the revenue. It also supports the requirements of charging and billing being subcontracted to a third-party. This paper proposes that standard-based interfaces and shared information model, and a well-accepted development methodology are keys to enabling co-operation between SPs. It presents a requirement analysis and a federated accounting management system architecture, which are based on the recommendations laid down by TMForum, IPDR, OMG and IETF organisations. The architecture supports mediation, rating, charges aggregation, settlement, and online billing.

1   Introduction

As broadband networks and UMTS infrastructure are more widely deployed, IP-based services are set to become more advanced and will be provided in customized manner. As a result, the demands of e-business are going to drive rapid innovation and SPs are going to provide new services in a B2B (business-to-business) environment. Recent surveys such as [1] and [2] chart these developments in a B2B context. The emergence of the B2B market is also influencing the way services are provided, charged and billed. An important feature in this development is the usage of composite services (several service bundled in one). Composite services consist of several types of services and can be provided by ISPs, virtual private network (VPN) and application service providers (ASP). In this environment, SPs face two important challenges: (1) operating services and maintaining QoS across multiple administrative domains; (2) integrating the charges for various services that make up a composite service. These challenges manifest themselves in a number of ways. For example, new types of B2B interactions have emerged mainly at the levels of service operations

K.C. Almeroth and M. Hasan (Eds.): MMNS 2002, LNCS 2496, pp. 12–24, 2002.
© Springer-Verlag Berlin Heidelberg 2002

management. New requirements for customer support, Quality of Service (QoS) maintenance, charge settlement and billing have also emerged [3]. SPs have also acknowledged the emergence of a new stakeholder in the existing business model. The EU-sponsored IST project FORM in which the work presented in this paper was carried out termed this new stakeholder *inter-enterprise service provider* or IESP.

The IESP can function as a portal to a wide array of services (simple or composite). It can also function as a service retailer or as a specialised service provider who composes new services on customers' demand and deal with the customer queries and bills on behalf of other SPs. This role of IESP adds a new dimension to Billing business model, which is, outsourcing of Billing operations management. Charging and billing is something without which SP businesses will not be commercially viable [4, [5]. Outsourcing Billing is proving to be effective because billing operations are increasingly becoming a specialised and automated task.

The core management operations that SPs require involve customer support, QoS management, charging, billing, and SP settlement [13]. The IESP can play a crucial role in providing them where it deals with customer queries and SLAs (Service Level Agreements) on behalf of SP [6]. It can also do the settlement of the charges amongst SPs if they collectively provided the service and present the bill to the customer. Here one can see three functional areas in operation: (1) *customer support and SLA management*; (2) *QoS management*; (3) *charging and billing*.

1.1   Related Works

Organisations such as TMForum (Telemanagement Forum), IPDR (Internet Protocol Detail Record) and IETF, OMG (Object Management Group) and ETSI (European Telecommunication Standards Institute) have come up with guidelines to develop OSS in these three functional areas. The work presented in this paper is relevant to these organisations; hence a brief introduction to their works is given in this section.

TMForum through its work on TOM (Telecom Operations Map) [7] and its successor eTOM [8] has produced a map of operations processes that can be used for the development of three functional areas mentioned above. Within TOM, these functional areas are called *F*ulfilment, *A*ssurance and *B*illing (or *FAB*).

The main goals of IPDR organisation are to define an open, flexible record format (the IPDR Schema) for exchanging usage information and essential parameters for any IP transaction [9]. For the specification of interfaces between OSSs (operation support system) and BSSs (business support system), the IPDR organisation has adopted the core functional roles and interfaces that TMF's TOM [7] has identified.

The AAA (Authentication, Authorisation, Accounting) WG of IETF has also produced a set of RFC on accounting management protocol and services [10], [11]. The AAA group can be compared to TOM process flow-through where OSS is regarded as a complete process chain. In the chain *F*ulfilment feeds relevant information into *A*ssurance, which in turn feeds relevant information into *B*illing (FAB). FAB themselves roughly correspond to Authentication, Authorisation and Accounting. Of these three broad areas, this paper focuses on the *Billing* area of TOM or *Accounting* sub-group of AAA WG.

Having introduced the paper, an outline of the rest of the paper is given here. Section 2 presents the concept of the federated accounting management. Section 3 describes the business context and presents requirement analysis model. Section 4 presents the federated accounting information model. Section 5 describes the federated accounting system architecture in details. Section 6 outlines the technology used to implement the system architecture. Section 7 concludes this paper and discusses the future work.

2   Federated Accounting Management Concept

This section introduces the concept of federated accounting management and briefly describes its main characteristics.

Distribution of Operational Processes and Use of Interdomain Interfaces: Service mediation, rating, and billing processes are distributed over several administrative domains. These processes interoperate by the means of well-defined interfaces. Interfaces may also exist at the boundary between two domains, in which case they are also called *Reference Point*. The processes mentioned here are already widely known through the TOM map where they are parts of the Billing process [7]. Interfaces between processes have also become known through the work of IPDR Operational Model [9]. However interfaces between domains are not covered in sufficient details by TOM and IPDR and still require further investigation. This paper presents the design of interdomain interfaces (see Sect. 5).

Inter-working of Fulfilment, Assurance and Billing Processes: These three processes take part in so-called end-to-end process flow. Although the Fulfilment and Assurance are separate functional areas in their own right, they co-operate with the Billing process. Federated accounting management incorporates this end-to-end process flow where Fulfilment and Assurance provide Billing with SLA and QoS details. This enables the service provider to apply different tariffs for different types of subscriptions or QoS provided.

A More *Inclusive* View of Accounting Information: Federated accounting management holds a more inclusive view in which usage information and charges details together form a part of accounting information. IPDR organisation is working on a standardised information model. However, the work of IPDR is confined to producing specification of usage information exchanged. The concept of federated accounting management complements the work of IPDR organisation by providing rationale for and specification of charge details as a part of federated accounting information model (see Sect. 4).

Use of Differential Tariffs: Charging regime uses tariffs that vary with customer types, QoS or any other factor that SPs choose to use. An earlier work by authors on this can be found in [12].

Charge Aggregation and Payment Settlement: In federated accounting management several third-party providers collectively provide their services. IESP acts on behalf of both customer and third-party providers. It aggregates charges and invoices the customer for all the services used; a single invoice is sent to the customer. IESP may also do the settlement for all third-party providers. Work on supplier-provider settlement is currently being addressed in eTOM [8].

3   Business Context and Functional Requirements Analysis

This section presents the business context, actors involved in federated accounting management and the roles they play (see Fig. 1). The information exchanged between various roles is also shown. This is followed by a description of operations processes involved in federated accounting management. Thereafter key functional requirements that the architecture implements are presented as a use case diagram.

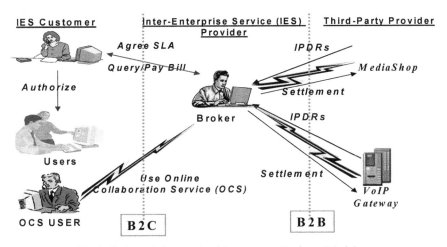

Fig. 1. Federated Accounting Management Business Model

In the business context, the IESP ensures that the customer (or *IES Customer* in Fig. 1) has access to a variety of services that it needs. They are provided by many SPs (*third-party provider* in the Fig. 1), who are IESP's partners. OCS (online collaboration service) is one such service, which packages MediaShop and VoIP services in single application. MediaShop is multimedia contents distribution service.

The *IES Customer* is the subscriber of IES and negotiates and signs a SLA with the IES Provider. It can be a business (organisation) or a private customer. It receives and pays bills for the services used. *End-User* is a person who uses Inter-Enterprise Service. End-user may be a private user or he/she may work for the IES Customer.

The *IESP*, as the customer-facing SP, is responsible for SLA handling, tariff negotiation, customer care and accounting aspects of the services offered to the customer by the IESP's partners in a value chain. It provides the IES Customer with access to communication, application, and information services, which are in turn provided by third-party providers (i.e., IRS Provider). IES Provider performs the task of charging and billing of service usage and charge settlement among IES Customers and third-party SPs. IES Provider acts as a service retailer and maintains contracts with third-party providers and does the final payment settlement.

The *IRS (Information Retrieval Service) Provider* is a third-party provider that provides its services to IES Customer. The third-party providers must be able to charge the IES Customer for service usage, details of which are sent to the IESP as *IPDR documents* (also shown Fig. 1). IESP incorporates the various IPDR documents by means of aggregation and rating processes and provides a consolidated bill to the

IES Customer. In order for interaction to occur between the IESP and third-party providers, IPDR Master schema and specifications are used as a shared information schema and a set of interfaces that all parties support.

3.1   Operations Processes Involved in Federated Accounting Management

Fig. 2 illustrates the federated accounting management operations processes in the context of the FAB of TOM [7]. Fig. 2 is based on an original version of FAB figure [7]; various aspects of federated accounting management have been added to original FAB figure and illustrated in Fig. 2. An enhanced version of IPDR XML Schema [9] is used to model accounting information (or E-IPDRs shown in Fig. 2) that is exchanged between various business processes. Sect. 4 discusses the enhancement done to Master IPDR Schema.

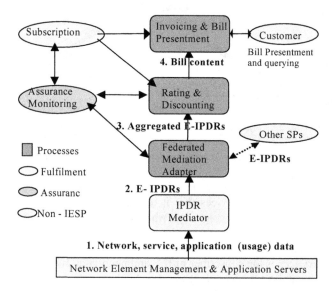

Fig. 2. Federated Accounting Management Operations Process

3.2   Functional Requirements and Use Case Model

A comprehensive list of functional requirements is discussed in [12]. The authors have worked on those requirements and narrowed them down to a set of requirements that must be addressed in the design. The narrowed set includes the following requirements and the use case diagram (see Fig. 3) models them:

1. Usage-based charging and real-time response levels.
2. Support for convergence of services (e.g., voice and data).
3. Adaptable federated service mediation facility.
4. Support for a variety of OSS and service value chain.

5. Charge detail aggregation of composite services.
6. Automated inter SP domain accounting and settlement.
7. Interaction with legacy billing systems.
8. Increased demand for guaranteed QoS and related discounting.
9. Rapid service deployment.

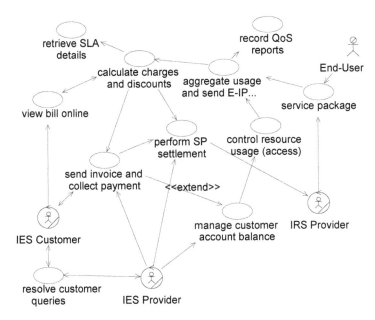

Fig. 3. Federated Accounting Management Use Case Model

Up to this point, this paper has presented the business context and key requirement. The following sections present the information model and design of the accounting management system.

4   Federated Accounting Information Model

This section presents the federated accounting information model. Before providing the details of the model, a brief rationale for developing it is given. If accounting management facilities are to be distributed then the SPs must use an information model that: (1) adapts easily to new services; (2) maintains consistency of information during exchange; (3) helps SP in using the information generated by other SPs with little or no effort. Clearly, a common structure, semantic, and syntax of information is crucial in a successful acceptance and functioning of federated accounting management and this is where the federated information model comes into play.

4.1   Enhancements to IPDR Master Schema

The governing idea behind federated accounting management is to support distribution of service mediation and rating facilities across several SP domains. A note for those readers who are familiar with FAB of TMForum, this support means enabling accounting management at BSS level. This is the level at which rates are applied, charges calculated and bills presented.

This is required for the aggregation of charges when a service package is provided to the customer. This package is an agreement that allows the customer to use many services. Several SPs may be involved in providing the package. Clearly SPs have a stake in the bill payments that IESP receives from customer. SPs themselves may want to calculate charges for the services that they contribute towards the service package. IESP's role in this scenario is to aggregate charges and do SP payment settlement. Therefore SPs require means by which they can exchange usage data as well as charges in a single IPDR document. This requirement means that information model must be able to support exchange of usage data as well as charge details.

In order to meet this requirement, this paper proposes federated accounting information model. The model is an enhancement on Master IPDR Schema [9] with a CE (charge entry) has been added to the latter. This enhancement enables IESP to the charge aggregation and settlement in a multi-SPs environment.

The CE holds information such as the charge that the customer owes to SP, discounts provided by the SP, etc. These details are received by IESP and used during SP settlement and payment. If several SPs send their charge details, all charges are aggregated and user pays a single bill for a service package.

The Master Schema that the IPDR organisation has produced does not provide for such requirements because it is outside the scope of the organisation. The federated accounting information model, which is based on Master IDPR Schema, does provide for such requirement. SPs can use CE (charge entry) E-IPDR document (E stands for *enhanced*) to include charge details and transfer them with IESP.

4.2   Federated Accounting Information Service-Specific Using UML Notations

It must be noted that IPDR information model and all model derived from it are implemented using XML Schema Recommendation. This essentially gives us three schemas, which follow from each other in this order: (1) Master IPDR Schema; (2) Federated Accounting Information Schema; (3) Federated Accounting Service-specific Schema.

Master IPDR Schema: This is the output of IPDR organisation and the basis for all service-specific schemas and federated accounting information schema. This schema has a service-specific part, which can be adapted to any service. SPs can use this schema and adapt its service-specific part to any service for which usage mediation is required. Since federated accounting information schema is based on Master IPDR schema, it is worthwhile to mention it here. For a fuller description, please refer to IPDR specification [9].

Federated Accounting Information Schema: This schema is essentially the Master IPDR Schema, plus the CE element. The CE element is optional and gets populated when SP wishes to calculate its own charges, leaving charge aggregation to IESP.

Federated Accounting Service-Specific Schema (see Fig. 4): This schema inherits all the elements of Federated Accounting Information Schema, including CE. It is adapted to provide for and record usage events that are specific to a service. For the development of federated accounting management system, two service-specific schemas have been developed; they are for MediaShop (shown in Fig. 4) and VoIP service. Usage attribute specific to these two services are added to the ones that are inherited from federated accounting information schema. The usage information forms the content of *E-IPDR Document*.

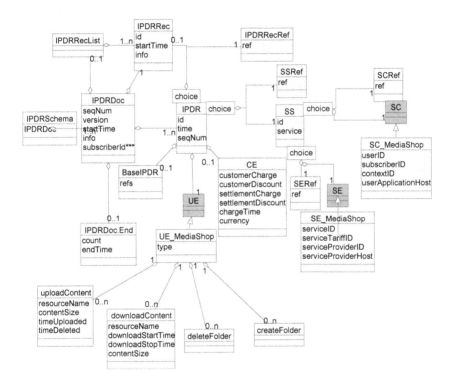

Fig. 4. Federated Accounting Service-Specific Schema for MediaShop Service

Fig. 4 serves three purposes. Firstly, it illustrates how Master IPDR Schema has been used to implement federated accounting information model. One can see the position and contents of CE element in the Fig. 4. Secondly, it also illustrates how federated accounting information model can be specialised to a particular service or network. It also shows how usage information generated by MediaShop can be modelled. Finally, to best of authors' knowledge, no UML diagram of IPDR Master Schema exists. Therefore the Fig. 4 allows UML users to see how various XML elements of IPDR Schema fit together to form a complete E-IPDR document.

As the reader will see in the next section, federated accounting service-specific schema is an integral part of the system architecture and E-IPDR documents are the information objects communicated at the interfaces such as interdomainAcctMgmt, Rating Bureau Service Interface. All E-IPDR documents are XML instance documents. Information objects (mainly usage and charge details) are integrated under a single tree-shape structure. Integration is done at the level of federated accounting management system boundary. Objects and structure are shared by all system interfaces, a shared information schema.

5   System Architecture

This section provides the definitions of components and interfaces of the federated accounting management systems architecture. The architecture is specified using UML (Unified Modelling Language) therefore a mapping of the components and interfaces onto to UML artefacts, namely boundary class, control class and information object is also briefly discussed (see Fig. 5).

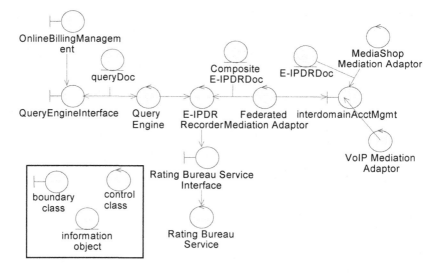

Fig. 5. Components of Federated Accounting Management System Architecture

An interface can be considered a *boundary class*. A component itself can be considered a *control class*. The term boundary has a strong connotation of something *facing outside* or an *interface*. Among other matters, an interface deals with communication protocols. If communication protocol changes, we need to change the interface; we need not change the component that offers the interface.

The term control class has a strong connotation of something that *receives things* and *manipulates* them without paying much attention to how they will be sent to other components. The *things* that control objects manipulate are *information objects*. A component deals with co-ordination task, leaving communication task to its interface. A component can have its own state, change its state independently of other components, and can send external event whenever it wishes to do. If co-ordination task changes we may need to change the component but we can still use the same interface offered by the component.

It co-ordination work is not complicated and sizeable enough then we may not need control object at all. A boundary object will be enough to do communication as well co-ordination.

5.1   Interfaces (Boundary Objects)

InterdomainAcctMgmt: This interface resides between IESP and third-party providers and supports usage mediation in a federated SPs environment. This interface is provided by the Federated Mediation Adaptor (FMA) component. Mediation Adaptors (MAs) can use this interface to send E-IPDR documents to FMA. **OnlineBillingManagement:** This interface resides between IESP and IES Customer. This is the customer entry point to the charging information stored by the IESP.

5.2   Components (Control Objects)

Federated Mediation Adaptor (FMA): This component supports collection and aggregation of E-IPDR documents and generation of a composite E-IPDR document. The documents are aggregated under a single usage session (or parent session), which denotes the beginning and end of service package use.
MediaShop Mediation Adaptor (MA): MediaShop MA collects usage data, records the usage events, generates an E-IPDR document, and sends it to FMA.
VoIP Mediation Adaptor (MA): The main role of VoIP MA is to collect usage data, record the usage events, generate an E-IPDR document, and send it to FMA.
QueryEngine: It ensures the availability of all recorded IPDR information.
E-IPDR Recorder: The IPDR Recorder takes upon the role of IPDR documents recorder/transmitter. It implements method specifies in the IPDR "Protocol Primitives and Parameters" specification (Push, Pull, Subscribe, etc).
Rating Bureau Service (RBS): RBS applies tariffs, calculates discounts and calculates charges for individual services that make up a composite service, for example, OCS (i.e., Online Collaboration Service mentioned in Sect. 3). Then all individual charges are aggregated into a single composite service charge. Finally, RBS generates and stores a rated/discounted E-IPDR document.

5.3   Information Objects (E-IPDR Documents)

Composite E-IPDR Doc: This is a *list* of E-IPDR documents, each of which is an instance document of federated accounting service-specific schema. Its main role is to carry usage information detailing usage of a composite service, as opposed to usage information for a singleton or simple service.
QueryDoc: An XML instance document, containing end-user's query.
E-IPDR Doc: This is *single* E-IPDR document, based on federated accounting service-specific schema. Its main role is to carry usage information for a singleton service. This information is details of usage events that are generated when the end-user uses MediaShop or VoIP services.

6   System Integration and Technology Architecture

This section discusses how a prototype federated accounting management system was implemented. Fig. 6 shows the technologies that have been used to implement and integrate components of the prototype.

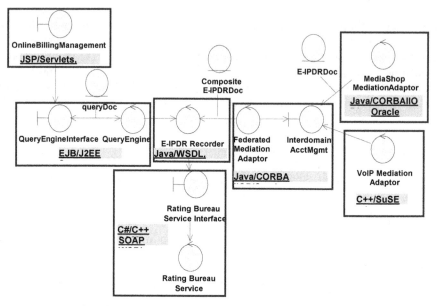

Fig. 6. Federated Accounting Technology Architecture

The main components (see Sect. 5.2) of the prototype were implemented using C++, Java, and C# and used IIOP, RPC COM/CORBA-SOAP for communication with one another. Interfaces were specified using CORBA IDL and WSDL.

Information objects (or E-IPDR and Composite E-IPDR documents) exchanged between components are XML instance document. They are modelled on federated accounting service-specific schema, which is specified using W3C XML Schema, Structure and Data Types. Oracle is used as storage for E-IPDR documents.

The technology described here has yielded many benefits. Java and EJB make architecture components highly portable. XML/WSDL allows service providers to deploy accounting components as Web-services and seamlessly exchange accounting information. Oracle enables direct mapping of IPDR structure (XML documents) onto database tables. SOAP binds IPDR documents and HTTP tightly, making document exchange them over the internet easy. OSP (Open Service Platform) is a service subscription and access management middleware, which is being developed by Fraunhofer-FOKUS. It is based on TSAS (Telecommunications Service Access and Subscription).

A number of lessons were learnt from the development and evaluation of the federated accounting system. Some important lessons are discussed here.

An interface at the boundary between two SP may possess more functionality then assigned during design phase. For example, interdomainAcctMgmt interface may also monitoring and recording network QoS deterioration. Interfaces implementations are kept simple because of the more complex structures (defined in XML) that are passed.

Standardised information model (i.e., IPDR Master Schema) proved to be useful in developing federated accounting service-specific schema. It also reconciles two differing sets of concerns (information-wise), service mediation and charge details that lead to a common goal, i.e., Billing.

There are trade-offs when using XML schemas, which are more complicated than DTDs (Document Type Definitions) but are richer and useful in expressing a vocabulary of federated accounting management business process.

7   Conclusions and Future Work

This paper has presented a requirement analysis model and architecture of federated accounting management system. The system presented has been developed and tested and evaluated in two trials. In order to ensure that components and interfaces provided the required functionality, test case result were mapped onto requirement captured in the requirement analysis phase. Mapping resulted in a set of key requirements that were important for the development of federated accounting management system. They are listed in Sect. 3.

One of the prime aims of the research and development was to validate the specification being developed in standardization community and feed the result into standardization process. It is fair to say that authors have successfully achieved this aim. Results obtained have been provided as contributions to a number of international organizations. A significant proportion of design specification has been provided as input to Telecom Domain Task Force of OMG, which is also developing a specification of federated charging and rating facility.

An initial business model and use cases have been provided to AAA WG of IRTF (Internet Research Task Force). A contribution containing intermediate business model and informational model has been provided to TMForum through a TM World conference. There are further plans to provide an enhanced IPDR Master Schema as an input to IPDR organization.

Several areas in which future work can be carried out have identified. Authors consider the use of XML and Webservice technologies (e.g., XSLT, WSDL, SOAP) for component and interface definitions an important area for future work. Therefore further research into Web service technologies will be carried out.

Use of XMI and XSLT in transforming technology-neutral system architecture to a technology-specific system is essential if federated accounting management is to appeal to E-commerce. Another area, which is gaining acceptance, is ebXML. It will be used for the definition of federated accounting management business process.

Further development will also be carried out into a generic approach to aggregated services mediation. In this generic approach, functionality will be added to FMA component, thus making them adaptable to several different types of communication protocol and technologies. Components and interfaces will be further enhanced to support QoS and a guaranteed delivery of E-IPDR documents.

Last but not the least, the authors would like to thank the members of PLATIN group (Fraunhofer-FOKUS Germany) and TSSG group (WIT Ireland) for their constructive comments. This research work was carried out under the auspices of EU-sponsored IST project FORM (IST-1999-10357). More information on FORM can be obtained from www.ist-form.org or from the authors.

References

1. Varshney, et al, "Voice Over IP", Communications of ACM, Jan 2002,Vol 45,No 1.
2. Bartholome, Lloyd, et al, "A Practical Approach For Implementing E-Commerce Programs in Business School", Communications of ACM, January 2002, Vol. 45, No. 1.
3. Howard-Healy, "Billing the future of content", Billing, Issue 7, September/October 2000.
4. Browne, "Have you got money to burn?", Telecommunications International, Aug 2001.
5. Whitworth, "The Unknown World of 3G Tariffs" Telecommunications International, Feb 2001.
6. Dobson "The SLA Battleground", Telecommunications International, March 2002.
7. Telecom Operations Map, Approved Version 2.1, TeleManagementForum, March 2000.
8. TMForum GB921: "eTOM: The Business Process Framework For The Information and Communication Services Industry", Members Evaluation Version 2.0, October 2001.
9. Network Data Management – Usage (NDM-U): For IP-based Service, Version 2.6, October 2001, IPDR Organisation.
10. RFC 2924: Accounting Attributes and Record Format, Category: Informational, Authors: N. Brownlee, A. Blount, September 2000.
11. RFC 3127: Authentication, Authorization, and Accounting: Protocol Evaluation, Category: Informational, Authors: Mitton, Johns, Barkley, Nelson, Patil, June 2001.
12. Bharat Bhushan, et al, "Federated Accounting: Service Charging and Billing in a Business-to-Business Environment", IM2001: 2001 IEEE/IFIP International Symposium on Integrated Network Management Proceedings, Seattle, May 2001.
13. Huston, Geoff, "Interconnection, Peering and Settlements: Part-I", The Internet Protocol Journal, Volume 2, Number 1, March 1999.

Policy-Based Quality of Service and Security Management for Multimedia Services on IP Networks in the RTIPA* Project

Valérie Gay[1], Sandrine Duflos[1], Brigitte Kervella[1], Gladys Diaz[2], and Eric Horlait[1]

[1] LIP 6 : Laboratoire d'Informatique de Paris 6,
8, Rue du capitaine Scott, 75015 Paris, France
{Valerie.Gay, Sandrine.Duflos, Brigitte.Kervella, Eric.Horlait}@lip6.fr

[2] L2TI – Institut Galilée – Université Paris 13,
99 Av. J. B. Clément, 93430 Villetaneuse - France
Gladys.Diaz@galilee.univ-paris13.fr

Abstract. This paper summarizes the research work that has been conducted in the context of the RTIPA project on policy-based QoS (Quality of Service) and security management for distributed multimedia services. It presents an architecture allowing the derivation of policies from the service level down to the network level. It is a step towards an end-to-end QoS and security management for distributed multimedia services running on the new generation of IP networks.

1   Introduction

Enabling end-to-end QoS and security management of distributed services is a research topic that has been going on for some years now. Services are getting adaptive and QoS-aware and the network is now able to deal with different levels of QoS and security. However, there is still a gap between the services and the network, and achieving end-to-end QoS and security for distributed applications is still bringing some challenges to the middleware and network research communities.

In the framework of the RTIPA project [1], our role was to reduce that gap and to make a step towards end-to-end QoS and Security management for distributed multimedia services running on the new generation of IP networks.

In the project we dealt with policy-based network management therefore we naturally focused our research on a policy-based solution. The major part of current standardization works on policy-based management is done at the Internet Engineering Task Force (IETF) and are positioned at the network level. The IETF proposes a centralized management [2]. This model is composed of several entities: the Policy Repository (PR) where policies are stored, the Policy Decision Point (PDP)

---

* RTIPA: Real-Time Internet Platform Architectures, ITEA (Information Technology for European Advancement) project

K.C. Almeroth and M. Hasan (Eds.): MMNS 2002, LNCS 2496, pp. 25-35, 2002.

that decides the policies to apply, and Policy Enforcement Points (PEP) that enforce the policies. At the network level, IETF also defined an information model: The Policy Core Information Model (PCIM) [3] [4]. It has also defined extension for QoS management: The QoS Policy Information Model (QPIM) and the QoS Device Data path Information Model (QDDIM) [5] [6]. For security management, the IPsec Configuration Policy Model (ICPM) [7] describes the information for policy management. Other research works propose solutions to specify, manage and enforce policies at network or middleware level. Examples are found in [8] that describes a solution for IPsec policies, [9] that bases its solution on the Corba Security framework [10] and [11] that proposes an object-oriented solution to manage and enforce policies expressed in a language called Ponder [12].

Our work presents an architecture for end-to-end QoS and security management of distributed multimedia services. It focuses on the top-down aspects of the policy management and its relationships with security and QoS managers. It also describes how it could be implemented on an Ipv6 network that takes into account the service level policies thanks to a refinement process.

This paper describes in Section 2 an architecture for policy-based management of QoS and security for multimedia services. Section 3 describes the policy refinement process. Section 4 presents how the policies are supported at the network level on the RTIPA platform. Section 5 concludes on open issues and perspectives

2   An Architecture for Policy-Based QoS and Security Management

Our architecture is presented in Fig. 1. It is separated into three abstraction levels: service, middleware and network. Fig.1 only highlights the elements and interactions we are discussing in this paper. Other managers that do not appear in the figure include the billing, mobility and Service Level Agreement (SLA) managers. At the service level, QoS, security, and policy rules are expressed in high-level terms understandable by the end-users. A QoS contract specifies the service requirements and offerings in terms of QoS and security. Its granularity can vary from 'per service' to 'per flow type'. The service level policy rules can express general administration rules (such as routing policy rules in the case of network management) in high-level terms. The policy manager maps them onto middleware policy rules. The service level QoS, policy and security requirements and offerings are translated into middleware level policy rules (using the middleware QoS, security and policy managers) to be integrated into the new set of middleware policy rules.

The middleware policy manager checks the policy rules and resolves the conflicts. Feedback can be provided to the application level and can lead, for example, to the re-negotiation of QoS or price or to the adaptation of the content.

The QoS and security managers check if the different QoS and security requirements specified at the service level can be met by the infrastructure and provide feedback to the application on the status of the infrastructure with respect of the application QoS and security. The resource manager [13] has a view of the available resources. It enables the QoS and security managers to know if their QoS and security can be fulfilled. Especially for real-time service it is important to have strict resource management policies so the real-time QoS requirements are valid during the lifetime of the service.

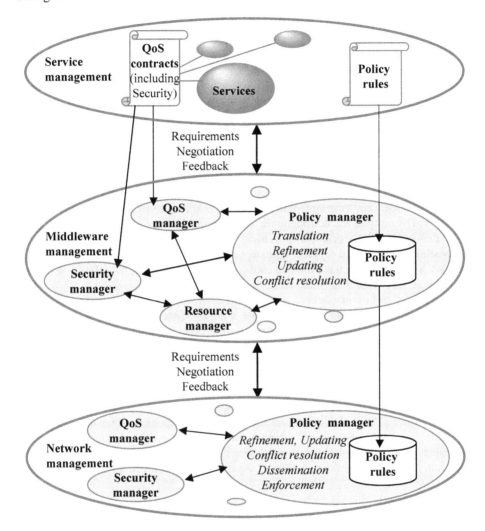

Fig. 1. Policy-Based QoS and Security Management Architecture

The middleware level policy rules are then translated into network-level policy rules. The network policy manager adapts the rules to reflect the requirements it gets from the other network managers (such as a network QoS manager). It is disseminating the rules and enforcing the policies. It resolves the conflicts between the policy rules and provides feedback to the middleware managers.

QoS management and mapping have been discussed in our previous work [14]. In that paper, the content of the QoS contracts are detailed, they express the QoS requirements and obligations of the distributed services. The QoS manager [13] monitors the network QoS and can initiate operations like QoS re-negotiation in case of QoS violation. It checks if the environment can and will fulfill the contracts. It requests the resource manager for certain resources (e.g. buffer, CPU-time, Audio-device) that can be allocated to a certain service. There is a need of cooperation of QoS managers in different domains.

The goal of the security manager is to provide the necessary security that is required by the multimedia service. The security manager analyses and translates these requirements, expressed in the QoS contract at service level, in security parameters depicting the security aspects to provide. For example, in the case of a Video-on-Demand (VoD) service, a minimum of security is necessary to protect the audio/video streams against a fraudulent listening. In such a case confidentiality is necessary. The resource manager is checked with to see if a security protocol can set this security aspect. If yes, it sends the parameters to the policy manager that integrates them in the middleware level policy rule. In order to produce the network level policy rules, the network level security manager must be able to provide the security protocols and cryptographic algorithms available to set the security required. In our VoD example, the confidentiality parameter becomes ESP and (3DES, DES) ESP being the IPsec protocol providing confidentiality and 3DES and DES a proposition of associated cryptographic algorithms. The security and policy managers interact a last time for the protocol configuration, in our example IPsec, when the network policy rule is disseminated.

In case the policy managers cannot resolve the conflicts, the security managers must be able to provide an alternative solution (e.g.: security parameters re-negotiation at middleware level or proposition of others protocols and cryptographic algorithms at network level) to produce a new policy and to secure the service. If it is not possible the service should be turned off.

The managers shown in Fig. 1 would typically be located on every node and cooperate among each other to manage the distributed multimedia service. We are not describing their internal mechanisms in this paper.

Policy rules [15] evolve through a life cycle (specification, refinement, static and dynamic conflict resolution, dissemination, enforcement, updating (includes disabling, withdrawing and deleting). Actions related to this life cycle are shown in Italics in Fig. 1. In the following section, we focus on the refinement process.

3   The Policy Refinement Process

This section describes the policy translation and refinement process from the middleware to the network levels. Our work is based on the TMN (Telecommunications Management Network) architecture defined by the ITU-TS [16] and the research work of [17]. The different managers presented at middleware level derive from the service level the rules to be generated and included in the middleware-level policy rules. A possible template for the middleware level policy is described in Table 1 where <ConfigurationType> is the network configuration type (e.g.: point to point, multicast, star, fully meshed.), <TransportService> is the requested transport service (e.g., ATM, SDH/PDH, IP), *<ApplicationType>* is the requested application (real player, Netscape, video on demand), *<SourceUser|user..*>* and *<DestinationUser..*>* are the identified users who will participate to the application. *<QualityType>* is the requested QoS level (e.g.: premium, gold, silver, bronze). *<SecurityConfiguration>* is the requested security configuration including confidentiality, authenticity (integrity and authentication of packet sender), mutual authentication, non-repudiation, tunnel mode and anti-replay.

The different parameters values are checked by the middleware managers described in the previous section (e.g.: are the recorded members known by the service? is the requested security configuration correct?)

Once the request is validated, it can be translated into a middleware-level policy rulerepresented here under the form "If condition Then provide configuration" that will support the implementation of the QoS and security requested.

Table 1. Middleware level policy

IF SourceUser|users = *<SourceUser|user..*>* AND DestinationUser = *<DestinationUser..* (Optional)* > AND ApplicationType = *<ApplicationType>* THEN PROVIDE *<ConfigurationType>* of *<TransportService>* for *<ApplicationType>* with Guarantee *<QualityType>* Quality and *<SecurityConfiguration>* Security

The middleware level policies are only understandable at that level. They use middleware-level parameters such as a specific security configuration (such as confidentiality) or the users' name. Some parameters do not have to be managed by the network because they are dealt with at a higher level but the rest of the parameters have to be converted in network level parameters. In the RTIPA project, our network is based on IPv6 therefore we are using IP Diffserv and IPsec [18] [19] [20] [21] at network level. A simplified translation table is presented in Table 2

Table 2. Simplified Translation from Middleware to Network-Level Parameters

	Middleware level parameters	Network level parameters
User	*<Users>* (e.g.: End-User1)	*<UserIpAddress>* (e.g.: 2.2.2.2)
Application	*<ApplicationType>* (e.g.:VoD)	*<PortNo> <QoSDirection> <ConnectionType> <InterfaceIPAddress>* (e.g.: 8000, uni, unicast, 2.2.0.0))
Configuration and transport	*<ConfigurationType>* and *<transport type>* (e.g. point to point, IP)	Identical
QoS	*<Quality Type>* (e.g.: gold)	*<PhBType>* (e.g.: AF11)
Security	*<SecurityConfiguration>* (e.g.: confidentiality)	*<Sec-prot>*, *<C-Algo>*, *<A-Algo>*, *<Mode>*, *<No-Replay>* (e.g.: ESP, (3DES, DES), NULL, IPsec_transport, NULL)

In Table 2 and Table 3, *<UserIpAddress>* corresponds to the users IP addresses, *<PortNo>* is the port used, *<QoSDirection>* is the QoS direction (unidirectional or bi-directional) the *<ConnectionType>* is the connection type (e.g. unicast, broadcast, multicast) and *<PhBType>* is the desired Per-Hop behavior. *<Sec-Prot>* is the IPsec security protocol used (AH or ESP), *<C-Algo>* is a list of algorithms used for confidentiality (e.g.: {private, key cryptography} or NULL), *<A-Algo>* is a list of algorithms used for authenticity (e.g.: {digest function, public key cryptography} or signature cryptography or NULL), *<Mode>* is the security mode (tunnel or transport) and *<No-Replay>* is set to True or False to indicate that it can or cannot be replayed.

For instance, the security parameters, expressed at the middleware level, will be replaced by the IPsec security protocol (Sec-Prot), a list of algorithms used for confidentiality (C-Algo), a list of algorithms used for authenticity (A-Algo), the security mode (tunnel or transport) used for the creation of secure tunnel (e.g. VPN) and the anti-replay protection (No-Replay). Furthermore, a user will be replaced by its IP address, the QoS type by the corresponding DiffServ PHB (Per Hop Behavior) type, etc. This modification of parameters allows the co-ordination of the policy implementation in the whole network. The new policy rule template is shown in Table 3.

Table 3. Network-Level Policy

IF SourceIPaddress|UserIPaddresses = *<SourceIPaddress|UserIPaddresses1..*>* and   SourcePortNo|UserportNo=*<SourcePortNo|UserportNo>*and DestinationIPAddress   =   *<DestinationIPAddress..(optional)>*and DestinationPortNo =*<DestinationPortNo (optional)>* THEN CONNECT with *<QoSDirection>* and <ConnectionType> from|among *<SourceIPAddress!..*>* at *<SourcePortNo|UserPortNo>* to *<destinationIPAddress!..*(optional)>* at *<DestinationPortNo1 (optional)>* with *<PhBtype>* and *<Sec-Prot>*with *<C-Algo>* and *<A-Algo>* and *<Mode>* and *<No-Replay>*

A last step is necessary to disseminate and enforce the policies rules in the different network entities. Only the rules and parameters of concern for the entity where the policy will be enforced are disseminated.

Table 4. Network-Level Policy for Dissemination to the Network Elements

IF SourceIPaddress|UserIPaddresses = *<SourceIPaddress|UserIPaddresses1..*>* and SourcePortNo|UserportNo = *<SourcePortNo|UserportNo >*and DestinationIPAddress = *<DestinationIPAddress..(optional)>* and DestinationPortNo = *<DestinationPortNo (optional)>* THEN SET at *<InterfaceIpaddress>* With *<PhBtype>* and *<Sec-Prot>* with *<C-Algo>* and *<A-Algo>* and *<Mode>* and *<Anti-Replay>*

For example for a videoconferencing service, when two users from distinct domains (managed by distinct entities) communicate, each entity receives the IP address of the other user. This policy rule allows the definition and the establishment of security associations between the communicating entities to ensure an end-to-end security. Table 4 presents the policy that will be implemented in the network elements. The keyword SET makes it clear that the objective is no longer to provide something but to set something to certain values. The *<interfaceIPAddress>* represents where the policy must be enforced. It generally represents an edge router on which a set of *<UserIPAddress>* is connected.

This is a first step towards automatic translation. Ideally, the refinement process could be automated through the use of a translation table as depicted in Table 2 but the translation process is more complex than that. In addition there is a need to resolve conflicts and to deal with the fact that some resources might not be available.

4 Network Level Prototyping

In the RTIPA project, we worked on different aspects of the architecture. One of our task was to study languages mapping between applications using SMIL [22][23] and the middleware level. However, the network level was the only really stable basis for the implementation. Standards on network policy management exist and the choice of technology had been made [24]. It is therefore on that level that we chose to demonstrate some aspects of our architecture. Our objective was to integrate QoS and security policies using Traffic Designer, a network-level tool developed by Qosmos [25].

This section describes how Traffic Designer is used to support policy-based QoS and security management at the edge routers level. The architecture of the Traffic Designer (TD) and its interactions with the different managers of our architecture are depicted in Fig. 2.

Traffic designer is an integrated tool able to provide actions on the flows (classification, prioritization, throughput guarantee, forbiddance, tagging of packets, counting, analyzing and spying) based on a set of rules. This set of (policy) rules integrates the policy rules that have been derived as described in section 3 (Table 4).

Traffic designer is composed of a classifier (*TD classifier*), a filter (*TD filter*) and five action modules (*TD QoS*, *TD Firewall*, *TD cryptography*, *TD Diffserv* and *TD Monitor* and its related *TD log database*).

The *TD classifier* takes as input packets or packet flows and gives as an output the highest level of protocol the packets belongs to. This allows us to provide rules on those particular applications.

The *TD filter* applies the rules (including our policy rules) and redirects the packets to the action modules if appropriate. Examples of rules are:

- IF (udp_dport=1024..65535) AND (tcp_dport=1024..65535) Then goto Firewall (rule based on the header fields)
- IF (http_mime=" image/gif ") AND (smtp_attach=" application/pdf") Then provide 20 Kbps (rule based on the application properties)
- IF (flow_content=*topsecret*) then goto Firewall (rule based on the packet content (not advised))
- IF (client to server) then...(rule based on the direction of a TCP connection).

The *TD QoS* module is able to shape the traffic, to apply queuing mechanisms and to recover the unused bandwidth. It gives the possibility to guarantee a minimum or a maximum throughput, to tune the maximum waiting delay for the packets, to provide priorities within a queue (e.g. LIFO). The packets can then be tagged depending on applicative criteria. It enable us, in particular, to guarantee bandwidth to mission critical applications and establish classes of traffic depending on the protocol used and the user involved.

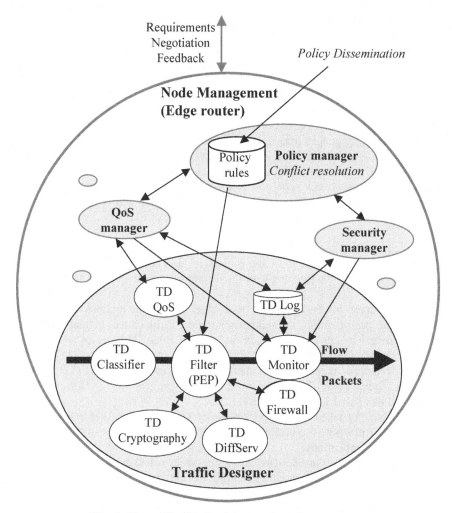

Fig. 2. Use of Traffic Designer at the Edge Routers

The *TD firewall* (security) can drop packets. It provides us with functionalities to protect the application against hackers, to filter per protocol or per application URL and keywords, to position alarms on certain event. This security aspect is interesting but not sufficient for our security needs.

To enforce our security policy rules we need another action module, the *TD cryptography* module that is currently under development. This new module will provide a user-transparent cryptography (multiple key system, choice of the key depending on the application or of the user). When available, this feature will be studied in order to know if it can be used for the cryptographic algorithm management.

The *TD Diffserv* module adapts the flow to DiffServ.

The *TD Monitor* provides information and statistics in its *TD log database* (number of packets/bytes, instant/average/peak throughput, percentage of bandwidth used, zoom on a particular traffic type and spying, discovery based on applicative criteria). The syntax used to query the database is a simplified subset of SQL. Some examples are:

- SELECT (tcp_sport, ip_saddr)
  FILTER (tcp_proto=http) AND NOT (ip_saddr=" webserver ")
  Result:
  o 8080   192.168.2.5   79pkt, 10,5Kbps, 4342octets
  o 7979   192.168.2.8   4 pkt, 2,1 Kbps, 324 octets

- SELECT (smtp_sender)
  FILTER (smtp_subject=" *big brother*") OR (smtp_subject=" *loft story*")
  Result:
  o Anne.Aunime@qosmos.net 79 pkts, 0 Kbps, 4342 octets
  o Joel.Noyeux@qosmos.net   458 pkts, 2,1 Kbps, 33424 octets
  o Jean.Aymard@qosmos.net   2303 pkts, 0 Kbps, 23423 octets

The policy manager acts on the *TD filter* to enforce the policy rules. The QoS and security managers of the edge router interact with the *TD Monitor* to describe the information to track. They can then query the *TD Log database* to get the information they need and if necessary they can provide a feedback to the network, middleware and service levels.

5   Conclusion: Open Issues and Perspectives

This paper has presented our research work done in the context of the RTIPA project to manage QoS and security for distributed multimedia services running on IP networks. Some open issues still remain.

The services have a range of QoS requirements and offerings well identified. Various protocols and mechanisms exist to support QoS in distinct architectures. But the problem is how can we mix and match their capabilities to provide a complete QoS and security management? For example, at the network level, some incompatibilities appear between the IPsec and Diffserv protocols.

The refinement of high-level policies (service level policies in our architecture) is another issue: it is difficult to automate. It is likely to remain partially a manual process since it requires a large amount of knowledge. Also, what happens when the different rules cannot be validated (conflict between the rules...) or when the network cannot support the low-level policy? What sort of feedback should be provided to the user and will there be renegotiations of the QoS and security requirements and offerings? If it is the case, a relationship binding the different policy abstraction levels, as in [26] with the parent/child relationship is essential.

In this article, we have depicted a simplified version of QoS and security policy rules but a problem is observed during inter-domain communications. The domains do not have necessarily the same way to represent policy, QoS and security. Several policy specification languages exist such as [27],[28],[29],[30],[31]. They provide flexibility and permit to express policies through different approaches (logical, graphical, etc.). Ponder [12] is the most suitable language for our solution. It integrates QoS and security policies, it is mature and an implementation is currently available. Another candidate for the security aspect would have been the Security Policy Specification Language (SPSL). There is a need for a global agreement on the policy language, and this not only at the network level, to be able to implement an end-to-end policy-based QoS and security management.

Our objective is to continue this research work and to extend this architecture to SLA and mobility management. The work on security is further detailed in another paper [32].

Acknowledgements

The authors would like to thank the members of the RTIPA project, Qosmos and the APS group of the university of Twente for their valuable comments on this work.

References

1. RTIPA   http://www.extra.research.philips.com/euprojects/rtipa/   or   http://www.itea-office.org/projects/facts_sheets/rtipa_fact_sheet.htm
2. R. Yavatkar et al., A Framework for Policy-Based Admission Control, RFC 2753, January 2000
3. B. Moore et al., Policy Core Information Model - Version 1 Specification, RFC 3060, February 2001. http://www.ietf.org/rfc/rfc3060.txt.
4. B. Moore et al., Policy Core Information Model Extensions V.7, http://www.ietf.org/internet-drafts/draft-ietf-policy-pcim-ext-07.txt, March. 2002.
5. Y. Snir et al., Policy QoS Information Model, Policy framework Working Group, Internet Draft, http://www.ietf.org/internet-drafts/draft-ietf-policy-qos-info-model-04.txt, November 2001.
6. B. Moore et al., Information Model for Describing Network Device QoS Datapath Mechanisms, Policy framework Working Group, Internet Draft, http://www.ietf.org/internet-drafts/draft-ietf-policy-qos-device-info-model-08.txt, May 2002.
7. J. Jason et al., IPsec Configuration Policy Model, Internet Protocol Security Policy Working Group, Internet Draft, February 2002.
8. J. Zao et al, Domain Based Internet Security Policy Management, Proceedings of DARPA Information Survivability Conference and EXposition 2000 (DISCEX '00), January 2000.
9. R. Chandramouli, Implementation of Multiple Access Control Policies within a CORBASEC Framework, 22th National Information Systems Security Conference NISSC'1999.
10. Corba "Security Service" Specification v 1.7, OMG, March 2001 (ftp://ftp.omg.org/pub/docs/formal/01-03-08.pdf)
11. N. Dulay et al., A Policy Deployment Model for the Ponder Language, 7th IFIP/IEEE International Symposium on Integrated Network Management (IM'2001), Seattle, USA May 2001.

12. N. Damianou et al., Ponder: Language for Specifying Security and Management Policies for Distributed Systems, The Language Specification Version 2.3, October 2000. http://www-dse.doc.ic.ac.uk/Research/policies/ponder/PonderSpec.pdf

13. P. Leydekkers et al., A Computational and Engineering View on Open Distributed Real-time Multimedia Exchange, In Lecture Notes in Computer Science - Number 1018 - Springer Verlag - ISBN: 3-540-60647-5 - Proceedings of Network and Operating System Support for Digital Audio and Video (NOSSDAV'95), Durham, New Hampshire, USA, April 1995.

14. P. Leydekkers and V.C.J. Gay, ODP View on Quality of Service for Open Distributed Multimedia Environments, In 'Quality of Service - Description, Modelling and Management', A. Vogel and J. de Meer editors. Proceedings of the 4th International IFIP Workshop on QoS, Paris, March 1996.

15. M. D. J. Cox and R. G. Davison, Concepts, Activities and Issues of Policy-Based Communications Management. BT Technology, Vol 17 No 3 July 1999.

16. Jajodia S. et al., Principles for a Telecommunications Management Network, ITU-T M.3010, February 2000.

17. H.J. Tjaja, SLA Enforced by Policy, masters thesis, KPN/Twente University internal report, 2001.

18. K. Nichols et al.., Definition of the Differentiated Services Field (DS Field) in the IPv4 and IPv6 Headers, RFC 2474, December 1998.

19. S. Kent and R. Atkinson, IP Authentication Header, RFC 2402, November 1998.

20. S. Kent and R. Atkinson, IP Encapsulating Security Payload (ESP), RFC 2406, November 1998.

21. S. Kent and R. Atkinson, Security Architecture for the Internet Protocol, RFC 2401, November 1998.

22. J.van Ossenbruggen et al., Towards Second and Third Generation Web-Based Multimedia. In: The Tenth International World Wide Web Conference, May 2001, Hong Kong

23. SMIL 2.0 documentation http://www.w3.org/TR/2000/WD-smil20-20000921/

24. M. Riguidel, Introduction to Policy Management, RTIPA Technical Report, 2000.

25. www.Qosmos.net

26. D. Marriott, PhD Thesis, Policy Service for Distributed Systems, Department of Computing, Imperial College, London, 1997.

27. N. Damianou, A Policy Framework for Management of Distributed Systems, PhD Thesis, Imperial College of London, February 2002.

28. T. Koch et al., Policy Definition Language for Automated Management of Distributed Systems, Proceedings of the Second International Workshop on System Management, IEEE Computer Society Press, 1996.

29. J. Hoagland, Specifying and Implementing Security Policies Using LaSCO, the Language for Security Constraints on Objects, PhD Thesis University of California, Davis Department of Computer Science, 2000.

30. M. Hitchens et al., Tower: A Language for Role Based Access Control, Policy 2001, LNCS 1995, pp.88-106, 2001.

31. Jajodia S. et al, A Logical Language for Expressing Authorizations. In Proceedings of the IEEE Symposium on Security and Privacy. Oakland, CA, USA: IEEE Press, 1997. p. 31-42.

32. S. Duflos et al., An Architecture for End-to-End Policy-Based Security Management, Submitted to the eighth IFIP/IEEE International Symposium on Integrated Network Management (IM 2003), March 2003.

Formal Modeling of Service Session Management

M. van Le, B.J.F. van Beijnum, and B.L. de Goede

Department of Computer Science,
University of Twente, The Netherlands.
{le,beijnum,goede}@cs.utwente.nl

Abstract. This paper proposes a concept to apply modeling tools to Multi-Provider Telematics Service Management. The service architecture is based on the framework called "Open Service Components" which serves as building blocks to compose end-to-end telematics services in terms of service components offered by different service providers. Our work presented in this paper contributes to the abstract way of modeling end-to-end Service Management using Architectural Description Language and an underlying Formal Description Language.

1 Introduction

Today telematics services are becoming increasingly complex. For instance, new services are being introduced by integrating existing services. Also, in the provisioning of a service session, many different 'service components' have to cooperate in order to establish the end-to-end service session to users. Moreover, instead of having the ability to manage individual service components, end-to-end service provisioning will require the management of the cooperation between these components in a service session. One of the complicating aspects is that in the provisioning of the end-to-end service, multiple providers are involved. Hence, inter-domain management is required. With the advent of user mobility and in-session seamless roaming capabilities new challenges in end-to-end service management are faced [1, 3, 4].

To deal with the complexity of service management, and to arrive at new management solution we envisage an increasing need for the application of existing (formal) modeling and analysis methods. In this paper we present the application of such a method and tools for a (simple) multimedia service provisioning scenario. In future work, specific management issues will be addressed for this and other more complex scenarios, specifically we will address service accounting issues.

The modeling and analysis method selected for this paper consists of the architecture description language (ADL) and a formal specification language (FSL). The ADL Darwin is used to express the service in terms of 'components' and the relations between them. To specify the behavior of each component, the formal specification language FSP (Finite State Processes) is being used. The Service Session Management model of the scenario considered basically specifies the coordination of activation, modification and termination needed for the end-to-end service session.
The remainder of this paper is organized as follows:

K.C. Almeroth and M. Hasan (Eds.): MMNS 2002, LNCS 2496, pp. 36–48, 2002.
© Springer-Verlag Berlin Heidelberg 2002

Section 2 discusses a scenario of multi-provider service architecture based on "Open Service Components Architecture Framework". Section 3 describes Service Session Scenario and associated Management Model. Section 4 presents the modeling method applied. Section 5 presents the model and some preliminary analysis results of the service session scenario. Finally, section 6 provides with conclusions and outlooks on future work.

2 A Service Architecture

The idea of *Open Service Component Architecture Framework* (OSCAF) is based on operational relevance. The framework is based on the observation that end-to-end services are built from 'service components' [2]. The services offered are mandated by a Service Level Specification (SLS), which is an agreed technical specification of the offered service. This technical specification determines the offered functionality and quality of service characteristics (the SLS is possibly parameterized, thus controllable to some extent by users). The means to offer a service is through the use of service components. In OSCAF four different classes of service components are distinguished, these are:

- *Connectivity Service Components* - Connectivity service components provide the distant exchange of information between geographically dispersed points. Thus, CSCs cover a very broad range of components, varying from bit-pipes, data-links, host-to-host communication, reliable inter-process communication channels, and the exchange of application messages.
- *Network Service Components* - Network service components offer functionality additional to connectivity service components. Concrete examples of network service components are time dependent routing, number translation, closed user groups, DNS, authorization and authentication. It is possible that different actors provide connectivity service components and network service components.
- *Enabling Service Components* - The execution of Application Service components is being supported by Enabling Service components that provide features related to selection, visibility, accountability and other facilities like adapting shape and language to users' needs.
- *Application Service Components* - Application service components maintain, generate and provide information or functional capabilities intended for users. Examples are Video, MP3, Web-pages etc. However, the range is much wider. For instance: e-mail, relational database, ticket reservation, virtual workspace and the like.

The *open* character of a decomposition as illustrated in Figure 1 is prerogative for seamless service interworking with other Service Providers. An *integral* approach of Telematics Service Component Management is to arrive at optimal cooperation of the mentioned classes of services.

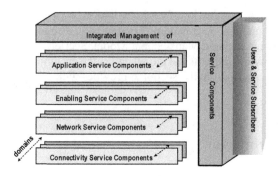

Fig. 1. Open Service Component Architecture Framework

2.1 Service Session Life Cycle

Three service life cycles can be identified in [2] in the context of operational lifetime, namely: *Implementation Life Cycle, Subscription Life Cycle and Service Session Life Cycle*. The implementation cycle involves: formulation of business plan, analyzing service characteristics, planning network resources, testing software, installing the service, etc. The subscription cycle is concerned with: contracts toward new service users, providing service users with relevant usage instruction, exchange of cost related data about service users with other domain, etc. The service session cycle involves the actual usage of services.

The service session life cycle consists of the following phases:

- *Service Session Invocation* - The service user invokes the Service Session Management by means of a service request. The requested service may be a composition different service components.
- *Service Session Negotiation* - This step enables the negotiation of appropriate service components to establish an end-to-end service session. The parameters of negotiation can be specified in a SLA (QoS, Price, etc.). The Service Session Management makes a selection of service component(s) to build up an end-to-end service session.
- *Service Session Creation* - Since the service session management is assumed to be capable to negotiate, select and drop service components offered by the negotiating service providers, this step confirms the participation of the selected service providers in the provisioning of a service session.
- *Service Session Provision* - Upon the reception of service component confirmation, service instances can be set-up and provisioned by the service providers. Parallel to service provisioning, service accounting can be started to account for the delivered service components. Further, service monitoring is essential to provide feedback to service providers about the delivered QoS, this information can have effect on the adjustment of the price that the user has to pay.
- *Service Session Termination* - Service session termination is the releasing of a session. Termination may be initiated by the service user or by a service provider.

3 A Service Scenario

3.1 Content Retrieval Service

The process of service component delivery from a service provider to a service user may be divided into two aspects: service usage and service provisioning. Seen from the service usage, two important management information exchanges are generated: the service request from the user to the service provider and the service termination. Seen from the service the service provisioning, service management information must be interchanged between service providers to arrive at end-to-end service. We assume the participation of following actors:

- Mobile Network Operator (MNO)
- Application Service Broker (ASB)
- Content Providers (CPs)
- Connectivity Service Broker (CSB)
- Internet Service Provider (ISP)

3.2 Content Retrieval Service Management

Previous definition of Service Session Life Cycle raises a number of research questions concerning multi-provider service management. A few are listed below:

- How to define clearly the service management boundary within which a service component is being delivered?
- What management functions are required at each domain in order to cooperate with other domains?
- What kind of information needs to be exchanged at each step during the session life cycle?
- How can the coordination of local management functions be organized in an end-to-end service management context?

In principle, two management models from the two extreme ends of multi-provider service management spectrum are conceivable: cascade and hierarchical service management.

Cascade service management is a management structure where user's service invocation is (re)directed to a content provider and the content provider figures out how to provision the requested service without further interaction with other involved actors. A good example of cascade service management is the current "best effort" Video-on-Demand (VoD) service through the Internet. In most of the cases, the content provider injects an amount of packets into the network and these have to find their way to the next hop until they reach the end terminal. Cascade service management does not concern about the dependency of service components as a whole and the end-to-end service session management.

Hierarchical service management is a management structure where the handling of service invocation is processed and monitored. Contrary to the former, hierarchical service management has an end-to-end significance concerning service provisioning and the dependency of service component management functions. Other management structures are certainly possible. However, for a comprehensive presentation of our modeling approach, a hierarchical management structure will be discussed further in detail.

The service management topology illustrated in Figure 2 reflects the management architecture to be modeled in section 5. Three classes of management function are distinguished:

1. *Component Management Function* (CMF) represented by a dot: components having this class of management function can only act as managed entity.
2. *Sub-Integral Service Management Function* (sub-ISMF) represented by a square with an internal dot: components having this class of management function can act as managed entity as well as managing entity.
3. *Integral Service Management Function (ISMF)* represented by a filled square: component having this class of management function always acts as managing entity.

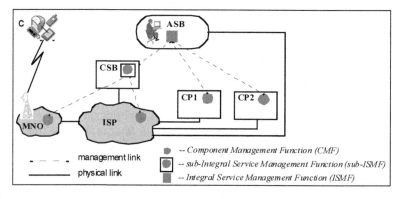

Fig. 2. Service Management Topology

In addition, Table 1 provides brief descriptions of the management functions and management information exchanged between managing en managed entities. The table describes how components interact and what service session management information should be exchanged.

In the chosen management model, ASB is assumed to have the information about which CP it should contact. ASB negotiates the requested content and the corresponding QoS level with both CP1 and CP2. There is a case where both CP1 and CP2 agree to provide the service component, then ASB will need to make a choice between one of the two service components offered. This situation is conceivable in practice when the prices of the service offered by CP1 and CP2 differ. The Service Component Provisioning is managed at local level, this means that if an actor confirms to the integral- or sub-integral management that the requested service component can be provided and service component creation confirmation message is received from the integral- or sub-integral management, then the actor must ensure a continuous provisioning of the service component (e.g. the final mapping of service confirmation message to network elements). These kinds of local management functionality are treated as "internal" management activities of a service component, which are not relevant for the modeling of service session management.

Component	Management Function	Management Information Exchange	Interact with
C	- send service request	- content M + Q1 or Q2	- ASB
	- terminate service	- termination message	- ASB
ASB	- negotiate the requested content and the corresponding QoS level	- content M + QoS level	- CP1 *and* CP2
	- negotiate the required network resource a the end-to-end transmission of the content	- QoS, source CP1 and CP2	- CSB
	- select service components and integrate these to obtain an end-to-end application service	*non*	*non*
	- inform C if the requested service can be delivered or not	- service confirmation message	- C
	- create connectivity and application service provisioning	- service creation message	- CSB, CP1 *or* CP2
	- abort service provisioning when needed	- service return message	- CSB, CP1 *or* CP2
	- terminate service	- service termination message	- CSB *and* CP1 or CP2
CP1, CP2	- respond to ASB if the requested content and the corresponding QoS is available	- content M + Q1 or Q2	- ASB
CSB	- negotiate network resource to destination C	- service negotiation message	- MNO
	- negotiate network resource from source CP1 and CP2	- datin1, datin2, Q1 and Q2	- ISP
	- respond if the requested end-to-end connectivity can be provided or not	- service confirmation message	- ASB
	- create connectivity service provisioning	- service creation message	- MNO *and* ISP
MNO	- respond to CSB if the requested connectivity service can be provided or not	- service confirmation message	- CSB
ISP	- respond to CSB which connectivity service can be provided	- service confirmation message, Q1 or Q2, datin1 or datin2	- CSB

Table 1. Management Functions and Management Information Exchange

4 Modeling Method and Tools

4.1 Modeling Methodology

State of the Art formal modeling methods can be applied to the previously presented service scenario and its management. More recently Architectural Description Languages have emerged. In review, the modeling concepts and tools relate as shown in Figure 3.

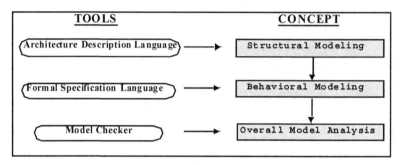

Fig. 3. The Modeling Concept

First, an Architecture Description Language (ADL) is used to express the structural aspect of a service architecture. The structural modeling step describes entities involved in an architecture and how they are connected to each other, through which interface, etc. A structural model should represent the topology of service relationships between the involved actors. Moreover, a structural model should contain the following information:

- Which actor is responsible for which class of service component;
- Through which interface should a certain service be provided;
- How end-to-end service is provisioned;
- Clear distinction of different class of interactions (e.g. basic signaling, accounting signaling, data stream, etc.);

In the area of software engineering, ADLs have been identified as promising approach to bridge the gap between requirements and implementation in the design of complex systems [5]. A few well-known ADLs among system designers are: Darwin, Meta-H, Rapide, Wright. In addition, some of the ADLs support the capability to specify dynamic structures, a capability needed to capture roaming users.

Second, the structural model is enriched with a behavior specification using a Formal Specification Language (FSL) that enables the behavioral modeling. The behavior of each component is specified in terms of process algebra.

Third, to gain confidence in the correctness of the system, Model Checker is used once the behavioral model has been specified. Model checking techniques are especially aimed at the verification of reactive, embedded systems, i.e. systems that are in constant interaction with the environment. These techniques allow the designer to verify that a mathematical model of a system satisfies logical properties depicting correct system behavior [6]. The followings summarize important aspects of model analysis:

- Consistency: does the behavior of an entity conform the protocols, which are being used to interact to other entities?
- Completeness: is any part missing in the system? (or, could we remove some parts and still being able to make sure that the system still function properly?)
- Refinement: can one architecture be substituted for other?
- Verification: does an implementation conform the architecture?
- Performance and Reliability: can the server handle the expected demand? will average response time meet the requirements? which entity is the bottleneck? how would server/database replication affect the server's performance?

The model-checking step does not only help to analyze the behavioral model, it also provides good comprehension of the system in order to arrive at the management design.

4.2 Languages and Tools

Most of ADLs have some formal semantics, which allows model checking. Darwin uses *Finite State Processes* (FSP), whereas Wright uses *Communicating Sequential Processes* (CSP). Both FSP and CSP are formal specification languages. Meta-H and Rapide use their own specification languages [7, 8, 9, 10]. Although limited in the number of states that can be captured and analyzed, Darwin/FSP is easy to use and therefore well suited as initial choice for this study.

Darwin Architecture Description Language has been successfully applied in the area of software engineering to describe the structure of distributed telematics systems [11]. Darwin is a declarative configuration language, which may be used to describe the overall architecture of a distributed system as a hierarchical composition of interconnected components. Each Darwin component is an instance of a component type. The component interfaces are defined in terms of provided or required service. Components are connected by a fixed set of connector types. The effect of binding a provided service with a required service that corresponds to the composition of the subcomponents, and a configuration corresponds to the parallel composition of the components. Darwin has the ability to specify dynamically changing architectures: new components may be created as the result of the invocation of a particular kind of provided service [12, 13, 14].

To obtain the Darwin description of the Content Retrieval Service as illustrated in Figure 2, we make use of the Software Architect's Assistant (SAA) [15], a visual programming tool that supports the construction of distributed programs through the design of their architectures. SAA generates Darwin description from a graphical representation of the system.

Given the overall structure specified in Darwin, this Darwin description can be parsed to an FSP specification using FSP's composition constructs. The behavior of each component can be specified in FSP. The combination of the two gives the entire system specification in FSP. For overall model analysis the tool LTSA is used [16].

5 Modeling of Service Management

5.1 Modeling of the Structure of the Content Retrieval Service

From the structural view, each involved actor is modeled as an independent component. Interaction between two components takes place through "binding". Distinction between two types of bindings is made explicitly, namely: *signaling binding* and *data binding*. Further, we chose to model unidirectional bindings for clarity purposes of management information exchanging.

Figure 4 depicts the graphical representation of the service architecture and the corresponding Darwin description. Management information exchange is enabled by unidirectional signaling bindings, "sig1_*name*" indicates an initiated interaction of a component, whereas "sig1_*name*" indicates an absorbed interaction of that same component.

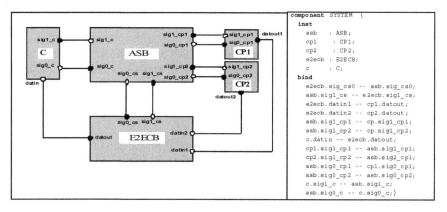

Fig. 4. Compositional Service Architecture

The refinement of the end-to-end Connectivity Broker component (E2ECB) is shown in Figure 5. The choice to model CSB, MNO and ISP as sub-components has to do with the separation of concern in terms of provided service components. In doing so, ASB delegates a portion of management tasks to CSB that needs to take care of the end-to-end connectivity service.

The CP1 and CP2 offer their application services physically through data interfaces *datin1* and *datin2*, respectively. Once the data arrives at ISP, it is transmitted through one single data binding in the direction of MNO and then C.

To summarize, the model contains the following parameters that govern the number of end-to-end service provisioning scenarios and therefore the number of states:

- 1 content in a single segment: M
- 2 content providers: CP1 and CP2
- 2 QoS levels: Q1 and Q2
- 2 data interfaces: datin1 and datin2

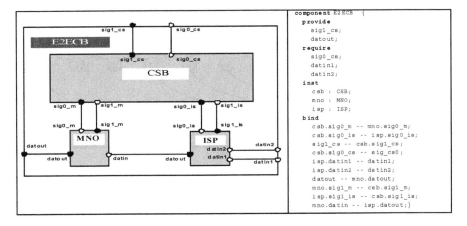

The following code appears in the figure box on the right:

```
component E2ECB {
provide
  sig1_cs;
  datout;
require
  sig0_cs;
  datin1;
  datin2;
inst
  csb : CSB;
  mno : MNO;
  isp : ISP;
bind
  csb.sig0_m -- mno.sig0_m;
  csb.sig0_is -- isp.sig0_is;
  sig1_cs -- csb.sig1_cs;
  csb.sig0_cs -- sig_cs0;
  isp.datin1 -- datin1;
  isp.datin2 -- datin2;
  datout -- mno.datout;
  mno.sig1_m -- csb.sig1_m;
  isp.sig1_is -- csb.sig1_is;
  mno.datin -- isp.datout;}
```

Fig. 5. Refinement of E2ECB component

5.2 Specifying the Behavior of the Service Components

The system behavior is modeled as a Labeled Transition System (LTS) with shared actions to synchronize processes. It is important to keep in mind the recurrence of the processes running in a system during the behavioral modeling phase, where "life" is created within each primitive[1] component. In terms of finite states processes, once a service session life cycle is terminated, all processes must return to the initial state.

The behavioral model of CP1 is shown in Figure 6 together with its corresponding FSP specification. The result of the system's overall behavior is a composite LTS:

$$|| \ \text{SYSTEM} = (\text{asb:ASB} \ || \ \text{cp1:CP1} \ || \ \text{cp2:CP2}|| \\ \text{e2ecb:E2ECB} \ || \ \text{c:C})$$

$$\text{where} \quad || \ \text{E2ECB} = (\text{csb:CSB} \ || \ \text{mno:MNO} \ || \ \text{isp:ISP})$$

The behavior of primitive component CP1 is relatively simple compared to other components in the model. CP1 is illustrated here as example to provide an idea about how the behavior of a primitive component can be described and graphically displayed as a finite state machine using LTSA.

LSTA provides two principle options to analyze a system: safety- and progress analysis:

- *Safety Analysis* checks system's deadlock, which is generally a bad state from which no further actions can be executed. Deadlock might occur in case a component cannot finish it session life cycle before the start of another session.
- *Progress Analysis* checks system's property to ensure that whatever state the system is in, there is always the case that a specified action will eventually be executed.

In addition to basic analysis options, one can also check system 's property with some pre-defined requirements. For instance, the responsiveness property of an accounting system ensures that accounting must stop whenever provision failure occurs.

---

[1] without decompositions capability

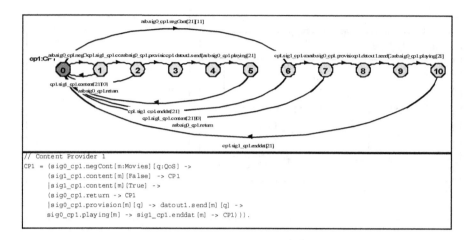

Fig. 6. Content Provider's behavioral model

In order to gain confidence in the correctness of the model, we first run the reachability analysis to check for deadlock in the system. A summary of the reachability analysis is given in Figure 7.

```
Compiled: ASB; Compiled: CP1; Compiled: CP2;
Compiled: CSB; Compiled: MNO ;Compiled: ISP
Composition: E2ECB = csb:CSB || mno:MNO || isp:ISP
State Space: 107 * 11 * 39 = 2 ** 17
Composing...; -- States: 221 Transitions: 342
...
Compiled: E2ECB
Compiled: C
Composition:
SYSTEM = asb:ASB || cp1:CP1 || cp2:CP2 || e2ecb:E2ECB || c:C
State Space: 216 * 11 * 11 * 221 * 11 = 2 ** 28
Analysing...
Depth 32 -- States: 1063 Transitions: 2036;Memory used: 3648K
No deadlocks/errors
```

Fig. 7. Reachability Analysis

As indicated, there is no deadlock in the system. However, reachability does not guarantee that a system's behavior completely meets the system's requirements. Therefore, all possible service scenarios must be examined with respect to expected management functionalities of each component. According to the system's degrees of freedom, ASB must manage in total 64 operational service scenarios, namely:

[M:1]x[QoS:2]x[CP:2]x[Availability:2]x {[DataInter-
face:2]x[QoS:2]x[Availability:2]} = 64

Where [Availability] is a YES *or* NO response of a managed entity in responding to a managing entity about the availability of the requested service component.

5.3 Example of End-to-End Service Provisioning

As mentioned previously, the behavioral modeling results in 64 operational service scenarios. Figure 8 provides the message sequence diagram of a scenario to illustrate how the Service Session Life Cycle mentioned in section 2 can be followed to obtain an end-to-end service provisioning.

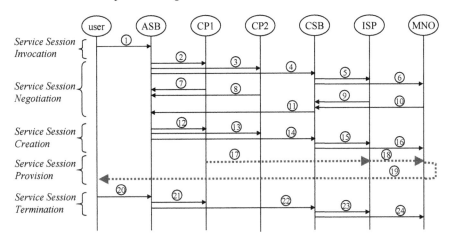

Fig. 8. Message Sequence Diagram of a service-provisioning scenario

- *Step 1* – The user invokes a service.
- *Step 2* and 3 – ASB negotiates the requested content and the corresponding QoS.
- *Step 4* – ASB negotiates the required network resource for the end-to-end transmission of the content.
- *Step 5 and 6* – CSB negotiates network resource at ISP and MNO
- *Step 7 and 8* – CP1 and CP2 respond positively to ASB.
- *Step 9 and 10* – ISP and MNO respond positively to CSB.
- *Step 11* – CSB responds positively to ASB about the availability of the end-to-end connectivity service.
- *Step 12* – ASB creates the application service component offered by CP1.
- *Step 13* – ASB informs CP2 that it the offered service component is dropped.
- *Step 14* – ASB creates the end-to-end connectivity service offered by CSB.
- *Step 15 and 16* – CSB creates the connectivity service components offered by ISP and MNO.
- *Step 17 to 19* – The actual end-to-end service is being provisioned.
- *Step 20* – The user terminates the ongoing service.
- *Step 21 and 22* – ASB terminates the application and end-to-end service components.
- *Step 23 and 24* – CSB terminates the connectivity service components.

6 Conclusions and Future Work

In our study we focus on the service management aspects, we abstract from the physical relations by looking at the *service relations* between the actors. We decompose telematics service management in a multi-provider environment in such a way that application of formal method results in an operational relevant behavioral model. The proposed concept serves as a basis for further application of formal method in the area of Service Management to investigate crucial properties of end-to-end Service Management Systems in order to arrive at a secure and optimal management system design.

As far as the future work is concerned, we aim at exploring the possibility to include mobility aspects in the modeling of multi-domain Service Management. As mentioned, Darwin has the ability to specify dynamically changing structures, which can be useful to describe the mobility of the customer when roaming from one to another domain and the system's behavior as a result of the user's mobility. Future extensions of the work presented here include also the modeling of multi-domain Accounting Management and property verification of service session management and its associated session accounting management.

Reference

1. Shingo Ohmori , "*The concept of future generation mobile communication based on broadband access technology*", IEEE Communication Magazine, Dec. 2000.
2. B.L. de Goede, "*Operational Management of Telematics Systems and Services*", ISBN: 90-365-1709-5, Dec. 2001.
3. Lewis, D.A.: "*A framework for the development of service management systems for the open service market*", PhD thesis, UCL, Mar. 2000.
4. Q. Kong et al: "*A Management Framework for Internet Services*", CiTR technical journal-Vol.3, 1998.
5. J. Kramer, J. Magee, "*Explosing the skeleton in the Coordination Closet*", Proc. of the 2nd International Conference on Coordination Models and Languages, Sept. 1997.
6. R. Allen: "*A Formal Approach to Software Architecture*", PhD thesis, 1997.
7. "*Rapide Overview*", http://pavg.stanford.edu/rapide/overview.html
8. "*The Wright Architecture Description Language*", http://www-2.cs.cmu.edu/afs/cs/project/able/, Canergie Mellon - School of Computer Science,1998.
9. "*Darwin - An Architecture Description Language*", http://www.doc.ic.ac.uk/~jsc/research/, Dept. of Computing, Imperial College, Apr. 1997.
10. "*Meta-H Language and Tools*", http://www.htc.honeywell.com/ projects/dssa/dssa_tools.
11. H. Fossa: "*Implementing Interactive Configuration Management for Distributed Systems*", International Conference on Configurable Distributed Systems, Annapolis MD, May 1996.
12. J.Kramer: "*Analysing Dynamic Change in Software Architectures - A Case Study*"; 4th International Conference on Configurable Distributed Systems, Annapolis, May 1998.
13. N. Dulay, "*Darwin Refererence Manual*", Dept. of Computing, Imperial College", 1994.
14. J. Magee, N. Dulay, J. Kramer, "*Specifying Distributed Sofware Architecture*", Proc. of the 5th European Software Engineering (ESEC'95), Sept. 1995.
15. K. Ng, et al: "*A Visual Approach To Distributed Programming*", in Tools and Environments for Parallel and Distributed Systems , A. Zaky and T. Lewis (Eds.), Kluwer Academic Publishers, Feb. 1996.
16. J. Magee, J. Kramer: "*Concurrency: State Models & Java Programs*", Wiley, 1999.

Network Requirement for Management of Multimedia over Wireless Channel

Bing Zheng[1] and Mohammed Atiquzzaman[2]

[1] New Focus Inc
5215 Hellyer Ave., San Jose, CA 95138.
Email:zhengbin@ieee.org
[2] School of Computer Science
University of Oklahoma, Norman, OK 73019-6151.
Email: atiq@ou.edu

Abstract. Wireless channels have a high channel bit error rate and limited bandwidth. The high bit error rate degrades the quality of multimedia transmission, and also increases the buffer size requirement at the client. In this paper, we propose a novel *selective retransmission scheme* for multimedia transmission over wireless ATM networks using the ABR service. Our objective is to develop a simple cost effective scheme which offers quality of service for MPEG compressed video transmitted over a noisy wireless channel. We have developed an analytical model to determine the networking requirements and receiver buffer size for our proposed scheme for transmitting multimedia over wireless ATM.

1 Introduction

The transmission of multimedia over wireless channel is becoming a research topic of growing interest [1,2,3]. With the emergence of next generation high speed wireless ATM networks, it is expected that multimedia will be the main source of traffic in future wireless ATM networks. Wireless transmissions use radio as the transmission media which is easily affected by environments such as buildings, moving objects, and atmosphere, etc., giving rise to issues such as effective bandwidth allocation.

The ATM Forum has standardized four service classes: Constant Bit Rate (CBR), Variable Bit Rate (VBR) including real time VBR and non-real time VBR, Available Bit Rate (ABR) and Unspecified Bit Rate (UBR). CBR has the highest quality of service guarantee and the highest service cost. However, ABR offers cost effective service at an acceptable quality of service, flexible bandwidth allocation, and has a high utilization of network bandwidth. We will therefore, investigate the effectiveness of using the ATM ABR service to transport multimedia over a wireless ATM network. By combining the advantages of ATM and wireless, it is possible to implement a wireless ATM network which will offer high speed, quality of service, and mobility to future multimedia users [4,5,6].

Networked multimedia applications include remote education, video-on-demand, tele-shopping, home game entertainment, etc. Because of traffic characteristics such as high bit rate, video will be the dominant traffic in multimedia

K.C. Almeroth and M. Hasan (Eds.): MMNS 2002, LNCS 2496, pp. 49–61, 2002.
© Springer-Verlag Berlin Heidelberg 2002

streams, and hence needs to be managed efficiently [7]. Video must be compressed (for example, MPEG) to reduce the required transmission rate. In contrast to data, multimedia can tolerate a certain level of error. Therefore, although a wireless network has a high bit error rate when compared to a wireline network, it is possible to cost effectively transmit multimedia over wireless networks with acceptable quality of service (QoS).

In their experimental studies on effective algorithms for video transmission over a wireless channel [8], the authors studied the go-back-W retransmission scheme with window size W. They also considered the receiver buffer size for single retransmission. Their experimental results have shown that retransmission without FEC can improve the video transmission quality. However, their studies did not present detailed theoretical model and analysis of their retransmission scheme. Since the effectiveness of a retransmission scheme depends on the network parameters such as channel bit error rate, channel transmission rate, and video parameters such as the video frame size, it is very important to study the relationship between these parameters and the effectiveness and efficiency of retransmission schemes. Moreover, to sustain continuous video display at the receiver considering transmission over a noisy channel, continuous monitoring of the network status is required to prevent transmission collapse. Finally, during the time taken for retransmission, the receiver can only decode the buffered data upto the errored frame. To prevent starvation at the receiver (resulting in frozen display), the receiver buffer must have a minimum fill level to sustain continuous display during retransmission. The minimum fill level thereafter decides the minimum receiver buffer size. The longer the retransmission time, the larger the minimum fill level. Since the retransmission time depends on the channel bit error rate, the minimum receiver buffer size depends on the channel bit error rate. The authors in [9] have reviewed several error resilient video coding methods for MPEG-2 transmission over wireless ATM networks. They found that in a WAN testbed, the cell losses and wireless packet losses occur independently.

The high bit error rate of wireless channels raises a number of challenging issues for multimedia transmission over a wireless ATM network. Such issues include techniques to ensure a continuous display at the receiver in spite of errors in the received video. Currently, errors are compensated mainly by Forward Error Correction (FEC) which employs redundant bits to passively correct errors at the receiver. Although FEC can correct some errors without retransmission, it needs extra bandwidth to transmit a lot of redundant bits for correction. This lowers the utilization of bandwidth which is expensive for wireless channels. Furthermore, implementing FEC requires a lot of computing power at the receiver, thereby increasing the cost of the receiver. Additionally, complicated error concealment algorithms will have to be implemented at the receiver for different error types [10]. All of the above issues may prevent cost effective wide scale commercial deployment of wireless multimedia receiver if FEC is used at the receiver. Therefore, new schemes for error correction at the receiver are required for widespread deployment of cost effective multimedia transmission over noisy wireless links.

In this paper, a new *selective retransmission scheme* is proposed for multimedia transmission over noisy wireless channels in order to ensure acceptable video quality at the receiver and allow the design of a cost effective receiver. Since multimedia can tolerate a certain level of error with little effect on picture quality, our scheme sets a threshold on the number of errored cells, and to decide whether retransmission is required. To prevent the receiver from starvation (i.e. ensuring a continuous display), a receiver buffer is required.

Our *objective* is to develop an efficient error handling scheme for wireless transmission of multimedia, and to show that the scheme results in a cost effective wireless receiver. The *significance* of our scheme is that it does not require powerful computing capability and complicated error correction algorithm to be implemented at the wireless receiver. The wireless receiver will require simple hardware and thereby reduce the receiver cost. Our scheme also offers a method to monitor the status of the transmission system to check if the conditions to maintain transmission are satisfied. Our performance measure is maintaining a continuous display at the wireless receiver.

The rest of the paper is organized as follows. In Section 2, we propose the system stack model and our proposed selective retransmission scheme. Analysis of a multimedia wireless system using our proposed scheme is performed in Section 3. In Section 4, the minimum receiver buffer size is derived. Numerical results obtained from our analysis are given in Section 5, followed by conclusions in Section 6.

2   System Model and Proposed Retransmission Scheme

In this section, we describe the system model and the operating principle for our selective retransmission scheme. It will be used in Section 3 to derive values of network parameters and the size of receiver buffer to sustain continuous display at the receiver. As shown in Figure 1, the system consists of a multimedia server and receivers connected by a wireless ATM network using the ATM ABR service. The protocol stack consists of four layers as shown in Figure 2.

MPEG compressed video consists of I, P and B frames. The frames are grouped to form a special structure called Group of Picture (GoP). Each GoP includes an I frame followed by a number of P and B frames. A GoP is denoted by $MmNn$ which represents a total of n frames in the GoP with $m-1$ number of B frames between the I/P or P/P frames. At the decoder, error in a received I frame will affect all the frames in the GoP, while error in a received P frame will affect the quality of the subsequent P and B frames. An error in a received B frame only affects its own quality. Therefore, I frame is the most important, while the B frame is the least important. To maintain the quality of video at the receiver, *we propose the following retransmission scheme based on errors in the received video stream at the receiver.*

– If the number of errored cells in an I frame is higher than an acceptable error threshold for the I frame, the cells belonging to the I frame are discarded, and the I frame is retransmitted from the multimedia server;

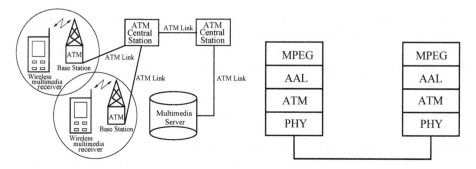

Fig. 1. The element of wireless ATM network for multimedia application.

Fig. 2. The protocol stack for MPEG video transmission over ATM wireless networks.

- If the number of errored cells in a P frame is higher than the acceptable error threshold for the P frame, the P frame is discarded and is retransmitted;
- Errored cells in B frames are discarded and are not retransmitted.

In the next section, we develop a mathematical model to analyze our proposed scheme, to derive the network requirements to sustain a continuous video display at the receivers, and to determine the minimum size of the receiver buffer. In our discussion, we assume:

- The wireless channel has a bit error rate which is independent of the traffic pattern and the channel transmission rate;
- Each bit has equal probability of being errored during transmission. Moreover, each cell has equal probability of having errors;
- The channel has fixed round trip time between the server and receiver;
- The ATM ABR service is used to transmit multimedia [7], i.e. the amount of bandwidth available to the application changes over time depending on the network congestion level.

3   System Analysis

In this section, we develop a mathematical model to analyze our proposed retransmission scheme. First, we define the following variables.

3.1   Notation

ρ: Channel bit error rate of the wireless link;

S_I, S_P and S_B: Average size of I, P and B frames respectively of MPEG video;

N: Number of bits in the payload of a cell (For an ATM cell, $N=48*8$);

N_I, N_P and N_B: Average number of cells belonging to I, P and B frame in a GoP;

d_I, d_P: Threshold for the acceptable number of errored cells in I and P frames respectively;

p: Probability that a cell has error;

W_I: Probability that an I frame is errored given that an error has occurred;

W_P: Probability that a P frame is errored given that an error has occurred;

$P_I(d_I)$: Probability that an I frame needs to be retransmitted, called *I frame transmission failure probability*;

$P_P(d_P)$: Probability that a P frame needs to be retransmitted, called *P frame transmission failure probability*;

T_d: Fixed round trip time (FRTT) from server to receiver;

T_r: Average successful retransmission time for an errored frame, called the *average system recover time interval*. This is the average time required for successful retransmission;

τ_f: Average time interval between consecutive frame errors, called *average system failure time interval*;

λ: Channel transmission rate;

$\mu(t)$: Multimedia playback rate at time t;

C_{min}: Minimum receiver buffer size.

3.2 Average System Failure and Recover Time

Since the probability of a bit being in error is ρ, the probability that the payload of a cell has no error is $(1 - \rho)^N$. Therefore, the probability p that a cell is in error can be expressed as:

$$p = 1 - (1 - \rho)^N \tag{1}$$

The probability $P_I(d_I)$ that an I frame needs to be retransmitted is the probability that the number of errored cells in the frame is higher than the threshold d_I. Therefore, $P_I(d_I)$ can be expressed as:

$$P_I(d_I) = 1 - \sum_{i=0}^{d_I} \binom{N_I}{i} p^i (1 - p)^{N_I - i} \tag{2}$$

where $\sum_{i=0}^{d_I} \binom{N_I}{i} p^i (1 - p)^{N_I - i}$ represents the probability of the I frame having upto d_I errored cells. Similarly, $P_P(d_P)$ can be expressed as:

$$P_P(d_P) = 1 - \sum_{j=0}^{d_P} \binom{N_P}{j} p^j (1 - p)^{N_P - j} \tag{3}$$

Given that a frame is in error, the probability that the frame is an I frame is proportional to the size of the I frame in a GoP. Therefore, W_I can be expressed as:

$$W_I = \frac{S_I}{S_I + S_P(\frac{n}{m} - 1) + S_B \frac{m-1}{m} n} \tag{4}$$

where the denominator represents the size of a GoP. Similarly, we can obtain the expression for W_P as:

$$W_P = \frac{S_P}{S_I + S_P(\frac{n}{m} - 1) + S_B \frac{m-1}{m} n} \tag{5}$$

If an I frame is in error, the average time T_r^I for successful retransmission is expressed as:

$$T_r^I = (T_d + \tau_s^I)(1 - P_I(d_I)) + 2(T_d + \tau_s^I)P_I(d_I)(1 - P_I(d_I)) + \ldots\ldots$$
$$= \frac{T_d + \tau_s^I}{1 - P_I(d_I)} \tag{6}$$

where $\tau_s^I = \frac{S_I}{\lambda}$ is the time required to transmit an I frame into the wireless channel. Similarly, T_r^P for successful retransmission of a P frame can be expressed as:

$$T_r^P = \frac{T_d + \tau_s^P}{1 - P_P(d_P)} \tag{7}$$

where $\tau_s^P = \frac{S_P}{\lambda}$ is the time to transmit a P frame into the channel.

Therefore, the average system recover time (T_r) is the statistical sum of the I and P frame recover times T_r^I and T_r^P with weights W_I and W_P respectively. Therefore, T_r can be expressed as:

$$T_r = T_r^I W_I + T_r^P W_P \tag{8}$$

Because a wireless channel has significant error rate, let's say that an error happens after time τ_f which is defined as the average system failure time. Since the acceptable error thresholds are d_I and d_P for I and P frames respectively, the average system failure time is:

$$\tau_f = \frac{\min(d_I, d_P)}{\lambda \rho} \tag{9}$$

where the λ is the available bandwidth of the ABR connection.

An interactive receiver can perform VCR like interactive functions such as stop, playback, fastforward (FFW), and fastbackward (FBW) which are represented by a state transition diagram as shown in Figure 3. In the FFW/FBW state, the receiver will consume data at a higher speed than the playback state. Therefore, in response to a FFW/FBW request, the sever will request higher bandwidth than is required in normal playback. The bandwidth λ required by the server is decided by the level of interactivity of the receiver and the available bandwidth.

Let's denote the stop, playback, FFW and FBW states of the receiver by 0, 1, 2, 3, and the state transition probability from state i to state j (where $0 \leq i, j \leq 3$) is represented by θ_{ij}. If stationary state probability vector for the receiver is $X = (X_0, X_1, X_2, X_3)$, X can be obtained by solving the following equation [11]:

$$X_0 = \frac{1}{1 + \theta_{0,1}/\theta_{1,0}(1 + \theta_{1,2}/\theta_{2,1} + \theta_{1,3}/\theta_{3,1})}$$

$$X_1 = \frac{\theta_{0,1}}{\theta_{1,0}(1 + \theta_{0,1}/\theta_{1,0}(1 + \theta_{1,2}/\theta_{2,1} + \theta_{1,3}/\theta_{3,1}))}$$

$$X_2 = \frac{\theta_{0,1}\theta_{1,2}}{\theta_{1,0}\theta_{2,1}(1 + \theta_{0,1}/\theta_{1,0}(1 + \theta_{1,2}/\theta_{2,1} + \theta_{1,3}/\theta_{3,1}))} \qquad (10)$$

$$X_3 = \frac{\theta_{0,1}\theta_{1,3}}{\theta_{1,0}\theta_{3,1}(1 + \theta_{0,1}/\theta_{1,0}(1 + \theta_{1,2}/\theta_{2,1} + \theta_{1,3}/\theta_{3,1}))}$$

For interactive multimedia, the expected channel transmission rate $E[\lambda(t)]$ is therefore expressed as the statistical sum of the playback rate, fastforward rate, and fastbackward rate with weights X_1, X_2 , and X_3.

$$E[\lambda(t)] = [X_1 + k(X_2 + X_3)]\mu(t) \qquad (11)$$

where k is the FFW/FBW speed factor implying that the channel transmission rate is k times that of the normal playback rate.

3.3   System Model and Dynamics

If the receiver receives a frame with the number of errored cells exceeding the threshold, the server will retransmit the corresponding frame by switching to the retransmission state. Therefore, the status of the system can be divided into two states as shown in Figure 4:

-   State 0: the *normal state* in which multimedia is continuously received at the receiver;
-   State 1: the *retransmission state* in which the system is retransmitting a frame. The receiver consumes data upto the errored frame and then waits until the successful arrival of the retransmitted frame.

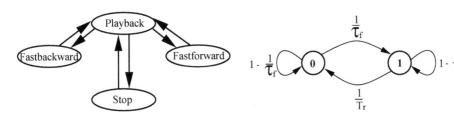

Fig. 3. The interactive operation state at receiver.

Fig. 4. The state diagram of the server-client type wireless multimedia transmission system.

From Figure 4, the state transition matrix M is expressed as:

$$M = \begin{bmatrix} 1 - \frac{1}{\tau_f} & \frac{1}{\tau_f} \\ \frac{1}{T_r} & 1 - \frac{1}{T_r} \end{bmatrix} \tag{12}$$

Let $V = (V_0, V_1)$ denote the long term stationary state vector, which satisfies the stationary equation:

$$V = VM \tag{13}$$

By solving the stationary equation, the steady state probabilities are obtained as:

$$V_0 = \frac{1}{1 + \alpha} \tag{14}$$

$$V_1 = \frac{\alpha}{1 + \alpha} \tag{15}$$

where $\alpha = \frac{T_r}{\tau_f}$. In order for the system to work satisfactorily, it should be at state 0 most of the time, i.e., $\alpha << 1$. This implies:

$$\frac{T_d + \tau_s^I}{1 - P_I(d_I)} W_I + \frac{T_d + \tau_s^P}{1 - P_P(d_P)} W_P \ll \frac{\min(d_I, d_P)}{\lambda \rho} \tag{16}$$

If $\mathrm{Det}(M) = 0$, there is no non-trivial steady state solution, i.e., the system does not have any long term stationary state. In this case, the system will not work properly; this gives the critical condition that the system will be down:

$$T_r \tau_f = T_r + \tau_f \tag{17}$$

Because T_r and τ_f are related to channel bit error rate, channel transmission rate, multimedia frame size, GoP structure, acceptable error threshold, FRTT, etc., by monitoring and dynamically adjusting these parameters during multimedia transmission, we can satisfy acceptable quality of service and prevent the video transmission from collapse. For example, ATM ABR service offers the possibility of adjusting channel transmission rate during transmission by requesting bandwidth using the Resource Management (RM) cell.

4   Minimum Receiver Buffer Requirement

For MPEG video, the decoding of P and B frames in a GoP depends on the I frame in that GoP; the decoding of a B frame depends only on the P frames preceding and following the B frame. Therefore, an error in an I or P frame propagates to all other frames in the GoP. The decoder at the receiver will deplete the buffered data until the damaged frame is recovered. Assuming that the system failed at time t_1, to sustain a continuous display at receiver, the amount of buffered data $C(t_1)$ must satisfy:

$$C(t_1) = \int_{t_1}^{t_1 + T_r} \mu(t) dt \tag{18}$$

By using the average expression, let $E[\mu(t_1)]$ denote the average value of $\mu(t)$ for $t_1 \leq t \leq t_1 + T_r$. Then $C(t_1)$ can be expressed as

$$C(t_1) = T_r E[\mu(t_1)] \tag{19}$$

The minimum amount of buffered data also sets the minimum receiver buffer size C_{min}:

$$C_{min} = T_r E[\mu(t_1)] \tag{20}$$

By substituting the expression for T_r into Equation (20), we get:

$$C_{min} = \left(\frac{T_d + \tau_s^I}{1 - P_I(d_I)} W_I + \frac{T_d + \tau_s^P}{1 - P_P(d_P)} W_P \right) E[\mu(t_1)] \tag{21}$$

From Equation (21), the minimum receiver buffer size is decided by the playback rate, the FRTT, the link rate, and the frame failure probability.

5   Numerical Results

In this section, we present results to evaluate the performance of our proposed scheme and show its effectiveness in multimedia transmission over wireless ATM. The average system failure time interval versus the level of user interactivity is shown in Figure 5. As expected from Equations (9) and (11), with an increase in the fastforward/fastbackward probability of the user, the required channel transmission rate also increases. This results in more data bits being transmitted in unit time, i.e. higher probability of error happening in unit time. Therefore, the average system failure time interval decreases.

The average system failure time interval versus the channel bit error rate is shown in Figure 6. As pointed out in Equation (9), the average system failure time interval is inversely proportional to the channel bit error rate.

The average system failure time interval versus the cell error threshold is shown in Figure 7. The average system failure time interval linearly increases with an increase in the cell error threshold which depends on the QoS acceptable by the user.

The I frame and P frame failure probability versus channel bit error rate is shown in Figure 8. As the channel bit error rate increase, the frame failure probability increase abruptly. Since the size of I frame is much larger than that of P frame, the I frame failure probability is much more sensitive to the channel bit error rate than the P frame.

The I frame and P frame failure probabilities versus cell error threshold are shown in Figure 9. As the cell error threshold increase, the frame failure probability decrease abruptly. This enables us to properly choose the cell error threshold to compensate for the the channel bit error rate which in turn reduces the number of retransmissions and increases the network bandwidth utilization.

The average system recover time interval versus channel bit error rate is shown in Figure 10. When channel error rate is relatively small, the average

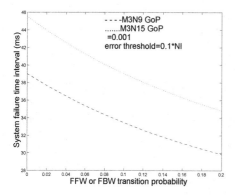

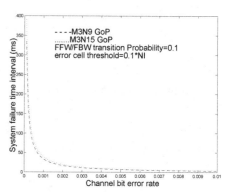

Fig. 5. Average system failure time interval versus the receiver's level of interactivity.

Fig. 6. Average system failure time interval versus the channel bit error rate.

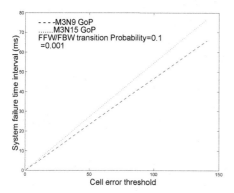

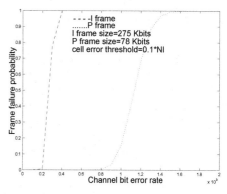

Fig. 7. Average system failure time interval versus cell error threshold.

Fig. 8. I & P frame failure probability versus channel bit error rate.

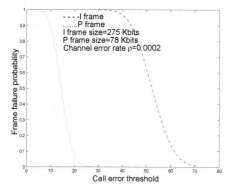

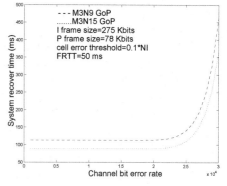

Fig. 9. I & P frame failure probability versus the cell error threshold.

Fig. 10. Average system recover time interval versus channel bit error rate.

retransmission time is almost constant. As the channel bit error rate increases to some area, the average retransmission time increases sharply.

The system recover time interval versus receiver's level of interactivity is shown in Figure 11. As the level of interactivity increases, the transmission rate increases, the time to inject a frame into network decrease, and the average retransmission time decreases.

The average system recover time interval versus the I frame size is shown in Figure 12. As the I frame size increases, the probability of I frame transmission increases with an associated increase in time to inject an I frame into network. Therefore, the average retransmission time will increase.

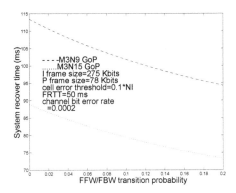

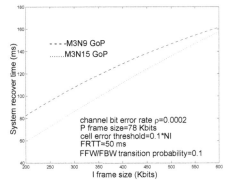

Fig. 11. Average system recover time interval versus user's level of interactivity.

Fig. 12. Average system recover time interval versus I frame size.

The minimum receiver buffer size versus channel bit error rate is shown in Figure 13. As described in Equation (20), the minimum receiver buffer size is proportional to the average system retransmission time. Therefore, when the channel error rate is low, the minimum receiver buffer size is almost constant. As the channel bit error rate increases, the minimum receiver buffer size increases abruptly in order to maintain a continuous display at the receiver.

The minimum receiver buffer size versus the user's level of interactivity is shown in Figure 14. Since interactivity only affects the channel transmission rate, its effect on receiver buffer size is relatively small.

The minimum receiver buffer size versus the I frame size is shown in Figure 15. As the I frame size increases, the frame transmission failure probability increases, the time needed to inject the frame into the network increases, and the required channel transmission rate increases resulting in an increase in the minimum receiver buffer size as shown in Equation (21).

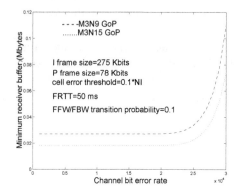
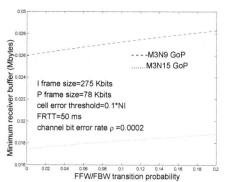

Fig. 13. Minimum receiver buffer size versus channel bit error rate.

Fig. 14. Minimum receiver buffer size versus receiver's level of interactivity.

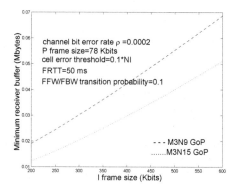

Fig. 15. Minimum receiver buffer size versus I frame size.

6   Conclusions

In this paper, we have proposed a new selective retransmission scheme for multimedia transmission over noisy wireless channel using the ATM ABR service. We analyzed the system requirements and minimum receiver buffer size for providing acceptable QoS to the user. We conclude that the average system failure time interval decreases with an increase in the channel error rate and level of user interactivity. The I frame has a much higher transmission failure probability than the P frame for a given channel bit error rate.

The average system recover time interval has tight relationship with the channel bit error rate and the frame sizes of video, but has little effect on the level of user interactivity. By choosing an acceptable cell error threshold for a given channel error rate, our proposed selective retransmission scheme requires a small receiver buffer to cost effectively transmit multimedia over a wireless channel with a bit error rate less than 10^{-4}.

Our investigation on the effect of coding on the performance of our proposed algorithm shows that for multimedia over a noisy wireless channel, a large GoP structure has a better performance than a small GoP structure.

References

1. Lombardo, A., Palazzo, S., Schenbra, G.: Management of wireless ATM networks loaded by mobile ABR source traffic. In: Globecom, Brazil (1999) 2758 – 2762   49
2. Kwok, Y.K., Lau, V.: A quantitative comparison of multiple access control protocols for wireless atm. IEEE Transactions on Vehicular Technology **50** (2001) 796 – 815   49
3. Kwok, Y.K., Lau, V.: Performance evaluation of multiple access control schemes for wireless multimedia services. IEE Proc - Communications **148** (2001) 86–94   49
4. Acampora, A.: Wireless atm: A perspective on issues and prospects. IEEE Personal Communication **3** (1996) 8–17   49
5. Raychaudhuri, D.: Wireless ATM networks: Architecture, system design and prototyping. IEEE Personal Communication **3** (1996) 42–49   49
6. Ayanoglu, E., Eng, K.Y., Karol, M.J.: Wireless ATM: Limits, challenges, and proposals. IEEE Personal Communication **3** (1996) 18–36   49
7. Zheng, B., Atiquzzaman, M.: Traffic management of multimedia over ATM networks. IEEE Communications Magazine **37** (1999) 33–38   50, 52
8. Batra, P., Chang, S.F.: Effective algorithms for video transmission over wireless channels. Signal Processing: Image Communication **12** (1998) 147–166   50
9. Zhang, J., Frater, M.R., Arnold, J.F., Percival, T.M.: MPEG-2 video services for wireless ATM networks. IEEE Journal on Selected Areas in Communication **15** (1997) 119–128   50
10. Sun, H., Zdepski, J.W., Kwok, W., Raychaudhuri, D.: Error concelment algorithms for robust decoding of MPEG. Signal Processing: Image Communication **10** (1997) 249–268   50
11. Zheng, B., Atiquzzaman, M.: Multimedia over high speed networks: reducing network requirement with fast buffer fillup. In: IEEE GLOBECOM'98, Sydney (1998) 779–784   55

Agile Systems Manager for Enterprise Wireless Networks

Sandeep Adwankar and Venu Vasudevan

Networks and Infrastructure Department,
Motorola Labs,
1301, E. Algonquin Road,
IL02-2240, Schaumburg, IL 60196,
sandeep.adwankar@motorola.com, venuv@labs.mot.com

Abstract. Advances in enterprise wireless networks with wireless LAN along with the need for a pervasive computing is leading to a very large growth in a number of managed elements. The conventional management model of a centralized manager does not work well in this highly evolving network that is characterized by mobility and intermittent connectivity. This paper motivates a need for an agile systems manager, one that is resource and network aware and redistributes the management logic within a "virtual" management station to operate effectively in changing network conditions. This paper proposes mobile agent based approach for systems management infrastructure that can deploy, reconfigure, load balance and react to environment change autonomously. The paper presents a performance management implementation for managing a mid-sized network composed of combination of wireless and wired network elements. The paper presents experimental results that show significant advantages of the agile management system over the conventional management system.

1 Introduction

With emergence of a wireless LAN, distinction between "fixed" (wired) and mobile wireless enterprise is blurring, which has implications on systems management. System management approaches for wired networks have relied on the fact that they have a relatively fixed set of network elements (and topology), connected together with high-bandwidth links. The wireless enterprise has existed in a different universe of protocols, hardware and management mechanisms. Now, with the ability of mobile laptop or handheld to enter an enterprise and "plug-in" to (and disconnect from) the fixed network, the network has a continually changing element set and topology, and a mixed breed of network links with different bandwidth capabilities. Over time, the wireless subset of this network is likely to become a significant fraction even in fixed enterprises, due to the difficulty in installing and expanding wired networks to accommodate personnel and organizational changes in an enterprise.

Additionally, the mobile workplace and associated mobile devices places new challenges on systems management such as coordination of software upgrades across

K.C. Almeroth and M. Hasan (Eds.): MMNS 2002, LNCS 2496, pp. 62-76, 2002.
© Springer-Verlag Berlin Heidelberg 2002

both static and mobile devices, load balancing and performance monitoring of dynamic network architectures.

Managing a dynamic network with conventional centralized management model will become progressively more cumbersome, and motivates the need for agile management architecture, where the management system re-organizes based on the changes in network. This paper explores elements of agile management, and proposes an agent based management architecture that exhibits such agility. The following attributes characterize an *agile* systems manager (ASM) :

- **Dynamic and Distributed**

An agile systems manager has management logic distributed throughout the network and location of manager components can be changed. The definition of manager includes all devices from which one can retrieve enterprise systems data and network data and can perform management operation. NEW management functionality can be incrementally added with self-distributing components.

- **Decentralized and Fault-tolerant**

The architecture is inherently decentralized, as there is no centralized management station where all intelligence is located and hence there is no central point of failure. This is particularly important for wireless networks as both managed elements and manager components can be intermittently connected. The architecture does not assume that all management agents are dumb and perform only get or set. The management functionality is distributed as autonomous components having their own fault recovery process.

- **Resource-Aware**

The agile systems manager is network and resource aware. It positions the management components according to dynamic network characteristics. The network-aware components are placed closer to managed hosts to conserve bandwidth of most frequent management operations. The management components requiring more CPU resources are placed on hosts having spare CPU computing cycles.

- **Mobile and Adaptive**

Agile management components have built-in mobility with operator-configurable rules that enable them to find the best location to migrate to for optimal operation. Manager composition and topology continually responds to a continually updated, dynamically discovered network topology. Reactive mobility allows an agile systems manager to survive attacks without the need for centralized, manual operator procedures.

- **Scalable**

The conventional management system micro manages due to central intelligence, thus it is not very scalable. The agile systems manager being decentralized; is able to scale and move to different administrative domains and send only useful and critical data to network operators. At the same time, operator has observability to all elements of the agile systems manager.

This paper presents our experiences in build an Agile Systems Management platform, whose capabilities are leveraged in an adaptive performance manager. The capabilities of the management platform are equally relevant to configuration and fault management problems. The rest of the paper is organized as follows. Section 2 introduces systems architecture of ASM. Section 3 gives overview of the ASM infrastructure and its capabilities of dynamic configurability and self-adaptation . Section 4 describes a network performance management application that leverages the platforms self-configuration capabilities. Section 5 describes discovery phase in the ASM and provides experimental results that shows more than 40% improvement in discovery operation due to mobility. Section 6 describes dynamic characteristics of performance monitoring with results. Section 7 discusses fault tolerance aspects and experimental results showing resilience of ASM under denial of service attack. Section 8 presents related work and Section 9 concludes with directions of future work.

2   Architecture of Agile Systems Manager

In a conventional systems manager, all management functions are centralized into manager platform. In ASM, management functions are distributed in components that have infrastructure substrate as a base. All components are autonomous and do not depend on centralized intelligence to perform management operations. The primary components of ASM are shown in Figure 1.

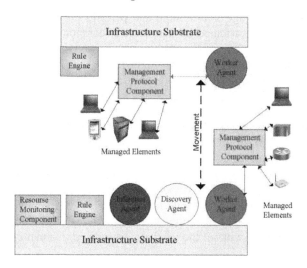

Fig. 1. Agile Systems Manager Architecture

2.1 Worker Agent

The worker agent is a primary management activity component of ASM. Worker agents are distributed throughout the network and they use management protocol components to invoke management operations on managed elements. Worker agents communicate with other agents using Tuple Space based protocol supported by the infrastructure substrate. The store-and-forward nature of tuple spaces allows communicating agents to reside on intermittently connected devices.

A worker agent carries a rule certificate, which encapsulates agent-specific policies for optimal location, and migration and cloning criteria. R rule certificates provide application reconfiguration policies to be defined and enforced in distributed fashion on a per agent basis.

The Performance Monitoring (PM) agent is a type of worker agent implemented to monitor performance of a set of managed elements. A graphical interface is associated with PM agents for debugging purposes. This allows the PM application developer to visually track agent movement, and potentially tune their rule certificates to optimize migration patterns. A snapshot of PM agent monitoring four hosts in 145.1.80 subnet is shown in Figure 2. This PM agent monitors ipInReceives, total number of input datagrams received from interfaces, including those in received in error and icmpInEchos, number of ICMP echo messages received.

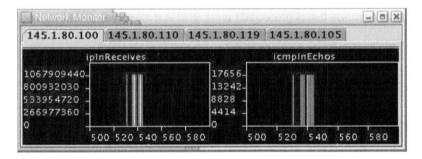

Fig. 2. PM Agent monitoring input packets and ICMP packets of 4 hosts in 145.1.80 network

2.2 Discovery Agent

The discovery agent dynamically discovers all active and manageable elements in the assigned domain by continuously monitoring the network. It provides this information to other agents in the system like worker agents and inference agent. The discovery agent maintains a list of active elements and manageable elements. It continuously monitors the network to check if any element becomes active and if so, it puts it in the active list. The discovery agent also monitors if any active element becomes manageable (due to start of management agent) and if so, puts it in the manageable element list.

In case of discovery system, our approach was not to come up with clever discovery algorithm, but to come up with mechanism that can perform multiple localized efficient discovery operations in terms of time taken for discovery. Discovering a manageable element is two-step process:

1. Finding whether the element is active. The discovery agent has a ping like implementation, in which a socket connection is tried with the element. If there is no route to host or if the host is unknown, that element is considered inactive.

2. Finding presence of SNMP agent on an element. The discovery agent creates a SNMP session, establishes the active element as peer and performs SNMP get operation on that active element. If this operation is successful, it identifies a working SNMP agent on that element with appropriate MIB.

2.3 Inference Agent

The inference agent serves both as an entity that makes high-level inferences from collected telemetry, and as the console for network operators to control and observe deployed network management applications. It interacts with worker and discovery agents to maintain (and log) an accurate view of network topology and state. Figure 3 shows the snapshot of an inference agent showing an agent-based view of the managed system. The *Agent View* panel on Figure 3 shows a mapping between agents and the hosts they manage. The *Monitor Data* panel shows telemetry on a per host basis. This telemetry is information that is processed (aggregated and averaged) by PM agents.

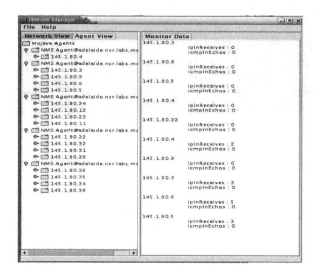

Fig. 3. Inference Agent showing Agent view and monitor data

The Inference agent can make use of monitor data to infer things such as top 10 nodes generating maximum network traffic or top 10 nodes under denial of service attack.

2.4 Management Protocol Component

Worker agents use a management protocol component (e.g. SNMP, CMIP or IIOP) to execute management operations on managed elements. This component allows other agents in the system to be agnostic about the underlying physical management protocol.

3   Infrastructure Substrate in ASM

The infrastructure substrate provides a number of support services to enable decentralized resource-aware, network-aware adaptation. To achieve this, it relies on the capabilities provided by the Mojave mobile agent system [2] [3]. Mojave supports a two-layer model of agents: a functional part and a policy (rule certificate) part. This model is key to enabling customizable adaptation policies, which can be enforced in a decentralized manner. The rest of this section describes the various components of Mojave and the role they play in architecting agile, auto-configuring systems management applications.

3.1 Pod

The Pod is an agent execution engine of the ASM. It provides runtime context and support services for the agent execution. To every incoming agent, pod provides a thread of execution, access to rule engine and resource monitoring component. Each pod is implemented as a Jini[5] service and is registered with a lookup service, thus each pod is able to find presence of other pods. Agents query host pod (i.e. pod where they are currently executing) to determine the places (pods) where they can move.

3.2 Resource Monitoring Component

The resource monitoring component makes ASM network and environment aware. Worker components make mobility or clone decisions based on resources available on a network and a host. The resource information such as bandwidth, delay, CPU spare cycles, available memory, network topology is gathered by a resource monitoring component and is made available to a number of worker agents. A resource monitoring component is associated with rule certificates of different worker agents.

3.3 Rule Engine

A rule engine on a pod tracks rule certificates of all agents in the pod. The XML based rule certificate consists of a set of event-action rules, with the event describing environmental conditions that can cause an agent to take some action, and the action clause describing what the agent needs to do. The rule engine maintains relationship with rules certificates, resource monitoring components, and agents. The rule engine is responsible for parsing rules, adding rules to the engine, firing rules and triggering agents.

3.4 Communication Mechanism

A pod needs communication infrastructure to transport an agent from one pod to another. Agents need a way to communicate with another agent or group of agents. A tuplespace satisfies this network middleware requirement by providing capability of network communication buffer. The tuplespace is a globally shared, associatively addressed memory space that is organized as a bag of tuples. A tuple is a vector of typed values or fields. An agent can register with a tuple space with a specific tuple template. It will then receive callback, if another agent writes tuple of same template to the tuple space, allowing it to communicate with group of agents. Pods use same mechanism to transport agents. They register with the tuple space with a template having a serialized agent as one of the field. When any pod writes serialized agent to the tuple space, it will receive callback of serialized agent. The Liaison is an entity that implements ASM's interface to the tuple space. IBM TSpaces [9] was used as a tuple space implementation.

3.5 Lookup and Leasing Mechanism

Pods and agents need mechanism to find other pods in the system. It also needs mechanism to remove outdated references for non existent pods or agents that did not or could not clean up. Jini provides architecture and implementation of lookup and leasing mechanism. So when agent service is plugged into a network of Jini services, it advertises itself by publishing an AgentProxy, a Java object that implements the agent functionality. The Pod finds this agent by looking for an object that matches agent attributes. When it gets the service's published object, it downloads agent code it needs and hands it over to an agent manager in a pod to start the agent in a new thread.

4   Network Performance Management

The network performance management application is built to show one example of agile systems manager that demonstrates self-installation, self-reconfiguration and load-distribution aspects in real world environment. The managed network for performance management is an array of subnetworks each having around 255 hosts connected by Ethernet and wireless LAN.

The overall performance monitoring (PM) task is to measure the network stress. The network stress is an operator configurable function and is defined as a function of different network parameters like IP packet traffic, ICMP in/out, TCP/UDP connections for hosts, bandwidth and latency. This performance monitoring task is performed for a network from a "management station" which itself is a collection of leased computers. Thus the management application runs on machines that are not dedicated to this management task. Therefore, the PM task has to share cycles with either other systems management tasks, or in the case where PM task is running on regular user machines, with non systems management tasks. The management task runs over some subset of the 255 machines on which pods are installed.

The PM task is divided into a group of identical PM agents, which are type of worker agents. Each PM agent monitors subset of IP addresses in the 255 node subnetwork. The network operator responsible for this system, instantiates the inference agent and provides list of subnetworks to be monitored. The network operator also customizes XML rule certificate for PM agent. The agent rule certificate contains rules for

- **Cloning**

The clone rule certificate lists maximum number of managed elements a single PM agent can monitor before it needs to take action to create clone for itself.

- **Mobility**

If load on a host pod is more than that specified in the loading function (combination of parameters like number of processes, CPU spare cycles, available memory etc.), then the agent tries to find a pod with lesser loading function and move there. Thus, agent can move to host having higher computational availability.

The rule certificate for mobility to protect agent under denial of service attack is shown below:

```
<watchFor action='move'>
  <podState>
      <sentry name = "ICMPSentry" op="GREATER" value="40" value-
      Type="Integer">
              com.motorola.mojave.snmp.sentry.ICMPSentry
      </sentry>
  </podState>
</watchFor>
```

This rule certificate relies on ICMP [10] resource monitoring component. With this rule, if ICMP packets for a pod are more than specified threshold (In this 40) then assume it is a denial of service attack, so move agent to another pod. Incoming agent will hand over this rule certificate to pod. The rule engine associates a resource monitoring component (ICMPSentry) monitoring ICMP packets with this rule certificate. The ICMPsentry will periodically sample ICMP packet count and if the sample value exceeds threshold, it will notify the rule engine. The rule engine performs dependency checking of this rule with all other rules contained in the rules certificate. If that leads to firing of the rule then action corresponding to that rule i.e. moving agent to another pod is executed. The rule Engine performs this check for all agents having rules about ICMP packet count.

5   Managed Element Discovery in ASM

The element discovery process is common for all types of network management activities. The discovery process is a continual process for detecting presence of any new managed element. The discovery process is usually first to start in the ASM and it requires setup of the ASM as shown in Figure 4. The steps for initial startup of agents are described below. The network operator starts infrastructure substrate that starts Jini lookup service, tuple space server and pods.

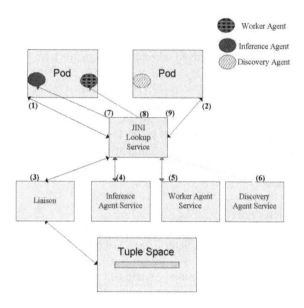

Fig. 4. Lookup Mechanism in JINI based Infrastructure Substrate

Steps 1,2: Pods register with Jini lookup service with certain name as attribute.
Step 3: The liaison which acts as wrapper for tuple space registers with the lookup service.
Steps 4,5,6: The network operator starts Jini agent services for all types of agents. These agent services register with lookup service and are responsible for starting as many agents of that type.
Step 7: The network operator starts inference agent on a pod.
Steps 8,9: The network operator starts PM agent and discovery agent in the pod.

PM agents and discovery agents establish a path of communication by registering for event channels with liaison (tuple space). A discovery agent is created on a pod that may not be on the subnetwork to be managed. The discovery agent queries host pod for presence of pods on the specified subnet. If a pod is found, discovery agent moves to the specified subnet. This move operation significantly reduces the subnet discovery time as shown in Figure 5. This figure shows the comparison of time taken when discovery agent discovers managed elements in subnet 145.1.80 while executing on another subnet 173.23.93 compared to time taken when it is moved and executed from a pod on 145.1.80 subnet. Thus there is improvement of more than 40% in the same discovery operation time due to mobility.

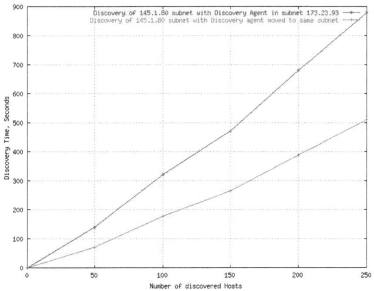

Fig. 5. Comparison of discovery time for discovery agent in same network with when it moved to different subnet

6 Performance Monitoring in ASM

The performance monitoring of a network in the ASM is accomplished by a set of distributed PM agents. These PM agents are created and positioned dynamically depending on a network topology, presence of infrastructure substrate in the monitored network and a rule certificate of a PM agent. The network operator starts a PM agent (Step 7 in Figure 4) and creation and positioning of new PM agents is achieved using cloning and movement of this agent. Figure 6 shows these clone and move phases in the ASM. The inference agent is not shown in the figure to reduce complexity, but it is listening to events from the discovery agent.

The clone, move operations steps as shown in Figure 6 are described below.

1. The discovery agent discovers presence of new active, manageable host.

2. The discovery agent writes the IP address of that host in the tuple space.

3. The PM agent is registered for listening to such tuple template. There will be eventRegister callback on the PM agent, as tuple of that template is written to the tuple space. The PM agent receives this tuple as part of callback and obtains IP address of newly discovered host. The clone rule for PM agents is "If number of monitored hosts for an agent exceeds specified limit, clone the agent". Thus, if the specified limit is four, then maximum number of hosts that PM agent can monitor is four. If clone rule is not triggered, then the PM agent monitors this host. It opens a new SNMP session, establishes the new host IP as peer and starts periodic SNMP "get" for performance variables.

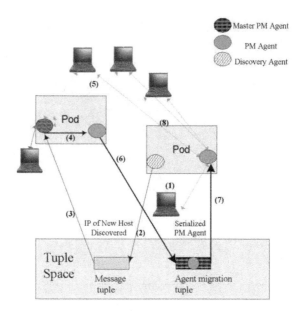

Fig. 6. Clone and Mobility in ASM

4. The discovery agent continues to send discovery events with new IP addresses and if number of hosts being monitored exceeds specified limit (say four), then PM agent clones and becomes master and creates a cloned PM agent and assigns a disjoint set of IP addresses (maximum of four, in this case) to the cloned PM agent.

5. The cloned PM agent becomes slave agent responsible for those set of IP addresses. This clone operation causes an event to be sent to the inference agent and it accordingly updates its internal data structures and correspondingly the operator GUI.

6. The cloned PM agent uses distance metric resource monitoring component (described in next subsection) to locate itself near hosts it is managing. The cloned PM agent will make call to the host pod to move itself to the new pod. The host pod will serialize the agent and will write the serialized agent in the tuple space.

7. The tuple space will invoke callback on registered pods, the new pod will take serialized PM agent tuple and will reconstruct agent object, allocate a thread of execution.

8. The cloned PM agent creates SNMP session for assigned hosts and starts monitoring those hosts.

6.1 Distance Metric Resource Monitoring Component

Distance metric resource monitoring component is used to determine the optimal location of PM agents. Since a PM agent is monitoring performance of set of hosts, it is best located at a location near to all or majority of hosts.

PM agents can execute only on agent execution engines i.e. Pods. The PM agent's task is to monitor a given set of hosts. To minimize latency in monitoring, PM agent should be moved to a pod that is closest in terms of time taken to monitor those set of hosts. The distance metric component finds such a pod. It finds this pod by following way: The distance metric component determines presence of pods from Jini lookup service. From each of these pods it initiates connection to set of hosts and gathers latency information. The pod that gives the least value for latency is the best pod to move to.

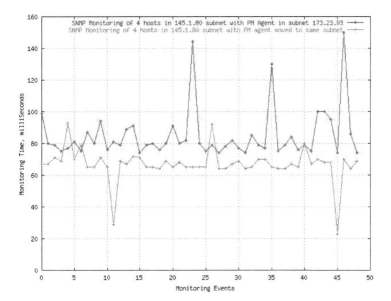

Fig. 7. Comparison of monitoring time of PM agent in different network with when it moved to same network

The Figure 7 shows the benefit of mobility of the PM agent. The PM agent using distance metric resource monitoring component moves from a different subnet to subnet on which managed host are present. There is improvement of more than 15% because of this mobility. In the case of PM agents, the increase in benefit is smaller compared to that observed for discovery agent. This is because the task accomplished by PM agent is significantly less in complexity compared to that of the discovery agent.

7   Observations of ASM

ASM based performance management is performed on two subnetworks consisting of both wired and wireless nodes over number of days. It was observed that the ASM is considerable stable with regular plug in and out of wireless LAN nodes.

7.1 Fault Tolerance and Load Balancing

The master PM agent has responsibility for recreating each of the failed cloned agents. The inference agent is responsible for recreating each of the failed master PM agent. The mechanism used for making inference agent fail-safe is by providing standard passive replication with the help of a backup inference agent.

The ASM load balances itself with the help of the mobility rules in PM agent certificates. If the operator needs to monitor the performance of four IP subnets, PM and discovery agents are dispatched to each of the four subnets and they perform the local processing by looking at large number of network parameters. These distributed PM agents send only parameters that exceed the operator specified threshold to the operator's management console leading to a scalable solution.

7.2 Experimental Observations of Agent Operations

The Table 1 shows time taken by agents in operations such as creation, movement and cloning [15]. The last two observations show the survivability aspects of ASM. The denial of service attack is launched on host by sending very large number of ICMP packets using flood ping. For three PM agents it took ten seconds to stop their execution on machine under attack, find safe machine with a pod, which satisfies load function, move to that pod and resuming operation from that safe machine. It took 20 seconds to move 11 PM agents to safe pods on the network.

Table 1. Performance Analysis of ASM

Agent Operations	Time in Seconds
PM, Inference agent creation at a remote place	4
Discovery agent creation at a remote place	1
PM agent movement between two different hosts	4
PM agent clone operation on a same host	1
PM agent traversal across 11 hosts (10 Moves)	44
Movement of 3 PM agents simultaneously in response to the denial of service (DOS) attack on the host.	10
Movement of 11 PM agents in response to the DOS.	20

7.3 Security

The security concerns is mobile agents technology are pertinent to mobile agent implementation and scope. In our mobile agent implementation, we leveraged J2SE security manager. Each agent execution engine has comprehensive Java policy file, which governs the set of operations that agent, can perform. Since we scope agile systems manager for "enterprise networks", agents and pods are assumed to have trusted relationship. Thus any agent created by a network operator is able to execute on any pod. Mojave should be able to leverage the security improvements in Jini (e.g. Davis) as they are made available to the community at large.

8   Related Work

Goldszmidt et al. [1] describes an approach of distributed management with help of programs that can be dispatched to remote processes and can invoke delegation procedure stored. However, unlike in the ASM, the delegation procedures themselves are not downloadable. IBM's NetScript [12] adopts a script based approach for providing mobility in systems management, with HTTP as the agent transport. Netscript uses a variant of the Basic language for agent scripting. The known security weaknesses of Basic make it less likely that it will gain traction as a systems management scripting language.

Pinheiro et al. [2] describes a way of using mobile agents for demonstrating aggregation network concepts. They outline a demand driven dataflow for the aggregation and filtering. The aggregation nodes in the dataflow graph are implemented using mobile agents.

Sumatra [13] is extension of Java that supports resource aware mobile programs. The resource monitor component in ASM is similar in concept to the Komodo, a distributed resource monitor.

There are many reported works in mobile agents [16], but we found that there are significantly few reported studies like [15] outlining experimental results and performance measurements. There are even fewer studies that demonstrate mobile agents implementation results over enterprise networks of meaningful size. Secondly, most of the published studies [15] target particular mobile agent systems, whose performance naturally differs depending on implementations. Many of these studies however fail to measure actual benefits of mobility to applications. In our work, we principally focused on creating "agile" systems manager for self-configuration and self-deployment and we measured the extent of benefits that mobility to offers to usual management operations such as discovery and performance management.

9   Conclusion

In this paper, we described why changing enterprise network architectures motivate new agile systems management architecture. We then described the necessary components of agility (e.g. application level auto-configuration, resource and network-awareness), and how an agile systems manager can be constructed over a tuple-space based agent system. Empirical data from a performance management prototype shows an improvement of 40% in the discovery process, and 15% in the performance management task.

Our current work is focused on making ASM pervasive. This involves bring downsizing components of the ASM to fit on resource constrained devices such as cell phones and PDA's. This enables anytime, anywhere management of enterprise networks from thin mobile devices. A particular challenge is supporting significant "control bandwidth" on mobile devices, whereby they can initiate and monitor complex customized management actions.

References

1. G. Goldszmidt, Y. Yemini. Distributed Management by Delegation. In 15th International Conference on Distributed Computing Systems, IEEE Computer Society, June 1995.
2. R. Pinheiro, A. Poylisher, H. Caldwell. Mobile Agents for Aggregation of Network Management Data, Third International Symposium on Mobile Agents, October 1999.
3. V. Vasudevan, S. Landis. Malleable Services, 34th Hawaii International Conference on Systems Sciences, January 2000.
4. V. Vasudevan, S. Landis, C. Jia, S. Adwankar. Malleable Services. OOPSLA Workshop on Experiences with Autonomous Mobile Objects and Agent Based Systems, October 2000
5. K. Thompson. JiniTM Technology Surrogate Architecture Specification. http://developer.jini.org/exchange/ projects/surrogate/
6. W. Keith Edwards. Core JINI. Prentice hall, Sept 1999
7. U. Warrier, L. Besaw, L. LaBarre, B. Handspicker., The Common Management Information Services and Protocols for the Internet. RFC 1095, Internet Engineering Task Force, Oct 1990.
8. S. Adwankar. Mobile CORBA. 3rd International Symposium on Distributed Objects & Applications, September 2001.
9. AdventNet. SNMP Agent Toolkit. http://www.adventnet.com.
10. IBM. TSpaces project home page. http://www.almaden.ibm.com/cs/TSpaces
11. K. McCloghrie, M. Rose. Management Information Base for Network Management of TCP/IP-based internets:MIB-II. RFC 1213, Internet Engineering Task Force, March 1991
12. A. Mohindra, A.Purakayastha, D. Zukowski, M. Devarakonda. Programming Network Components Using NetPebbles: An Earlly Report, Usenix COOTS, April 1998.
13. A. Purakayastha, A. Mohindra. Systems Management with NetScript, LISA, December 1998.
14. A. Acharya, M. Ranganathan, J. Saltz. Sumatra: A Language for Resource-aware Mobile Programs, Spring Verlay Lecture Notes in Computer Science.
15. M. Dikaiakos, M. Kyriakou, and G. Samaras. Performance Evaluation of Mobile-Agent Middleware: A Hierarchical Approach, 5th IEEE International Conference on Mobile Agents, December 2001.
16. A. Bieszczad, B. Pagurek, T. White. Mobile Agents For Network Management, IEEE Communication Surveys, 1998

System Performance of HiperLAN/2

K. Haider and H.S. Al-Raweshidy

Communication Systems Division,
Department of Electronics, University of Kent @ Canterbury,
Canterbury, Kent, UK, CT2 7NT, England
kh15@ukc.ac.uk, H.Al-Raweshidy@ukc.ac.uk

Abstract. Standards for broadband wireless multimedia communications in the 5 GHz band have being developed in Europe as well as in the US and Japan. HiperLAN/2 is a radio based local area networking solution that is intended for connecting mobile users with the backbone network wirelessly. HiperLAN/2 is being developed by ETSI (European Telecommunications Standards Institute). This paper will present HiperLAN/2's system design and performance. Furthermore, comparison is made with the American standard the IEEE 802.11(a).

1 Introduction

Wireless technology have enjoyed an increase demand from the general public as well as from business and other professional users, these range from cellular phones to high-speed digital networks supporting high speed computer communications.

HiperLAN/2 (H/2) is an upcoming standard, which is being specified by the ETSI/BRAN project. High Performance Radio Local Area Network type 2 (HiperLAN/2) is one of the wireless broadband access networks, shall provide high-speed communications between mobile terminals and various broadband infrastructure networks. HiperLAN/2 system operates at the 5GHz region. The frequency allocation in Europe is: 5.15-5.35 GHz, lower band (indoor use only) and 5.47-5.725 GHz, upper band (indoor and outdoor use). HiperLAN/2 can be used as an alternative access technology to a 2nd and 3rd generation cellular network. One may think of the possibility to cover hot spots (airport, hotels, etc.) and city areas with HiperLAN/2 and the wide area with GSM and WCDMA technologies. In this way, a user can benefit from a high performance network wherever it is feasible to deploy HiperLAN/2 and use GSM, WCDMA elsewhere. One of advantages of HiperLAN2 is that it could be connected to any backbone network, ATM, IP, Ethernet etc. HiperLAN/2 system is likely to be deployed in a wide range of environments, such as buildings, exhibition halls, airport, industrial buildings and outdoor deployment.

K.C. Almeroth and M. Hasan (Eds.): MMNS 2002, LNCS 2496, pp. 77-88, 2002.

2 High Speed Transmission

One of the main features in HiperLAN/2 system is the high transmission rate that could get up to 54 Mbps [1]. Orthogonal Frequency Division Multiplexing (OFDM) is a type of multicarrier modulation which uses overlapped orthogonal signals to divide a frequency-selective channel into a number of narrow-band flat-fading channels. Instead of transmitting the data symbols sequentially at a high symbol rate on a single carrier, a block of symbols is encoded using the Fast Fourier Transform (FFT), and transmitted in parallel over a number of subchannels.

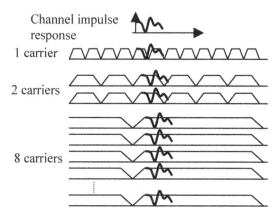

Fig.1. The advantage of muticarrier transmission

The sub-carriers are spaced by the inverse of the symbol period, so making them orthogonal. Individual sub-channels will have a symbol period longer than the multipath delay spread, therefore OFDM is useful for avoiding multipath interference. If a particular sub-channel has high noise then it can be de-activated, hence reducing the effects of fading and interference.

By increasing the number of transmitted carriers the data carried on each carrier reduces and hence the symbol period increases. This means that the Intersymbol Interference (ISI) affects a smaller percentage of each symbol as the number of carriers increase and hence the symbol period increases.

The sub-carriers are said to be orthogonal if

$$1/t \int e^{jwm_1t} * e^{-jwm_2t} dt = 1 \qquad \text{if } m_1 = m_2$$
$$= 0 \qquad \text{else}$$

where t is the useful symbol period, m_1 and m_2 are subcarrier number. Orthogonality is achieved by using a symbol period equal to subcarrier spacing ($\approx 1/312khz$).

3 Physical Layer

The transmission format on the physical layer is a burst, which consists of a preamble part and a data part. There are 19 channels in Europe, 9 channels for indoor and 10 channels for indoor and outdoor. Each channel is 20 MHz wide. Total subcarriers are 64 per channel, reflecting on the 64-point IFFT used at the transmitter end of HiperLAN/2 system. 52 subcarriers are used per channel, of which 48 are used for data transmission and 4 for pilot in order to estimate the fading channel.

Each channel, 20MHz wide, is divided into 52 sub-channels, about 300Khz wide each

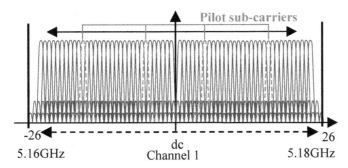

Fig.2. Sub-carrier allocation in each channel

The sub-carriers are number spread from –26 to 26 (Total of 52 Subcarriers), subcarrier number zero is dc meaning no data will be transmitted on it. Pilot subcarriers are numbered ±7 and ±21, as shown in figure 2. All 52 subcarriers are transmitted in one OFDM symbol, the duration of each symbol is 4μsec. This OFDM symbol consists of two parts, the cyclic prefix part (800 nsec) and the useful data part (3.2 μsec). The length of the useful symbol part is equal to 64 samples.

The cyclic prefix is a cyclic extension of the useful part and it is inserted before the useful part. The cyclic extension is a copy of the last 16 samples of the useful part. The reasons behind using a cyclic are to maintain receiver carrier synchronization and to model the transmission channel by convolving between the OFDM signal and channel response.

The air interface of HiperLAN/2 is based on time division duplex and dynamic time division multiple access, which allows for simultaneous communication in both uplink and downlink within the same time frame called MAC frame. The duration of the MAC frame is 2ms and comprises transport channels for broadcast control (BCH), frame control (FCH), access control (ACH), downlink (DL) and uplink (UL) data transmission and Random access (RCH).

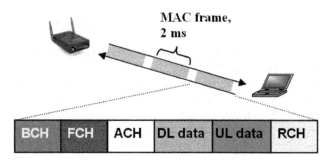

Fig.3. MAC frame structure

In order to improve the link capability due to different interference situations and distances of terminals to the access point (AP), a link adaptation scheme is applied [2], by using various modulation schemes on the subcarriers and puncturing of convolutional codes, the data rate can be varied.

Seven physical layer modes are specified [3], of which the first six are compulsory, where as the last which uses 64 QAM is optional.

Table 1. Physical layer modes of HiperLAN/2

Mo	Modulation	Code	Bit	Bytes/sym
1	BPSK	1/2	6Mbps	3.0
2	BPSK	3/4	9Mbps	4.5
3	QPSK	1/2	12Mbps	6.0
4	QPSK	3/4	18Mbps	9.0
5	16QAM	9/16	27Mbps	13.5
6	16QAM	3/4	36Mbps	18.0
7	64QAM	3/4	54Mbps	27.0

Forward error control is performed by a convolutional code of rate 1/2 and constraint length seven. Code rates 3/4 and 9/16 are obtained by puncturing. The puncturing codes for code rate 3/4 and 9/16 are 111111110111101111 and 110101 respectively.

4 Transport Channels

The broadcast channel (BCH), 15bytes long, contains control information that is sent in every MAC frame and reaches all mobile terminal (MT). Information such as the power levels, starting point and length of the FCH and RCH, network and AP ID.

The frame control channel, multiple of 27 bytes frames depending on the number of MT requests of resources, contains the exact description on the allocated bandwidth, in DL and UL, for the requested users in current MAC frame.

Access feedback channel, 9 bytes long, conveys information on previous access attempts made in the RCH.

All the above channels are transmitted in downlink only (AP to MT).

Uplink and Downlink traffic, bi-directional, consists of Protocol Data Unit (PDU) trains to and from MTs. A PDU train consists of DLC user PDUs (U-PDU of 54 bytes with 48 bytes of payload) and DLC control PDUs (C-PDUs of 9 bytes) to be transmitted or received by one MT. The C-PDUs and data PDUs are referred to as short and long transport channel respectively.

The random access channel, uplink only and it is 9 bytes long. Used by the MTs to gain bandwidth from the AP in the next MAC frame so data could be transmitted.

5 Convergence with other Systems

HiperLAN/2 system will be used in Airports, Large shopping malls, Train stations, etc, in order to connect the mobile user with the core network wirelessly. The core network could be Ethernet, ATM, IP or UMTS, i.e. HiperLAN/2 will be used with variety of services and protocols. This is possible due to the flexible architecture that defines a convergence layer (CL) between the core networks and the data link control (DLC) layer [4]. The CL adapts the Higher Layer Protocol to the DLC layer.

Data units that are transmitted within these protocols may differ in length. The CL in HiperLAN/2 segments and reassembles (SAR) theses data units (U-PDUs) with fixed length 48 bytes, which are then passed down to DLC and physical layer.

The number of OFDM symbols varies depending on the mode chosen, the higher the mode the fewer number of OFDM symbols required in order to transmit a Long or Short transport channels.

If mode 1 was chosen, i.e. 3 bytes per OFDM symbol, the number of symbols required in order to transmit a 54 byte data PDU is 18 symbols, if mode 4 was chosen then the required number of symbols is 6 per U-PDU.

All modes could be used to transmit the U-PDUs, but only modes 1, 2 and 4 are used to transmit C-PDUs. The U-PDU size is fixed, 54bytes, then for all modes, the "bytes per OFDM symbol" will go into 54 bytes.

In case of C-PDUs where the PDU size is 9 bytes, modes 3, 5, 6 and 7 have "bytes per OFDM symbol" sizes that will not go into the C-PDU. U-PDUs which are detected to be in error after the convolutional decoding are automatically requested for a retransmission (ARQ).

Two different codes are defined in HiperLAN/2 [5]: U-PDUs are protected by the CRC-24 with generator polynomial $g(x) = x^{24} + x^{10} + x^9 + x^6 + x^4 + x^3 + x + 1$ C-PDUs are protected by the CRC-16 with generator polynomial $g(x) = x^{16} + x^{12} + x^8 + x^7 + x^6 + x^3 + x + 1$. The minimum hamming distance for both codes is 6, which is the highest achievable at each case [6].

Using the cyclic redundancy check (CRC) would dramatically reduce PDU error probability.

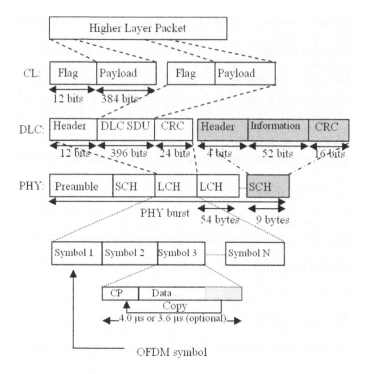

Fig.4. The transformation from data units from upper layer to OFDM symbol in HiperLAN/2 physical layer

6 Radio Network Functions

In order to support a number of radio network functions HiperLAN/2 standard defines measurements and signalling. These radio network functions are link adaptation, dynamic frequency selection, power control, multi-beam antenna and handover. All algorithms are vendors specific.

6.1 Dynamic Frequency Selection

HiperLAN/2 is a time-division duplex (TDD) system where the interference between the downlink and uplink can never be avoided. The Dynamic Frequency Selection (DFS) allows several operators to share the available spectrum. The DFS has to provide a good frequency plan already shortly after the installation of a new H/2 system. For fairness, the frequency plan established by the DFS should aim in providing individual cell with the same radio quality. A quick reaction due to sudden fades in the link is not desirable in order to avoid frequency reselections. The frequency reselection rate indicates the stability of the system and therefore it is preferable to be kept as low as possible. The task of DFS is to select a single carrier for each cell to ensured a reliable communication with small tolerable interference from other cells. Each access point has been allocated a number of frequencies, for example

F_1, F_7, F_{13}. From time to time the access point orders the mobile terminal to measure the radio signals received from the neighbouring access points. The MT will then report the measurements to the AP on each measured frequency. If the neighbouring AP uses a frequency near the frequency that the current AP is using then this will cause high interference to the MT. The AP will provide the MT with all the frequencies that it has been allocated and asks the MT to take interference measurements for each one with the neighbouring APs. The AP will choose the frequency that has the lowest interference level compared to other frequencies, as reported by the MT, and uses it for later transmissions. The respective protocols [7] specify that the AP controls the measurement period, the frequency on which to measure, the MTs which are requested to measure. Current quality $q(f)$ of the frequency f is [8]:

$$q(f) = -(R(f)_{UL} + \overline{R}(f)_{DL}) \div 2 \qquad (1)$$

where $\overline{R}(f)_{DL}$ is the mean value over all values $R(f)_{DL}$ calculated for each MT having reported its measurement. $R(f)_{UL}$ is signal measurement measured in AP in the uplink. These quality values $q(f)$ are filtered (using first order recursive filter with filter renewal coefficient C = 0.1) then frequency f becomes the long term mean quality measures $Q(f)$. The current frequency f_0 is kept when $Q(f) < Q(f_0) + M$ for all frequencies. Where M = 1dB, which is the margin if $Q(f)$ has exceeded $Q(f_0)$ by then carrier frequency f will be used rather than f_0. During these measurements, the AP will stop any data transmission to the MT. The data will be saved and will not be forwarded until the measurements are completed.

6.2 Power Control

Power control is needed in order to reduce the interference between HiperLAN/2 system and satellite system. It also reduces the complexity of the AP, for example by not needing to have an Automatic Gain Control (AGC). The transmit power P_{MT} of each MT is separately controlled within the range -15dBm $\leq P_{MT} \leq$ 30dBm. The minimum acceptable received signal strength at the AP is –71 dBm. The AP transmits power ranges from -15dBm $\leq P_{MT} \leq$ 30dBm. But the AP requires more accuracy.

6.3 Link Adaptation

The radio quality is totally dependent on the radio environment. As the environment gets worst, traffic in surrounding cells increases for example, the carrier to interference ratio (C/I) degrades. The link adaptation scheme adapts the physical robustness based on link quality measurements. Thus the physical mode is dynamically selected for the SCH and LCH in each transmitted MAC frame.

It is performed in both directions, in downlink and uplink in order to minimise the usage of an interfered carrier. In uplink, the AP measures the signal quality and informs the MT which mode to use in next transmission. In the opposite side, the MT measures the signal received from the AP and then informs the AP on the type of mode to use for the downlink transmissions. However, it is at the AP where the final decision is made, it decides which mode to use for downlink and uplink transmissions.

6.4   Multi-beam Antenna

In order to improve the link budget and improve the carrier to interference ratio (C/I) HiperLAN/2 system employs multi-beam antenna. The MAC protocol and the frame structure in HiperLAN/2 allow up to seven beams to be used. The MT informs the AP on which beam it will receive information from, i.e. it is MT initiated. The selection is based on constant monitoring the link performance, by measurements on the broadcast fields transmitted by each beam.

6.5   Handover

The mobility of the mobile user causes the variation in the link quality and in the interference levels. As the interference level increases the noise level increases.

When such effect occurs the best solution is to allow the Mobile Terminal (MT) to change the AP that it is currently connected with to other AP that provides better S/N ratio. This process is called Handover. Handover is a process used in order to recover the signal quality and to reduce the noise level. It is Mobile Terminal (MT) initiated, i.e. the MT performs the measurements and informs the Access Point for a handover process.

There are three types of Handover in HiperLAN/2 system.

Sector handover (Inter-Sector). During the Sector Handover only the antenna sector of the AP shall be changed.

Radio handover (Inter-APT/Intra-AP Handover). During the Radio Handover the MT changes the transceiver it is currently connected to, to other transceiver at the same AP.

Network handover (Inter-AP/Intra-Network Handover). As the MT moves from one AP coverage area to another it will request Handover to the new AP.

The MT uses the AP with the best radio signal as measured by the signal to noise ratio. As the MT moves around towards the boundary of the associated AP's coverage area, it may detect that there is an alternative AP with better radio transmission performance than the AP that it is currently connected/associated to.

The MT will then order a handover to the new AP. All connections will be moved to this new AP resulting in the MT staying associated to the HiperLAN/2 network and can still continue its communication.

7   System Performance

During the standardization process, exhaustive simulations have been conducted for selecting the parameters and performance analysis. Channel models have been developed for standardization. They were derived from measurements in typical indoor and outdoor environments [9].

Table 2. Channel models for HiperLAN/2

Channel model	r.m.s delay spread	Rice factor on first tap	Environment
A	50 ns	-	Office NLOS (no light of sight)
B	100 ns	-	Open space / Office NLOS
C	150 ns	-	Large open space NLOS
D	140 ns	10dB	Large open space LOS
E	250 ns	-	Large open space NLOS

Figure 5 shows the irreducible PER versus delay spread for few data rates. The figure shows the tolerable delay spread from each mode [10]. This is the minimum possible PER for certain delay spread, for which all packet errors are caused by Intersymbol Interference (ISI) due to the path delays exceeding the guard interval time of the OFDM symbol.

It could be concluded that as the bit rate increases the tolerable delay spread reduces. Taking the case when the PER is equal to 1%, the tolerable delay spread for the 54Mbps rate is estimated 120 ns, for the 27 Mbps bit rate the tolerable delay spread is 260 ns and finally for the 12Mbps bit rate the tolerable delay spread is 450 ns, which is the highest tolerable delay spread compared to other modes.

From the results shown in figure 5, it could be said that the 54 Mbps bit rate could be used in office buildings as it could tolerate delay spread of 120 ns, refer to table 2, where as the 12Mbps rate could be used in indoor and outdoor environments.

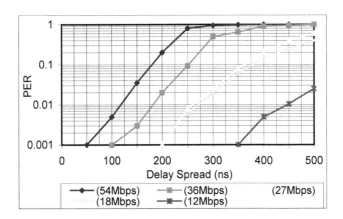

Fig.5. PER against Delay spread

Error rate performance at the presence of co-channel interference is shown in figure 6 below. The results shown are only applicable for channel model A (50 ns delay spread).

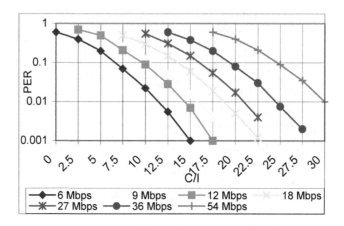

Fig.6. PER against C/I

The performance differences between all modes could be understood from figure 6 above. As the bit rate increases the required C/I for a certain error rate gets higher. Except for mode2, 9 Mbps, where its performance degrades below mode 3, which is 12 Mbps. This is due to the dominating effect in terms of C/I performance by worst performance of the code rate 3/4 compared to the rate 1/2, i.e. the C/I is dominated by the worst performance from the code rate of 3/4. The respective C/I requirement is between 6.2 dB and 30 dB, as shown in figure 6, depending on the mode, since the reasonable point of operation for packet services may lie between PERs of 1% and 10%. Link adaptation technique is performed by measuring the received signal, and then depending on the calculated C/I the best mode, with the highest throughput, is chosen. Taking for example, at one instant of time the measured C/I from a received signal is 17.5 dBs, hence Mode 6 will be chosen for the next signal transmission. This is one of the main advantages of HiperLAN/2 system, the best mode is always chosen which causes reduction in the interference level.

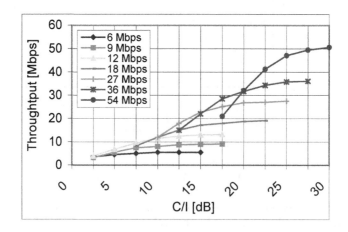

Fig.7. Link throughput against C/I for channel A

8 Comparison

In the 5 GHz band, there is another wireless system that is expanding rapidly in US, the IEEE 802.11(a) which will be well harmonized with HiperLAN/2 in physical layer. The upper layers are designed using different concepts.

IEEE 802.11(a) uses Carrier Sense Multiple Access with Collision Avoidance (CSMA/CA) as a channel access technique, where as HiperLAN/2 is based on reservation access which is scheduled by the access point. Both systems use OFDM technology as a modulation technique due to the advantages stated earlier. The physical layer Mode 5 of HiperLAN/2 and IEEE 802.11(a) differ in the rate and hence the code rate used. In IEEE 802.11(a) the fifth mode has a bit rate of 24 Mbps with 16QAM modulation type and 1/2 rate coder. There is an extra mode used in IEEE 802.11(a), where the bit rate is 48 Mbps, the modulation type used is 64QAM and 2/3 coding rate. Both system's throughput were compared and showed that H/2 had better system performance than IEEE 802.11(a). Additional mode supported in IEEE 802.11(a) will help to improve throughput in some scenarios, to reach H/2.

HiperLAN/2 leads 802.11(a) by using Dynamic Frequency Allocation (DFA) technique and Transmit Power Control (TPC) in order to have coexistence with radar systems that operate in the upper part of the European 5GHz band.

9 Conclusion

Current wireless communication systems are deployed in every possible spot in order to serve as many users as possible. At the hotspot areas, where the maximum concentration of users are situated current wireless systems still have problems in providing the required coverage area. HiperLAN/2 system will solve these problems. It will mainly be used in these hotspot areas and in office buildings in order to connect the mobile user with the core network wirelessly at high bit rates, which may reach up to 54 Mbps.

The report has shown the physical layer structure of HiperLAN/2. The advantages of using OFDM technique are also been looked at. System's performance under different delay spreads and interference levels also been looked at and shown that the system has good power efficiency technique as HiperLAN/2 has high flexibility in adjusting the link modulation and coding types (hence varying the physical bit rate) that suites the link performance accordingly.

References

1. www.hiperlan2.com
2. Furuskar et al., System Performance of EDGE, a Proposal for enhanced Data Rate in Existing Digital Cellular Systems, in Proc. IEEE VTC'98.
3. ETSI BRAN, HiperLAN Type 2, Physical (PHY) layer, TS 101 475, April 2000.
4. ETSI BRAN, HiperLAN Type 2; Data Link Control (DLC) layer Part 2: Radio Link Control (RLC) Sublayer, TS 101 761-2, April 2000.
5. TS 101 515-1 Ver.1.x.x Broadband Radio Access Networks (BRAN), HiperLAN Type 2:Data Link Control (DLC)Layer, Part1:Basic Data Transport Functions.

6.   F.J.Mac Williams, N.J.A. Sloane, The theory of error-correcting Codes, north-Holland Publishing company, New Yort.
7.   TS 101 761-2 Broadband Radio Access Networks (BRAN), HiperLAN type 2, Data Link Control (DLC) Layer, Part 2: Radio Link Control (RLC).
8.   C.Johanson, J.Naslund, M.Madfors, Adaptive Frequency Allocation of BCCH Frequencies in GSM, Proceedings 45th, IEEE VTC 1995, pp. 107-111.
9.   J. Medbo, H. Hallenberg and J.E. Berg. Propagation Characteristics at 5 GHz in Typical Radio-LAN Scenarios, proc. Of VTC' 99 Spring (Houston), pp. 185-189.
10.   Richard Van Nee, Ramjee Prasad, OFDM for Wireless Multimedia Communications (Artech House 2000)

Streaming Media Congestion Control Using Bandwidth Estimation[1]

Nadeem Aboobaker, David Chanady, Mario Gerla, and M.Y. Sanadidi

Computer Science Department, University of California, Los Angeles
{nadeem, chanady, gerla, medy}@cs.ucla.edu

Abstract. The fundamental challenge in streaming media over the Internet is to transfer the highest possible quality, adhere to the media play out time constraint, and efficiently and fairly share the available bandwidth with TCP, UDP, and other traffic types. This work introduces the Streaming Media Congestion Control protocol (SMCC), a new adaptive media streaming congestion management protocol in which the connection's packet transmission rate is adjusted according to the dynamic bandwidth share of the connection. In SMCC, the bandwidth share of a connection is estimated using algorithms similar to those introduced in TCP Westwood. SMCC avoids the Slow Start phase in TCP. As a result, SMCC does not exhibit the pronounced rate oscillations characteristic of traditional TCP, thereby providing congestion control that is more suitable for streaming media applications. Furthermore, SMCC is fair, sharing the bandwidth equitably among a set of SMCC connections. An important advantage is robustness when packet losses are due to random errors, which is typical of wireless links and is becoming an increasing concern due to the emergence of wireless Internet access. In the presence of random errors, SMCC is also friendly to TCP New Reno. We provide simulation results using the ns2 simulator for our protocol running together with TCP New Reno.

1   Introduction

TCP has successfully supported data applications with end-to-end reliable in-order packet communication. With the increase in link bandwidth over the past decade many multimedia applications that stream video and audio over the Internet have emerged. The popularity of such applications has caused multimedia data to be increasingly present in the Internet. Protocols must be developed that fairly share network bandwidth between multimedia and other connection types such as TCP, UDP, etc.

Multimedia is generally not transferred using the pure TCP paradigm because the services provided by TCP are more beneficial to applications requiring reliable data transfer, such as the Web, E-mail, and FTP. The latter applications place greater priority on reliable delivery, rather than the data transfer time. In contrast, the video

---

[1] This research was supported by NSF Grant ANI 9983138

K.C. Almeroth and M. Hasan (Eds.): MMNS 2002, LNCS 2496, pp. 89-100, 2002.

streaming application has stricter transfer latency requirements. The key distinguishing characteristic of such applications is that audio and video data needs to be continuously played out at the client end. This associates a play out time with each transferred data packet. If the packet arrives late, it is useless to the application, and might as well have been lost. A sending rate that does not fluctuate dramatically is therefore more suited for multimedia communications.

SMCC estimates the bottleneck bandwidth share of a connection at the client (receiver) side, using algorithms similar to those introduced in TCP Westwood [4,5,10]. The client does not send acknowledgements to the sender for each received video packet. Instead, a negative acknowledgment (NACK) is returned to the sender when the client perceives a packet loss. This NACK serves two purposes. First, it is a request for retransmission of the lost packet. Depending on whether it can be delivered on time the sender may or may not retransmit the packet. Secondly, in SMCC, a NACK carries to the sender the current Bandwidth Share Estimate (BSE). Thus a NACK message conveys a measure of congestion, and the sender adjusts its sending rate accordingly.

At all times, the sender mimics TCP's congestion avoidance phase by increasing its sending rate by one packet per round trip time (RTT) until a NACK message is received, upon which the sending rate is set to the BSE. After this readjustment in the sending rate, the server resumes a linear sending rate increase of one packet per RTT.

As will be shown in the remainder of this paper, each SMCC sender gets an accurate estimate of the connection's fair share of the bottleneck bandwidth, and effectively adjusts the sending rate to the changing estimate. This enables the receiver to continuously play out the delivered media, albeit at varying quality, even under highly dynamic network conditions. SMCC is also a fair protocol in that it shares the bottleneck bandwidth fairly among a set of SMCC connections. Finally, SMCC behaves well in random loss environments, since the bandwidth estimate is robust to sporadic packet loss, unlike TCP Reno-like adaptive schemes, which tend to overreact to random errors with significant throughput degradation. Moreover, SMCC is TCP friendly when packet losses are due to random errors.

The remainder of this paper is organized as follows: Section 2 overviews related work. Section 3 presents SMCC, the streaming protocol proposed in this paper. This is followed by an evaluation of SMCC bandwidth estimation accuracy, throughput performance, fairness, and its friendliness to TCP, all in Section 4. Section 5 concludes by summarizing results and discussing current and possible future research directions.

2   Related Work

Recent research has focused on designing TCP friendly protocols that meet the demands of multimedia applications. In many cases these efforts have produced multimedia protocols that behave very similar to TCP.

Time-lined TCP (TLTCP) [11] is one such protocol that adheres strictly to the TCP congestion mechanism, while allowing data to be associated with deadlines. Once the deadline of a section of data has passed the rest of the data associated with that deadline is dropped. Although this protocol eliminates some of the timing issues introduced by TCP, it still adheres to the reliability and in-order delivery constraints of TCP, which hinder the transfer of streaming media.

SCTP [7] adapts the basic mechanisms of TCP congestion management to multimedia traffic requirements. SCTP allows the disabling of in-order packet delivery and reliable packet delivery, in times of network congestion. However, SCTP still employs the slow-start mechanism of TCP, leading to undesirable sending rate fluctuations.

RAP [13] also mimics the additive increase multiplicative decrease congestion scheme of TCP. While in congestion avoidance phase, the sending rate is increased by one per round-trip-time. Upon detection of congestion, the sending rate is multiplicatively decreased. RAP filters out the throughput variation, caused by the multiplicatively sending rate reductions, by relying on receiver buffering strategies.

Feamster et al. [3] extend the RAP protocol by using non-AIMD algorithms along with receiver buffer management to further reduce sending rate oscillations. Their SQRT algorithm in particular improves throughput variations by reducing the sending rate by sqrt(window size), as opposed to AIMD algorithms where the reduction in transmission rate is proportional to the window size.

TCP Friendly Rate Control (TFRC) [6] adjusts the server's sending rate upon congestion according to a TCP throughput equation. This equation includes packet loss rate (due to congestion) and RTT, which are monitored and maintained at the receiver. TFRC, however cannot handle random losses in the sense that such losses will cause unwarranted loss of throughput.

One key design distinction between SMCC and the protocols mentioned above is that SMCC does not require the acknowledgement of every data packet. This is a significant saving since multimedia data packets are typically small in size, ~200 bytes. Requiring a 40byte acknowledgment for each data packet automatically adds a 20% overhead to the protocol.

An issue that has recently been addressed in the Rate Control Scheme (RCS) proposed by Tang et al. [14] is robustness of the rate adaptation algorithm to high link loss rates on wireless channels with high Bandwidth X Delay products. Such cases correspond to satellite links as well as wireless access links to remote Internet servers. This scenario is likely to attract considerable interest as wireless Internet access to multimedia services is gaining popularity. The RCS scheme is a clever mechanism based on dummy packets to distinguish between congestion loss and random loss. The proper operation of RCS, however, requires the implementation of a priority level "below TCP best effort" in the router. Such support is not provided by most Internet routers. SMCC on the other hand provides robustness to random errors by virtue of the intrinsic insensitivity of the Bandwidth Share Estimate to isolated losses. No extra network level support is required.

3   Streaming Media Congestion Control Protocol (SMCC)

The protocol we propose in this paper, SMCC, 1) is able to adapt the sending rate according to the connection estimated bandwidth share, 2) is fair to existing connections, and 3) does not suffer from pronounced sending rate oscillations typical of most window protocols.

There is no congestion window in SMCC, although SMCC adjusts its sending rate so as to mimic TCP's congestion avoidance phase with its linear bandwidth probing, i.e. one extra packet is sent per round trip time so long as no congestion is detected. When congestion is encountered in SMCC, the sending rate is reduced to the current Bandwidth Share Estimate (BSE), and linear probing is continued. Never is the sending rate dropped to 1 packet per round trip time following a timeout, as in TCP, unless the current BSE dictates this value. In other words, the "slow-start" phase with exponential growth as in TCP is not present in SMCC.

3.1   SMCC Sender Operation

After connection setup using a three-way-handshake between SMCC server and client is complete, the sender starts to send media data. In our implementation, we assume the network can handle the lowest quality sending rate, and use that rate as the initial sending rate.

The initial round trip time estimate is gathered from the handshaking process. After each successive RTT, the sender increases the sending rate by one packet. This has the effect of mimicking TCP congestion avoidance phase. The sender readjusts its RTT estimate once every round trip time, by requesting an acknowledgement for the first data packet in every new RTT window.

Whenever the sender receives a NACK, it resets the sending rate to the BSE contained in the NACK message (the BSE computation is discussed below), and resumes linear probing. The sender can determine if there is sufficient time to retransmit the lost packet, based on information it gets from the client regarding the receiver's current buffer and current play out time.

3.2   SMCC Receiver Operation

With each data packet received, the client may recalculate the BSE. Upon receiving a data packet that the sender requests to be acknowledged, the receiver sends an ACK for that packet. As mentioned above, this message exchange is used to set the RTT at the sender side. Once a lost packet is detected, a NACK message is sent containing the current bandwidth estimate. As noted above, it is the sender's responsibility to determine if the packet should be retransmitted.

3.3   Bandwidth Calculation in SMCC

Just as in TCP Westwood, the Bandwidth Share Estimate, i.e. the estimate of the rate to be used by the sender in order to share the bottleneck bandwidth fairly, is determined by exponentially averaging rate samples. However, where TCP Westwood measures ACK arrivals at the sender, SMCC uses the inter-arrival time between two subsequent packets at the client (receiver) to calculate a rate sample on the forward path of the connection. The advantage of the SMCC approach is that it measures the rate on the forward path of the connection, filtering out the effects of congestion on the reverse path.

Basically, the client side calculates the connection bandwidth share using the Receiver Based Packet Pair (RBPP) method described in [12]. RBPP requires the use of two consecutively sent packets to determine a bandwidth share sample. The adherence of SMCC to the RBPP sequence number requirement is fundamental for not overestimating bandwidth share and thus enhancing fairness and friendliness of SMCC.

A second constraint is to make sure that 'time compression' has not occurred on the consecutive packets. Here we define time compression as occurring when the difference between arrival times of the packets is less than the difference between sending times of the packets [12]. If the packets are time compressed, they are not used in the BSE calculation, as the resulting estimate would be too aggressive. The intent is to estimate bandwidth only up to the server's (sender) instantaneous sending rate, even if more bandwidth is available.

If two consecutively received packets have passed the two tests above, they are used to calculate a bandwidth sample as follows:

$$\text{Bandwidth} = s_2 / (a_2 - a_1) \qquad (1)$$

Where s_2 is the size of the second packet, a_1 and a_2 are the arrival times of the first and second packet respectively. This bandwidth sample is then used just as the rate estimation in TCP Westwood; it is plugged into the exponential filter to produce the current BSE.

4   Experimental Results

We performed several simulation experiments to assess the performance of SMCC with respect to throughput, fairness, and TCP-friendliness. Unless otherwise stated, all simulations use the topology depicted in Figure 1, with all connections going through the same bottleneck link using RED queue management, and sending data in the same direction. Simulations were run for 200sec. To filter out transient system behavior, all simulations were run for 100 seconds before measurements were taken. Table 1 shows the constant configuration parameters.

Table 1. Simulation properties

Delay of all side links	3ms
Side links capacity	5Mbps
Bottleneck buffer	10*RTT*bottleneck B/W
FTP/SMCC data packets	200 bytes
FTP/SMCC ack packet size	40 bytes
Min. Threshold	0.05*Bottleneck buffer
Max. Threshold	0.5*Bottleneck buffer
q_weight	0.002

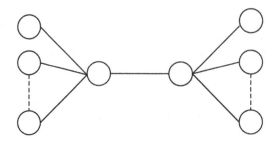

Figure 1. Simulation Topology

4.1   Accuracy of Bandwidth Estimation

First, we want to verify the accuracy of SMCC's bandwidth estimation.   This is achieved by changing the link capacity during the lifetime of a SMCC connection. We alter the link capacity by introducing CBR traffic at different rates over the bottleneck link. Figure 2 shows how SMCC adapts to changing bottleneck bandwidth with no competing SMCC or TCP connections. The figure shows both SMCC's BSE value, and its throughput as a function of time.   The figure shows that SMCC calculates the BSE accurately to within 10% of the available bottleneck bandwidth.

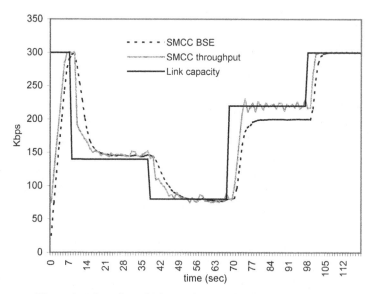

Figure 2. Adaptation of BSE to changing bottleneck bandwidth

4.2   Throughput Behavior

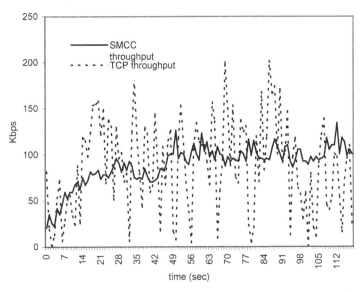

Figure 3. Throughput curve of 1 SMCC and 1 FTP/TCP New Reno connections

Figure 3 plots the throughput curve of one SMCC and one TCP New Reno connection, in 1-second intervals for a 120 second simulation. A total of 5 TCP and 5 SMCC connections were present, but only one throughput curve of each type of connection is shown if Figure 3. The bottleneck capacity was 1Mbps, with a 10msec delay, thus the fair share per connection is 100Kbps. Figure 3 shows that while still receiving its fair share value of 100Kbps, SMCC's throughput curve is much smoother than TCP New Reno's oscillatory sending rate. This is because SMCC does not reduce its sending rate by one half or to a minimum of one packet per round trip time as TCP does. Rather, SMCC adjusts its sending rate to the BSE, and never performs an exponential rate increase. Thus, SMCC takes longer to reach the fair share value, but it does not suffer from pronounced sending rate oscillations, and is thus suitable for streaming media such as audio and video.

TCP was originally designed to work in a totally wired environment, where a packet loss meant that a buffer overflow occurred somewhere in the network, and therefore, served as a sign of congestion. However, in the case of lossy links, packets may not only be lost due to congestion, but also due to random errors. TCP Reno incorrectly interprets this event as congestion, and unnecessarily reduces its window size with consequent reduction in throughput. This prohibits TCP from fully utilizing the error-prone link.

SMCC is more robust to random loss because of the relative insensitivity of bandwidth estimation to sporadic errors. In fact, the loss of an isolated packet has only marginal impact on the bandwidth estimation. No time out and slow start are incurred in SMCC.

To illustrate the robustness of SMCC in the wireless domain, Figure 4 presents results from a simulation with one SMCC and one TCP New Reno connection running over a 0.3Mbps bottleneck link with 35ms delay, and an error rate varying from 1 to 20%. We see that SMCC is able to maintain a large percentage of the 150Kbps fair share value independent of the error rate, while TCP throughput continues to degrade as the error rate increases.

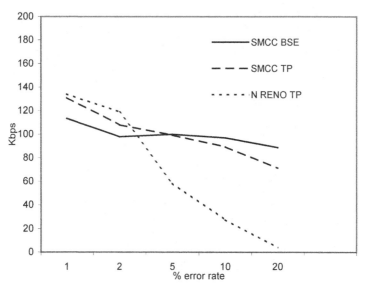

Figure 4: 1 SMCC versus 1 TCP New Reno connection running over a 300Kbps bottleneck lossy link with a 35ms delay

4.3   Fairness

The fairness of a protocol is a measure of how a number of connections running the same protocol share the bottleneck bandwidth. The fairness of SMCC is studied below by simultaneously running 10 SMCC connections. The time averaged throughput and BSE of each connection is shown in Figure 5. The results show that the connections vary little in their throughput and BSE averages. We also ran experiments changing the number of connections from 2 to 50. The bottleneck capacity is scaled to maintain a fair share value of 100Kbps, while the delay was held constant at 10ms. All runs showed good fairness behavior: Jain's Fairness Index was higher than .99 for all runs.

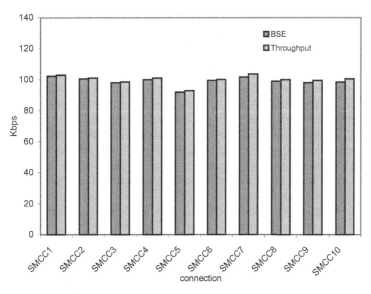

Figure 5: Time Averaged BSE and Throughput on 10 SMCC connections

4.4   TCP Friendliness

We also tested friendliness for a variety of network conditions, including number of flows, bottleneck link delay, bottleneck bandwidth, and random errors. Varying the number of flows did not show significant impact on friendliness. Therefore we will limit our discussion in this section to how bottleneck delay, bandwidth and random errors impact friendliness. All simulations in this section were performed using a balanced set of 10 SMCC and 10 TCP New Reno connections.

We use the Efficiency/Friendliness Tradeoff Graph introduced in [4] to better visualize the efficiency/friendliness tradeoff behavior when introducing SMCC connections to share a common bottleneck link with TCP New Reno connections. The following two experiments produce a single point on the graph:

1. A simulation with 20 TCP New Reno flows is run for calibration, to establish a reference value. The throughput of each flow, and the total link utilization, are measured.
2. Another simulation is then run with half of the TCP flows replaced with SMCC flows. The new throughput and utilization are measured.

Let t_{R1} be the average throughput of the TCP New Reno flows in the first simulation, and U1 be the total link utilization. Similarly, let t_{R2} be the average throughput of the TCP New Reno flows in the second simulation, and U2 be the total link utilization by all connections, that is SMCC as well as TCP connections. We then define:

$$\text{Efficiency Improvement } E = U2/U1 \tag{2}$$

$$\text{Friendliness } F = (t_{R2}/t_{R1}) \tag{3}$$

For each network scenario of interest, E and F are determined and an (F, E) point is placed on the Efficiency / Friendliness Tradeoff graph. We expect that, in most cases, an increase in Efficiency (E) is compensated for by a decrease in Friendliness (F).

We performed a set of experiments, varying the bottleneck capacity from 5 to 20Mbps. The bottleneck delay was also varied between 10, 50, 100 and 150ms. We also introduced random dropping of packets over the bottleneck link to simulate random loss associated with data transfer over a wireless channel.

Figure 6 shows the efficiency/friendliness tradeoff behavior when SMCC connections share a bottleneck link with TCP New Reno connections. Each curve in Figure 6 corresponds to fixed bottleneck bandwidth and error rate. Moreover, the points on each curve represent the impact of sequentially changing the bottleneck delay. For convenience, the arrows mark the direction of increasing bottleneck delay.

We see that for all three 0% error rate cases, as the delay increases, SMCC reduces TCP's throughput without any resulting gain in efficiency. The reason for this is that in these scenarios there is not much room for improvement in efficiency, since TCP by itself can achieve a high utilization of the bottleneck link. There is a friendliness problem in the current version of SMCC, represented by the flat portions of the 0% error curves. This is one area of further needed enhancement, and can be addressed by applying adaptive share estimation methods, as in [4,5], as opposed to the current packet pair model. The packet pair model and the associated available bandwidth estimation have been shown to be too aggressive at times. Results presented in [4,5] have shown major improvements in friendliness using the rate estimation model.

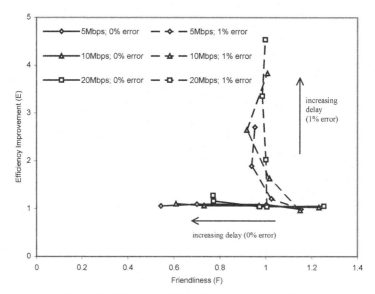

Figure 6: Efficiency / Friendliness tradeoff graph

Figure 6 also shows that SMCC is friendly to TCP New Reno in the random error case (wireless scenario).

As we mentioned in Section 4.2, when a packet loss is due to random error, TCP unnecessarily reduces its window size, with consequent reduction in throughput. This prohibits TCP from fully utilizing the capacity of an error-prone link. This inefficiency is more pronounced as the bandwidth X delay product increases.

In SMCC, the loss of an isolated packet has only marginal impact on the bandwidth estimation, thus it achieves a higher utilization of an error-prone link. When SMCC connections are introduced, they readily use the residual bandwidth that TCP is incapable of utilizing. This is apparent in Figure 6 where the 1% error rate curves show that SMCC remains friendly to TCP irrespective of bottleneck capacity and delay. Furthermore, the gain in total utilization resulting from the introduction of SMCC increases as the bandwidth X delay product increases.

4.5   Comparison of SMCC to Other Streaming Protocols

As mentioned in Section 2, the common challenge for any streaming protocol is to adjust its sending rate to an appropriate value once congestion occurs. Most protocols so far proposed adhere to the multiplicative decrease paradigm of TCP. Others, such as TFRC attempt to calculate the throughput that TCP would achieve on the same connection, and use that calculation to set the sending rate. The drawback of these methods is that in striving to achieve the same throughput as TCP with lower sending rate oscillations, such protocols can inherit the fundamental limitations of TCP. [13] shows that the RAP protocol using fine-grain rate adaptation can achieve the same throughput as TCP regardless of the bottleneck delay. Similarly, TFRC [6] is based on an underlying control equation that ensures that the protocol uses no more bandwidth, in steady-state, than a TCP conforming protocol running under comparable conditions. From figures 5 and 6, we see that in the random error cases, achieving the same throughput as TCP, leaves the bottleneck link severely underutilized.   SMCC allows the streaming application to access this unused bandwidth in these cases, without hindering existing TCP connections. As wireless Internet access becomes increasingly popular and technology increases the capacity of links, this issue will become increasingly important.   Naturally, in the attempt to improve utilization, SMCC at times also grabs bandwidth from TCP (and vice-versa). We plan to address these issues in depth in future work.

5   Conclusion

This paper has presented Streaming Media Congestion Control (SMCC), a protocol based on bandwidth estimation concepts, which provides smooth sending rate changes and good utilization when available network bandwidth fluctuates. SMCC is fair with respect to other SMCC flows. It is reasonably friendly to TCP, particularly with lossy links. SMCC mimics the linear probing for additional bandwidth in TCP congestion avoidance phase.   Upon detection of a lost packet, which the receiver explicitly

NACKs along with the current BSE, the sender adjusts its sending rate to the current Bandwidth Share Estimate. SMCC mimics the Congestion Avoidance phase of TCP congestion control, but never the Slow Start phase.

SMCC dictates the sending rate of a streaming media application, but not the quality of the stream. The quality adaptation is a separate issue. It not only depends upon the current sending rate, but also upon the receiver's buffer, and the user preferences and profile as well.

The resulting behavior shows that SMCC throughput is quite smooth, as compared to the fluctuating behavior of conventional TCP. This is a desirable property for video streaming applications. Robustness to link errors and random loss was also demonstrated via simulations.

Areas of further research include: friendliness of bandwidth estimation method particularly when congestion, not random error, is the predominant cause of packet losses; and the extension to multicasting applications (both single and multi-source). This protocol will also be tried on interactive media, although the tight time delay constraints will introduce more stringent buffer space requirements.

References

1. I.F Akyildiz, G. Morabito, S. Palazzo. TCP Peach: A New Congestion Control Scheme for Satellite IP Networks, IEEE/ACM Transactions on Networking, Vol. 9, No. 3, pp. 307-321, June 2001.
2. D. Bansal, H. Balakrishnan, S. Floyd, and S. Shenker. Dynamic Behavior of Slowly-Responsive Congestion Control Algorithms. In Proceedings of Sigcomm 2001.
3. N. Feamster, D. Bansal, and H. Balakrishnan. On The Interactions Between Layered Quality Adaptation and Congestion Control for Streaming Video. 11th International Packet Video Workshop, Kyongju, Korea. May 2001.
4. M. Gerla, M. Sanadidi, K. Ng, M. Valla, R.Wang. Efficiency/Friendliness Tradeoff in TCP Westwood. ISCC 2002, Taormina, Italy.
5. M. Gerla, M. Sanadidi, M. Valla, R. Wang. Adaptive Bandwidth Share Estimation in TCP Westwood. To appear in Globecom 2002, Taipei, Taiwan.
6. M. Handley, J. Padhya, S. Floyd, and J. Widmer. TCP Friendly Rate Control (TFRC): Protocol Specification. Internet Engineering Task Force, July 2001.
7. Internet RFC 2960
8. K. Lai, M. Baker. Measuring Link Bandwidths Using a Deterministic Model of Packet Delay. Proceedings of SIGCOMM 2000.
9. A. Mahanti, D. Eager, M. Vernon, and D. Sundaram-Stukel. Scalable On-Demand Media Streaming with Packet Loss Recovery. ACM SIGCOMM Aug. 2001.
10. S. Mascolo, C. Casetti, M. Gerla, M. Sanadidi, and R. Wang. TCP Westwood: Bandwidth Estimation for Enhanced Transport over Wireless Links. In Proceedings of Mobicom 2001.
11. B. Mukherjee and T. Brecht, Time-lined TCP for the TCP-friendly Delivery of Stremining Media, Proceedings of ICNP 2000.
12. V. Paxon. Measurements and Analysis of End-to-End Internet Dynamics. Ph.D. thesis, University of California, Berkeley, April 1977.
13. R. Rejaie, M. Handley, D. Estrin. RAP: An End-to-end Rate-based Congestion Control Mechanism for Realtime Streams in the Internet. University of Southern California, Information Sciences Institute. July 1998.
14. J. Tang, G. Morabito, I. Akyildiz, and M. Johnson. RCS: A Rate Control Scheme for Real-Time traffic with High Bandwidth-Delay Products and High Bit Error Rates. Infocom 2001.

Signaling Protocol for Session-Aware Popularity-Based Resource Allocation*

Paulo Mendes[1][2], Henning Schulzrinne[1], and Edmundo Monteiro[2]

[1] Department of Computer Science, Columbia University
New York, NY 10027, USA
{mendes,schulzrinne}@cs.columbia.edu
[2] CISUC, Department of Informatics Engineering, University of Coimbra
3030 Coimbra, Portugal,
{pmendes,edmundo}@dei.uc.pt

Abstract. The Differentiated Services model maps traffic into services with different quality levels. However, flows are treated unfairly inside each service, since the Differentiated Services model lacks a policy to distribute bandwidth between flows that form the same service aggregate traffic. Therefore, we present a signaling protocol that fairly distributes the bandwidth assigned to each service, among scalable multimedia sessions in a multicast environment. Fairness is achieved allocating bandwidth based upon the audience size of each session. We evaluate the efficiency of the proposed protocol using theoretical analysis and simulation.

Keywords: QoS; multicast; differentiated services; scalable sessions; fairness.

1   Introduction

Current popular Internet multimedia applications, such as RealNetworks Sure-Stream and Microsoft Windows Media, stream the same content at different rates, depending on receiver capabilities. However, even if they use multicast, each stream in this multi-rate encoding contains a complete encoding, thus wasting bandwidth. This problem can be solved by using scalable encoding [17,9]. Scalable encoding divides a video stream into cumulative layers with different rates and importance. Thus, the stream rate is then the sum of its layers. Sources send only one stream to all receivers, mapping each layer to a different multicast group. All layers belonging to the same stream form a *session*.

Due to their real-time characteristics, scalable sessions need quality guarantees from networks, namely: *inter-session* fairness, the ability to guarantee a fair distribution of bandwidth between sessions sharing a service; *intra-session* fairness, the ability to respect the importance of each layer of a session; and punishment of *high-rate* sessions, i.e., sessions with a rate higher than their fair share

* This work is supported by POSI-Programa Operacional Sociedade de Informação of Portuguese Fundação para a Ciência e Tecnologia and European Union FEDER

K.C. Almeroth and M. Hasan (Eds.): MMNS 2002, LNCS 2496, pp. 101–113, 2002.

of bandwidth. The current Differentiated Services (DS) model [3] aggregates traffic into services with different priorities at the boundaries of each network domain. Among the services DS can provide, the Assured Forwarding PHB (AF) [5] is ideal for transporting scalable sessions, since flows are assigned different drop precedences. Although AF services provide intra-session fairness, the DS model lacks the other two properties. Therefore, we propose a protocol named *Session-Aware Popularity-based Resource Allocation* (SAPRA) that allows a fair allocation of resources in each DS service. SAPRA provides inter-session fairness by assigning more bandwidth to sessions with higher audience size, and intra-session fairness by assigning to each layer a drop precedence that matches its importance. SAPRA has a punishment function and a resource utilization maximization function. The former increases the drop percentage of high-rate sessions during periods of congestion. The latter avoids waste of resources when sessions are not using their whole fair share: the remaining bandwidth is equally distributed among other sessions. To achieve its goal, SAPRA adds agents and markers to edge routers. Agents manage sessions to provide inter-session fairness; markers deal with layers, providing intra-session fairness. Only edge routers are changed, since SAPRA handles individual traffic aggregated in each service. The behavior of agents and markers is described and evaluated in [13]. In this paper, we describe and study the SAPRA signaling protocol used by agents to exchange information about sessions, allowing a fair distribution of resources in the path of each session.

The remainder of the paper is organized as follows. Section 2 briefly describes work related to SAPRA. In Section 3, we describe the SAPRA protocol. Section 4 presents a theoretical analysis and simulation of SAPRA. Finally, Section 5 presents some conclusions and future work.

2   Related Work

The amount of resources reserved for each DS service depends on service-level agreements (SLAs) between domains. The management of multicast traffic can be done with static SLAs for flows with more than one egress router. However, since multicast traffic is both heterogeneous and dynamic, static SLAs needs over-provisioning of resources in the domain. As alternative, dynamic SLAs can be used. These can be managed by bandwidth brokers (BB) or intra-domain signaling protocols to reserve resources where they are needed. However, these approaches do not distribute reserved service resources across several domains, among sessions that constitute the service aggregate traffic. To solve this issue some proposals present inter-session fairness mechanisms based on the max-min fairness definition [2], but this definition cannot exist with discrete set of rates [15]. Sarkar et al. present a fairness algorithm [16] that considers discrete set of rates, but does not consider the population of sessions, and its scalability and efficiency is not proved for Internet-like scenarios. Audience of sessions is pondered by Legout et al. [10], but their proposal does not consider intra-session fairness for scalable sources, requires changes in all routers, does not maximize resources, and does not punish high rate flows. Li et al. [11] present another inter-session fairness mechanism, but it is also based on the max-min fairness definition, assumes only one shared link, and does not consider audience of sessions and the importance of their layers.

3   SAPRA Protocol

In this section we describe SAPRA. We assume that edge routers have an accurate notion about resources reserved for each service, being the mechanism implemented in each domain a policy issue beyond the scope of this paper. Multicast branch points can be located in edge and interior routers, but receivers are attached only to leaf edge routers.

SAPRA is most suited for long-lived scalable sessions with large audience size, such as Internet TV and periodic near-video-on-demand systems [1]. Each layer is identified by a source-specific multicast (SSM) channel [6]. SAPRA also integrates non-scalable sessions and unicast traffic. The former are treated like scalable sessions with one layer, and the latter as sessions with one layer and one receiver.

Not all DS domains have to implement SAPRA, because SAPRA messages are exchanged between SAPRA-speaking agents. However, receivers in non-SAPRA domains do not count toward the session population and thus sessions with a big audience outside of SAPRA domains have a small share of resources.

Receivers can join sessions by, for instance, listening to Session Announcement Protocol (SAP) [4] messages. Receivers first join the multicast group for the most important (lowest) layer and then increase their reception quality by joining additional (higher) layers. Each layer requires all layers below it. Agents in leaf edge routers use IGMPv3 "State-Changes" reports, issued when receivers join a layer, to measure the local audience size of each session.

SAPRA allocates resources to sessions, rather than managing multicast groups without concern about their relationship. If the structure of sessions would be kept hidden, agents would not be able to implement inter-session fairness, markers would fail to provide intra-session fairness, and sessions would have lower and less stable quality levels. We propose two methods for agents in leaf routers to collect information about the composition of sessions, using consecutive address ranges and IGMP extensions. With SSM, multicast addresses are locally allocated by each source, from a pool of 2^{24} addresses in IPv4 and 2^{32} addresses in IPv6. For the first method, each sender allocates consecutive multicast addresses to all layers inside a session and keeps a gap of at least one address between sessions. Since receivers join layers sequentially, an agent can detect a new session if its multicast address differs by at least two from any other session address. Alternatively, if the number of layers per session can be bounded, the address bits can be divided into high-order session and low-order layer bits. For the second method, we add the address of the most important layer to IGMPv3 [7], using the "auxiliary" data field. The address of the most important layer then identifies the session. For both methods, agents deduce the relationship between layers in a session by the order receivers join them. Details can be found in [13].

We define downstream as the direction from sources to receivers, and the opposite as upstream. We also define the *Downstream Fair Rate* (DFR), the *Local Fair Rate* (LFR) and the *Used Fair Rate* (UFR) of sessions in a link. DFR is the fair rate that a session has downstream that link, LFR is the fair rate of the session in the link and UFR is the lesser of LFR and DFR. By using UFR instead of LFR, sessions that do not use downstream resources do not waste local bandwidth.

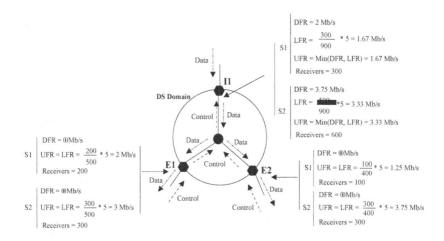

Figure 1. Fair rate computation in edge routers

Fig. 1 shows how agents compute the UFR of two sessions, S_1 and S_2, in a domain with three edge routers. This computation requires information about sessions population and DFR, which agents collect from downstream neighbors using the SAPRA signalling protocol. As we described in [13], agents compute the LFR dividing the resources of the shared service among sessions by assigning more resources to sessions with bigger audience size. For instance, assuming that the service has $5\,Mb/s$ in each link, the LFR of S_1 is $1.25\,Mb/s$ in E_2, since S_1 has 100 receivers and the total population is 400. If most of the sessions have few receivers, SAPRA allocates a small share of resources to each session, which can be useless to assure the minimum quality level that the source wants to provide to receivers. If agents are informed about this requirement, for instance by BB, they can compute a zero LFR for new sessions, assuring a minimum share to existing sessions. This can be an extension to SAPRA, considering pricing issues, which is beyond the scope of this paper.

In this example, the UFR of each session is equal to its LFR at egress routers, since we assume an infinite DFR. At the ingress router, the population of a session is the sum of its receivers in each egress router and its DFR is the maximum value of its UFR in each egress router. This maximum value satisfies the heterogeneous requirements of receivers downstream different egress routers without congesting links downstream the domain, since packets will be dropped at egress routers in conformity with the local UFR.

In each downstream link of edge routers, UFRs are passed to the marker. Packets are marked in or out of profile depending on the relationship between the estimated rate and the UFR of sessions, being marked out of profile starting by the least important layer [13].

3.1   Overview of Protocol Operation

Agents use two messages, UPDATE and SYNC, to propagate information. UP-DATE messages deliver the UFR and population size of each session to upstream neighbors, allowing agents along the path to compute fair rates. SYNC messages propagate information about the quality of sessions to downstream neighbors. When session listeners get a SYNC message, they can adapt to quality changes.

Messages are exchanged only between neighboring agents, increasing scalability. For robustness, SAPRA runs over TCP, eliminating the need to implement fragmentation and re-transmission. UPDATEs are forwarded using routing information of the Border Gateway Protocol (BGP) [14] and SYNCs follow the path of the UPDATEs in reverse, similar to RSVP PATH and RESV messages.

Agents send messages periodically. Messages include information about non-stationary sessions, i.e., sessions whose state changed significantly since the last time they were included in a message. So, agents do not send any message if there are only stationary sessions. The minimum state variation is set to 25%, which appears to be a good compromise between the number of messages and the propagation of accurate information. This restriction allows the use of 1 s intervals, improving the protocol accuracy: since sessions are long and their population normally varies significantly only when they begin and end, intervals as short as 1 s are enough to propagate significant state changes. To avoid synchronized messages, intervals are varied by a small random of 10%.

As an alternative, agents could send messages, not periodically, but only after receiving a message of the same type, a SYNC from the upstream neighbor in the path to the session source, or an UPDATE from each downstream neighbor where that session is present. However, this approach increases UPDATEs propagation delay since agents can take a long time to gather information about each session from all downstream neighbors. This happens, for example, when there is a different number of routers between the agent and each neighbor, or when neighbors send information about the same session at different times.

UPDATE messages are triggered when an agent receives the first join from local receivers or the first UPDATE. Stationary sessions are identified by the variation of their population or UFR, considering the total population and total UFR in the link where the UPDATE is going to be sent. When a session ends, its information is always included in the next UPDATE allowing the immediate release of unnecessary state in upstream agents. Sessions have hard-state, since state starts and ends with the reception of UPDATEs. However state is also refreshed by periodic complete UPDATEs that include information about all sessions. This soft-state property makes SAPRA cope with routing changes and link failures, so the default values for the interval of complete UPDATEs and for the time agents wait before deleting state were chosen based upon BGP variables: the former is 30 s, the value of the BGP keep_alive_time variable, and the latter 90 s, the value of the BGP hold_time variable. When agents receive complete UPDATEs, they only update the state of those sessions whose DFR varies more than 25% to avoid computations that do not affect the local distribution of resources. The population size is always updated, to avoid cumulative rounding errors.

SYNC messages are triggered when an agent with local sources receives the first UPDATE, or when an agent without local sources receives the first SYNC. Stationary sessions are identified by the variation of their quality. In this paper, we consider that the quality information carried by SYNCs is the UFR of sessions. If the source of a session is local, that information is the UFR of that session in the downstream link, otherwise it is the minimum value between the local and upstream UFR.

3.2   Example of Protocol Operation

Fig. 2 illustrates how SAPRA works, by using two sessions, S_1 and S_2. We label edge router i as r_i, the agent on that router as a_i, and the link between r_i and r_j as (r_i, r_j). The notation $U_n@t$ indicates that the nth UPDATE is being sent at time t; $Y_n@t$ has a similar meaning for SYNCs. We assume that intra-domain links have 10 Mb/s of bandwidth and inter-domain links (r_1, r_2), (r_5, r_8) and (r_4, r_6) have 5 Mb/s, 3 ,Mb/s, and 4 Mb/s of bandwidth, respectively.

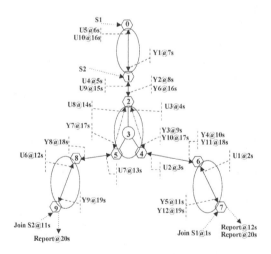

Figure 2. Protocol operation

When receivers join S_1, a_7 sends U_1 toward a_0. The reception of U_4 at a_1 triggers the sending of SYNCs, since a_1 has a local source. However, since the source does not belong to S_1, a_1 does not send a SYNC at second 6. The first SYNC is sent by a_0 toward a_7 at second 7, with 4 Mb/s as minimum UFR of S_1 on the tree, the UFR on (r_4, r_6). Receivers on r_7 get a reports 11 s after having joined S_1. When receivers join S_2, a_1 receives U_9 at second 15. At that moment, S_1 and S_2 have an UFR of 2.5 Mb/s on (r_1, r_2). Since the minimum UFR of S_1 decreased more than 25%, a_1 sends U_{10} to a_0 at second 16. At the same time, a_1 sends Y_6 with the UFR of S_2. Since the UFR of S_1 differs more than 25% from the value sent in the previous SYNC, Y_6 also includes the UFR of S_1. The agent a_2 sends Y_7 to a_5 with the UFR of S_2 and Y_{10} to a_4 with the UFR of S_1. Hence, a_9 receives the UFR of S_2 8 s after receives joined the session and S_1 receivers on r_7 get a second report at second 20. After second 20, messages are suppressed, because there are no changes in population or in fair rates. However, agents send a complete UPDATE at second 30, the default interval.

4   Protocol Evaluation

4.1   Theoretical Analysis

To evaluate SAPRA, we analyze the memory required to store state, the bandwidth overhead, the time to update UFR of sessions in all agents, and the time to notify receivers about the quality variation of their session.

For N sessions, agents need to store $O(N)$ of state. The stored state does not depend on the number of receivers, increasing SAPRA scalability.

The bandwidth overhead is reduced, because some messages can be suppressed and they are only exchanged between neighbors. This means that the overhead is independent from the network size, being dependent only on the number of sessions and the size of intervals. We analyze the protocol for a worst-case scenario with short intervals (1 s) and high number of sessions (1,000). We assume that all sessions are present on all links, that each session has three layers with total rate of 1.8 Mb/s, and that their population is very dynamic, with significant changes every second. Sessions are decribed by their Id, source address and fair rate (12 bytes), and layers by their Id, group address and number of receivers (12 bytes). Since UPDATEs carry 48 bytes (session plus three layers) and SYNCs 12 bytes (only session) per session, the control rate between two agents is 480 kb/s. Also because the total data rate in a link is 1,800 Mb/s, the ratio between control and data rate is of 0.03%. Even with low-rate sessions the overhead is insignificant: if we assume a data rate of 64 kb/s, the protocol overhead is of 0.75%.

The time taken to update UFR of sessions in all agents depends on the number of agents in each session path and if agents were already triggered to start sending messages. Time required to notify receivers depends on one additional factor: if the minimum UFR of the session, in the path to its source, increases or decreases. The maximum time to update UFR of a session is given by $(n_a - 1) a_s$, and the maximum time to deliver a report to its receivers by $(2(n_a - 1) + 1) a_s$, where n_a is the number of agents in the session path and a_s the sending interval. This maximum time occurs only during the first update, because the first UPDATE triggers all agents to start sending messages being delayed by the total a_s in each agent. After this, the delay is lower than a_s. So, for a path with six domains and 12 agents, the maximum time required to update UFR is 11 s and receivers get their first report 23 s after joining their session. We assume that there is only one DS domain per Autonomous Systems (AS) and that a path can have a maximum length of six AS, since the percentage of longer paths is very low. For instance, a November 2001 study of 60,978 different Autonomous Systems (AS) [18] showed that there are only 0.5% of paths with size of seven AS and 0.1% with size of eight AS.

When the UFR increases, if it remains higher than the upstream fair rate in all agents, the minimum UFR is only established by the agent closest to the source, and so the time required to notify receivers is proportional to the path length. Hence, notifications are faster when the minimum UFR is decreased by an agent that is not the agent closest to the source, because that agent immediately sends a SYNC and so n_a is lower than the number of agents in the path. This is possible because in each stabilized network branch the upstream fair rate in each link is equal to the minimum UFR on the branch. If changes happen in different branches at the same time, stabilization of fair rates is achieved first in each branch and only afterwards in the entire network. On the one hand, slower notification of higher minimum UFR leads to a higher stability, since receivers only join layers when resources of their session are updated in the entire path. On the other hand, faster notification of lower minimum UFR optimize resource utilization, since receivers leave layers more quickly, reducing network traffic.

4.2   Simulations

In this section we present simulations (using NS) that show SAPRA ability to allocate resources across several domains. We use a scenario with ten domains, one domain per AS as shown in Fig. 3, where the longest path has six domains.

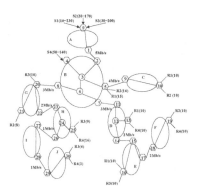

Figure 3. Simulation scenario

The topology has four sessions, S_1 to S_4, in different domains. Domains have multicast branches either in ingress or interior routers, and receivers either in ingress or egress routers. Due to lack of information about traffic distribution among ASs, we use the distribution of addresses by AS distance [18] to decide upon receiver locations. Hence, we place 26%, 40%, 26%, 9%, and 2.5% of receivers in domains at a distance of two, three, four, five, and six domains from their source, respectively. In Fig. 3, $R_x(Y)$ denotes Y receivers of S_x.

We assume that service capacity in inter-domain links is equal to the link bandwidth and that intra-domain links have enough bandwidth to avoid congestion. We also assume that each queue has a size of 64 packets, which is the default value in Cisco IOS 12.2, and that interior routers have FIFO queues, since these are the simplest ones. We use data packets with 1,000 bytes since this is a value between the MTU of dial-up connections, 576 bytes, and the MTU of ethernet and high speed connections, 1,500 bytes. Since control messages are exchanged between routers, UPDATE and SYNC packets have a size of 1,500 bytes, which is the default MTU in Cisco routers.

Session S_1 spans seconds 10 through 230, S_2 20 to 170, S_3 30 to 200, and S_4 50 to 150. Each session has three layers with total rate of 1.8 Mb/s. The most important layer has 303 kb/s, the medium 606 kb/s, and the least important one 909 kb/s. Although SAPRA supports any number of layers, three layers provide a good quality/bandwidth trade-off and additional layers provide only marginal improvements [8]. The simulation covers 240 s, which is enough to identify transient state when sessions start and end. For simplicity, we assume that receivers of the same session join and leave simultaneously. For longer simulations, sessions remain stable for a longer time and the time needed for their state to stabilize does not change. Results for 600 s simulations are available in [12].

We analyze the protocol efficiency based on the session rate monitored by S_1 receivers and the minimum UFR they get from SAPRA, Fig. 4 a), and based on the UFR of sessions on (r_7, r_{11}), Fig. 4 b). Results for the remainder sessions and inter-domain links are available in [12].

Fig. 4 a) shows that the rate of S_1 is always kept below its minimum UFR, with the exception of the rate monitored by r_{13} receivers from seconds 29 to 89. This happens because the UFR of all sessions on (r_7, r_{11}) is always lower than the service capacity on that link, as is shown in Fig. 4 b), and so a percentage of out of profile packets from all sessions pass through r_7 allowing r_{13} receivers to get a rate higher than the minimum UFR. Nevertheless, Fig. 4 a) also shows that S_1 rate on r_{13} decreases in that interval. This is due to the punishment mechanism that filters S_1 when this session is identified as high-rate session during the congestion of (r_7, r_{11}).

Fig. 4 b) shows that SAPRA is able to distribute resources in each link, decreasing UFR of sessions to release resources for new sessions or increasing them to grab resources that were used by sessions that ended. The only irregular behavior is the initial variation of the UFR of S_4. This happens because in this simulation a_7 gets information about receivers of S_4 on r_{13} and r_{19} at different moments: at second 51, a_7 has only knowledge about receivers on r_{13}, because

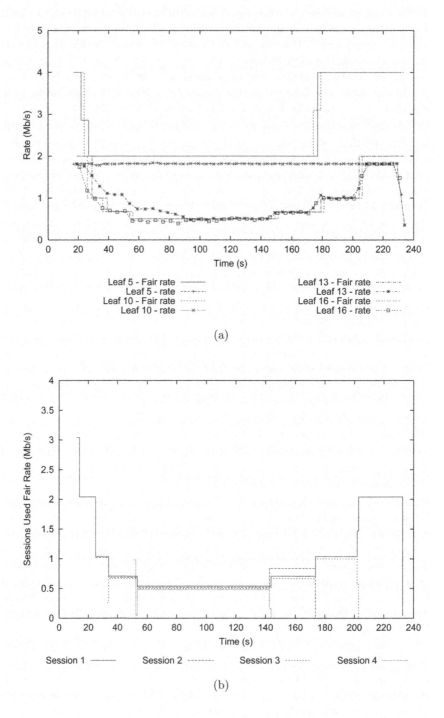

Figure 4. a) rate and minimum UFR of S_1; b) UFR of all sessions on (r_7, r_{11})

the UPDATE from a_{13} arrives to a_7 first than the one from a_{19}. At that time, the LFR of S_2, S_3 and S_4 is 0.6 Mb/s and the one of S_1 is 1.2 Mb/s, since S_1 has 20 receivers, and S_2, S_3 and S_4 have 10 receivers each. However, since S_1 has a DFR of 0.6 Mb/s, it releases 0.6 Mb/s from its LFR, which are used to increase the UFR of S_2 and S_3 until their DFR is reached (0.667 Mb/s). The remaining released bandwidth is used to increase the UFR of S_4 to 1.06 Mb/s. Although ten receivers joined S_4 on r_{19}, this happens at the time (second 50) a_{19} is sending an UPDATE. Thus the agent might not have information about some receivers when the message is sent (in this case, a_{19} has only information about the first receiver). Therefore, at second 52, a_7 gets information about only one receiver on r_{19}, and thus, the UFR of S_4 is reduced to 0.06 Mb/s (its UFR on link (r_{14}, r_{15})). After second 53, a_7 already knows about all S_4 receivers on r_{19} and so the UFR of S_4 increases to 0.5 Mb/s.

Next, we analyze the efficiency of SAPRA updating the UFR of sessions in all agents, and notifying receivers when S_1 and S_2 start and end. When receivers join S_1, the ones closer to the source take relatively more time to get their first report than the ones closer to the leaves. This time is proportional to the distance to the source, since it is their first UPDATE that triggers upstream agents. When receivers join and leave S_2, the time that SAPRA takes to notify S_1 receivers also depends on the variation of the minimum UFR of S_1, in addition to the session path length to their leaf router. Tab. 1 shows more clearly these times than Fig 4 a).

Table 1. Notifications of S_1 receivers

	router 5	router 10	router 13	router 16
S2 starts at second 20	27 s	24 s	29 s	25 s
S2 ends at second 170	177 s	179 s	179 s	181 s

Although r_5 receivers are notified about the minimum UFR of S_1 at second 27, Fig. 4 shows that they get a transient UFR of 2.8 Mb/s at second 21. This happens because changes occur at the same time in the branches from the source to r_5 and from r_5 to r_{10}, when receivers joined S_2 on r_5 and r_{10}, which means that the stabilization of UFR of S_1 is achieved first in each branch and only after in the entire path to r_{10}. This transient value is the minimum UFR in the branch upstream r_5 before second 21, but it is not the minimum UFR in the entire path to r_{10}, since the UFR of S_1 on the branch from r_5 to r_{10} was not considered yet upstream of r_5. Fig. 5 shows how the minimum UFR of S_1 is stabilized in the entire path to r_{10} after being computed in each branch.

When a_5 gets a SYNC at second 21 with an UFR of 2.8 Mb/s, it sends a notification to receivers on r_5, since this is the current minimum UFR of S_1 in the path from the source. At that time, S_1 has an UFR of 2 Mb/s on the branch from r_5 to r_{10}, which correspond to the UFR computed by a_5 on (r_5, r_9) after received an UPDATE from a_{10}. At second 22, a SYNC is sent toward a_{10} with an UFR of 2 Mb/s, since this value is lower than the upstream fair rate on a_5

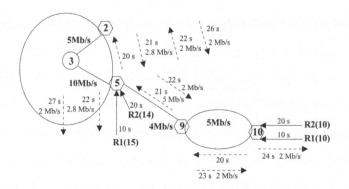

Figure 5. Messages after joining S_2

(2.8 Mb/s) and it is different from the fair rate previously sent (4 Mb/s). At the same time, a_5 also sends an UPDATE with an UFR of 2 Mb/s toward the source and so r_5 receivers get, at second 27, a report with the final minimum UFR for S_1 (2 Mb/s). When a_5 gets this SYNC, it does not sent another SYNC toward a_{10}, because this value is equal to the one sent in the previous SYNC.

When S_2 ends, the UFR of S_1 becomes higher than its upstream fair rate in all links, and so, only the agent closest to the source includes the new UFR of S_1 in a SYNC. So, receivers closer to the source are notified first, as shown on Tab. 1, and the notification time increases downstream by $O(n_a x a_s)$, where n_a is the number of agents and a_s is 1 s.

5   Conclusions and Future Work

This paper describes and evaluates SAPRA, a protocol that distributes resources among sessions proportionally to their audience size. SAPRA also notifies receivers about the quality of their sessions, allowing them to adapt to quality variations. Theoretical analysis and simulation results show that SAPRA requires a small amount of storage state, has small bandwidth overhead, and is efficient keeping the rate of sessions below their fair share, updating the fair share of sessions and notifying receivers. Although SAPRA aims mainly to distribute services resources with fairness, it also provides information about the quality of sessions and their population, which can be used to settle SLAs in each domain or define cost allocation policies.

As future work, we will define a receiver-driven adaptation mechanism, where receivers adapt when they receive network reports, a cost allocation scheme based on SAPRA and also study SAPRA in mobile environments, where the location of receivers change frequently.

References

1. Charu C. Aggarwal, Joel L. Wolf, and Philip S. Yu. Design and analysis of permutation-based pyramid broadcasting. *Multimedia Systems*, 7(6):439–448, 1999. 103
2. Dimitri Bertsekas and Robert Gallager. *Data Networks*. Prentice-Hall, Englewood Cliffs, New Jersey, 1987. 102
3. S. Blake, D. Black, M. Carlson, E. Davies, Z. Wang, and W. Weiss. An architecture for differentiated service. Request for Comments 2475, Internet Engineering Task Force, December 1998. 102
4. M. Handley, C. Perkins, and E. Whelan. Session announcement protocol. Request for Comments 2974, Internet Engineering Task Force, October 2000. 103
5. J. Heinanen, F. Baker, W. Weiss, and J. Wroclawski. Assured forwarding PHB group. Request for Comments 2597, Internet Engineering Task Force, June 1999. 102
6. H. Holbrook and B. Cain. Source-specific multicast for IP. Internet Draft, Internet Engineering Task Force, March 2001. Work in progress. 103
7. H. Holbrook and B. Cain. Using IGMPv3 for source-specific multicast. Internet Draft, Internet Engineering Task Force, March 2001. Work in progress. 103
8. Jun ichi Kimura, Fouad A. Tobagi, Jose-Miguel Pulido, and Peder J. Emstad. Perceived quality and bandwidth characterization of layered MPEG-2 video encoding. In *Proc. of SPIE International Symposium*, Boston, Massachussetes, USA, September 1999. 109
9. Mathias Johanson. Scalable video conferencing using subband transform coding and layered multicast transmission. In *Proc. of International Conference on Signal Processing Applications and Technology (ICSPAT)*, Orlando, Florida, USA, November 1999. 101
10. Arnaud Legout, Joerg Nonnenmacher, and Ernst Biersack. Bandwidth allocation policies for unicast and multicast flows. In *Proc. of the Conference on Computer Communications (IEEE Infocom)*, New York, New York, USA, March 1999. 102
11. Xue Li, Sanjoy Paul, and Mostafa Ammar. Multi-session rate control for layered video multicast. In *Proc. of Multimedia Computing and Networking*, San Jose, California, USA, January 1999. 103
12. Paulo Mendes. "SAPRA: Session-Aware Popurality-based Resource Allocation fairness protocol". http://www.cs.columbia.edu/~mendes/sapra.html. 109, 109
13. Paulo Mendes, Henning Schulzrinne, and Edmundo Monteiro. Session-aware popularity resource allocation for assured differentiated services. In *Proc. of the Second IFIP-TC6 Networking Conference*, Pisa, Italy, May 2002. 102, 104, 104, 105
14. Y. Rekhter and T. Li. A border gateway protocol 4 (BGP-4). Request for Comments 1771, Internet Engineering Task Force, March 1995. 105
15. Dan Rubenstein, Jim Kurose, and Don Towsley. The impact of multicast layering on network fairness. In *Proc. of SIGCOMM Symposium on Communications Architectures and Protocols*, Cambridge, Massachussetes, USA, September 1999. 102
16. Saswati Sarkar and Leandros Tassiulas. Fair allocation of discrete bandwidth layers in multicast networks. In *Proc. of the Conference on Computer Communications (IEEE Infocom)*, Tel Aviv, Israel, March 2000. 102
17. David Taubman and Avideh Zakhor. Multirate 3-D subband coding of video. *Journal of IEEE Transactions on Image Processing*, 3(5):572–588, September 1994. 101
18. Telstra. "AS 1221 BGP statistics". http://bgp.potaroo.net/as1221/bgp-active.html. 108, 109

A Scalable Video Server Using Intelligent Network Attached Storage[1]

Guang Tan, Hai Jin, and Liping Pang
Internet and Cluster Computing Center
Huazhong University of Science and Technology, Wuhan, 430074, China
{tanguang, hjin, lppang}@hust.edu.cn

Abstract. This paper proposes a new architecture, called intelligent network attached storage, for building a distributed video server. In this architecture, the data intensive and high overhead processing tasks such as data packaging and transmitting are handled locally at the storage nodes instead of at special delivery nodes. Thus an unnecessary data trip from the storage nodes to the delivery nodes is avoided, and a large amount of resource consumption is saved. Moreover, these "intelligent" storage nodes work cooperatively to give a single system image to the clients. Based on the architecture, we design our admission control and stream scheduling strategies, and conduct some simulation experiments to optimize the system design. The simulation results exhibit a near linear scalability of system performance with our design. Some implementation issues are also discussed in this paper.

1. Introduction

The incredible progress of multimedia and network technology enables one to build *Video-on-Demand* (VoD) system delivering the digitized movies to PCs or set-top-boxes of its subscribers. In order to support hundreds or thousands subscribers, the server for VoD service must be a high performance computing system. While many systems are built on a single high performance computer, more and more people tend to run this service on a cluster system composed of off-the-shelf commodities for their cost-effectiveness and fault-tolerant capability, and this area has attracted increasing attention of the researchers.

In designing a video server, one major concern is to pump a huge amount of data from disks to many clients at the same time, which is a great challenge due to the relatively slow I/O facilities. Most of the existing schemes are to develop a highly efficient parallel file system (e.g., Tiger Shark File System [14], xFS [4]) to achieve a satisfactory I/O bandwidth. In these systems, data is partitioned into stripes and distributed across storage nodes. When needed, they go through one delivery node, or a proxy [19] in parallel, where they are encapsulated into packets according to a certain protocol like RTP (*Real-time Transport Protocol*), and finally sent to clients for playing back. A typical data flow process is shown in Figure 1.

---

[1] This paper is supported by Wuhan Key High-Tech Project under grant 20011001001.

K.C. Almeroth and M. Hasan (Eds.): MMNS 2002, LNCS 2496, pp. 114-126, 2002.

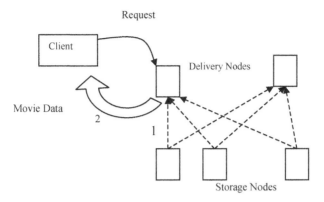

Fig. 1. Data flow in a traditional video server. In real implementations, the delivery nodes can also be storage nodes, or even machines independent of the server system.

One characteristic of this kind of systems is that the required data generally makes two trips on its way to clients: from the storage nodes to the intermediate nodes, and then to the clients. This makes the internal network or the processing capability of intermediate nodes potential bottlenecks for system performance. Even though high-speed network infrastructure like Gigabit Ethernet or Myrinet is adopted and the CPU speed is increasing rapidly, the scalability of this kind of systems is quite limited.

Our solution to this problem is to remove the first data trip between the storage nodes and the intermediate nodes (indicated by the dashed lines in Fig. 1) by offloading the latter's function to the former. If the storage nodes can work in a cooperative manner that makes the data from multiple independent nodes looks like from one machine, the clients can enjoy the video service without any loss on QoS. For the server side, a great amount of resource consumption is saved.

This idea is similar to the concept of active disk [1][23], intelligent disks [16], or network attached autonomous disks [2][3] in some ways. The common point is to push the basic processing closer to the data, providing a potential reduction in data movement through the I/O subsystem. This method is being applied to various applications such as database, data mining, image processing. Especially it is employed in multimedia streaming service [9]. Our structure however, has the following differences: while these systems have only small processing engines attached to the disks performing some simple operations, our storage nodes are capable of handling more complicated problems specific to one application, such as admission control, load balancing and automatic failover. Compared to some of these systems' relying on clients to do some special task such as data block mapping and data pulling in predefined syntax, our system hides all the data locating details in itself, and therefore gives a single system image to the clients. This makes our scheme more adaptable in real internet world.

The rest of this paper is organized as follows: section 2 presents the system architecture and discusses some specific problems related to video server. Section 3 describes our simulation experiments and demonstrates some simulation results, reveling the relationship between server system parameters and the system performance.

Section 4 discusses several implementation issues. Section 5 evaluates some related work, and finally section 6 ends with a conclusion and the future work.

2 System Architecture

The system architecture is illustrated in Figure 2. The storage system in this figure can be realized by different hardware platforms, e.g., a regular workstation or active disks attached to a network [1]. In this paper we take the first approach and use the term disk and storage node with no difference.

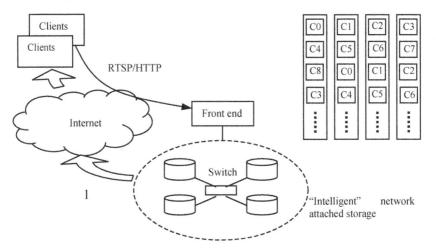

Fig. 2. System architecture. The video server system comprises of two major components: front-end machine and the "intelligent" network attached storage.

The basic function of the front-end machine, which is the only entry-point of the system, is to accept the client requests and instruct storage nodes to retrieval the requested data and send it back to client directly. Usually it is implemented as a RTSP daemon or HTTP daemon, depending on the protocol adopted to carry the interaction commands between the clients and the server.

When the front-end machine accepts a client's request, it first processes the authentication. If passed, the request will be broadcasted to the attached disks, which will translate it to a set of sub-requests and schedule them according to their own task scheduler. The front-end machine collects the scheduling results and makes a comprehensive decision, which is to be sent to the clients, and then it schedules the storage nodes to arrange their playing tasks.

Besides, the front-end machine takes care of redirecting the clients' feedback to appropriate storage nodes to adjust the transmission quality. It is also the global manager of the UDP ports used by storage nodes. These problems will be further discussed in section 4.

2.1 Data Organization

The storage system is the container of movies and takes responsibility for packaging and transmitting of media data. Movies are partitioned into segments (movie clip) of equal playing time (except the last one) and interleaved across disks. Each segment has two replicas in order to achieve fault tolerance and load balancing. The segments of one movie are placed in a round robin fashion with the first one at a randomly chosen storage node, and the beginning nodes are different for one movie's two replicas. An example of the data layout is illustrated in Figure 2.

In this paper, each movie segment together with its processing code is regarded as an object. Similar to traditional concept of object, this abstract also has its own features. The attributes, data, and processing code of the object are all separately stored in disk as different forms: clip index file, clip file, and program file respectively. The clip index file is a text file recording all the clip items of one movie. It is named as xxx.index, where xxx is the corresponding movie file name, and the content of the index file is a table-like file illustrated in Table 1.

Table 1. An example of index file LifeIsBeautiful.mpg.index

Clip No.	Clip Name	Range	Buddy Location	Next Location1	Next Location2
0	LifeIsBeautiful.0.mpg	$0 - 5{:}00$	Node5	Node3	Node6
4	LifeIsBeautiful.4.mpg	$20{:}00 - 25{:}00$	Node5	Node3	Node6
...	...	...	...	...	...

In table 1, the Buddy Location refers to the location of another replica of the same movie segment, and the Next Location1 and Next Location2 point to the places of the next segments in playing time. These parameters serve as pointers when one object needs to interact with another one. The pointers link up all the objects into a well-organized data structure, as shown in Figure 3.

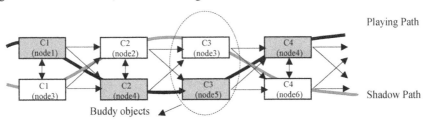

Fig. 3. Linked object lists. The sequence of grey blocks on the black curve represents the storage nodes to play the consecutive segments of one movie, and the blank blocks on the grey curve composes the shadow path.

With this structure, a movie's playing back is in fact a sequence of object operations: the first object retrieves and transmits its data, then it tells the next object to transmit next segment, and then next one, until all the objects finished its task. We call the sequence of objects participating in the real playing back a "playing path", and the remaining objects of this movie compose a "shadow path". The shadow path accompanies the playing path and periodically pulling information like normal playing time, RTP sequence number, RTP timestamp, etc., as checkpoints. When one object crashes, its buddy object will resumes its work using the latest checkpoint data. We call the failover process "path switching". The playing path and shadow path is shown in Figure 3 and the path switching process is illustrated in Figure 4.

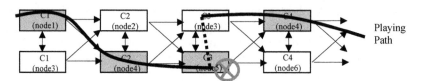

Fig. 4. Path switching upon a node failure. Node2 resumes the playing back of one movie when node5 fails in the middle of clip3.

2.2 Admission Control and Stream Scheduling

As an important issue for a system providing real-time service, admission control and resource allocation have been hot issues [13][15][17]. While it can enjoy some of the optimizations brought by these researches, our system has some particular features to take into account in its design.

Since a movie is partitioned into multiple segments, the task of playing a movie is divided into a set of sub-tasks, each representing the playing of one segment. A movie-playing request is translated into a set of sub-requests to the storage nodes according to the movie index files. All the sub-requests must be scheduled by the storage nodes before their corresponding sub-tasks are accepted, and the scheduling results jointly determine the result of the request.

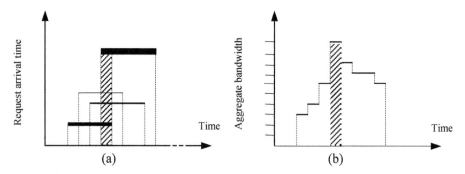

Fig. 5. Scheduling table and aggregate data bandwidth. In (a), each line represents a sub-task, or a streaming, and the width of the line indicates the resource requirement of this task.

To schedule sub-requests, each storage node maintains a scheduling table recording all the playing tasks being currently executed or to be executed. An example of the scheduling table is illustrated in Fig. 5(a). Our admission control and streaming scheduling are based on the peak value of the system load, defined as the aggregate data bandwidth of all the streams. Fig. 5(b) presents the aggregate data bandwidth vs. time. Denoting the bandwidth of individual task by b(T), the aggregate bandwidth at time t by B(t), and the beginning time and ending time of one task by bgn(T) and end(T), respectively. We define the peak value of system load in a time range of a task as:

$$L(T_{new}) = Max \; B(t) = \sum_{T \in \{T | T \in \Phi \; \wedge \; bgn(T) \leq t \leq end(T)\}} b(T) \quad + b(T_{new}),$$

$$bgn \; (T_{new}) \leq t \leq end \; (T_{new}) \tag{1}$$

where Φ is the set of tasks that have been already arranged in the scheduling table.

If $L(T_{new})$ exceeds a certain upper bound (typically determined by the local disk I/O bandwidth and network interface bandwidth), this sub-request is rejected. Based on this, the admission control process is handled as follows: if one sub-request is rejected by both storage nodes owning the corresponding segments, the whole request is rejected. If only one storage node can admit this sub-request, the sub-request is assigned to this node for movie retrieval. If both storages nodes can admit this sub-request, the one with smaller $L(T_{new})$ will be selected as the operator of this segment in the movie playing back. All the scheduling results should be returned to the front-end machine for comprehensive decision. The algorithm is given in Figure 6.

```
RequestSchedule()
{
   int Decision = ACCEPTED;
   if( current overall data bandwidth + bandwidth of new request
       > maximum system outbound bandwidth)
      return REJECTED;
   Broadcast the new request to storage nodes;
   for (int i = 0; i < NumClips; i ++)
     Receive scheduling result and store it in result[i];
     for (int i = 0; i < NumClips; i ++)
        if result[i] = REJECTED {
              Decision = REJECTED;
              break;
      }
   if (Decision == ACCEPTED)
     Send PLAY commands to the storage nodes, asking them to ar-
     range the playing tasks;
   return Decision;
}
```

(a)

```
SubRequestSchedule()
{
   Receive request from front-end machine;
   Look up the clip table and map the request to a set of sub-
      request: subreq[nclip];
```

```
for (int i = 0; i < nclip; i ++)
/* A schedule result contains the evaluated load in the
 * time period of given sub-request, and a very large
 * value means the sub-request is rejected */
    result[i] = Schedule(subreq[i]);
for (int i = 0; i < nclip; i ++){
    if local IP < Buddy IP of clip i
        Send result[i] to the buddy object;
else {
    Receive result from the buddy object as result1;
    Compare result and result1, select a smaller one and re-
    turn it to the front-end;
}
}
```

(b)

Fig. 6. Request scheduling and admission algorithm: (a) Algorithm for front-end machine, (b) Algorithm for storage node. These two parts work in a coordinated fashion to make a final decision regarding admission and stream scheduling. For simplicity, the error handling is omitted.

The above discussion is based on the assumption that the streams are constant bit rate and the local admission control adopts a threshold-based deterministic policy, that is, calculates the expected resource requirement using worst-case evaluation and gives a deterministic result regarding admitting or rejecting. Our decision model, however, is not limited to these assumptions. Since each storage node is an autonomous entity, it can use whatever algorithm to process the admission control, as long as it gives a deterministic or probability-based result to the front-end machine. If a probability-based policy is adopted, the final admission probability should be

$$P = \prod_{i=1}^{n} P_i \qquad (2)$$

where n is the segment number of a given movie and P_i is the probability of admitting object i given by its storage node.

3   Design Optimization

To optimize the design, we develop a simulation model to study the relationship among some basic system parameters, such as segment length, number of storage nodes, and the overall system performance. We also conduct experiment to demonstrate the scalability of this architecture.

In the simulation, a process called front process represents the front-end machine accepting request from a request producer, and several other processes called back process represent the storage nodes scheduling and executing the "playing" tasks. There is no real media data processing and transmitting; and the load values are calculated from the scheduling table using the assumed parameters described below.

Though simulating in a simplified environment, we believe that the model can correctly reflect the behavior pattern of the major system components based on the assumption given below.

3.1 Simulation Assumptions, Parameters and Performance Metrics

Without loss of generality, we make some assumptions and parameterize the simulation model as follows:

(1) The arrival of clients' requests is a steady Poisson stream with arrival rate $= \lambda$;
(2) Movie number $M = 200$, movie duration is conform to uniform distribution between 110 and 130 (minutes), with the average value $T = 120$; and the movie selection pattern is conform to Zipf distribution ($\alpha = 1$) [6];
(3) All requests ask for const-bit-rate streaming service, with data bandwidth $= b$;
(4) The admission control adopts a threshold-based policy. The threshold numbers of streams for the whole system and individual storage node are S_{server} and S_{disk}, respectively;
(5) Number of storage nodes is N;
(6) Request number $Rn = 1080$.

We use the following simulation metrics:

(1) Request satisfying rate R

It is defined as the ratio of accepted requests to all the client requests issued. Given a request arrival rate, this metric reflects the service capability of the server system. Another implication of this metric is the average system data throughput B, which can be derived from:

$$B = \lambda T \cdot R \cdot b \qquad (3)$$

(2) Maximum concurrent stream number C

It reflects the peak performance of the system while guaranteeing the quality of service.

3.2 Simulation Results and Analysis

3.2.1 Scalability Test

We fix $S_{disk} = 45$, and the clip length $= 8$ (minutes). Varying the number of storage nodes and computing the system's servicing capability, we have Figure 7.

The figures exhibit a near linear scalability of the servicing capability of our system. Using equitation (3), we also learn that the average data throughput has a linear scalability with the scale of the system.

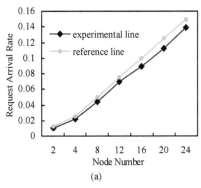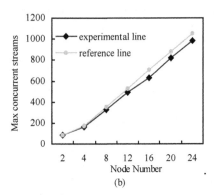

Fig. 7. System scalability vs. system performance. Here the Request Arrival Rate is the maximum arrival rate that makes the service's satisfying rate no less than 97.5%.

3.2.2 Relationship between System Parameters and System Performance

The purpose of this experiment is to find out the relationship between some basic system parameters and the overall system performance. We studied two parameters, clip length and replica number of movies, called replicate degree. For the former parameter we vary the clip length and computing the satisfying rate and number of maximum concurrent streams, showing in Figure 8.

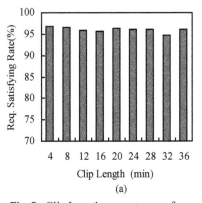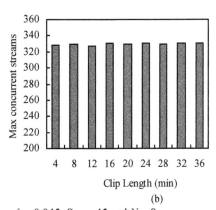

Fig. 8. Clip Length vs. system performance. Here $\lambda = 0.045$, $S_{disk} = 45$ and $N = 8$.

From Fig. 8 we can see the length of clip have only slight influence to the system performance. This phenomenon is probably due to our assumption that the client requests arrive as a steady Poisson stream, which has a characteristic that the numbers of request appearing in two different time ranges are independent stochastic variables. So a single long clip has the same effect as a group of short clips in assigning the playing task, though they occupy different periods of playing time in the time axis of one movie.

To find out the relationship between replicate degree and the system performance, we examine 4 different patterns for the replicate degree setting in simulation: (1) Single replica. Each movie has only one replica; (2) Double replica. Each movie has two replicas; (3) Variable replica 1. Each one of the top 10 (most frequently accessed) movies has replicate degree of 3, and the remaining movies have replicate degree of 2; (4) Variable replica 2. Each one of the top 10 movies has replicate degree of 3, each one of the top 11-70 has replicate degree of 2, and the remaining movies have replicate degree of 1.The simulation results are presented in Fig. 9.

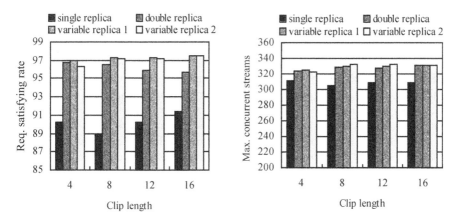

Fig. 9. Replicate degree vs. system performance

In Fig. 9 (a), there is a distinct improvement in system performance from single replica scheme to double replica scheme. This means that doubling the replica number will benefit much to system performance. From double replica scheme to variable replica 1 scheme, however, there is not much performance improvement, which suggests that the addition of replicas on the base of double replica scheme only bring quite limited benefit.

Compared with the second and third schemes, the variable replica 2 scheme has comparable performance. This implicates that the load balancing on the hot movies has significant influence on system performance, while the effort on balancing the load on cold movies has little gains. Therefore, the reduction in replica number of cold movies, which occupy the majority in the movie library, will have little negative influence on system performance. This result appears to be a valuable suggestion in real deployment: when the QoS for cold movies are not so critical, the cost on data storage can be reduced by (200-20-60)/400= 30% without performance degradation.

4   Implementation Issues

In a typical video service system, the server serves as a data provider and clients as data consumers. Most of the data transmission takes place from the server to clients, making it possible to scale up the one-way data bandwidth. However, some data (such as those required by RTCP) must be sent to the server as necessary information for adjusting the transmitting quality. These data should arrive at the appropriate storage node of the server via the front-end machine. As the data manipulation of one movie is changing from one storage node to another, the front-end machine needs to know where the operation on a movie is occurring when the feedback of a client comes. We add a port-mapping table in the OS kernel (our experimental platform is Linux Kernel 2.4.2). It receives messages from storage nodes and accordingly updates its mapping table so as to redirect the incoming UDP packets destined for some port to the appropriate receiver.

Another practical issue is the scalability of the system. Since the major responsibility of the front-end machine is to maintain the RTSP or HTTP connections, performing only very sparse interaction (like PLAY, PAUSE, TEARDOWN, etc. commands), and to direct the incoming RTCP packets. The overhead of the front-end machine is very low, and it can easily handle hundreds of concurrent VoD sessions. However, when the number of simultaneous clients exceeds 1000 or more, the front-end machine is very likely to become a performance bottleneck, as it is the single entry point of the whole system. A solution to this problem is to use multiple front-end machines to share the load. The available approaches include Dynamic DNS [8], One-IP technology [11], etc. Layer 4 switching technology can also be used to enhance the processing capability of front-end machine.

5   Related Work

Microsoft's Tiger [5][7] is a special-purpose file system for video servers distributing data over ATM networks. To play a video stream, Tiger establishes a multipoint-to-point ATM-switched virtual circuit between every node and the user. This mechanism achieves high parallelism for data retrieval and transmission. But the reliance on ATM network also brings a disadvantage: when receiving data from the server in a network environment other than ATM, front-end processors may be needed to combine the ATM packets into streams.

CMU-NASD [9][12] achieves direct transfer between client/drive in a networked environment. It exports a pure object-based interface to clients, and clients can contact with disks directly in a secure communications channel. Multimedia file accessing is experimented on this platform, but the emphasis is put on developing a file system, and VoD service as an Internet application conforming to a set of industrial standards is not considered.

C. Akinlar and S. Mukherjee [2][3] proposed a multimedia file system based on network attached autonomous disks. The autonomous disks, implemented using regular PC-based hardware, have specific modules called AD-DFS in their operating system kernels. When a client requests a file, the disks send data via their own network interfaces. But the client needs particular module in its OS kernel to understand the block-based object interface exported by AD-DFS. Like the NASD, the client must issue multiple network connections to the disks when accessing a file expanding several disks.

Parallel Video Server [20][21] employs an array of servers to push data concurrently to the client stations. Unlike our design to exploit parallelism among multiple streams, it attempts to achieve data retrieval and transmission parallelism within individual stream. One disadvantage of this architecture is the data distribution is not transparent to the clients. Client-side re-computing is needed to mask the data lose in playing back when server node fails [21].

6   Conclusion and Future Work

We introduced our new architecture for building a distributed video server, called intelligent network attached storage. In this architecture, the network attached disk acts as an "intelligent" entity with its own policy to determine admission and stream scheduling. Each data segment is regarded as an object with its own processing method. The data of multiple objects is processed locally at the storage nodes and then delivered to remote clients in a consecutive manner among the storage nodes. By cooperation of movie objects the system achieves a single system image to clients. Based on this architecture, we studied several issues related to video service such as admission control, stream scheduling, data placement policy, and conduct simulation experiments, which shows a near linear scalability in servicing capacity.

Our future research is to further optimize the system performance. This includes studying the relationship between the movie accessing pattern and appropriate data striping and placement schemes, for example, system performance when the input requests are a non-stable Poisson stream, system performance in presence of object failures, etc. We also attempt to study the issues on software model. How should the software be partitioned between the delivery nodes and the storage nodes? What a protocol the storage nodes should use to interact with each other? How to support both real-time and non real-time applications effectively? To provide structural support for a wider range of data intensive applications based on this architecture, all these issues need to be explored.

References

1. A. Acharya, M. Uysal, and J. Saltz. "Active Disks". *Proceedings of International Conference on the Architectural Support for Programming Languages and Operating Systems.* 1998
2. C. Akinlar and S. Mukherjee. "A Scalable Distributed Multimedia File System Using Network Attached Autonomous Disks". *Proceedings of 8th International Symposium on Modeling, Analysis and Simulation of Computer and Telecommunication Systems*, 2000. Page(s): 180 -187

3. C. Akinlar and S. Mukherjee. "Bandwidth Guarantee in a Distributed Multimedia File System Using Network Attached Autonomous Disks". *Proceedings of Sixth IEEE Real-Time Technology and Application 2000 Symposium*. RTAS 2000. Page(s): 237–246

4. T. E. Anderson, M. D. Dahlin, J. M. Neefe, D. A. Patterson, et al. "Serverless Network File Systems". *ACM Transactions on Computer Systems*, February 1996

5. K. Argy. "Scalable multimedia servers". *IEEE Concurrency*, Volume 6, Issue 4, Page(s): 8-10, Oct.-Dec. 1998

6. R. L. Axtell. "Zipf Distribution of U.S. Firm Sizes". *Science*. Sept. 7, 2001, Vol. 293.

7. W. J. Bolosky et al. "The Tiger Video Fileserver", *Proc. of Sixth Int'l workshop on Network and Operation System Support for Digital Audio and Video*, 1996.

8. T. Brisco, "DNS Support for Load Balancing", RFC 1794, http://www.landfield.com/rfcs/rfc1794.html

9. Carnegie Mellon University. "Extreme NASD". http://www.pdl.cs.cum.edu/extreme/

10. Cisco Local Director, Cisco Systems, Inc., http://www.cisco.com/univercd/cc/td/doc/pcat/ld.htm

11. P. Damani, P. E. Chung, Y. Huang, C. Kintala, and Y. Wang. "ONE-IP: Techniques for Hosting a Service on a Cluster of Machines". *Proceedings of 6th International World Wide Web Conference*, April 1997

12. G. A. Gibson, D. F. Nagle, K. Amiri, and et al. "File Server Scaling With network-attached secure disks". *Proceedings of the ACM International conference on Measurement and Modeling of Computer Systems (Sigmetrics'97)*, June 1997

13. A. Hafid. "A Scalable Video-on-Demand System Using Future Reservation of Resources and Multicast Communications". *Computer Communications* 21 (1998), Page(s): 431-444

14. R. Haskin and F. Schmuck. "The Tiger Shark File System". *Proceedings of COMPCON*, Spring 1996

15. X. Jiang and P. Mohapatra. "Efficient Admission Control Algorithms for Multimedia Servers". *Multimedia Systems*, 7:294-304, 1999

16. K. Keeton, D. Patterson, and J. Hellerstein. "A Case for Intelligent Disks (IDISKs)". *ACM SIGMOD Record*, September 1998

17. E. W. Knightly and N. B. Shroff. "Admission Control for Statistical QoS: Theory and Practice". *IEEE Network*, March 1999

18. J. B. Kwon, H. Y. Yeom. "An Admission Control Scheme for Continuous Media Servers using Caching". *Proceeding of IEEE International Performance, Computing, and Communications Conference, 2000*. IPCCC'00. Page(s): 456-462

19. J. Y. B. Lee. "Parallel video servers: a tutorial". *IEEE Multimedia*, Volume 5 Issue 2, April-June 1998, Page(s): 20–28

20. J. Y. B. Lee. "Concurrent Push – A Scheduling Algorithm for Push-Based parallel Video Servers". *IEEE Transactions on Circuits and Systems for Video Technology*. VOL. 9, No. 3, April 1999

21. J. Y. B. Lee. "Supporting Server-Level Fault Tolerance in Concurrent-Push-Based Parallel Video Servers". *IEEE Transactions on Circuits and Systems for Video Technology*. VOL.11, No.1, January 2001

22. Linux Virtual Server Project, http://www.LinuxVirtualServer.org/.

23. E. Riedel. *Active Disks – Remote Execution for Network-Attached Storage*. Doctoral Dissertation. School of Computer Science, Carnegie Mellon University. 1999

On Proxy-Caching Mechanisms
for Cooperative Video Streaming
in Heterogeneous Environments

Naoki Wakamiya, Masayuki Murata, and Hideo Miyahara

Graduate School of Information Science and Technology, Osaka University
1-3 Machikaneyama, Toyonaka, Osaka 560-8531, Japan
{wakamiya, murata, miyahara}@ist.osaka-u.ac.jp

Abstract. In this paper, we investigate mechanisms in which proxy servers co-operate to provide users with low-latency and high-quality video-streaming services. The proxy is capable of adapting incoming or cached video blocks at the user's request by means of transcoders and filters. On receiving a request from a user, the proxy checks its own cache. If an appropriate block is not available, the proxy retrieves a block of a higher quality from the video server or a nearby proxy. The retrieved block is cached, its quality is adjusted to that which was requested as necessary, and is then sent to the user. Each proxy communicates with the others and takes the transfer delay and video quality into account in finding the appropriate block for retrieval. We propose several caching mechanisms for the video-streaming system and evaluate their performance in terms of the required buffer size, the play-back delay, and the video quality.

1 Introduction

To provide fascinating video content without irritating, disappointing, or discouraging the viewer, mechanisms that accomplish low delays and high quality for the streaming service are required. Proxy caching [1], which was originally proposed for WWW (World Wide Web) systems and is now widely deployed, provides savings on bandwidth, load balancing, reduced network latency, and better content availability. The technique thus appears to be helpful in the context of video steaming.

However, existing caching architectures are not intended for video streaming services; they are thus not directly applicable to video delivery. One problem in the caching of video streams is the size of video objects. For example, two hours of video encoded as MPEG-2 at the lowest coding rate and quality takes up 1.35 Gbytes. The buffer in the proxy-cache server is of limited size, it may, for example, only be capable of caching ten or so streams. Segmentation of the video stream, into `blocks`, `segments` or `frames`, provided the basis for the proposals made in earlier research work on proxy-cache mechanisms for video-steaming services [2,3,4,5]. Retrieving, caching, and sending video streams on a per-segment basis makes effective use of the cache buffer possible and obtains a high probability of cache hits.

A problem, however, that arises with video streams which are segmented in some way is the strict requirements on the timing of block delivery. Since conventional web

K.C. Almeroth and M. Hasan (Eds.): MMNS 2002, LNCS 2496, pp. 127–139, 2002.
© Springer-Verlag Berlin Heidelberg 2002

browsing does not impose any requirements in terms of temporal QoS, except for the so-called eight-second rule, the proxy is allowed ample time to find and retrieve requested objects. On the other hand, once a user starts to watch a video stream, the service provider must guarantee the continuous delivery of the blocks of video so that there are no interruptions or freezing during play-back.

A further issue is the heterogeneity among clients. The available bandwidth and the capacity of the access links differ from client to client. Client systems are also diverse in terms of their capabilities. Since receiving and decoding a video stream places large loads on the network and on the client system, the affordable video rate, i.e., the quality, also differs from client to client. Users may have preferences in terms of perceived video quality. Two teams have introduced a proxy-cache server which is capable of video-quality adjustment as a solution to the heterogeneity issue [3,6]. The proxy adjusts the quality of retrieved or stored blocks to requests and provides clients with blocks of a satisfactory quality.

In this paper we propose proxy-caching mechanisms for streaming-video services. Several papers [2,3,4,5,6] describe valid ways of achieving a low-delay and high-quality video-streaming service. However, none provides a solution to all of the problems outlined above and explained in the next section. Our proposal is based on our own previous research [6], and takes into account the segmentation and prefetching of the data, and the client-to-client heterogeneity. More importantly, we propose a new mechanism for cooperation among video proxy-cache servers. In this paper, on the basis of research in that area, we describe a generally applicable idea for the provision of more effective and higher-quality video-streaming services in the *heterogeneous* environment. To the best of our knowledge, insufficient attention has been given to this point. We tackles the problem of how the requested block should be provided to the client, and what the quality of the block must be. The mechanisms proposed in the paper are somewhat general, but provide a good starting point from which we are able to see how several basic techniques may be combined to accomplish an effective video-streaming service in a heterogeneous environment.

The organization of the rest of this paper is as follows. In section 2, we present our assumptions on the video-streaming system and briefly summarize the related issues that have been considered in this work. The basic mechanism of proxy caching with video quality adjustment is introduced in section 3. In section 4, we give the results of some preliminary evaluations. Finally, we summarize the paper in section 5.

2   System Model and Related Issues

In this section, we start by illustrating our video-streaming system. We then summarize the issues in relation to a cooperative video-streaming service for an environment with heterogeneous clients.

2.1   A Video-Streaming System with Proxies

The video-streaming system considered in this paper consists of an originating video server, several heterogeneous client systems, and proxy-cache servers which are capable of video-quality adjustment. Several video streams are prepared and placed in the local storage of the video server, which communicates with the proxies. Each proxy further communicates with a number of designated clients and neighboring proxies. Communications among the entities of this system for the video streaming are according to the RTSP/TCP protocol stack. The video streams are segmented into blocks. Delivery of the blocks from the originating server to the proxies and to the clients takes place in RTP/UDP sessions.

A client obtains information on a video-streaming service through the SDP. If the user decides to receive the service, the client sets up an RTSP session with the designated proxy-cache server, which is typically the closest such server to the client, and informs the proxy server about the client's requirements in terms of the video stream. The information includes the desired level of video quality, which is determined by both the user's preferences and the limitations of the client system, including its processing capability and any multimedia equipment that is available, the size of the dedicated buffer for prefetching, and, if possible, the available bandwidth.

On receiving the PLAY request from the client, the proxy searches its local cache for a corresponding block of video. If it does hold such a block and the proxy is able to satisfy the client request in terms of video quality (this constitutes a "cache hit"), the proxy applies any video-quality adjustment that is needed. Note that the cache is only hit if the block is both held and is of the same quality as has been requested or of higher quality. The block is then sent to the client in an RTP/UDP session. If, on the other hand, a "cache miss" occurs, the proxy retrieves the block from the most appropriate server, which is selected from among the the originating server and the other proxy-cache servers. The proxy then deposits the block in its local cache, adjusts the block's quality as required, and then sends the block to the client.

At the same time, the proxy predicts the blocks which will be required in the near future, and retrieves them in anticipation of client requests. This mechanism is called prefetching [3,6] and provides a way of avoiding breaks in the play-back of the video stream. Prefetching was originally developed for WWW systems in general, but is particularly effective when used with video objects.

The client is equipped with a prefetch buffer in which the delivered blocks are initially stored. Play-back by the client is delayed until sufficient blocks are thought to have been stored. The client then begins to read the blocks from the buffer for play-back. At the same time, the client deposits new blocks, as they arrive, in the buffer.

2.2   Related Issues and Relevant Previous Works

Several research issues are involved in the building of the video-streaming system which we have introduced in the previous subsection. In this subsection, we introduce those issues and some relevant work, and then explain the solutions we have selected.

Segmentation of video streams :   When we considered the structure of a coded video stream and its frame-by-frame mode of play-back, we decided to use a block of several video frames in segmentation [6]. Such frame-based segmentation is preferable when we are employing RTSP as the communications protocol for video streaming. For the proxy to retrieve specific blocks from the other servers, a PLAY request must specify the range of the video stream in terms of an SMPTE relative timestamp, a normal play timestamp, or an ISO 8601 timestamp. Employing frame-based segmentation allows us to easily derive appropriate range parameters from the order of a block in the sequence, since each block corresponds to a certain number of frames and we know the period of one frame, e.g., 1/24 second.

Adjusting video quality : Of the mechanisms for the adjustment of video quality, which are sometimes called transcoders or filters, we have tended to concentrate on the quantizer-scale-based approach [6]. The originating server generates a video stream of the finest possible quality by using the smallest quantizer scale, i.e., $Q = 1$. The originating server requantizes the blocks if the proxy's request was for block of lower quality and then sends them to the proxy. The proxy also adjusts cached and retrieved blocks when a lower quality has been requested by another proxy or the client. Note that we do not intend to limit the adjustment of video quality to the quantizer-scale-based technique, since this sometimes leads to sudden jumps in the level of quality due to diverse quantizer scale. Yeadon et al. [7] report on a range of useful and scalable ways of controlling the quality of encoded video streams. The layered coding algorithm inherently enables the quality adjustment.

Locating the appropriate server : To locate a server which is appropriate to handle a request for missing blocks, the originating server and the proxy-cache servers need to communicate with each other and to maintain up-to-date information. The information includes the blocks that are available and their quality, the round trip time and the available bandwidth between the proxy-cache server and the other servers. Extending the messages of the well-known inter-cache communications protocols, including ICP, CARP, and WCCP [1] to include information on the quality of the cached blocks and other performance metrics makes them applicable to video-streaming services.

The proxy estimates the block size, propagation delay, and throughput and thus obtains as accurate a prediction of the transfer time as is possible. The block size can be derived by using a traffic model for coded-video streams [8] or the information provided by the server through out-of-band communications. The latest research activity in network measurement, monitoring, and telecommunications engineering has provided us with several tools and methods for obtaining information on network conditions. Any of the methods may be applied to the proxy servers, as long as this is easy to apply and the selected method provides accurate estimates. For example, latency may be estimated by a means of *ping*, *echoping* and so on. The throughput of a session between two servers may be measured by using *pathchar*, *pchar*, or and any other suitable methods. Employing the TCP-friendly rate-control protocol [9,10] as the underlying rate-control mechanism simplifies the estimation of latency and throughput.

Cache management : Since the proxy server's cache buffer is of finite size, a less important cached block must sometimes be replaced by a newly retrieved block. On the contrary to the LRU and LFU algorithms which implicitly track the pattern of client requests [11], the algorithms proposed in earlier work [3,6] explicitly track the client requests and determine the blocks to be kept and to be thrown away on the retrieval of a new block. Those blocks which are located at the beginning of the video, those which are currently being watched by clients, and those which are considered likely to be requested in the near future are regarded as important and are not replaced. Of the

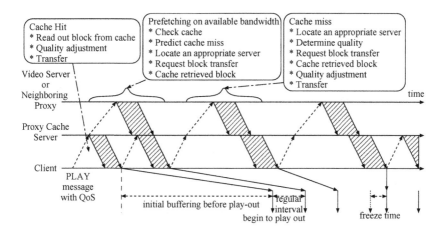

Fig. 1. Behavior of the proposed system

other blocks, those closer to the end of the stream are labeled as being lower priority and become the first victims when replacement is required.

Prefetching : Introducing prefetching mechanisms to the proxies and clients of the video-streaming system conceals the effects of variations in network conditions on delays in the transfer of data and increases the time that is available for finding and retrieving requested blocks with the desired quality. The proxy prefetching mechanism we present in this paper predicts future cache misses and prefetches blocks of the appropriate quality on the basis of requests from the client request and of the number of blocks in the client's prefetch buffer.

3   A Proxy Cache with Video-Quality Adjustment

Our system consists of an originating server, cooperative proxies, and heterogeneous clients. To simplify the discussion, we have concentrated on the case where clients concentrate on a single video stream. Our mechanism is, however, applicable to cases where the video-streaming system is providing multiple video streams to individual users. The basic behavior of the system is illustrated in Fig. 1. Although video streaming according to the RTSP does not necessarily require block-by-block requests, we have assumed that the client explicitly informs the proxy server of a requested level of quality per block. Of course, we are also able to employ implicit quality notification, where the server continues to apply the most recently requested level of quality to subsequent blocks and does not wait for new requests.

3.1   The Cache Table and Remote Table

The proxy server has two tables. Information on the locally cached blocks is maintained in one, referred to as the cache table, while the other, the remote table, is for information on the caching of blocks at other servers. One such pair of tables is organized for each video stream.

The cache tables maintain information on the cached and non-cached blocks of video streams. A block consists of N frames. Each entry in the cache table corresponds to one block of the stream and consists of a block number i, the quality of the block $q(i)$ in the cache, and a list of markers $M(i)$ for the cached block i. Larger values of $q(i)$ indicates higher levels of video quality while a zero means that the block i is not cached in the local buffer. After a block has been received, the corresponding $q(i)$ is replaced by the quality of the newly retrieved block. The list of markers $M(i)$ is a set of identifiers of proxy servers.

The remote table in a given proxy holds information on the other servers. Each entry in the remote table corresponds to the name of a server (e.g., server k, $k = 0$ indicates the originating server). It includes the estimated latency d_k^S and the estimated throughput r_k^S for the connection, along with the list of blocks available on that server and their respective quality $O_k(i)$. The table is built and maintained by exchanging QUERY and REPLY messages.

When a proxy receives a first request from a new client, it sends a QUERY message to a multicast address which is shared by all of the servers. The proxy sets a TTL for the QUERY message and thus limits the scope of neighboring servers that will respond to the query as in SOCCER [2]. The QUERY message informs the other servers of the video stream which the proxy is requesting and a list of the blocks it expects to require in the near future. On receiving the query, the proxy server k searches its local cache for the blocks which are listed in the QUERY message, and sets marks $M(i)$ for the blocks in its cache table. After a block has been marked, it leaves the scope of block replacement. Those blocks not being declared in the message are un-marked for the proxy. The server k then returns a REPLY message which carries a timestamp and the list of $O_k(i) = q(i)$ values for those blocks it holds which were in the list included with the query. The blocks indicated in the inquiries about quality are those which are currently requested by clients and subsequent I blocks. The window of inquiry I is defined as a way of restricting the range of blocks to include in a single inquiry and preventing all blocks from being locked. I blocks from the beginning of the stream are also listed in the QUERY message to prepare for new clients that will request the stream in the future [5].

The interval at which a proxy sends QUERY messages must be neither too short nor too long. The proxy issues a QUERY message when the end of the prefetching window, which is later explained, of any client finds an entry $O_k(i)$ which is zero. In addition, we also introduce a timer to force refreshing of the remote tables. Timing reaches expiry every $(I - P - 1)N/F$ where P is the size of the prefetching window, N is the number of frames in a block and F the frame rate, respectively.

3.2   Block Retrieval Algorithm

The block-retrieval algorithm determines the levels of quality of the blocks that will satisfy client requests and the way that the proxy-cache server provides the block to the client. The client sends request messages to its designated proxy server on a per-block basis as shown in Fig. 1. The client j's request for the block i is denoted by $q_j(i)$.

On receiving a request $q_j(i)$, the proxy determines how the requested block should be provided to the client on the basis of the cache table, the remote table, the available bandwidth r_j^C, the latency d_j^C to the client j, the number of video blocks stored in the client's prefetch buffer p_j, and the client's persistence or tolerance on the video quality degradation β_j. The bandwidth r_j^C which is available for sending the block i to the client j and the one-way delay d_j^C for this transfer are determined in the same way as the estimated throughput r_k^S and the estimated latency d_k^S for the server k. The number of video blocks in the client j's prefetch buffer is denoted by p_j and is included in the request from the client to the proxy. At the beginning of a session with a proxy by a client, the proxy is notified of the client's persistence on the video quality, i.e., the parameter β_j. When the client chooses $\beta_j = 1$, the proxy is obliged to provide the client with blocks of a level of quality that is in accordance with the request. On the other hand, a value of β_j close to zero means that the client is tolerant of lower quality but is placing tight restrictions on the punctual or in-time arrival of blocks. Finally, we assume that the proxy knows the size of a block i with a level of quality q, $s(i, q)$.

The quality, for a block i, that the proxy is able to offer to a client j is derived as

$$q_j^P(i) = \min(q(i), q_j^{Pmax}(i)), \tag{1}$$

where $q_j^{Pmax}(i)$ indicates the maximum quality with which the block i is deliverable to the client j without making the client's prefetch buffer underflow. Reading of video data from the prefetch buffer is block by block and a reception of a block must be completed before the first frame of that block is required. The sending of a next required block to the client j must be finished before all blocks which are stored in the client's prefetch buffer have been consumed. Thus $q_j^{Pmax}(i)$ is derived by using the following equation;

$$q_j^{Pmax}(i) = \max(q | 2d_j^C + \frac{s(i, q)}{r_j^C} \leq \frac{p_j N}{F} - \Delta). \tag{2}$$

Here, Δ has been introduced to avoid risky control and to absorb unexpected delay jitter and errors in estimation of delay and throughput. At the beginning of the session, the client employs a large value of p_j, independently of the actual number of blocks in the prefetch buffer, and intentionally sets the quality $q_j(i)$ to as low as possible in order to store as many blocks as possible to avoid unexpected delays. This is maintained until sufficient blocks have been prefetched or the client begins play-back. On receiving a request $q_j(i)$, the proxy starts by examining its own cache table. If $q_j^P(i) \geq \beta_j q_j(i)$ (i.e., the cache is hit), the proxy is able to satisfy the client by providing a cached block. The block is immediately sent to the client with a level of quality $\hat{q}_j(i) = \min(q_j(i), q_j^P(i))$.

If the cache is missed and the given proxy decides to retrieve the block from the other server, the given proxy sends a request message to the proxy chosen by algorithms that will be described later. The proxy keeps track of requests it has sent out in lists of the form $Q_k = \{q_n^{Q_k}\}$. The nth entry in such a list, $q_n^{Q_k}$, corresponds to the quality setting of the nth request sent to a server k for the retrieval of a block b_n. An entry is added to the list Q_k whenever the given proxy sends a request to the server k and is removed from the list on completion of the retrieval of the block. The lists are referred to when the cache is missed on the client's request. The proxy compares $q_j(i)$ with the quality of the blocks that the proxy has already been requested of the other servers. To save on bandwidth, the proxy provides the client with the block in the list if the mth request in the list Q_k is for the block i, i.e., $b_m = i$, the quality satisfies the client request, i.e., $q_m^{Q_k} \geq \beta_j q_j(i)$, and the given proxy is expected to finish retrieving the block in time, i.e., $2d_j^C + \frac{\sum_{n=1}^m s(b_n, q_n^{Q_k})}{r_k^S} \leq \frac{p_j N}{F} - \Delta$. The quality of the block i provided to the client j is given as $\hat{q}_j(i) = \min(q_j(i), q_m^{Q_k})$.

Otherwise, the proxy retrieves the block of desired quality from an appropriate server. The quality of block j that a server k can offer is derived by using the following equation.

$$q_{k,j}^S(i) = \min(O_k(i), q_{k,j}^{S max}(i)) \tag{3}$$

The maximum quality $q_{k,j}^{S max}(i)$ of a block i such that there is no starvation of the client j's prefetch buffer is derived by using

$$q_{k,j}^{S max}(i) = \max(q | 2d_j^C + \max(\frac{\sum_n s(b_n, q_n^{Q_k})}{r_k^S}, 2d_k^S) + \max(\frac{s(i, \hat{q})}{r_j^C}, \frac{s(i, q)}{r_k^S}) \leq \frac{p_j N}{F} - \Delta) \tag{4}$$

If there is no request in the list Q_k, $\sum_n s(b_n, q_n^{Q_k})$ becomes zero. In the same way as with $\hat{q}_j(i)$, the quality of the block to be provided to the client by the proxy, $\hat{q}$, is determined once the quality of the block that is provided to the proxy by the server, q, has been specified. The proxy sends the request for the block to that server among all of the neighboring servers, i.e., candidates to supply the block, which holds the block at the highest quality. To avoid retrieving a block of unnecessarily high quality, the quality requested for the block, $q_{k,j}(i)$, is limited to $\max_{l_m \leq i} q_m(l_m)$ where l_m corresponds to the block identifier requested by the client m that joined the service later than the client i. That is, the proxy retrieves the block of the minimum quality such that the future requests from the clients that succeed the given client on the block will hit its cache. If multiple servers are capable of supplying the block at the same quality, the proxy chooses the fastest of the servers.

If no server is capable of delivering the block in time and at a satisfactory level of quality, the proxy determines the server k which is capable of most quickly providing the given proxy with the block i at the quality $\beta_j q_j(i)$. In this case, the buffer starves and the continuity of video play-back is broken. The client j must wait for the reception of the block i over a period, which is referred to as the freeze time, given by

$$f_j(i) = \max(0, 2d_j^C + \max(\frac{\sum_n s(b_n, q_n^{Q_k})}{r_k^S}, 2d_k^S) + \frac{s(i, \beta_j q_j(i))}{\min(r_j^C, r_k^C)} - \frac{p_j N}{F} + \Delta) \tag{5}$$

3.3   Block Prefetching Algorithm

To achieve even more effective control, the proxy prefetches blocks in accordance with client requests. On receiving a request for a block i, the proxy consults its cache table and checks the lists Q^k from block $i + 1$ to $i + P$ to find a potential future cache miss. The parameter P determines the range of the prefetching window. When the proxy finds that a block $j > i$ has been cached or requested in a form with a lower level of quality than $\beta_j \cdot q_j(i)$, it attempts to prefetch the block in a finer quality form. If two or more such unsatisfactory blocks are detected, only that block which closest to the ith block is chosen and prefetched. A request for prefetching that has arrived at the server k overwrites the preceding prefetch request and will be served only when no request for typical block retrieval of cache-missed blocks is waiting.

The quality of the block m that the server k is able to offer to the client j is derived by using the following equation;

$$q_{k,j}^R(m) = \min(O_k(m), q_{k,j}^{Rmax}(m)) \tag{6}$$

where $q_{k,j}^{Rmax}(m)$ stands for the maximum quality which is deliverable, in time, to the client in time and is given as

$$q_{k,j}^{Rmax}(m) = \max(q|d_p \leq \frac{(p_j + m - i)N}{F} - \Delta) \tag{7}$$

Due to limited space, we omit the detailed explanation of prefetching mechanisms. The expected transfer delay d_p is appropriately derived taking into account the condition, i.e., how block i is provided to the client j. For each of candidate servers, the offerable quality of the block m is calculated. In a similar way to the retrieval of a block i, the most preferable server is chosen on the basis of the quality of available blocks and the block-transfer delay.

3.4   Cache Replacement Algorithm

The proxy makes a list of blocks to be discarded on the basis of its cache table. Those blocks which are located in windows of inquiry and marked by the other proxy servers are placed beyond the the scope of replacement. Reference to the blocks about which the inquiry was made is expected in the near future, i.e., in IN/F seconds. The marked blocks should not be dropped or degraded in order to maintain consistency of the remote tables that the other proxies hold. In addition, retention of the first I blocks is also considered important as a way of hiding the initial delay [5]. The rest of the blocks are all candidates for replacement. Of these, the block which is closest to the end of the stream is the first to be a 'victim', i.e., to be assigned a reduced level of quality or discarded. Let n be the identifier of this block.

The proxy first tries lowering the quality of the victim as a way of shrinking the block size and making a room for the new block. The space which may result from this adjustment is limited to $\max_{l_m < n} \beta_m q_m(l_m)$, that is, to the highest value for minimum tolerable quality in the client requests for blocks that precede the victim. If the adjustment is not sufficiently effective, the victim is discarded from the cache buffer. If this is still insufficient, the proxy moves on the next victim.

When all of the candidate victims have been dropped and there is still not enough room, the proxy identifies the least important of the protected blocks. The last P blocks of the successive marked blocks are only for use in prefetching and may thus be considered less important since the prefetching is given a lower priority by the servers, as was explained in subsection 3.3. The proxy starts the process of trying degradation of quality and dropping blocks at the block closest to the end of a video stream. Finally, if all of the attempts described above fail, the proxy gives up on storing the new block.

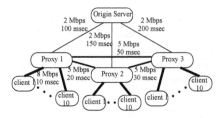

Fig. 2. The model used in simulation

4   Evaluation

In this section, we describe some of the results we obtained in our preliminary experimental evaluation of the system described above. The network we employed is depicted in Fig. 2. The originating server is behind a wide-area network or the Internet, and the proxy servers are located in an ISP network. There are ten clients in the local network of each proxy server. The one-way delays and the available bandwidth for each session are indicated beside the respective connections. Although the available bandwidth and one-way delay fluctuate greatly under realistic conditions, we have employed static values so that we are able to clearly observe the behavior obtained by applying the control mechanisms in various way. Clients start their subscriptions one after another in accordance with the given numbers and the inter-arrival time of the first PLAY messages issued by the clients follows an exponential distribution with an average of 30 minutes.

The video stream is 90-minutes long and is played back at 30 fps. The stream is divided up into one-second blocks, that is, $L = 5400$ and $N = 30$. The one-second block is too short and is a somewhat unrealistic assumption, but our proposed mechanism still provides satisfactory performance improvement under this difficult condition, as is described later. Ten levels of quality are available and the respective block sizes are given by $\forall i \; s(i, q) = \frac{qN}{F} \times 10^6$ bits. The window sizes are $P = 10$ and $I = 20$ blocks. These windows mean that a proxy predicts a cache miss ten seconds in advance of the block being required and that QUERY and REPLY messages are exchanged every ten seconds. The time prepared for errors Δ is set to 2 seconds and the proxy tries to leave 60 frames in the client's prefetch buffer. The period of initial waiting time is set to 4 seconds, that is, the client waits for 4 seconds before beginning to play a requested stream back. During the initial wait, the requested quality $q_j(i)$ is set to its lowest level, and the client then randomly determines the quality requirement on a block-by-block basis. In the experiments, a probability of 10% was assigned to each event of the client increasing or decreasing $q_j(i)$ by one, while retaining the same value for $q_j(i)$ was assigned a probability of 80%.

In the following description, we focus on the performance which was observed at proxy 2 and describe the results for the four different schemes which we applied for purposes of comparison. One is referred to as "Independent w/o Prefetch"; in this approach proxies always retrieve the missing or unsatisfactory blocks from the originating video server and proxy prefetching is not employed. "Independent w/ Prefetch" corresponds

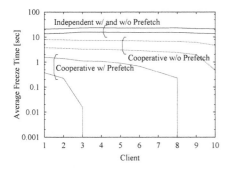

Fig. 3. Average freeze time

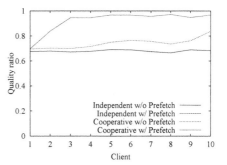

Fig. 4. Average quality ratio

to the case where independent proxies are coupled via the prefetching mechanism and retrieve blocks from the originating server in accordance with client requests. "Cooperative w/o Prefetch" and "Cooperative w/ Prefetch" indicate the cases where the proxies cooperate in providing the stream of video data. The prefetching mechanism is absent from the former approach and present in the later. The "Cooperative w/ Prefetch" corresponds to our proposed mechanism. In all four schemes, proxies are capable of video-quality adjustment to accomplish the effective use of cached data.

4.1   Infinite Buffer Case

We start by considering the case where the proxy servers are equipped with infinitely large cache buffers. A cached block is thus never discarded, but is replaced by a block of the same sequence number and higher quality. Figure 3 summarizes results for cases where the clients persist in guaranteeing the quality requirements, i.e., $\beta = 1.0$, and where the clients are made tolerant of quality degradation, i.e., $\beta = 0.6$. For each pair of lines for a scheme, the upper line corresponds to the case of $\beta = 1.0$ and the lower does to the case of $\beta = 0.6$. Results for the independent schemes are almost the same and it is impossible to tell difference. The comparison is in terms of the average freeze time $f_j(i)$ (see Eq. (5)).

Figure 3 shows that, the average freeze time of the independent schemes is much greater than that of the cooperative scheme regardless of the prefetching mechanism. This is because the proxies in the independent schemes are forced to retrieve blocks from the distant originating server even though other proxy servers may be holding the blocks in their local caches and thus most of the bandwidth between the originating server and the proxy is taken up by the retrieval of blocks. The performance of the cooperative scheme is improved when the proxies prefetch blocks for which a cache miss would otherwise be expected. However, the maximum of the average freeze times for our proposed mechanism is quite long, at 1.57 seconds. This value is for client 1, which is the first client of proxy 2. Since there are no corresponding blocks in the cache of proxy 2's cache, the client is forced to wait for about 1.57 seconds every time it move on the next block.

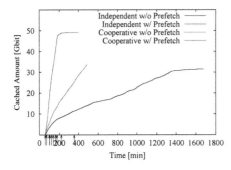 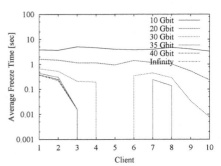

Fig. 5. Amount of cached data   **Fig. 6.** Variation in average freeze time

The freeze time is improved by the lower value of β, regardless of the scheme which is applied. With our scheme in particular, the maximum freeze time fell to 0.37 seconds for client 1. A continuous video-streaming service was provided to the client 4 to client 10 since blocks of sufficient level of quality are stored in the cache buffers. In addition, there is less loss of quality and the clients are able to enjoy a higher quality of video streaming. Figure 4 depicts the average quality ratio which was defined as the ratio of the quality of the delivered block to the requested level of quality in the case of $\beta = 0.6$. For example, the ratios of quality are 0.70 for the first client and 0.97 for the last, even though a ratio of 0.60 is approved. Even if $\beta = 0.2$ is chosen, the first user suffers from a ratio of 0.40, while the others are able to enjoy video play-back with a quality ratio that is more than 0.85. On this basis, we conclude that intentionally employing a lower β leads to a comfortable streaming service with no unnecessary loss of video quality.

4.2   Limited Buffer Case

Figure 5 depicts transitions in the amount of data cached by proxy 2. The arrows on the x-axis indicate instances where the first PLAY requests have been issued by clients. As shown in the figure, the size of the buffer required for our scheme is about 49 Gbits. Figure 6 summarizes the results of a comparative evaluation of various cache capacities for use with our scheme. Comparison between Figs. 3 and 5 shows that as long as the buffers in the servers for our scheme are larger than 20 Gbits, the average freeze times for our scheme are obviously shorter than those for the other schemes. For clients 1 to 3, increasing the buffer capacity from 35 Gbits provides a small reduction in discontinuities in video play-back. The other clients, however, are freed from annoying breaks when each proxy is equipped with a cache buffer that has a capacity of more than 40 Gbits. With 35-Gbit buffers, clients 7 and 8 suffer from freezing that lasts for a few hundreds milliseconds. This is because cached blocks are being degraded to make a room for freshly retrieved blocks but these two clients require blocks of higher quality than do the preceding clients. Thus, we are able to conclude that the preferable buffer capacity in this case is as much as 40 Gbits. Note that further performance improvements would be expected if the users choose lower value for β.

5   Conclusion

In this paper, we have proposed a new scheme for video streaming in which proxies that are capable of video-quality adjustment retrieve, prefetch, cache, and deliver video blocks in a cooperative manner. Simulation demonstrated that our scheme is effective in reducing the freeze times and in providing high-quality blocks to clients. Our scheme is applicable to any video-streaming service that employs a coding algorithm which allows segmentation and adjustment of quality. However, areas for further research remain. There is room for improvement, for example, in terms of the protection of blocks against replacement, which leads to a problem of scalability. We have to further investigate the practicality of our scheme, since several assumptions were made for the control mechanisms. In addition, the effect of such control parameters as I, P, β, δ, and the initial waiting time on performance was not fully evaluated in work reported in this paper. We will be able to derive an algorithm to determine these effects in an appropriate way. Furthermore, the system model employed in this evaluation is somewhat artificial. For this reason, we want to apply our scheme to a more generic network model.

References

1. G. Barish and K. Obraczka, "World Wide Web caching: Trends and techniques," *IEEE Communications Magazine*, pp. 178–185, May 2000. 127, 130
2. M. Hofmann, T. S. E. Ng, K. Guo, S. Paul, and H. Zhang, "Caching techniques for streaming multimedia over the Internet," *Technical Report BL011345-990409-04TM*, April 1999. 127, 128, 132
3. R. Rejaie, H. Yu, M. Handley, and D. Estrin, "Multimedia proxy caching mechanism for quality adaptive streaming applications in the Internet," in *Proceedings of IEEE INFOCOM 2000*, March 2000. 127, 128, 128, 129, 130
4. Z. Miao and A. Ortega, "Proxy caching for efficient video services over the Internet," in *Proceedings of Packet Video Workshop'99*, April 1999. 127, 128
5. S. Sen, J. Rexford, and D. Towsley, "Proxy prefix caching for multimedia streams," in *Proceedings of IEEE INFOCOM'99*, vol. 3, pp. 1310–1319, March 1999. 127, 128, 132, 135
6. M. Sasabe, N. Wakamiya, M. Murata, and H. Miyahara, "Proxy caching mechanisms with video quality adjustment," in *Proceedings of SPIE International Symposium on The Convergence of Information Technologies and Communications*, vol. 4519, pp. 276–284, August 2001. 128, 128, 128, 129, 129, 130, 130
7. N. Yeadon, F. Garcia, D. Hutchison, and D. Shepherd, "Filters: QoS support mechanisms for multipeer communications," *IEEE Journal on Selected Areas in Communications*, vol. 14, pp. 1245–1262, September 1996. 130
8. A. M. Dawood and M. Ghanbari, "Content-based MPEG video traffic modeling," *IEEE Transactions on Multimedia*, vol. 1, pp. 77–87, March 1999. 130
9. S. Floyd, M. Handley, J. Padhye, and J. Widmer, "Equation-based congestion control for unicast applications: the extended version," *International Computer Science Institute technical report TR-00-003*, March 2000. 130
10. M. Miyabayashi, N. Wakamiya, M. Murata, and H. Miyahara, "MPEG-TFRCP : Video transfer with TCP-friendly rate control protocol," in *Proceedings of IEEE International Conference on Communications 2001*, vol. 1, pp. 137–141, June 2001. 130
11. M. Reisslein, F. Hartanto, and K. W. Ross, "Interactive video streaming with proxy servers," in *Proceedings of First International Workshop on Intelligent Multimedia Computing and Networking*, vol. II, pp. 588–591, February 2000. 130

Using CORBA's Advanced Services to Enhance the Integrity of QoS Management Programmable Networks

Qiang Gu and Alan Marshall

Advanced Telecommunications System Laboratory,
School of Electrical & Electronic Engineering,
The Queen's University of Belfast,
Ashby Building, Stranmillis Road, BT9 5AH Belfast
Northern Ireland, U.K.
{qiang.gu, a.marshall}@ee.qub.ac.uk

Abstract. The development of wideband network services and the new network infrastructures to support them have placed much more requirements on current network management systems. Issues such as scalability, integrity and interoperability have become more important. Existing management systems are not flexible enough to support the provision of Quality of Service (QoS) in these dynamic environments. The concept of Programmable Networks has been proposed to address these requirements. Within this framework, CORBA is regarded as a middleware technology that can enable interoperation among the distributed entities founds in Programmable Networks. By using the basic CORBA environment in a heterogeneous network environment, a network manager is able to control remote Network Elements (NEs) in the same way it controls its local resources. Using this approach both the flexibility and intelligence of the overall network management can be improved. This paper proposes the use of two advanced features of CORBA to enhance the QoS management in a Programmable Network environment. The Transaction Service can be used to manage a set of tasks, whenever the management of elements in a network is correlated; and the Concurrency Service can be used to coordinate multiple accesses on the same network resources. It is also shown in this paper that proper use of CORBA can largely reduce the development and administration of network management applications.

1 Introduction

The provision of QoS-guaranteed network services on-demand requires a more advanced network management architecture. The use of programmable network architectures is a new approach aimed at increasing the flexibility and manageability of networks [6],[7],[8]. CORBA from the Open Management Group (OMG) provides an enabling environment with many useful facilities that can be applied to these architectures. In this paper, two of CORBA's services, the Transaction Service and the Concurrency Service, are used to improve the integrity of the network management system.

K.C. Almeroth and M. Hasan (Eds.): MMNS 2002, LNCS 2496, pp. 140-153, 2002.
© Springer-Verlag Berlin Heidelberg 2002

Sections 2, 3 and 4 give an overview of QoS, programmable network architectures and the CORBA standard respectively. Section 5 describes the problem with managing network elements that are both distributed and correlated. In section 6, a new management architecture based on CORBA's Transaction Service is proposed to address the problem. A case study with this architecture is given in section 7. Section 8 investigates CORBA's Concurrency Service, which can be used in multi-access scenarios. With regard to the common concern of CORBA's performance and other new network management architecture (i.e. WBEM), the authors have provided a discussion in section 9. Section 10 provides the conclusions of this work.

2   QoS Architectures

There is more than one way to characterize Quality of Service. Generally, QoS is the ability of a NE (an application, host, switch or router) to provide some level of assurance for consistent network delivery of specific network connections. Applications, network topology and policy dictate which type of QoS architecture is most appropriate for individual or aggregates traffic flows (connections). The evolution of IP networks from their current best-effort delivery of datagrams into guaranteed delivery of time sensitive services is still far from complete. Resource Reservation (RSVP)[15],[16] and Differentiated Services (Diffserv) [3] have been proposed as mechanisms for implementing Service Quality in IP based networks.

One apparent issue is that it is impossible to use just one router or switch in the network to achieve the guaranteed service. All the NEs will need to conform to the same configuration scheme and work cooperatively. For example, the end users only care about the end-to-end performance of a network application. They may have no idea of how many routers are being used to carry the traffic. But from network provider's point of view, in order to provide such a guaranteed service, all the routers along the path of an application must obey the same rules. If any of them fail to do so then it is impossible to achieve the guaranteed end-to-end service.

3   Programmable Network Architectures

The NEs in present day networks are mostly vertically integrated closed systems whose functions are rigidly programmed into the embedded software and hardware by the vendor. The paradigm 'Programmable Network' envisions the future telecommunications network as an open system that can be programmed to deliver QoS based network services e.g. voice, video and data in a customisable manner.

The framework considered here will be based on the emerging standard for open interfaces for Programmable Network equipment, namely the IEEE's P1520 reference model [10]. Figure 1 shows the architecture of this model. To date, most of the research in this area has tended to concentrate on the network generic services layer (between the U and L interfaces). An important feature of the research considered here, is the mapping of higher layer requirements onto actual physical resources in the network equipment. The current P1520 model considers that all the legacy network's resources (e.g. routing, scheduling, PHB etc) are abstracted into objects. However, P1520 has only defined the basic access APIs on network resources. There is not any definition for advanced business logics in P1520. Features such as transaction, concurrency and log are commonly used in centralized system. By using CORBA's rich set of services, programmable network architectures can also benefit from these features.

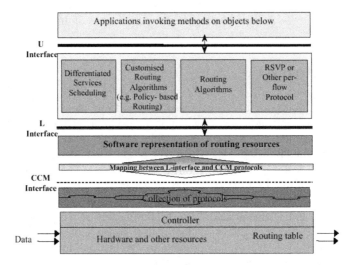

Fig. 1 IEEE P1520 Architecture [10]

4   CORBA as a Standard Middleware Solution

The Common Object Request Broker Architecture (CORBA) from Object Management Group (OMG) has been widely considered as the choice architecture for the next generation of network management [1],[2]. Until now, most research has focused on using CORBA to integrate incompatible legacy network management systems such as SNMP and CMIP [11], and the definition of specific CORBA services (e.g. Notification, Log). In addition to the basic features of CORBA, there are also some other CORBA services, which can be very useful for network management applications. In this paper, the use of the Transaction Service and Concurrency Service to achieve better QoS control is investigated.

It is widely accepted that transactions are the key to constructing reliable distributed applications. The CORBA Transaction Service supports the concept of transactions as atomic executions. In a distributed environment, these executions can span more than one NE. By either committing or rolling back, a transaction can always maintain a consistent state in a designated NE. The Transaction Service defines the interfaces that allow multiple and distributed objects to cooperate to provide atomicity. The Service provides transaction synchronization across the elements of a distributed client/server application. Its functionality includes: controlling the scope and duration of a transaction; allowing multiple objects to be involved in a single, atomic transaction; allowing objects to associate changes in their internal state with a transaction; and coordinating the completion of transactions.

The purpose of the Concurrency Control Service is to mediate concurrent access to an object such that the consistency of the object is not compromised when accessed by concurrently executing computations. In the context of network management, this can be access to a network resource by more than one distributed application. The Concurrency Control Service consists of multiple interfaces that support both transactional and non-transactional modes of operation. The user of the Concurrency Control Service can choose to acquire a lock on resources in one of two ways:

1.   On behalf of a transaction (transactional mode.) The Transaction Service implicitly acquires and releases the locks on a resource. After obtaining the lock, the client can access the resource exclusively. This prevents other users changing the same resource which may corrupt its integrity.
2.   By acquiring locks on behalf of the current thread (that must be executing outside the scope of a transaction). In this non-transactional mode, the responsibility for dropping locks at the appropriate time lies with the user of the Concurrency Control Service

5   Management of Correlated NEs

Two terms are used in this paper. A **management session** is one single interoperation between a network manager and a NE. Additionally, a **management task** is more user-oriented. A task should have a specific significance for the end users (i.e. achieve a meaningful function). The following example shows that sometimes, a task will have more than one session involved. Figure 2 shows a case study network. In this network, there are three video conferencing applications running between 3 pairs of server/clients. A network formed by router1 through router3 connects these applications. There are two bottlenecks in the network. One is the link between router1 and router2. The other is the link between router2 and router3. The three applications have the same traffic profile, labeled as traffic1, traffic2 and traffic3. Traffic n is the traffic between video_server_n and video_client_n. All the routers use the same criteria to classify the traffic, and Weighted Fair Queuing (WFQ) is used in each router to schedule the traffic for each application.

Initially, the weights for each type of traffic are the same in every router, which means they receive the same service from network. Because they share the same traffic profile, these applications have the same throughput and delay. If for some reason, the network administrator wants to give a certain flow (e.g. traffic2) lower delay, then this can be done by increasing the weight for that flow in the routers it passes through. In this test network, because the transmission and propagation delays for all the traffic are the same, end-to-end delay will mainly depend on the queuing delay in each router along the path.

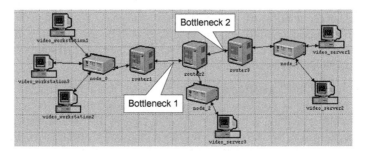

Fig. 2 Case Study Network

In this scenario, only the weight for traffic2 on router3 was increased. Traffic2 has lower queuing delay in router3. However, traffic2's queuing delay is increased in router2. As the result, there is no significant end-to-end delay improvement for traffic2.

The explanation for this phenomenon is that by increasing the weight for traffic2 on router 3, more traffic2 is forwarded to the downstream router2. Because the WFQ on router 2 still has its original weight, an increase in the delay is inevitable. In this example, the end-to-end delay is the meaningful performance statistics for the end users. Merely changing the weight on one router cannot achieve the desirable effect.

The example shows that some management tasks will need to have more than one NE involved. Every management session on an individual NE is only a part of the overall management task. The task may not be fulfilled if a session in the chain is not executed properly. It is therefore necessary that the manager be informed if a session failed. The manager can then take appropriate action to reverse the change of other successful sessions in the same task. The integrity of network is hence guaranteed. Because the manager and NEs are in different locations, there needs to be distributed coordination.

It can be expected that as the network scale and complexity increase, the synchronization of NEs will become more and more difficult. The services may be very dynamic. The provision of service may only span a relatively shorter term. This makes the network configuration in a very changeable. The network integrity is apt to be violated. As the result, no services can be guaranteed.

As well as the synchronization of data across NEs, it is also necessary to synchronize data across different network managers in the overall end-to-end connection. There will be more and more interactions between the sub-managers in a large network where topology and management relationships can vary quite dramatically. Therefore if one manager wants to affect the behavior of a number of others, the originator should be able to guarantee that all the changes affected on the other managers can be committed or rolled back as a whole. For example, a higher-level manager may wish to change the billing information on all its sub-managers. If only some have successfully updated to the new price schemes, unfairness may occur between clients residing in different management domains. To avoid this, the Transaction Service can be used to make sure all the customers receive the same price scheme.

The concept of distributed transaction is not available in either SNMP or CMIP. It is left to the system developer to make a management application transactional. This approach has several disadvantages. Firstly, without a standard distributed transactional mechanism, it is impossible to achieve interoperability in heterogeneous environments. Secondly, the management application developers need to write their own code to support distributed transaction, which is can be a very complex and error-prone task.

6   Using CORBA's Transaction Service to Enhance Network Management in a Distributed Environment

Figure 3 shows the architecture of using the CORBA Transaction Service in network management. In order to deploy it, there must be at least one CORBA server in the network with the Transaction Server running on it. The manager with Transaction-Service-compatible ORB installed is the client or, in the terms of Transaction Service, the originator. It can choose the participant NEs and the options of a transaction. During the transaction, the manager will invoke the method on all the other participants. At the beginning of the transaction, the participants will register their resources involved with the Transaction Server. The Transaction Server will then coordinate the participants during the transaction. All the participants take part in the two-phase commit protocol. If for any reason the change on one NE's resource fails, the NE can report the failure to the Transaction Server. This allows the Transaction Server to roll back all the changes on other transaction participants. Otherwise the transaction server can conduct all the participants to commit the changes. In either case, the integrity of the network is maintained.

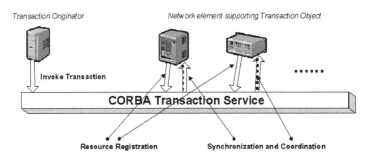

Fig. 3 Using CORBA Transaction Service in Network Management

Figure 4 illustrates an example where the CORBA Transaction Service is used to change the WFQ tables on all the routers along a path. In this example, the incoming packets to each router are classified according to certain criteria in each router. If the network provider wants to allocate a certain amount of bandwidth to a specific class of traffic along a path, then the network manager needs to contact all the routers along this path and change the settings on each of them. The network manager can invoke the appropriate methods on these routers' WFQ entities to change the classifying criteria and the bandwidth allocated for incoming packets.

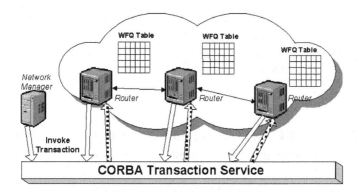

Fig. 4 Using CORBA's Transaction Service for Queue Configuration

To make the WFQ entities in each router accessible, they need to be wrapped into a CORBA object. Following code shows an example IDL code of such a queuing system.

```
// QueuingSystem.idl
#include "CosTransactions.idl"
module QueuingSystem{
  typedef unsigned long IP_ADDRESS;
  interface QueueProfile  {
    readonly attribute unsigned long queue_profile_id;
    attribute IP_ADDRESS source_addr;
    boolean queue_equ (in QueueProfile
in_queue_profile);
    // can be extended to support more complicate queue
classification
  };
  interface Queue  {
    readonly attribute unsigned long queue_id;
    attribute QueueProfile  queue_profile;
    attribute unsigned long weight;
    attribute float band_width;
  };
  typedef sequence<Queue> QUEUE_LIST;
  interface Queue_Sys: CosTransac-
tions::TransactionalObject,CosTransactions::Resource  {
    attribute unsigned long total_weight;
    attribute QUEUE_LIST queues;
    void add_queue_weight(in QueueProfile
in_queue_profile, in unsigned long weight);
    void add_queue_bandwidth(in QueueProfile
in_queue_profile, in float band_width);
    void remove_queue(in QueueProfile
in_queue_profile);
    void modify_queue_weight(in QueueProfile
in_queue_profile, in unsigned long new_weight);
```

```
      void modify_queue_bandwidth(in QueueProfile
in_queue_profile, in float new_bandwidth);
    };
};
// QueuingSystem.idl
```

The interface *QueueProfile* is used to specify the classification criteria. The interface *Queue* is used to specify the setting for a certain queue. The *Queue_Sys* is the interface that can be accessed to change all the configuration of queuing system (add a queue, remove a queue etc.). *CosTransactions::TransactionalObject* is the super class of all the objects, which need to be transactional.

7 Case Study

The test network described in Section 5 was used to study how to use the Transaction Service to enhance the QoS management in the Programmable Network. Two scenarios are compared. In the first the manager changes the weights of traffic2 on router3 and router2 without a Transaction Service. The weight on router3 is changed at 60 seconds and the weight on router2 is changed at 90 seconds. In the second scenario, the manager performs the same task via the Transaction Service. Figures 5 and 6 show the results of two scenarios respectively. It can be seen that in scenario 1, the end-to-end delay will only change after the weight for traffic2 on router2 was increased (at 90 seconds). While in scenario 2, the end-to-end delay for traffic2 makes a significant improvement after just 60 second.

It should be noted that in order to illustrate the difference between the transaction and non-transaction scenarios, the weight on router2 was deliberately changed in the first scenario. In the real network applications, this delay can be much shorter. However, when there are many NEs in a path, it will take very long time to do all the changes.

8 Using the CORBA Concurrency Service to Enhance Network Management in Distributed Environments

Concurrency is not a significant issue when most of the time, only one network manager would access a network element at a certain time point. The emergence of programmable network has greatly changed the above assumption. In order to provide more customizable services, the network providers may open some resources on network devices to third party providers or even end users. There will always be the possibility of more than one thread running simultaneously wishing to manipulate the same resource. There are two solutions for this problem:

■ Every network element has a build-in mutual exclusion (mutex) mechanism to protect critical data
■ Employ a third party concurrency service to serialize the access to the critical data in the network elements.

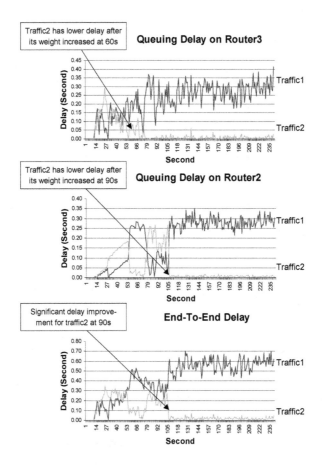

Fig. 5 Result of Changing Weight without Transaction Service

One obvious disadvantage of the first solution is that it requires that all the network elements upgrade their software to support concurrency. To achieve the complicated mutex mechanism in a network element with limited memory and CPU power might result in a significant decrease in its performance. By using a third party concurrency service in the network, all the network elements can continue to operate as before. They do not even need to know that there is some other service in the network coordinating the access to the critical data on themselves. These concurrency services can be run on a generic hardware and software platform with adequate memory and processing power. Such a platform (e.g. a workstation) can be the proxy for many network elements. This provides a very flexible approach to configuring the number, location and load of the concurrency services in the network.

Another potential disadvantage of the first approach is the incompatibility between different vendors and platforms. The same code may not be able to access the critical data in different devices because they have different concurrency API's. This problem will not occur in the second approach, whenever only one standard concurrency service API is used across the whole network.

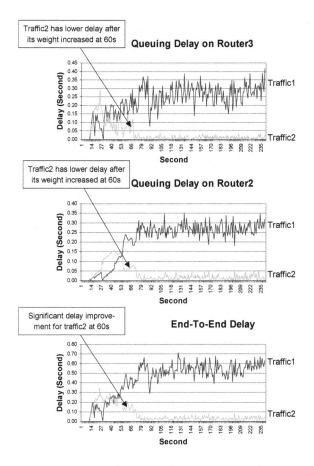

Fig. 6 Result of Changing Weight with Transaction Service

In this paper, CORBA's Concurrency Service is investigated as one choice for the second solution.

The use of CORBA's Concurrency service is very straightforward. Figure 7 shows its general application in network management. There are normally three steps. In step 1, the network element creates the *LockSet* on CORBA Concurrency server and associates it with the internal resource. There is no limit on the number of *LockSets* a network element can create. One Concurrency server can also serve any number of network elements. In step 2, if a client wants to access a certain network resource, it will firstly need to acquire the *LockSet* for that resource. If there are multiple accesses to a resource, the Concurrency Server will coordinate all of them. The Concurrency Server serves the requests and grant *LockSets* according to the mutual exclusion rule. In step 3, only the client that obtains the *LockSet* can then access the real network element resource. The others must wait for the release of *LockSet*.

The use of transaction and concurrency also raises the issue of deadlock within network nodes. This becomes exacerbated whenever the management system is dis-

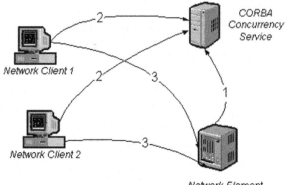

Fig. 7 Using CORBA's Concurrency Service In Network Management

tributed. There are however, a number of solutions to for it (e.g. deadlock prevention, deadlock avoidance, deadlock detection). CORBA's Concurrency Service also has a built-in deadlock avoidance mechanism – the *upgrade mode lock*. In addition to common read or write mode lock, an upgrade mode lock is a read lock that conflicts with itself. It is useful for avoiding a common form of deadlock that occurs when two or more clients attempt to read and then update the same resource. If more than one client holds a read lock on the resource, a deadlock will occur as soon as one of the clients' requests a write lock on the resource. If each client requests a single upgrade lock followed by a write lock, this deadlock will not occur.

9 Discussion

One common concern of CORBA-based applications is their complexity. CORBA's advanced services may be viewed as yet another sophisticated component in an already complex management system. It is very likely that the management system with CORBA's advanced Service will have higher overall complexity. However, compared to traditional network management architectures, this new approach has some advantages:

▪ In the traditional management system, almost all the intelligence is placed in the central manager. The NEs are more like dumb devices. Most decisions are made by the manager and sent to NEs. When the scale and complexity of network management applications increases, the manager will find itself in a very overloaded state. The development of embedded technologies (e.g. embedded JAVA, embedded CORBA) has made it possible to use a distributed computing approach to achieve the same functionality but with an alternative architecture. The idea of distributed computing is to spread the intelligence and load into the entire network. This is based on several assumptions. Firstly, it is cheaper to use multiple NEs to achieve the functionality of one single mainframe manager. Secondly, the NEs may have more knowledge of local environment and thus can have quicker and more accurate response. In the case of CORBA's Transaction and

Concurrency Services, the NEs installed with embedded ORBs will take a more active role in the management. With this approach the manager has much less functions to perform. The only thing the manager needs to do is to trigger the transaction at the beginning and wait for the result (e.g. commit or rollback) when it is finished. If the scale and the complexity of a network are increased, the extra load will be shared by newly added NEs. The manager's load will be maintained at an almost constant level.

- From the developers' point of view, to develop a distributed transaction or concurrency application can be a complex task. CORBA allows distributed application developers to enjoy the elegance of OO methodology. By using third party standard services, a large portion of development effort can be saved.

- One significant feature of CORBA is the reusability. It is very common that a protocol has more than one versions or releases. The early versions may not be able to satisfy all the requirements of a network application or may not predict the future requirements so some revised versions will be issued later. It is desirable that the development of new versions or new releases can use the work from old version or release as much as possible. By using the inheritance mechanism, the work in an old version or release can be easily reused.

In the development and deployment of network applications, there are two kinds of timescales. One is used to measure how fast an application can fulfill a particular service requirement (e.g. using an algorithm to manage the current network infrastructure and then provide end to end delay-constrained virtual links). The other is used to measure how fast an application with new service requirements can be developed and deployed into the current network environment. OMG has defined the standard for embedded and real-time CORBA. There are already some real-time CORBA implementations available. Regarding the timer of developing a new application, CORBA has undoubted superiority over the traditional protocols. And providing new services and applications to satisfy users' demand as soon as possible is just the key to win the competition in the current marketplace.

Recently, Web-Based Enterprise Management (WBEM) [13] and Common Information Model (CIM) [14] from Distributed Management Task Force (DMTF) is another trend of network management. Comparing to CORBA-Based architecture, both of them have their advantages and disadvantages.

WBEM uses XML and HTTP as transport encoding and protocol. Because of the popularity of HTTP in PC and Unix workstation, it is easier to add WBEM into enterprise where general workstations are the majority of network elements. Sun's Java Management eXtension (JMX) and Microsoft's Windows Mgmt Instrumentation (WMI) are all based on WBEM. However, it should be noted that fully functioned and extensible HTTP server is still not common in network devices (e.g. router, switch etc.). Another problem of HTTP is that it can only run on TCP/IP. CORBA uses GIOP as transport protocol. As a middleware, it is designed to be independent from underlying physical network protocol. This feature makes CORBA more flexible.

CIM is an approach to the management of systems and networks that applies the basic structuring and conceptualization techniques of the object-oriented paradigm. A management schema is provided to establish a common conceptual framework. The management schema is divided into these conceptual layers: core, common and extension. The language used to define CIM (e.g. MOF, XML) is the equivalence of IDL. The CIM schema is similar to the core classes in CORBA. The elegancy of IDL is that it is independent of any programmable language. As the same time, by using IDL compiler, the IDL code can be translated into any specific language and integrated with current code.

CORBA uses binary encoding for all the information. It is not friendly for end users. But it is easy for machine to manipulate the data. On the contrary, XML uses textual encoding. XML parsing is always necessary. So generally, information decoding of CORBA is more efficient.

10 Conclusion

This paper describes the use of CORBA's Transaction Service and Concurrency Service to enhance the management in Programmable Network environment. While it is very common that these two services are used together in an IT domain (e.g. enterprise database), this paper has shown that they can also be employed in the telecommunications network management domain, where they can cooperate to achieve better integrity and consistency than conventional network management techniques. The paper specifically describes how these advanced CORBA services can be deployed in future heterogeneous open and Programmable Networking environments in order to perform distributed management tasks such as configuring NEs to meet QoS targets.

Acknowledgements

The authors would like to thank the Industrial Research and Technology Unit (IRTU) of Northern Ireland for their financial support for the research carried out in this work. The technical support from NITEC (Northern Ireland Telecommunications Engineering Centre, of Nortel Networks) is also gracefully acknowledged.

References

1. Paul Haggerty and Krishnan Seetharaman The benefits of CORBA-based network management Communications of the ACM, 41(10), October 1998, pp. 73-79.
2. Luca Deri Network Management for the 90s ECOOP'96 Workshop on 'OO Technologies For Network and Service Management' Proceedings, July 1996.
3. S. Blake, D. Black, M. Carlson, E. Davies, Z. Wang, W. Weiss. An Architecture for Differentiated Service. December 1998.
4. QoS Protocols & Architectures, QoS Forum white paper, 1999
    http://www.qosforum.com/white-papers/qosprot_v3.pdf
5. Document formal/01-05-02 (Object Transaction Service specification, v1.2), OMG

6. David L. Tennenhouse et al. A survey of active network research, IEEE Communications Magazine, pages 80-86, January 1997.

7. Andrew T. Campbell et al. A Survey of Programmable Networks, ACM Computer Communications Review, April 1999.

8. David L. Tennenhouse and David. J. Wetherall, Towards an Active Network Architecture Computer Communication Review, Vol. 26, No. 2, April 1996.

9. IEEE P1520 Programming Interfaces for IP Routers and Switches, an Architectural Framework Document.
    http://www.ieee-pin.org/doc/draft_docs/IP/p1520tsip003-04dec98.pdf

10. Jit Biswas et. al., "IEEE P1520 Standards Initiative for Programmable Network Interfaces", IEEE Communications Magazine, Vol.36, No.10, October 1998, pp. 64-70.

11. OMG CORBA/TMN Interworking Specification, version 1.0
    http://www.omg.org/cgi-bin/doc?formal/2000-08-01

12. Document formal/00-06-14 (Concurrency Service stand-alone document), OMG

13. Web-Based Enterprise Management (WBEM) Initiative
    http://www.dmtf.org/standards/standard_wbem.php

14. CIM Specification v2.2
    http://www.dmtf.org/standards/documents/CIM/DSP0004.pdf

15. R. Braden, D. Clark, S. Shenker Integrated Services in the Internet Architecture: an Overview.. June 1994.

16. R. Braden, Ed., L. Zhang, S. Berson, S. Herzog, S. Jamin Resource ReSerVation Protocol (RSVP) -- Version 1 Functional Specification.. September 1997

Remote Multicast Monitoring
Using the RTP MIB

Julian Chesterfield, Bill Fenner, and Lee Breslau

AT&T Labs—Research
75 Willow Road
Menlo Park, CA 94025
{julian,fenner,breslau}@research.att.com

Abstract. Multimedia applications often involve one-to-many, or many-to-many, communication. These applications can be supported efficiently with network layer multicast. While multicast is a promising technology, monitoring multicast routing infrastructure and the performance of applications that use it presents challenges not found with unicast. In this paper we describe a monitoring architecture, and an implementation of the architecture, that uses application level monitoring to assess the performance of multicast-capable infrastructure. The architecture makes use of standards-based management technologies and allows both active and passive monitoring. The implementation has been tested extensively and provides a network operator with a network-wide view of multicast performance.

1 Introduction

IP multicast is an efficient way to provide support for one-to-many communication. Multicast was first used for distribution of real-time multimedia content in the Internet nearly a decade ago [6]. It experienced rapid deployment in the early 1990s, and it has been an active area for protocol development, resulting in several intra- and inter-domain protocols (e.g, DVMRP [9], PIM [8], MSDP [18]). Despite its initial promise and its ability to enable new applications, its growth slowed and it has yet to see widespread use in the Internet. Several issues have inhibited the deployment of multicast, including pricing models, security, and the complexity of routing protocols. One factor in particular, that has prevented wider deployment, is a lack of adequate management tools available to network operators. Without the kinds of tools available in the unicast domain, network operators find it difficult to monitor and debug their multicast networks.[1]

Management and monitoring of multicast networks is an inherently hard task. In contrast to the unicast domain, where a mature set of tools exists, multicast

---

[1] For simplicity, we use the term *multicast network* to refer to an IP network in which multicast forwarding is enabled on the routers. For the purposes of this paper, the particular multicast routing protocol employed – DVMRP, PIM, MOSPF, etc. – is not important.

K.C. Almeroth and M. Hasan (Eds.): MMNS 2002, LNCS 2496, pp. 154–169, 2002.

presents some unique challenges. First, whereas unicast traffic generally follows a single end-to-end path between a source and destination, multicast distribution involves transmission along a tree from a single sender to multiple receivers. Further, membership in a multicast group can be dynamic, so the tree itself can change over the lifetime of a multicast session, even if the topology is static. Finally, in contrast to unicast, the state needed to forward a multicast packet is not instantiated until a session is initiated, making it difficult to determine the status of multicast routing until traffic is flowing.

Early attempts to provide management functionality for multicast networks resulted in a set of ad hoc tools. These included *mtrace* [11], which provides information about the set of links on the path from a sender to a single receiver in a multicast tree, and *mrinfo* [19], a utility that returns information about a multicast router's local configuration. These tools provided only limited information about multicast configuration and operation, and were not always implemented on all multicast routing platforms. More recently, tools such as *mhealth* [14], which discovers and displays an entire multicast tree, have provided additional information for network operators. Similarly, multicast-related MIBs, which have been defined (e.g., [12,15,16]), further enhance the set of tools available for managing multicast. Nonetheless, the state of network management tools for multicast lags far behind what is available for unicast infrastructure and continues to impede deployment.

In this paper we present an architecture for remote management of multicast routing infrastructure and describe our implementation of this architecture. The goal of our work was to provide a tool that would give a network operator, from a single management station, a system wide view of the end-to-end performance of a multicast network. In designing this system, we were guided by several key requirements. First, we wanted a system that would be based on standard protocols. This facilitates integration with other management tools and leverages existing technology. Second, we desired a clean separation of functionality between data collection and data analysis. The purpose of this separation is to enable a data collection architecture based on Internet standards, while enabling independent development of analysis and management tools. Third, we wanted a monitoring architecture that allowed both passive monitoring of existing multicast sessions, while also permitting creation of test sessions and the artificial generation of multicast traffic. Finally, we wanted a system that supported both long term background monitoring, as well as active debugging of multicast sessions.

Our architecture and implementation, which we call RMPMon, meet these requirements. By combining known standard technologies, and extending existing management standards to enable a novel method of generating test traffic, our system can provide an operator responsible for managing a multicast network with better information than was previously available. Because it is based around standard technology, we believe RMPMon can facilitate the development of additional management tools for multicast and help further deployment of this promising technology. The rest of this paper is organized as follows. In the following section, we present relevant background about the standard protocols that we make use of in our architecture. In Sect. 3, we describe extensions to these protocols that provide additional building blocks for our system. The architecture, implementation and evaluation of our tool are presented in Sect. 4. We discuss related work in Sect. 5 and conclude with a discussion of future work in Sect. 6.

2   Background

We built RMPMon around two key Internet protocols: the Simple Network Management Protocol (SNMP) [5] and the Real-Time Transport Protocol (RTP) [27]. Using SNMP has several benefits. As the standard management protocol for IP networks, it is widely available in existing network management platforms, which provides the opportunity to integrate our tool into these platforms. In addition, we are able to leverage important features in SNMP, such as its security model, and we can take advantage of existing public domain implementations and focus on those pieces of functionality unique to our system. Finally, SNMP uses unicast transport, so we do not require multicast to be deployed everywhere between our management station and the systems we are monitoring.

RTP is a transport protocol for real-time applications which supports unicast and multicast applications. In the remainder of this section we present a brief overview of SNMP and RTP to provide background for the remainder of the paper.

2.1   SNMP

SNMP is used to manage a wide range of devices, protocols and applications in the Internet. Management information can pertain to hardware characteristics, configuration parameters or protocol statistics. For example, SNMP can query a router to determine the bandwidth of one of its interfaces or the number of packets that it has forwarded. SNMP is built around the concept of a Management Information Base, or MIB, which defines a set of managed objects for a device or protocol. A MIB consists of a set of objects, or MIB variables, related to the device or protocol being managed. Each object has a unique name, syntax and encoding, as well as a set of properties. The properties associated with an object determine whether the object is readable, writable, or both. Managed objects may be either static or dynamic. Static objects always exist while dynamic objects are created or deleted as a protocol or device changes state. For example, in the TCP MIB, the number of active TCP connections is a static object, whereas an object representing the state of a particular connection is dynamic.

A network management station uses SNMP to manage a remote device by communicating with an agent running on that device. The remote agent interacts directly with the managed objects on that device. SNMP defines several commands that are used between the management station and the remote agent. There are two categories of SNMP commands:

- The value of MIB variables are retrieved from a remote agent using the commands Get, GetNext, and GetBulk.
- The value of MIB variables can be set using the Set command.

In the simplest cases, the Set command can be used to configure parameters of a protocol or device. However, setting MIB variables can also cause other actions to be taken, making it a powerful tool in managing a remote client. This functionality is a key enabler in the system we describe later. We next describe how SNMP is used in the context of the RTP protocol.

2.2   RTP and Related MIBS

RTP is a transport protocol intended for use by real-time applications, such as video-conferencing and playback of recorded multimedia content [27]. Because these applications often involve more than two participants, RTP was defined to accommodate multicast communication. An RTP session is identified by a destination address, either multicast or unicast, and a destination port number. Within the context of multicast, a host can join the relevant multicast group to become a receiver of a session, or a host can transmit packets to the session address to become a sender to a session, or both.

Real-time sessions require timely delivery of data for the data to be useful, and these applications are assumed to be tolerant of modest amounts of packet losses. In addition, feedback in the form of acknowledgments or requests for re-transmission presents scalability problems for large multicast sessions. For these reasons, RTP does not provide reliable data transport. Nonetheless, some feedback among session participants can be useful to RTP-based applications, as a means to share state about performance, to identify sources, and for monitoring purposes. This functionality is provided by a companion protocol, RTCP. Session participants (both senders and receivers) periodically transmit RTCP packets. These packets are sent to the destination IP address of the session using a different port number than the data packets.

RTCP control packets include the following information:

- Each participant periodically transmits identifying information, such as user name and email address.
- Each receiver periodically transmits condition reports. These reports include the loss rate and an estimate of delay variance that the receiver experiences for each source.

Thus, every session participant learns the identities of all active participants as well as the loss rate and other performance statistics experienced by each receiver.[2]

---

[2] In order to limit bandwidth consumed by the control protocol, the frequency at which a participant transmits RTCP packets is inversely proportional to the number of session participants. The utility of RTCP reporting with very large sessions is an open question, and several ideas to address the scalability question have been proposed.

Management information for RTP is defined in an associated MIB [4]. The RTP MIB is organized into 3 tables.[3] These are the session table, the sender table, and the receiver table. Each entry[4] in the session table contains information about an active session at the host. Each entry in the sender table contains information about a sender to one of these active sessions. The session and sender fields provide a unique index for each entry in the sender table. Finally, each entry in the receiver table contains information about a single sender/receiver pair for each session. The session, sender and receiver fields provide a unique index for entries in the receiver table. The objects represented in these tables are all dynamic. That is, they are instantiated when a host joins a session, when a new sender is identified, or when a receiver report from a new session is received, respectively. The MIB variables in the receiver table include such things as the number of packets received, the number lost, and the measured delay jitter.

SNMP is used to query or set the values of these MIB variables. For example, by querying the receiver table, a management client can determine the loss rate experienced between a particular sender/receiver pair. In addition, using the Set command, a management client can create new entries in these tables. By creating an entry in the session table and setting a MIB variable to make that entry active, a management client can cause a remote agent to join a multicast group as a receiver. We use this functionality extensively in the management framework that we describe in Section 4.

3   RTP Sender MIB

RTP and the RTP MIB provide necessary building blocks for our management system. However, they are not sufficient to enable the entire range of functionality we required. Therefore, we defined a new MIB that extends the capability of multicast management to enable active monitoring. We refer to this new MIB as the RTP Sender MIB.

The RTP Sender MIB is an extension to the RTP MIB described above. The MIB describes data streams that are generated by a remote agent. Specifically, it contains a table describing the characteristics of the data streams, and links the source to an existing entry in the RTP MIB. Entries are indexed by a test name and a user name to provide user based access control. Each entry contains the following objects: packet generation rate, packet length, and outgoing interface. When an entry is set to active, the remote agent begins transmitting packets according to the parameters in the sender entry.

Allowing the generation of test traffic by remote agents has certain inherent security risks. This problem is addressed with a view based access control mechanism that is implemented, as described above, in the MIB. Only authenticated

---

[3] RFC 2959 actually defines 6 tables. The latter three provide reverse lookups to enable efficient indexing. Since they provide performance improvements, and do not directly address issues of functionality, we do not discuss them further here.

[4] In SNMP terminology, a table entry is referred to as a row.

users are able to create active streams on the agent, where the authentication is part of the SNMP security framework.

The active sender MIB provides an important function to the monitoring architecture. The management client can create a new entry in a remote agent's sender table and populate the MIB variables with appropriate packet generation statistics. The remote agent then generates traffic according to these parameters when the management client sets the entry to become active. In this way, the management client can generate test traffic at one or more remote agents and monitor receipt of this traffic using the RTP MIB.

4   RTP-Based Monitoring System

We now describe the management and monitoring system that we have developed. We begin with a high level description of the architecture of the system and its features. We next describe our implementation. Finally, we describe our experience with the implementation and present results of measurements we've gathered in our lab.

4.1   Architecture

The system we developed consists of two key components: remote agents running on managed devices (hosts or routers) that participate in the monitoring system and a management client. The remote agents implement the RTP MIB and the RTP Sender MIB, and they communicate with the management station using SNMP. In response to SNMP commands, they join RTP sessions as senders or receivers. As senders, they generate test traffic for controlled experiments. As receivers, they receive RTP data packets and RTCP control packets, and they maintain statistics about session participants and performance. Since these data are part of the RTP MIB, they can be returned to the management client in response to SNMP queries.

The management client communicates with remote agents via SNMP. The management client controls the monitoring by causing remote agents to join sessions as senders or receivers, and the remote agent collects statistics from the remote agents. The management station is then able to analyze the data and present it to a network operator in useful ways.

This architecture has several desirable features. First, the separation of functionality between the remote agents is a flexible design that enables extensibility. Rather than designing a monolithic system in which the data collection and analysis are tightly coupled, we have separated the two primary components. Hence, new management applications can be written that use the basic functionality provided by the remote agents in new and interesting ways.

Another key feature of the architecture is that by incorporating the RTP Sender MIB, it is capable of both active and passive monitoring. Passive monitoring is used to monitor actual user multicast sessions. In this case, the management client causes one or more remote agents to join the session as receivers.

These receivers monitor session performance (i.e., loss rate, delay jitter), and send and receive RTCP messages to and from other session participants.[5] Reporting information can then be returned to the management station. Note that RTCP receiver reports are transmitted to the session's multicast address and are seen by all receivers in a session. Therefore, by creating a single receiver at a remote agent, the monitoring system is able to collect information about all senders and receivers in a session, regardless of their location in the network. This presents the network operator with a network-wide view at very little overhead beyond the existing session traffic. Note, however, that even though RTCP receiver reports are distributed to all group members, using more than one remote agent to collect and report data may be useful. As an example, querying MIB values of more than one session participant allows consistency checking, which can identify situations in which routing problems prevent distribution of receiver reports to all session participants.

Passive monitoring provides performance information for actual user sessions. However, one of the difficulties of monitoring multicast infrastructure is that it is hard to assess performance when sessions are not active. Active monitoring fills this void. With active monitoring, rather than joining a user multicast session, a special session dedicated to monitoring is created. The management client uses the RTP MIB and RTP Sender MIB to create receivers and senders for this testing session. The traffic generation parameters of the sender or senders are controlled by the management station. In this way, the network operator is given a view of performance that is independent of user sessions.

This system can be used for both long term background monitoring as well as for reactive debugging. In the former case, a long running test session could be used to collect performance statistics over time. In the latter, network operators who are alerted to potential problems can create active sessions to help debug network problems.

4.2   Implementation

We have implemented the architecture described above in order to test our ideas and gain experience with them in both laboratory and production environments. One of our design goals was to leverage prior work and experience, concentrating our effort on those parts of the design unique to our system and easing the task of porting our implementation to other platforms. As such, we have taken extensive advantage of open source implementations that provide some of the needed functionality. In this section, we describe the implementation of both the remote agents and management station.

The remote agent is built within the AgentX framework [7], which supports extensible SNMP agents. Specifically, it allows a single master SNMP agent to run on a client and dispatch SNMP commands to subagents. AgentX defines the

---

[5] We anticipate that future extensions to the RTP MIB will allow the network operator to make a remote agent's participation in the session invisible to other session participants by setting its TTL to zero.

interface between the master and subagents. We implemented the remote agent as an AgentX subagent. The remote agent implements both the RTP MIB and RTP Sender MIB, and registers these MIBs with the master SNMP agent on the host. It also implements an RTP application. For the SNMP functionality, we used Net-SNMP, an open source SNMP library [20]. For the RTP functionality, we used the UCL RTP library, which implements RTP (including RTCP) for multicast as well as unicast sessions [23]. The remote agent is capable of acting as a sender or receiver of multiple RTP sessions. The application extracts relevant information to populate the MIB with session conditions in real-time.

We also implemented an application to serve as our management client. This application was built by extending the *Scotty* management application [28]. *Scotty* includes extensions to TCL that provide access to SNMP functions. In addition, it incorporates *tkined*, a graphical network editor designed for management applications. Thus, a user can manipulate a graphical user interface depicting agents in the network that are being managed. User interface actions then cause SNMP commands to be issued by the management client to the remote agents. Data collected by the management client can then be displayed in the user interface. We added functionality to *tkined* to enable management of the RTP agents. Scripts were written to allow simple activation of pre-configured sessions for debugging and real-time monitoring purposes. Additional functionality was added for monitoring existing RTP sessions.

4.3   Experience

RMPMon was originally developed on FreeBSD and has been ported to Solaris and HP-UX. We have tested it extensively in our lab, and it is now being evaluated for use by a major ISP. In this section, we describe its use in more detail and show results from its use.

Experiments.   As part of our debugging and analysis of the tool, we have performed many experiments with it in our lab. We now describe one such test. We use this test to demonstrate some of the tool's functionality and to gain some understanding of the overhead associated with it. We will then describe in less detail other uses of the tool.

Figure 1 shows a snapshot of the management client's graphical interface. The network operator can use this interface to dynamically create an object based network map and associate these objects with network devices. The map in the figure shows the topology used in the experiment we describe here. The test network consists of 14 Pentium III class PCs running FreeBSD 4.3. Three of these (cubix09, cubix10, and cubix11) are configured to act as routers for both unicast and multicast traffic. The remaining 11 are end hosts attached to one of six subnets. All host interfaces provide 100 Mbit/s switched ethernet connectivity. In order to simulate conditions of network loss, we used the *dummynet* software [10] to create artificial loss. *Dummynet* implements a configurable traffic shaper based on the FreeBSD firewall code, enabling a user to create virtual traffic

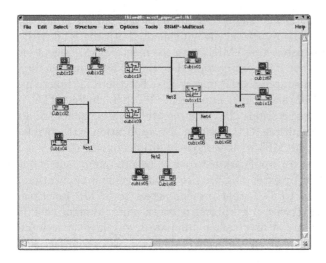

Fig. 1. Management Configuration

Fig. 2.   SNMP-
Multicast Menu

flow *pipes* based on a source and destination identifier and to configure certain characteristics for those flows. In this case, we used the pseudo-random fixed packet loss rate parameter to introduce 4% loss on the outgoing link from cubix09 to cubix10, the outgoing link from cubix10 to Net3, and the outgoing link from cubix11 to Net5. In this way, traffic between any pair of end hosts would traverse 0, 1, 2 or 3 lossy links.[6]

Once the network map is configured (Fig. 1), the experiment is controlled through the SNMP-Multicast pulldown menu shown in Fig. 2. For example, to start an RTP listener on a remote agent, the operator selects an object (e.g., cubix02) and then selects Start RTP Listeners on the pulldown menu. Similarly, remote senders are started via the Start RTP Senders option. For this experiment, we configured cubix02, cubix05, cubix07, and cubix16 as senders, each generating 64 kbps data streams. All of the end hosts were configured as receivers, and they all participated in RTCP exchanges. Cubix04 was selected as the host to be queried by the management client.[7]

The output of the experiment is shown in Figs. 3 and 4. Figure 3 shows a *Reception Quality Matrix*. We developed this tool by integrating the interface from the Reception Quality Matrix (which was originally implemented in version 4 of the Robust Audio Tool [22]) into our management client. The tool reports on connectivity between all senders and receivers, with each column representing a sender and each row representing a receiver. Each cell in the matrix indicates the loss rate between a sender and receiver. In addition, color codings indicate

---

[6] Configuring the loss is not done with the management tool. Rather, this is part of the general network setup for the experiment.

[7] Recall from Section 2.2 that we only need to query a single remote agent since all remote agents exchange RTCP receiver reports.

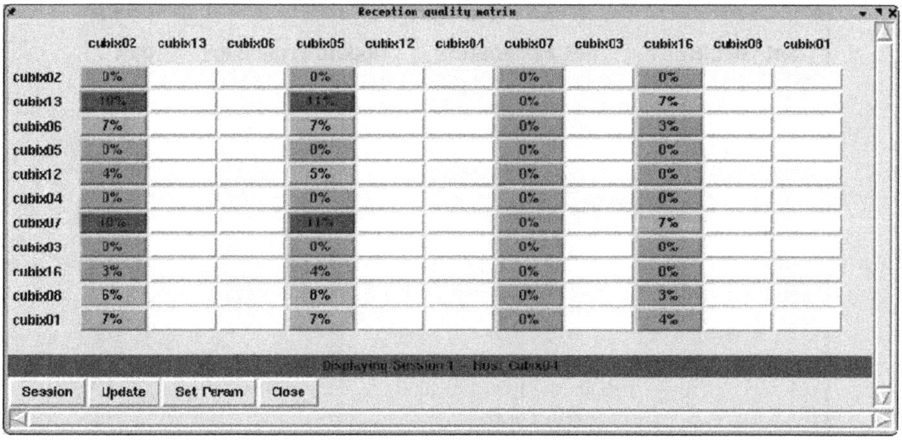

Fig. 3. Reception Quality Matrix

0-5% loss (green), 5-10% loss (orange), and loss over 10% (red), to assist in easy identification of problems.

Looking at Fig. 3, we see that the results are consistent with the experimental setup. cubix07 and cubix13, the two hosts on Net5, experience high loss (10-11%) for packets transmitted by senders cubix02 and cubix05. The paths between these senders and receivers traverse all three of the lossy links.[8] Paths that traverse two of the lossy links result in more moderate loss (e.g., 7% loss between cubix02 and cubix01), and single loss paths yield 3%-5% loss (e.g., cubix16 to cubix01). In all cases, hosts that are connected by paths that do not include links with loss report 0% loss.

In addition to reporting performance conditions in different places of the network, the tool can be used to deduce where in the network loss is occurring. For example, given that there is only a single link between cubix16 and cubix01, one can conclude that it is this link that is responsible for the loss. The loss between cubix02 and cubix01 can then be attributed in part to loss on the aforementioned link, and additional loss experienced on the link between cubix09 and cubix10.

A second tool that we developed is the *Loss Graph* tool which provides another view of loss rates. It periodically queries an agent to build up a series of values over time to indicate longer term performance of the agents. The tool takes a single source/receiver pair, and plots the reported loss at a user specified query interval. It also provides the facility to display the results over a variety of time scales. Figure 4 indicates the loss reported by host cubix07 from source cubix02 over a half hour time scale. The long timescale helps to draw attention to the trends over time, something that is not apparent from the snapshot results provided by the *Reception Quality Matrix*.

---

[8] Loss on these links is random, accounting in part for the slight variation between the expected loss rate, which is approximately 12%, and the reported loss rates.

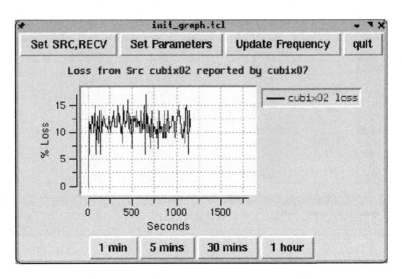

Fig. 4. Loss rate

Overhead. The kind of experiment described above could be used by a network operator to monitor performance in a production network. It is important to consider the overhead created by such monitoring. There are two kinds of overhead: packets generated by the test traffic (RTP and RTCP), and packets associated with SNMP traffic between the management client and the remote agents. The amount of RTP traffic is directly controlled by the network operator, who determines both the number of senders to instantiate and the rate at which they send. On network links of even moderate speed, it should be possible to accurately measure loss using fairly modest data rates.

In order to gain some understanding of the overhead caused by the SNMP traffic we measured the SNMP traffic between the management client and remote agents. The average aggregate rate for this traffic (including both directions) was approximately 4 kbps. However, this data is very bursty as a result of the management station periodically polling the remote agents. Polling resulted in transfer of about 10 kbytes of data, followed by a quiescent period. The overhead of SNMP traffic will obviously be impacted by the frequency of the polling and by the number of participants in the session being monitored.[9] While we can't draw

---

[9] The overhead need not grow linearly with the number of session participants. The tool queries a single session participant, and there is some fixed overhead associated with this query. The incremental cost of returning information about another receiver should be small. Further, for very large groups, the management client can have the flexibility to request information about a subset of session participants. Also note that for active monitoring, RMPMon need not scale to very large number of remote agents. A network operator can monitor performance across its network by deploying one remote agent per routing center, likely on the order of several tens of locations.

firm conclusions from one experiment, the results indicate that the overhead of the tool is likely minimal.

Further, we have not optimized the performance of our implementation. SNMP provides flexibility in how data is retrieved from remote agents. For example, an entire table can be retrieved with the GetBulk command, or a single object can be retrieved in one message. The optimal strategy depends on several factors, such as the percentage of objects in a table which are needed by the management station. We have not paid particular attention to these issues, concentrating on functionality rather than efficiency in our implementation. Simple analysis of packet traces in our experiments indicates that we can easily achieve a factor of 2 reduction in the overhead with a more careful implementation.

The decision to retrieve data from a single host connected to the session was motivated by the network configuration as well as implementation simplicity as far as SNMP management is concerned. This would not help in situations where RTCP packet loss is very high, or indeed where multicast connectivity is broken. For a small increase in SNMP traffic overhead, an efficient management client could selectively ask each member of the session for its own specific values. In the case of calculating loss, the RTP agent would return the MIB variables denoting lost packets and expected packets for each source that it hears. In this way, GetBulk requests might still be used for sessions with multiple senders to maintain low SNMP packet overhead, whilst retrieving more accurate information for the management station. This would provide the additional advantage of helping to detect active sources and receivers that are not ubiquitously heard by all members. A simple table view would highlight these inconsistencies.

Other Usage Scenarios. Above we described an experiment that demonstrated how RMPMon could be used to measure application level performance across a multicast network. We now mention some other ways in which it can be useful.

RMPMon can be used for passive monitoring of an actual user multicast session. In this case, the management station need only create one receiver somewhere in the network. By participating in the RTCP exchanges, this receiver collects session-wide information, which is returned to the management station via SNMP. This scenario demonstrates one of the advantages of our approach. If the receiver is located along the existing distribution tree, then no additional RTP traffic is distributed and no additional forwarding state is created. Using SNMP to retrieve reporting statistics from the agent is more efficient that having the management station receive both the RTP data packets and the RTCP control packets.

A second way in which RMPMon can be used is for consistency checking. In this scenario, every remote agent is asked for a list of active sources that it hears in the session. A simple consistency check across the data returned can indicate whether there is full, partial or no multicast connectivity to all relevant areas of the network.

RMPMon could be used in conjunction with other debugging tools. For example, *mtrace* can be used to debug problem areas in the case of poor connectivity between clients. This action can be initiated from the Reception Quality Matrix display. It might also help to identify routing anomalies in case data does not flow over the intended or preferred path.

RMPMon can also be used in conjunction with other tools that monitor multicast routing performance. For example, MSDP Source Active messages are triggered by data packets. If MSDP messages are being monitored, RMPMon can be used to generate multicast traffic at remote places in the network. A network manager can then verify that the proper MSDP messages are seen in MSDP protocol exchanges. Instantiating remote senders and receivers can also be used to verify that distribution trees are correct. For example, a receiver could be created and then terminated in order to verify that pruning is working correctly in a protocol such as DVMRP.

Additional management applications could be developed to extend the use of the tool. For example, rather than continuously displaying the reception quality matrix, the management client could monitor when certain thresholds of performance (e.g., loss rate) are crossed and alert the network operator.

5   Related Work

There has been a significant body of work in the area of multicast management and monitoring that has resulted in tools to support network, application, and session layer monitoring. Here we briefly review the work most closely related to ours. The interested reader is referred to [26] for a more in depth review.

The need for management tools became evident with the rapid growth of the MBone in the early 1990s. *Mrinfo* was an early tool that queried multicast routers for their adjacencies. Using this tool, one could then build a map of the multicast topology. Multicast traceroute, or *mtrace*, defined a protocol for querying routers along a path from receiver to source. This could be used to determine the path from sender to receiver, and ultimately an entire distribution tree. In addition, it can provide statistics about the number of multicast packets, and their loss rate, traversing a link. *Mtrace* remains an effective tool for debugging multicast reachability problems. Mantra [21] is a more recent system that determines multicast routing information by querying routers for this information. These tools all have the characteristic that they operate at the network level and retrieve adjacency or routing information from the routers themselves. Our work takes the alternative, and complementary approach, of monitoring performance information at the application level. There are tradeoffs associated with both approaches [21] and we believe that both kinds of tools are needed.

The earliest multicast debugging tools were developed outside the context of a general management framework. More recently, MIBs have been defined for multicast protocols. Tools such as *mrtree*, *mstat* and *mview* [17] are based on SNMP and take advantage of information in these multicast-related MIBs. As such, they represent a logical progression in the development of multicast tools.

`RMPMon` is also based on SNMP, and provides functionality not present in other SNMP-based tools.

The use of multicast in SNMP for communication between management stations and remote agents has been proposed [1]. This work is largely complementary to ours, as we have not focused on the communication channel between the management station and remote agents. One similarity is that both have mechanisms whereby the management station can cause a remote agent to join multicast groups. In `RMPMon` the multicast groups are used for communication between remote agents while in this other work the multicast groups are used for communication between the management station and the remote agents.

Ours is by no means the first work to use application level monitoring generally, or RTP-based monitoring, specifically. Rtpmon, RQM and *mhealth* are 3 tools that use RTCP reporting information in various ways. Rtpmon [24], developed at UCB, collects RTCP reporting information on a host and presents a loss matrix similar to the one we showed in Section 4.3. RQM, which provided the interface we used for our loss monitoring matrix, also collects RTCP reporting information for a session. *Mhealth* [14] is a tool that integrates both network layer information and application layer information to present both the multicast topology and end-to-end performance information. Our work extends the idea of using RTCP receiver reports embodied in all of these tools and embeds it into an SNMP framework. Incorporating it into a standard management framework provides several advantages, not the least of which is the ability to instantiate remote agents to participate in the monitoring.

The Multicast Reachability Monitor (MRM) [3] has been implemented on some commercial router platforms, and it has been used in an integrated framework for multicast monitoring that includes topology discovery and performance monitoring [25]. MRM is a protocol for generating test traffic on remote agents, providing functionality similar to what we achieve with the RTP Sender MIB. It represents an important development in the ability to monitor multicast routing infrastructure. We have borrowed this concept and used it within the context of SNMP. This allows us to take advantage of the authentication and access control available in SNMP, and it allows integration into a tool that allows both active and passive monitoring. SMRM [2] is another tool that is very similar to `RMPMon`. Like the MRM-based tool, SMRM allows a central management station to generate test traffic remotely and to collect statistics about performance. The primary difference between that work and ours is the use of RTP and its MIB in `RMPMon`. The use of RTP provides two primary advantages. First, it allows passive monitoring of multicast sessions that use RTP. Second, we leverage the reporting functionality of RTCP so that the management station can receive information about all receivers by querying a single remote agent.

6   Conclusions

In this paper we described a new tool for monitoring and managing multicast networks. The tool has several desirable features. It is based on standard technology and can thus be integrated with common management platforms. It enables remote monitoring of multicast infrastructure, using both passive and active tests. In addition, it does not depend on multicast connectivity between the management station and remote monitoring agents. We have demonstrated its use through testing in our lab environment, and it provides useful functionality at acceptable levels of overhead.

Our current implementation is a prototype that has served as a proof of concept. We see several opportunities for future work to build on the architecture and implementation we have presented here:

- Integrating new developments in the area of Source Specific Multicast (SSM) extensions would be a useful extension to the architecture. Monitoring SSM groups and providing the capability to generate IGMPv3 source include and exclude messages and monitor the resulting state in routers in the network will be key elements in managing single source distribution architecture networks. This will require updates to relevant MIBs in addition to implementation work on the remote agent software.
- We intended to integrate the functionality provided by the RTP Sender MIB into a generic traffic generation MIB currently being considered in the IETF [13].
- One of the reasons for basing our implementation on SNMP was to allow for integration of RMPMon into standard management platforms. For the prototype, we built a standalone management client. In the future, we will explore integrating our work into a common platform, such as HP Open View.

Multicast is a promising technology whose potential value has not yet been realized. The increasing demand for the delivery of multimedia content in the Internet may provide a push for multicast. If this is to happen, the long-known challenges of monitoring and managing multicast infrastructure will need to be solved. Several years of work have shown that this is indeed a difficult problem. We believe standards-based tools that allow for end-to-end performance monitoring of multicast infrastructure, like the one presented here, must be a part of the solution.

References

1. Ehab Al-Shaer and Yongning Tang. Toward integrating IP multicasting in Internet network management protocols. *Journal of Computer and Communications Review*, December 2000. 167
2. Ehab Al-Shaer and Yongning Tang. SMRM: SNMP-based multicast reachability monitoring. In *IEEE/IFIP Network Operations and Management Symposium*, Florence, Italy, April 2002. 167
3. Kevin Almeroth, Kamil Sarac, and Liming Wei. Supporting multicast management using the Multicast Reachability Monitor (MRM) protocol. Technical report, UCSB, May 2000. 167
4. M. Baugher, B. Strahm, and I. Suconick. Real-Time Transport Protocol Management Information Base. RFC 2959, Internet Engineering Task Force, 2000. 158

5. J. Case, K. McCloghrie, M. Rose, and S. Waldbusser. Protocol operations for version 2 of the simple network management protocol (SNMPv2). Request for Comments 1905, Internet Engineering Task Force, January 1996. 156
6. Stephen Casner and Stephen Deering. First IETF Internet audiocast. *ACM Computer Communication Review*, 22(3):92–97, July 1992. 154
7. M. Daniele, B. Wijnen, M. Ellison, and D. Francisco. Agent extensibility (AgentX) protocol version 1. RFC 2741, Internet Engineering Task Force, January 2000. 160
8. S. Deering, D. Estrin, D. Farinacci, Van Jacobson, C.-G. Liu, and L. Wei. An architecture for wide-area multicast routing. In *SIGCOMM Symposium on Communications Architectures and Protocols*, London, UK, September 1994. 154
9. Stephen Edward Deering. *Multicast routing in a datagram internetwork*. PhD thesis, Stanford University, Palo Alto, California, December 1991. 154
10. Dummynet. http://info.iet.unipi.it/~luigi/ip_dummynet/. 161
11. Bill Fenner and Steve Casner. A traceroute facility for IP multicast. Internet Draft, Internet Engineering Task Force, July 2000. 155
12. Bill Fenner and Dave Thaler. Multicast Source Discovery protocol MIB. Internet Draft, Internet Engineering Task Force, July 2001. 155
13. C. Kalbfleisch, R.G. Cole, and D. Romascanu. Definition of managed objects for synthetic sources for performance monitoring algorithms. Internet Draft, Internet Engineering Task Force, March 2002. 168
14. David Makofske and Kevin Almeroth. MHealth: A real-time multicast tree visualization and monitoring tool. In *Proc. International Workshop on Network and Operating System Support for Digital Audio and Video (NOSSDAV)*, Basking Ridge, New Jersey, June 1999. 155, 167
15. K. McCloghrie, D. Farinacci, and D. Thaler. Internet Group Management Protocol MIB. Request for Comments 2933, Internet Engineering Task Force, October 2000. 155
16. K. McCloghrie, D. Farinacci, and D. Thaler. IPv4 Multicast Routing MIB. Request for Comments 2932, Internet Engineering Task Force, October 2000. 155
17. Merit SNMP-Based MBone Management Project. http://www.merit.edu/~mbone/. 166
18. David Meyer and Bill Fenner. Multicast source discovery protocol (MSDP). Internet Draft, Internet Engineering Task Force, November 2001. Work in progress. 154
19. mrinfo. ftp://ftp.parc.xerox.com/pub/net-research/ipmulti/. 155
20. Net-SNMP. http://net-snmp.sourceforge.net/. 161
21. Prashant Rajvaidya and Kevin Almeroth. A router-based technique for monitoring the next-generation of internet multicast protocols. In *International Conference on Parallel Processing*, Valencia, Spain, September 2001. 166, 166
22. Robust Audio Tool. http://www-mice.cs.ucl.ac.uk/multimedia/software/rat/. 162
23. UCL RTP Library. http://www-mice.cs.ucl.ac.uk/multimedia/software/common/. 161
24. Rtpmon. ftp://mm-ftp.cs.berkeley.edu/pub/rtpmon/. 167
25. Hassen Sallay, Radu State, and Olivier Festor. A distributed management platform for integrated multicast monitoring. In *IEEE/IFIP Network Operations and Management Symposium*, Florence, Italy, April 2002. 167
26. Kamil Sara and Kevin C. Almeroth. Supporting multicast deployment efforts: a survey of tools for multicast monitoring. *Journal of High Speed Networks*, 9(3,4):191–211, 2000. 166
27. H. Schulzrinne, S. Casner, R. Frederick, and V. Jacobson. RTP: a transport protocol for real-time applications. RFC 1889, Internet Engineering Task Force, 1996. 156, 157
28. Scotty. http://wwwhome.cs.utwente.nl/~schoenw/scotty. 161

Active Technology as an Efficient Approach to Control DiffServ Networks: The DACA Architecture

Nadjib Achir, Nazim Agoulmine, Mauro Fonseca, Yacine Ghamri-Doudane, and Guy Pujolle

LIP6 - Pierre et Marie CURIE University
8, rue du capitaine Scott, 75015 Paris, France.

{Najib.Achir, Nazim.Agoulmine, Mauro.Fonseca, Yacine.Ghamri, Guy.Pujolle}@lip6.fr

Abstract. The objective of this work is to propose an architectural solution to achieve an efficient, distributed control and management of DiffServ enabled networks. DiffServ offers a scalable QoS provisioning solution but it introduces a certain amount of complexity in terms of management and control. The proposed solution is an alternative to the client/server policy-based approach put forward by the IETF[1], which assumes that complete predefined instrumentation is already implemented in DiffServ nodes. In this work, we suppose that DiffServ nodes offer an API with a minimum number of control functions. Based on this assumption, the proposed solution introduces a new control architecture to configure and control these nodes in a customized and flexible manner.

1. Introduction

One of the biggest challenges in present-day telecommunication networks is the deployment of high-quality, large-scale multimedia applications. Thus QoS management and control issues have become key points of ongoing research. While optical technologies such as WDM and DWDM allow broadband communications, end-to-end assurance of the bandwidth and the delay are still an open issue when using the IP protocol because of the bottlenecks occurring at access and intermediate nodes. Some standards and proprietary solutions have already been specified in an attempt to guarantee a certain level of QoS to end-user communications crossing a number of network devices. Among these solutions, we find RSVP/IntServ and DiffServ. While the former, based on per flow reservation [1], presents some scalability problems, the latter is a promising scalable solution [2,3]. It is based on aggregate classes of traffic where each class possesses a certain level of QoS. This approach processes packets according to the aggregate to which it belongs, not on a stream-per-stream base, which explains why it is scalable. The principal side effect of this approach is the complex management. In fact, in order to offer the target QoS, the DiffServ routers must be configured with great precision and a monitoring process is

---

[1] IETF : Internet Engineering Task Force

K.C. Almeroth and M. Hasan (Eds.): MMNS 2002, LNCS 2496, pp. 170-183, 2002.
© Springer-Verlag Berlin Heidelberg 2002

required to control the QoS provided. Actually, DiffServ does not provide a strict QoS but a relative one, so that if the desired QoS is not fulfilled, changes must be made in the configurations or in the conditioning algorithms. Looking at currently used DiffServ routers, the only way to configure them is to use a complex configuration command script. However, reconfiguration is based only on the existing capacity of the router, with the result that there is no way to add new functionalities dynamically without rebooting the system.

The aim of this work is to investigate the possibility of developing a new solution based on active networks (ANs) in an aim to make the management and control of today's IP networks more dynamic. The proposed solution is aimed at improving the DiffServ network architecture by implementing DiffServ functionalities as active components and control their service logic through policies. This solution will allow the current IP-based network architecture solution to be maintained while providing a more predictable and manageable network. Thus, ISPs will gain more control over the way network resources are used and consequently will be able to support their customers' requirements in what are called Service Level Agreements (i.e. contractual relationships between the customer and the provider) with far more efficiency.

This paper is organized as follows. Section 2 describes the DiffServ, policy-based management and active network technologies. The following section presents the objectives of our work while section 4 outlines the proposed architecture, its components and internal mechanisms. A number of elements concerning the implementation of this new architecture are given in section 5. Finally, a conclusion and suggestions for future work are presented.

2. Underlying Technologies

Three main technologies have been used to define the proposed architecture: DiffServ, Active Networking and Policy-based Management. These technologies are briefly introduced in this section.

2.1 QoS Management Using DiffServ

The IETF has specified the DiffServ architecture as a scalable QoS provisioning solution for the Internet. The proposed architecture introduces two main functionalities, namely   Packet Marking using the IPv4 ToS byte and the Per Hop Behavior (PHB) [2] treatment. In the first case, the ToS byte field of the IPv4 packet is replaced by a new field called the Differentiated Services Code Point (DSCP) which identifies the treatment to apply to this particular packet [3]. The packet marking process is performed by edge routers at the ingress of the network to order to achieve a target end-to-end QoS. At the core of the network, packets with the same DSCP value will be treated in the same way by core routers, this treatment is the PHB, which is related to a Traffic Conditioning Block (TCB). The latter corresponds to the packet scheduling, queuing, policing or shaping behavior of a node on any given packet belonging to a Behavior Aggregate (BA).

2.2   Policy-Based Management

The policy-based management (PBM) approach aims to automate the management of complex networks by defining high-level management objectives that are enforced in the network equipment as a set of policies [4]. Policies are a set of pre-defined rules that govern network resource allocation. The IETF has specified a policy management architecture [5] composed of a PEP[2] component, a PDP[3] component and a Policy Repository component. Based on the resource allocation policies, the network administrator defines a set of rules that describe these policies and saves them in a Policy Repository. The PDP monitors this repository and applies policies as necessary. The PEP component is a policy decision enforcer located in or closely to the network equipment. Finally, the IETF has defined a Policy Core Information Model (PCIM) that allows policy objects to be represented in the DMTF[4] consortium Common Information Model (CIM) [6].

2.3   Active Networking

The active networking technology emerged from discussions within the Defense Advanced Research Projects Agency (DARPA) research community [7]. Enabling the programmability of networks was expected to allow a flexible network architecture thereby facilitating the integration of new services and accelerating network infrastructure innovation. Two approaches exist: the first, the so-called "programmable networks" approach, has as its objective to open up network control to applications by means of standardized interfaces, the second, the "active packets" or "capsules" approach, allows application packets to carry their own processing.

3.   Objective of the Work

The objective of this work is to investigate the possibility of using active networks coupled with policy-based management to propose a new solution for deploying and controlling DiffServ networks. The main characteristics we introduce in order to reduce the complexity of DiffServ networks management and control [8] are (1) more flexibility in provisioning DiffServ services, (2) better control of the DiffServ process at different points of the various TCBs (scheduler, meter, shaper, etc.) and (3) optimization of the network by allowing the deployment of customized control functions capable of reporting information that will allow problems in the network to be anticipated. The solution proposed here aims to introduces configuration and control based on dynamic introduction, modification and deletion of mobile code directly in the DiffServ routers to implement configuration and control functions. An architecture is therefore proposed for organizing the overall activity of the operator and provide him with a set of tools that will facilitate management activities: DACA, or DiffServ Active Control Architecture.

---

[2] PEP: Policy Enforcement Point
[3] PDP: Policy Decision Point
[4] DMTF: Distributed Management Task Force

4.   The DACA Architecture

The proposed DACA architecture aims to facilitate and ideally automate the configuration of network equipment so that the provider does not have to do it manually for each node. This will avoid the administrator having to configure each router in the network individually to reflect a new or changing strategy. In present-day equipment, in a context of heterogeneous and high scale networks, these configuration tasks are very complex for the administrator. Reconfiguration of network equipments is a very fastidious task calling for highly skilled expertise.

The DACA architecture presented in Figure 1 provides a set of tools and functionalities allowing dynamic deployment and distribution of control services in an active network. It uses active codes and policies as basic paradigms to introduce specific functionalities rapidly and transparently in active nodes. The main control service in this work is DiffServ.

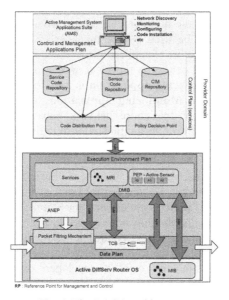

Fig. 1. The DACA architecture

4.1   Lifecycle of Differentiated Services

DiffServ deployment consists in specifying TCBs for ingress and core routers and implementing these TCBs in the network. We have identified four phases allowing configuration and assurance of the service:
- **Pre-service phase**: When an ISP has signed a SLA with a customer to provide a service with a certain QoS, the ISP administrator creates the corresponding policies in the policy repository.
- **Before-service phase**: The administrator must specify the exact TCB to be used for the customer or define a new one, depending on the service requested,

existing services and the state of the network. For example, if the network is overprovisioned, the administrator can decide to install only simplified versions of TCB.

- **In-service phase**: In this phase, the administrator can define high-level rules that will allow network utilization to be optimized. For example, if congestion occurs in the network for entire classes or a particular class, then a new complex TCB should be installed.
- **Post-service phase**: At this stage, the administrator is interested in customer care and, in particular, in SLA violation detection.

4.2   Component Description

The DACA architecture consists of a set of components distributed among five logical plans: the management and control applications plan, the provider control plan, the ADR OS plan, the active-router execution environment plan and, lastly, the active-router data plan. In the **management and control applications plan**, we find the applications that can be used by the manager to control the active DiffServ network. A non-exhaustive list of applications is: the **Configuration application** that helps the administrator to configure the local system as well as any remote active nodes; the **Network Discovering application** is used to discover the active network topology dynamically; the **Monitoring application** serves to monitor any target active node specifically or the entire network behavior; and, lastly, the **Code installation application** allows the administrator to define new control algorithms or management functions to be used in the network and to enforce them in any active node.

In the **provider active plan**, we find the following components: the **Active Management System (AMS),** i.e. the central point of management in the provider domain. All **management policies** are defined and stored in this system. It comprises a set of tools (for editing, distribution and management) that enables network manager to define the basic management and control functionalities to be deployed in the network. These functionalities concern the network level as well as the service level management. Each functionality can be developed on the basis of a service composition principle, which means that the manager can specify enhanced functionalities that are built on top of existing management components (information, services and sensor) already deployed in the managed active node. The **CIM Repository (CIMR)** is the virtual store that contains information about the network, the services, the customers, the SLA and so on. It also contains a description of the policies and of the association between all these objects. The **Service Code Repository (SCR)** is the virtual store containing active codes relating to DiffServ TCBs. Each code corresponds to a functionality that can be installed dynamically in the active node in order to implement a particular control function (classifier, meter, shaper, etc). The **Sensor Code Repository (SeCR)** is the virtual store that contains active codes relating to sensors. Sensors are management functionalities that can be installed dynamically in any active node in order to implement a particular management function (monitoring, event notification, summarization, etc).   The **Policy Decision Point (PDP)** is the decision-making component described in section

2.2 which is designed to monitor events in general (time, network, etc.) and trigger policy rules of which the condition part is verified with these events. **The Code Distribution Point (CDP)** is a component responsible for deploying service codes or sensor codes on behalf of the administrator or when a PDP requests it in order to perform a policy.

The **ADR OS plan** comprises the following components: the **Active DiffServ Router OS (ADR OS), i.e.** the active node. ADR OS runs an operating system which supports the active plan as well as the execution environment. Normally at this level we have the conventional **Management Information Base (MIB),** defined by the IETF SMI (System Management Information), which contains a set of objects representing different resources of the active node viewed as an IP router.

The following Execution **Environment Plan** comprises the following components: the **Dynamic MIB (DMIB),** a special active application which supports the local installation and management of active management services. In this case, therefore, it will support the installation and management of services, active sensors, and ADRs. Unlike the MIB, the DMIB offers a view of the ADR seen as an active node, i.e. a management information view as well as an active-services view. It can be extended on the fly with new objects and associated instrumentation. The **Managed Resources Information (MRI),** like the MIB, is a repository of information about each manageable resource in the ADR. Passive, it requires instrumentation to update the information. Active Sensors (AS) that push information into the MRI or any other function defined by the manager can apply the instrumentation. The **Services** are thus active control services available in the ADR that can be used by other components such active sensors. The services are allowed to use managed resources information, DiffServ services or active sensors. Not all services are active all the time. They need to be activated in order to be operational. An example is the FlowID update process, which sets up a FlowID table used at the ADR level by the filter. The **PEP active sensor** performs the PEP functions in the active router as presented in section 2.2. Its role is to enforce policy actions requested by the PDP and also local PDP functions, or LPDP. Thus it monitors managed resource information and applies management policies when events occur locally. Policies are defined in terms of rules with a condition part and an action part. The LPDP implements active sensors, individual processes that handle each rule. Each Active Sensor is responsible for performing one rule and monitoring the action part to verify whether it is valid. It uses other components of the architecture to monitor ADR resources (MIB, DMIB) and other active sensors to create a complex monitoring process. An active sensor can be active or passive, depending on whether its condition part is verified (all corresponding actions being applied) or passive in the sense that it is still monitoring the validity of the condition part.

Finally, in the **execution data plan**, we find the Packet **Filtering Mechanism (PFM)** and the **Traffic Conditioning Block (TCB),** which is defined in the DiffServ architecture. In order to optimize the performance of the system and not intercept all packets in the network, we have defined a packet filtering mechanism capable of intercepting and redirecting packets based on specific filters, which define the set of active applications installed in the active node.   From the data plan viewpoint, the installation, modification and removal of a TCB is transparent (depending, of course, on the performance of the system and how fast it is able to react to particular events).

4.3   Filtering Capsules in the Data Plan

When a capsule crosses the network, it goes through several active routers. If the capsule belongs to an active application whose protocol is deployed in a particular node, it should be handled by the active protocol before being forwarded to the following node. Not all active-application protocols will be installed in all active routers, so that the role of the PFM is to detect capsules to be captured and forward them to the EE[5] as fast as possible in order to avoid cumulative delay. The PFM uses a special FlowID table which identifies the installed set of active applications in order to select the capsules to be captured. The Flow ID is stored in an option field of the IPv4 packet or in the FlowID field of the IPv6 packet. To keep the FlowID table up to date, the so-called FlowID update service is activated. Its role is to monitor the installed active application protocols and update the FlowID by adding or removing an entry in the table (Fig.2).

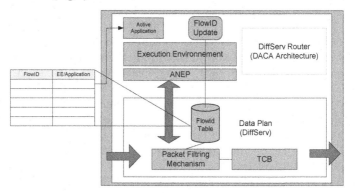

Fig. 2. FlowID table updates and packet filtering mechanism

PFM plays a central role in the architecture and, as such, has an important impact on the network performance. It therefore has to be installed as close as possible to the active router OS.

4.4   Monitoring ADR Resources

As stated at the beginning of the paper, it is important for the operator to have detailed information about the network behavior. The DMIB offers facilities for monitoring and notifying events dynamically, i.e. the information model is not static as in the classical IP management protocol SNMP (Simple Network Management Protocol) and its corresponding SMI. The DMIB offers the means to monitor any resource in the ADR efficiently using two APIs:

- **Dynamic Information Interface** (DInfo) is an object-oriented API that allows access to management information, service objects or active sensors. This API comprises five primitives: getAbout(), getVersion(), get(), set() and function().

---

[5] EE: Execution Environment

Of these, get() and set() make it possible to read and write the attributes of a particular managed object while function() allows a particular method to be applied to one or several particular managed objects.

- **Dynamic Management Information Base Interface** (DMIB) is an API to access DInfo objects. It is composed of the following primitives: getAbout(), getVersion(), get(), set(), function(), getObject(), nextObject(), restart(), and putObject(). It allows DInfo's objects to be manipulated for a particular management activity. To ensure the specific identification of each Dinfo object, the DMIB uses a specific ID similar to the SMI naming tree, whose leaves represent the DInfo objects.

Management applications have the possibility of creating specific information in the ADR and instrumenting them using these two APIs.

4.5   QoS Policy Definition

Policies are defined according to the SLS[6] agreed between the customer and the ISP. The negotiation process is not addressed in this work. We assume that this phase has been performed and that the SLS has been converted into a set of policy rules. These rules have a condition part and an action part. For example, if the ISP has made a commitment to provide a Gold Service to the customer on a certain Day/Time, then the policy rules will be defined as follows:

IF (PolicyTimePeriod == TimeValidityPeriod) **THEN** Provide Customer with a Gold Service.

This business level rule is converted into a network level rule identifying the customer flows at the ingress of the network and the corresponding DSCP value. It is created in the CIM repository and enforced in the ingress router.

IF (PolicyTimePeriod == TimeValidityPeriod) and (IPAddr IN Customer IP Address Set) **THEN** mark Flow with DSCP = Gold.

The basic concepts remain the same as those of IETF and DMTF policy work. However, in our proposal, it is also possible to use policies to deploy new services or sensors in the controlled router. For example, if an ISP has decided to shape the traffic aggregates of an AF Class only if more than 80% of the link capacity is used, then the policy rule will be defined as follows:

IF (LinkCapacityUsage > Threshold) **THEN** Install(Shaper (TBF(r,b)), AF).

This approach gives the operator a very powerful mechanism for efficiently controlling the network behavior, which does not exist in today's networks.

4.6   TCB Definition and Deployment

The service code of the DACA architecture described earlier contains a set of active codes which implements different algorithms of the DiffServ model. It provides the ISP with a very flexible approach for specifying the behavior of its network. The internal structure of this repository is described in Figure 3. The highest level of the

---

[6] SLS : Service Level Specification, set of performance parameters that agreed in a SLA.

tree is the abstract DiffServ active services. Under this entity, we find five different sub-trees, each treating one aspect of TCB: classifiers, meters, actions, droppers and schedulers. All these entities are containers for active codes that implement different types of algorithms.

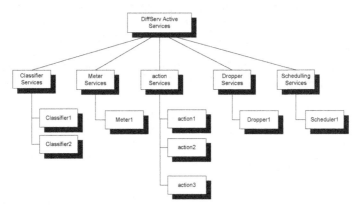

Fig. 3. TCB Active Services

The TCB in the DiffServ model consists of a set of TCB blocks connected in a specific sequence according to the desired behavior. Thus, in this case, the administrator defines the set of blocks to be deployed in the underlying routers in terms of his objectives. Once this has been done, the administrator asks the Code Distribution Point to install this path in the target node. This task is performed using a specific active installation protocol. The selected blocks are installed in the target routers and are then visible in the Service block at the execution environment layer of the active router. This installation affects only the capsules concerning this new TCB. In general, the manager will define various classes of TCB (called TCBClass). Each class will be assigned to a particular service and installed in the appropriate active node. A chain of DiffServ active services will compose each TCBClass.

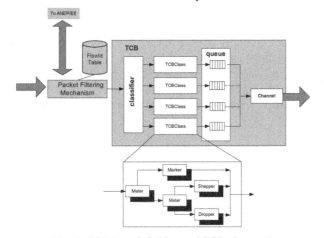

Fig. 4. TCBclass definition and TCB class path

When the Filter Service identifies a capsule belonging to an existing active application, it sends the capsule to the corresponding execution environment. If the capsule is not filtered, it is sent directly to the TCB block where is classified according to the DSCP and sent to the appropriate TCB. The TCBClass Service is composed of a set of TCBElem Services (Fig.4), each corresponding to a particular algorithm (i.e. meter, dropper, marker, etc.).

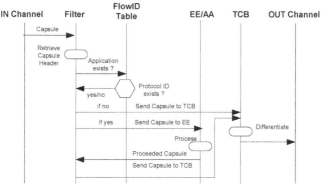

Fig. 5. Interaction process between the filter, the TCB and the FlowID table

If the administrator would like also to automate the installation and reconfiguration process and can do so by defining special policy rules dedicated to the installation of new TCBs. These rules allows the installation, modification or removal of TCBs according to a set of conditions such as the load on the network, performance data collected via the DMIB, etc. The interaction process between the Packet Filtering Mechanism, the TCB and the EE/Active Application that allows these functions to be carried out is described in the following Figure 6.

4.7   Sensor Deployment

When policies are introduced in the CIM repository, they are converted into a set of low-level policies, as described briefly in section 4.6. When a PDP detects the introduction of a new policy, it decides whether this policy should be handled locally or if it should be downloaded directly into the LPDP of the set of active routers concerned by the policy. The decision depends on whether the policy can be handled at the active router boundary. An example of a policy that can be handled locally is one that changes the configuration of the local metering algorithms of the active router depending on a Time Condition. A policy that can not be achieved locally is one that has a condition part containing a variable concerning the end-to-end delay between two access points. A sensor cannot resolve this information locally.

When the LPDP receives new policy rules to handle, it creates a new sensor that takes charge of the rules concerned. Depending on the condition part and the action part, the sensor could require functionalities that do not exist locally, which means that the LPDP may obtain these functionalities directly from the Provider Sensor Code Repository through the Code Distribution Point (CDP).

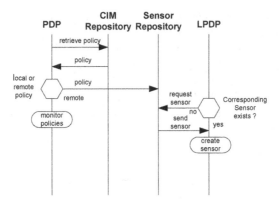

Fig. 6. Policy deployment using sensors

5.   Prototype Implementation

Implementation of the DACA architecture is performed using a set of Java classes developed on the top of the ANTS[7] toolkit [9] used in the Amarrage project [10]. This toolkit allows the straightforward and efficient deployment of a full Java-based active node on IPv6. The ANTS is based on a mobile code as well as remote-loading-on-request and cache techniques. It allows new protocols to be deployed dynamically in network nodes without synchronization. ANTS defines capsules as active packets that customize network services and active nodes. The active nodes process incoming capsules and maintain soft-store. ANTS has a flexible code distribution scheme in which code capsule fragments can be loaded on request into an active node. Capsules are injected into the network by Applications and forwarded to their destination with customized routines. Each time a capsule enters an active node, it is treated according to the specifications defined in its own code. In our implementation we also use the Active Network Encapsulation Protocol [11] to provide another mechanism for routing user packets to particular EEs. The ANEP header includes a "Type ID" field which are assigned to specific execution environments. If a particular EE or various EEs are present at a node, packets containing a valid ANEP header with the appropriate Type ID will be routed to the appropriate EE.

Classes in DACA implementation represents the components defined in the DACA architecture presented in Figure 1. The classes are developed as Java 2 classes that extend or interact with the existing ANTS native classes. The ANTS classes implement the EEs and the channels.

The first component extending the ANTS platform is the **ActiveQoS** class, which corresponds to the Data Plan in the DACA architecture and is connected to ANTS via four JAVA interfaces, *SendToEE*, *ReceiveFromEE*, *SendToChannel* and *ReceiveFromChannel*. The ANTS capsule is extended by **QoSCapsule**, containing two specific fields, *FlowID and DSCP* identifying the application that generates this capsule and the TCB that must be applied to it, respectively. The ActiveQoS Class

---

[7] ANTS : Active Node Transport System

consists of many classes. The first, the **Filter** Class, recognizes then intercepts the capsules belonging to active applications installed in the DACA node by checking the FlowId field in the QoSCapsule. If the capsule is not intercepted by the Filter class, then it is transmitted to the **Classifier** class, which checks the DSCP field and forwards the capsule to the appropriate **TCBClass**. The latter is a thread that contains a chain of **TCBElems** corresponding to the different algorithms of DiffServ. Each **TCBElem** present in the TCBClass applies a function "**exec**" to the capsule. This function is implemented as an abstract Java function which must be redefined for each particular DiffServ algorithm (i.e. meter, dropper, marker, etc). After that, the capsule is put in a buffer corresponding to the TCB queue. Lastly, we find the SchedulClass, which forwards the capsules to the output (i.e. to the ANTS channel). Like the TCBElem class, the SchedulClass class implements an abstract "**Schedul**" function which must be redefined for all the scheduling algorithms. The DACA architecture implements two types of scheduling algorithm, namely Priority Queuing and Round Robin Scheduling, but it is possible to implement others.

To allow the TCBElem and SchedulClass algorithms to be changed on-the-fly, the DACA architecture uses a hierarchic tree repository, the DMIB, to manage its classes. This repository is able to keep and to schedule Services and other classes such as the PEP services, active sensors, MIB, TCBElem, SchedulClass, etc. In order for a class to be kept in the DMIB, it has to inherit from the DInfo class presented in section 4.5.

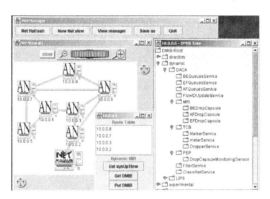

Fig. 7. Network discovery and code installation applications.

The GUI of the Active Management System of the DACA architecture implemented to manage the prototype is shown in Figure 7. It allows on-the-fly installation but also replaces, upgrades and deletes services and active sensors in all nodes of the DACA network.

The service and active-sensor repositories are currently implemented as class files in a directory while the CIM model is implemented as a straightforward file. Thus, three applications allowing the discovery of the active network topology are already operational, namely the manager of installed active services (e.g. TCB, Scheduler and active sensors), code installation and MRI object monitoring, as presented in Figure 7. Implementation is still under way to extend the existing components with new functionalities and to test the performance of the deployed network.

6.   Conclusion and Future Work

QoS and Service Level Agreement management are two important concepts for ISPs. As customer needs change, ISPs have to deploy a quality of service solution that is manageable and customizable in order to address different customers' requirements. The solution we propose here aims to integrate the advantages of DiffServ, Active Networking and policy-based management in a single architecture. The proposed DACA architecture offers the ISP operator a set of powerful tools allowing him to enforce a business strategy in the network in terms of policies and to optimize network utilization by maintaining better control over the DiffServ resources.

At the moment, this work is still progressing toward complete implementation over DACA architecture but initial results show how easy it is for an administrator to modify the DiffServ configuration and how very promising this architecture appears for the future. The next step, therefore, will be to finalize the implementation of the PDP and the PEP in order to deploy the policy-based management part of the architecture and test it in a real trial.

7.   Acknowledgments

This work was carried out partly within the framework of the Amarrage research project funded by the French Ministry of Research under the RNRT telecommunication research program. The authors express their thanks to the rest of the project team and, in particular, to the members of WP1 and WP4 for fruitful comments and discussion during the various meetings.

8.   Bibliography

1.   WROCLAWSKI J., « The Use of RSVP with IETF Integrated Services », RFC 2210, September 1997.
2.   BLAKE S., ET AL., « An Architecture for Differentiated Services », RFC 2475, December 1998.
3.   NICHOLS K., JACOBSON V., ZHANG L., « A Two-bit Differentiated Services Architecture for the Internet », RFC 2638, July 1999.
4.   RAJAN R., VERMA D., KAMAT S., FELSTAINE E., AND HERZOG S., « A policy framework for integrated and differentiated services in the Internet », IEEE Network Magazine, vol.13, no.5, pp.36-41, September / October 1999.
5.   DURHAM D., ET AL., « The COPS (Common Open Policy Service) Protocol », RFC 2748, January 2000.
6.   MOORE B., ELLESSON E., AND STRASSNER J.,"Policy Core Information Model -- Version 1 Specification", RFC 3060, February 2001.
7.   PSOUNIS K., « Active Networks: Applications, Security, Safety, and Architectures », IEEE Communications Surveys Magazine, 1st quarter issue, 1999.
8.   CISCO White paper, "DiffServ - The Scalable End-to-End QoS Model", www.cisco.com.
9.   AMARRAGE PROJET, http://www.telecom.gouv.fr/rnrt/projets/res_d41_ap99.htm.

10. WETHERALL D. J., GUTTAG J., AND TENNENHOUSE D. L., "ANTS: A Toolkit for Building and Dynamically Deploying Network Protocols", IEEE OPENARCH'98, San Francisco, CA, April 1998.
11. ALEXANDER D. S., et al., « Active Network Encapsulation Protocol », Draft, DARPA AN Working Group, July 1997.

Efficient Implementation of Packet Scheduling Algorithm on High-Speed Programmable Network Processors

Weidong Shi, Xiaotong Zhuang, *Indrani Paul, and Karsten Schwan

Georgia Institute of Technology, College of Computing, 801 Atlantic Drive
Atlanta, GA, 30332-0280
{Shiw, xt2000, schwan}@cc.gatech.edu
* indrani@ece.gatech.edu

Abstract. This paper describes the design and implementation of the Dynamic Window-Constrained Scheduling (DWCS)[1][2][3] algorithm to schedule packets on network processors. The DWCS algorithm characterizes multimedia streams with diverse Quality of Service (QoS) requirements. Earlier implementations of DWCS on Linux and Solaris machines use a heap-based implementation, which requires $O(n)$ time to find the next packet and send it out, and which frequently moves heap elements. For speed improvements and conservation of memory bandwidth, our design uses a Hierarchically Indexed Linear Queue (HILQ). The HILQ substantially reduces the number of memory accesses by scattering packets sparsely into the queue. Experimental results demonstrate improved scalability compared to a heap-based implementation in supporting thousands of streams with strict real-time constraints, while causing no loss in accuracy compared to the standard DWCS algorithm.

1 Introduction

Network technology is being pushed forward to satisfy the ever-increasing requirements of future applications. Real-time media servers need to serve hundreds to thousands of clients, each with its own Quality of Service (QoS) requirements. Critical QoS properties like packet loss rate, deadline and delay variance need to be maintained without compromising the processing speed of incoming data streams. Many papers [1][4][5] have addressed the problem of scheduling priority-ordered input packets that packets from different flows are processed in an appropriate order, the order being determined by the QoS requirement of each stream. Packets of less priority not able to meet their QoS may be dropped to save computing power or bandwidth for more urgent packets.

This paper presents an efficient implementation of the Dynamic Window-Constrained Scheduling Algorithm (DWCS) [1][2][3] on high-speed programmable network processors. DWCS is designed to guarantee the QoS requirements of media streams with different performance objectives. Using only two attributes, deadline and loss-tolerance, DWCS can maximize the network bandwidth usage and limit the number of packets that have missed deadlines over a finite window of consecutive packets. DWCS is also able to share bandwidth among competing streams in strict proportion to their deadline and loss-

K.C. Almeroth and M. Hasan (Eds.): MMNS 2002, LNCS 2496, pp. 184–197, 2002.

tolerance. Moreover, several traditional scheduling algorithms like Earliest Deadline First (EDF) [4], Static Priority, and Fair Queuing [5] can be simulated with DWCS.

Previous implementations of DWCS have been limited to Linux or cluster machines where computation resources are relatively plentiful compared to packet arriving rates. An earlier implementation of DWCS [3] uses a heap structure to store and select packets according to their deadline and loss-tolerance order. The computational complexity of this implementation is proved to be O(n), where n is the number of the simultaneously active streams in the system.

This paper considers the efficient implementation of stream scheduling on high-speed programmable network processors. The processors attain high processing speed by exploiting parallelism to hide memory latency. In the Intel IXP1200 network processor, for example, two Gigabit ports are supported by six microengines running in parallel. Each microengine contains four hardware contexts or threads. Memory operations and on-board computation can be performed concurrently by context switching. However, memory operations are time- consuming. Roughly, if the network processor is serving two Gigabit ports, one packet should be sent out every 500 – 600 microengine cycles (each microengine runs at 232 MHz), while each off-chip memory access takes about 20 cycles to complete. Although the latency can be somewhat hidden by context switching, memory intensive data structures like heaps or linked lists make it difficult to meet these requirements. An outcome is the need for new designs that address the limitation of memory-intensive data structures.

This is particularly important for packet scheduling algorithms [1][4][5], which rely on ordered queues or lists that must be updated, as packets arrive or are delivered. Specifically, to keep the queue or list ordered, with O(n) operations, where n is the number of elements in the queue, it becomes impossible to maintain an ordered queue (list) on the IXP network processor without major modifications in the packet scheduling algorithm while operating at Gigabit rates.

This paper addresses memory bandwidth limitations by holding the fact that memory space is of less concern than memory speed. The "Hierarchically Indexed Linear Queue" (HILQ) introduced in this paper reduces the time needed for packet ordering and priority adjustments by reducing the cost of both packet insertion and selection operations. It also eliminates the need to move data within memory by directly inserting packets into the queue that is intentionally kept sparse.

This paper is organized as follows. Section 2 discusses some of the related work. Section 3 presents the DWCS algorithm and discusses the previous implementations of DWCS. Section 4 introduces the IXP architecture. Section 5 describes the data structures and the implementation of HILQ. Section 6 presents the performance results and section 7 concludes the paper.

2   Related Work

There are many approaches to schedule a large number of streams. For instance, rate-monotonic [4] scheduling is based on the period of each task. The task with the shortest period gets the highest priority among all queued packets. Earliest Deadline First (EDF) [4] and Minimum Laxity First (MLF) are two variations of RM.

D.C.Stephens, C.R.Bernnett, H.Zhang[13] proposed the fast implementation of PFQ (Packet Fair Queueing) on ATM networks. They used a grouping architecture to reduce the cost of basic operations. Only a limited number of guaranteed rates are supported by the server. Flows with similar rates are grouped together. Inaccuracy of flow rates is introduced when approximating flows with fixed number of rates. Their implementation uses a hierarchical calendar queue for intragroup scheduling, which is somewhat similar to the HILQ structure used by us. However, they add packets to the list of the same slot (when a conflict happens), and only two-level hierarchical structures are supported. As a result, the scan operation on the calendar queue is costly when the number of slots increases. Since they implement of PFQ, no garbage collection mechanism is needed to improve concurrency.

In [14], a heap is implemented with hardware (ASICs), where the hardware supports operations at each layer of the heap. The three basic operations (read-compare-write) can be quickly performed by pipelined processing.

In [15], the authors design a *hash with chaining* data structure to accelerate flow table management for high-speed routers. The hash value is provided by a hardware hash function, and the entries competing for the same hash value are chained together. Their hash function can achieve uniform hashing without considering the stream properties of packets, while in our case, uniform hashing will cause the packets to cluster around certain values. *Purge when convenient* is used to reduce the overhead of deleting entries from the flow table.

3   DWCS Algorithm and Earlier Implementations

The DWCS algorithm is detailed in [1] [2] [3]. We briefly reiterate some of the main features of DWCS in this section. We also discuss a previous implementation of DWCS.

The DWCS algorithm can work as a network packet scheduler. It schedules packets from multiple streams by limiting the number of late or lost packets over a finite number of consecutive packets. This is most favorable for video or audio streams, where a limited amount of packet loss is tolerable over a fixed transfer window. DWCS can also be applied to the scheduling of processes for time-sensitive real-time tasks. The DWCS algorithm uses two parameters for each stream:

Deadline -- Deadline is the latest time a packet can commence service.

Loss-tolerance -- This is specified as a value x_i / y_i, where x_i is the number of packets that can be lost or transmitted late for every window, y_i, of consecutive packet arrivals in the same stream i.

DWCS transmits the packets in an order according to their loss-tolerances and deadlines. Packets of the same stream have the same original and current loss-tolerances and will be scheduled in the order of their arrival. When scheduled by DWCS, the priorities of each stream can be adjusted dynamically. Whenever a packet misses its deadline, the loss tolerance for all packets in the same stream is reduced to reflect the increased importance of transmitting a packet from this stream. This approach prevents starvation and tries to keep the stream from violating its original loss-tolerance. Table 1 lists the complete packet-ordering scheme according to the priority.

Table 1: Precedence amongst pairs of packets (from [1])

$x/y=0$	$x/y!=0$
EDF	EDF
Same deadline, lowest y first	Same deadline, lowest x/y first
Same deadline and y, FIFO	Same deadline and x/y, lowest y first
	Same deadline, x/y, y, FIFO

Every time a packet in a stream is transmitted, the loss-tolerance is adjusted for that stream. Also, every time a packet misses its deadline, the loss-tolerance is adjusted to give the stream a higher priority when the next packet comes. Formally, the pseudo-code for adjusting the loss-tolerance value is listed below in Figure 1.

```
For packets transmitted before deadline:
if (y'_i > x'_i) then y'_i =x'_i-1;
if (y'_i = x'_i=0) then x'_i =x_i; y'_i =y_i;
        For any packet misses its deadline:
If(x'_i>0) then
        x'_i =x'_i-1; y'_i =y'_i -1;
        if(x'_i = y'_i=0) then x'_i = x_i; y'_i = y_i;
else if(x'_i = 0) then
        if(x_i > 0) then y'_i = y'_i + ⌈(y_i -x_i)/ x_i ⌉;
        if(x_i = 0) then y'_i = y'_i + y_i;
```

Figure 1: Pseudo-code for packet processing (from [1])

R.West, Chris. Poellabauer [3] fully implemented DWCS on Linux machines. This implementation uses a circular queue for each stream. Packets of the same stream are added to the tail of the queue and removed from the head of the queue. Two heaps are set up for deadline and loss-tolerance. With the heaps, packet insertion can be done using heap sorting. Packet precedence comparison will follow the rules of Table 1.

DWCS checks streams for packets that have missed their deadlines every time a packet has been serviced. In the worst case, every stream can have late packets when the scheduler completes the service of one packet. The deletion of these packets from the loss-tolerance heap and the heap adjustment will cost $O(n\log n)$. Also, $O(\log n)$ time is required to find the next packet to be sent from the n streams. Thus, the current implementation on Linux with heap structure is not scalable as the number of active streams in the system increases. When the stream rate is low (more active streams coexist in the system) or the bandwidth is high compared to the stream rate, the two heaps will be adjusted frequently. Since more time is spent on insertion and selection, there will be further degradation in the throughput as the system is overloaded.

4   IXP Architecture

4.1   IXP Hardware

The IXP (Internet Exchange Processor) 1200 in Figure 2 is a network processor from Intel. The processor consists of a StrongArm core, which functions as a traditional microprocessor. Connected to this core are six microengines (RISCs), which are responsible for managing the network data. Both the Strong Arm core and the six microengines run at the same clock rate (232 MHz). Furthermore, all microengines connect to a high-speed bus (IX bus, 80 MHz) for receiving and transmitting packet data. On the other side of the IX bus are external MAC devices (media access controllers). The MAC devices can be either multi-port 10/100BT Ethernet MAC, Gigabit Ethernet MAC, or ATM MAC. Both the StrongArm core and the microengines can access all of the address space of the SRAM and the SDRAM.

4.2   Pipelined Processing

There are two choices in assigning microengines (µEs) to tasks. One is to duplicate the functionality of each µE, so that all µEs work in the same way to service the ports in a round robin fashion. The second choice is to assign the microengines with different tasks, so that each of them can work on one job. The second choice allows threads in different microengines to be chained to form a processing pipeline.

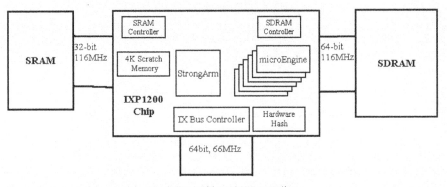

Figure 2: Block Diagram of IXP network processor

5   Hierarchically Indexed Linear Queue (HILQ) – Data Structure and System Design

5.1   Drawbacks of the Heap Structure

The current Linux implementation of DWCS has many drawbacks that make it unsuitable for network processors:

(i) The heap needs many memory operations. Selection and insertion each require $O(\log(n))$ time. In the worst case, when every stream may have packets that missed deadlines, $O(n\log(n))$ time will be needed to delete and rearrange the heap.

(ii) The loss-tolerance heap will potentially become a bottleneck when packet insertion, packet dropping and packet selection happen concurrently. Introducing locks on the loss-tolerance heap will further degrade the performance.

(iii) A centralized scheduler will surely become a bottleneck even with a small number of streams (5-10). To maintain Gigabit speed, a centralized scheduler should have a scheduling period within 500 – 600 microengine cycles (microengine runs at about 232MHz).

5.2   Assumptions

Several assumptions influence the HILQ data structure's design and implementation. They are as follows:

(i) The IXP network processor can have very large off-chip memories, and a well-established memory hierarchy from scratchpad to SRAM, to SDRAM and it offers specific hardware for hash operations, freelists, memory locks, etc. So, a well-established data structure may benefit from this architecture.

(ii) We choose a video/audio unified traffic, where the intervals between frames are in the range of tens to at most one hundred milli-seconds. In other words, the packet rate is as low as 20 – 60 packets/second for each stream. However, the number of streams can be extremely large (hundreds to thousands of streams). This paper addresses scalability in number of streams, but current implementation avoids the need of frame fragmentation and reassembly by scheduling MAC-layer packets.

(iii) Our implementation deals with systems that are not overloaded, where the average stay time or the average delay time for each packet (including queuing time and processing time) is much less than the packet inter-arrival time, i.e. when the input and output packet rates are balanced.

5.3   Data Structures

Previous researches on priority queues [13][14][16][17] used *heap* or *calendar queue* data structures. Calendar queues have a good average performance, especially when the queue is sparse. Our design can be thought of as calendar queue-like, since the "hash function" is not arbitrarily defined but based on the deadline and loss-tolerance. To search for the next packet to be sent, we traverse the queue linearly.

Figure 3 shows the overall data structure—the Hierarchically Indexed Linear Queue (HILQ). Level 0 is a continuous queue divided equally into 100 segments. Each segment represents one milli-second, i.e. all the packets with deadline in this milli-second are stored into the segment accordingly. Currently, 100 milli-seconds (segments) are included, which means we only look forward for this amount of time. 100 milli-second is sufficient for stream data, where inter-arrival times are typically much smaller. Also notice that the segments are organized as a circular queue, in a sense that it will loop back after segment 99. The transmission microengine will work on the current milli-second segment and then go forward to the next milli-second segment when all packets in the current segment have been serviced. The receiving engine will put the packets directly into the queue according to their deadlines. For packets with deadline 100 milli-seconds in the future, this structure will cause problems. For example, if the current time is 100.050s, the transmission engine will work on segment 50. For a packet with a deadline of 101.020s, it will be put into segment 20. The transmission engine proceeds linearly till segment 99 and then loops back to segment 0. It will reach segment 20 at time 101.20s. If we insert a packet with a deadline of 101.60s, then it will be erroneously put into segment 60, i.e. it will be processed at time 100.60s. Thus, our implementation does not support arbitrarily disordered streams.

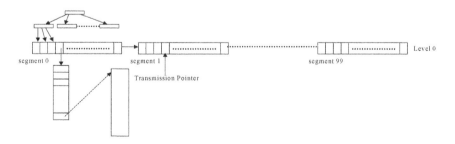

Figure 3: Hierarchically Indexed Linear Queue

Within each segment, a number of slots are created which is actually a mapping from the values of x and y. Figure 4 shows the structure inside each segment. First, to avoid the calculation of x/y, an x/y table is used to retrieve the value of x/y via a single memory operation. The size of the table depends on the ranges of permitted x and y values. The current implementation uses 50 distinct values in the x/y table. These 50 values are from 0 to 1 with a step of 0.02. Each x/y value is rounded to the nearest one among these 50 predetermined values. In other words, we may have up to 0.01 inaccuracy during the round off. We consider this amount of inaccuracy tolerable in practice. In our experiments, x can have an integer value between 0 and 19; y can have an integer value from 0 to 29.

Figure 4 shows the 1000 slots and the interpretation of each slot. Slots are ordered based on Table 1. The slots with smaller indices will be serviced earlier since they have higher precedence. If x/y values are identical, slots are ordered again by the value of x, the numerator. So, 20 slots for each of the 50 x/y values are added to the queue. Therefore, a total of 1000 slots are needed for each milli-second. Till this point, we have considered the precedence of x/y and x.

However, it is still possible that packets with the same values of x/y and x fall into the same milli-second interval. In reality, this happens when streams are quite regular. We also observe that streams tend to cluster around several x/y values as x/y values are adjusted during the transmission of streams. This requests the existence of an element queue (a FIFO queue) for each slot. Actually, each slot currently contains information (header pointer and element number) about the element queue if there are packets in this slot. Multiple packets belonging to the same slot will be ordered by their arrival times and placed into appropriate queue position.

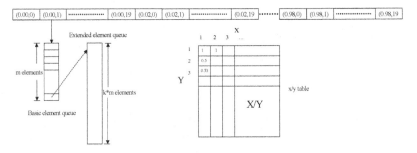

Figure 4: Elements inside a Segment

All three precedences have been taken into account in HILQ. To avoid frequent memory reallocation, there are two kinds of element queues for each slot, a basic element queue and an extended element queue. The basic element queue is created for a fixed number of packets, while the extended element queue is used only when the basic element queue is not large enough. Statistically, the extended element queue is rarely used. The two element queue structures can reduce memory needs while still providing enough support in the worst case. Memory usage is partly static and partly dynamic. The segments for each milli-second are allocated statically, whereas element queues (basic and extended) are dynamic data structures, which can be allocated on demand and released by the garbage collector.

5.4   Pipeline Stages

The microengines are assigned three kinds of functionality—receiving, scheduling and garbage collection. They all operate on the shared HILQ data structure, while the element queues reside in the IXP SRAM for low memory access latency. We develop microcode component for each functionality and assign them to different threads to form a processing pipeline.

5.4.1   Receiving Threads

When the network processor receives a packet, admission control will first check whether to accept it. Dropping packets by admission control is a violation of the DWCS rules. It can only happen when the system is running out of memory, which may occur when the system is overloaded.

Receiving threads also do some common processing on the packet header like modification to the protocol fields, etc. After that, the pointer to the packet is inserted into a proper place in the queue. In DWCS, three property values are used to direct the packet insertion—D(deadline), x and y. Suppose the current time is T_{now}(in milli-seconds), then the packet should be put into the segment with number $(T_{now}+D)\%100$. Then we will look up the value of x/y in the x/y table. In fact, the table stores the index number to the position inside the segment. Let the function LOOKUP do the mapping of the x/y table. We will insert the packet pointer into the element queue at the place LOOKUP(x/y)+x inside the segment.

If the packet is the first one in a slot, a new basic element queue is allocated from the freelist. If the basic element queue is full at the time a new packet is inserted, an extended element queue is allocated from the freelist.

5.4.2   Scheduling Thread

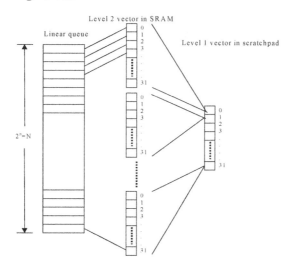

Figure 5: The Hierarchical Index Queue

The scheduling thread first works on the current milli-second segment and tries to send out all the waiting packets in this segment. The scheduling thread traverses the segment linearly. Certainly, there will not be any new packets put into the segment when the scheduling thread is working on it. Therefore, the search is unidirectional. We can also make use of the hierarchical index to skip empty positions quickly. When a packet is encountered, the scheduling thread will remove it from the queue, which includes resetting the pointer and releasing the element queue if needed. The x, y values of that stream should also be adjusted.

After servicing the packets in the current milli-second segment, according to the DWCS algorithm, we should go forward to send the packets in the future segments (we should not wait in the current segment, otherwise the computation power is wasted). However, the future segments are dynamically changing, when new packets are inserted into their deadline slots. We cannot simply search forward. If a new packet belongs to an earlier place than the current search position, the scheduling thread has to go back and send it. Note that this will not degrade performance because when time for the next segment comes, the scheduling thread will move to the next segment immediately. All the packets before the next segment will be dropped.

Figure 5 shows a two level hierarchical indexed queue that can further reduce search time ($n=10$, $N=2^n=1024$). The level-one vector is a longword (4 bytes) in the scratchpad (on-chip) memory. The level two vectors are 32 longwords in the SRAM. Each bit of the level-two vector corresponds to an element in the queue. Each bit in the level-one vector corresponds to a longword in the level-two vector. To search out the next element with a packet, it requires only two memory reads.

5.4.3   Garbage Collection Thread

The garbage collector is called every time the scheduler has moved to the next milli-second segment. It searches the processed milli-second segment, drops all packets in the segment, and adjusts the x/y values for the streams with dropped packets. Separate threads are used for garbage collection. Since scheduling and receiving threads will not work on the same data location as the garbage collector, we are sacrificing the accuracy of the DWCS algorithm. This is because, at the time garbage collector begins to work but packet-dropping has not been completed, the receiving threads are still using the old x/y values of the streams (those x, y values may be modified if packets are dropped by the garbage collector). The garbage collector can work extremely fast under light overload (a small number of packets are dropped), thus limiting the inaccuracy to a small range. When the system is under heavy load, packets will not be admitted by the receiving threads, automatically constraining potential inaccuracies.

6   Performance Evaluation and Analysis

We have implemented the HILQ algorithm with microcode. All experiments are conducted on the Intel-provided simulation environment—IXP1200 Developer Benchmark 2.0. The IXP1200 workbench supports two microcode testing modes, simulation and real hardware. The user's microcode program can be tested in either of these two modes. It is capable of simulating most IXP devices and microengines with high fidelity. It also has a cycle accurate IX bus model that can simulate receiving and sending traffic data. We want to demonstrate that our HILQ based DWCS performs well with high-speed connections like Gigabit Ethernet. All the experiments are simulated in the workbench with a SRAM configuration of 8MB and SDRAM configuration of 64MB.

To get an idea of how costly the SRAM operations are, we collected the data in Table 2 to show the distribution of one SRAM operation. We can observe from the figure that most of the SRAM operations need about 20 cycles to complete.

Table 2: Latency Distribution for SRAM Access (cycles)

Cycles of SRAM Access	19	21	23	25	27	29	31	33
Percentage of SRAM Access	64.7	10.3	8.7	7.5	2.9	2.4	1.9	1.0

In Table 3, we compare the number of memory accesses required in our algorithm with that of a simple heap-based implementation. It takes only one SRAM access for a heap-based scheduler to find out the next packet to be sent. However, maintaining the heap requires O(logn) steps, and there are two heaps in the original DWCS implementation. Each step of heap reorganization requires six SRAM accesses. HILQ minimizes the number of SRAM accesses as compared to the heap-based DWCS implementation. The number of SRAM accesses per stream is close to a constant for HILQ, while it increases logarithmically with the number of active streams for the heap-based DWCS. As shown in Table 3, SRAM access is expensive. Combining results in Table 3, we can conclude that a simple heap-based DWCS would not scale as well as the HILQ for a large number of streams.

Table 3: Memory Operation Comparison for Different Number of Streams

No. of streams		10	50	100	200	500	1000	2000
Memory	Heap	45.86	73.73	85.73	97.73	113.59	125.59	137.58
access#	HILQ	19.8	14.36	13.68	13.34	13.135	13.068	13.034

We test the scalability of the HILQ-based scheduler in simulation. There are two sets of tests, one without input packet traffic, and the other with input/output packet traffic. The objective of the first testing is to chart the actual scheduling overhead under different numbers of active streams. To obtain a large number of active streams, we use a separate microengine to generate a variety of pseudo-streams. In total, there are two microengines in use: one sends stream scheduling requests and the other runs the HILQ scheduler. Figure 6 shows the scheduling delay per active stream as we vary the number of active streams. It indicates that our HILQ-based DWCS scales well for a large number of active streams. As the number of streams increases, the average scheduling delay per active stream approaches 500 cycles/per stream. Readers may notice the high scheduling delay when the number of active streams is small (below 20). This is caused by a fixed amount of overhead in our HILQ scheduler. The scheduler has to read and check all indexes during a segment sweep even when there are only few active streams. Secondly, we want to show that the HILQ scheduler can actually produce high data throughput. Traffic is fed into the Developer Benchmark through a packet generator. We can adjust the packet speed and the number of streams through the packet generator and the configuration option in the simulator.

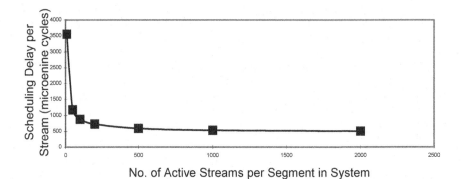

Figure 6: Scalability - No. of Active Streams vs. Average Scheduling Delay

We linked our HILQ scheduler with microcode that performs packet receiving and transmission. There are two microengines, which run the receiver code that pulls packets from a Gigabit Ethernet port, and two other microengines run the transmission code that sends packets to another Gigabit Ethernet port. One more microengine is used for the HILQ scheduler. The receiver thread pulls each packet from the wire and puts it into the scheduler queue. The HILQ scheduler scans each segment linearly and sends out the waiting packets to an output queue. The transmission thread reads from the output queue and puts the packet on the wire. To sustain a certain data rate, the scheduler has to complete a packet scheduling cycle within a time limit. Figure 7 shows the throughput vs. the scheduling cycle for different sizes of packets. The figure indicates that large packets allow a higher time budget for a packet scheduler. When the packet size is 1K, a packet scheduler with about 900 cycle scheduling overhead is still capable of supporting a Gigabit data link. However, for small packet size like 128 bytes and 256 bytes, throughput starts to drop even with small scheduling overhead.

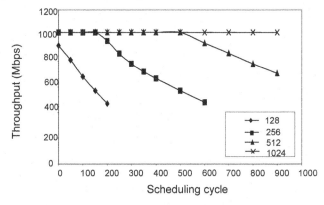

Figure 7: Throughput vs. Scheduling Cycles for Different Packet Sizes

One interesting result concerns the 512-byte packet size. There is about a 600 cycles time-budget for a packet scheduler to sustain a Gigabit link with a packet size of 512 bytes. This means that any packet scheduler that can schedule a packet in less than 600 cycles will not have a negative impact on the data rate. Since our HILQ has a limit of about 500 cycles, we anticipate that it should be capable of supporting Gigabit throughput for streams whose packet size are equal to or above 512 bytes. In Figure 8, the results indicate that with our HILQ implementation, the DWCS QoS scheduler is capable of supporting a Gigabit data link when the packet size is 512 bytes. For smaller size packets such as 256 bytes, the throughput is about 650MB/ps. This result is consistent with the scheduler time budget shown in Figure 7. For 512-byte packets, the scheduler is able to schedule about 260,000 packets per second. If each stream has only about 40 – 60 packets per second, our HILQ scheduler would be able to support about 4,000 – 6,000 streams. Note: Figures 6 and 7 refer to the number of active streams.

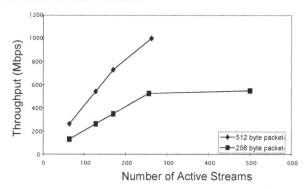

Figure 8: Throughput vs. No. of Active Streams for Different Sizes of Packets

The last result compares our DWCS approximation with the original DWCS. The single most important metric for evaluation is window constraint violation. Theoretically, DWCS does not have any loss tolerance violation when the bandwidth utilization factor is below 1.0 [2]. According to [2], the bandwidth utilization factor is computed as U = sum$((1-W_i)C_i/T_i)$, i = 1,2,…, n, where $W_i = x_i/y_i$, and C_i is the amount of time required to serve a packet of stream i and T_i is the request period of stream i. However, when U exceeds 1.0, there will be window constraint violations. Results in Figure 9 show that our DWCS approximation does not create more window constraint violations than the heap-based implementation when U exceeds 1.0. The results are collected from a simulation having 200 streams. Each stream starts with a random $W_i = x_i/y_i$ lying between 0.2 and 0.8. The range of x is 0 to 19 and the range of y is 0 to 29.

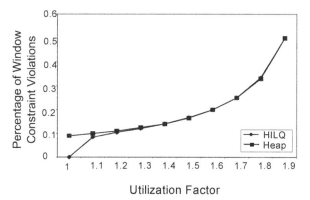

Figure 9: Comparison between HILQ and Heap Based Implementation under Different Utilization Factors

7   Conclusion

This paper proposes a fast algorithm to implement a multimedia stream scheduler on the IXP Network Processor. A data structure called Hierarchically Indexed Linear Queue meets the requirements of Gigabit speeds by exploiting certain architectural attributes. High performance is gained by integrating send/receive and garbage collection threads.

Our implementation can achieve O(1) packet insertion and selection time by hierarchically indexing a sparse queue and separation of the garbage collection threads. Although our design incurs a small amount of inaccuracy with regard to the standard DWCS specification, the inaccuracies are shown to be tolerable. Our performance results strongly support the benefits of HILQ by serving up to thousands of streams at Gigabit speeds.

8   References

[1] Richard West and Karsten Schwan, "Dynamic Window-Constrained Scheduling for Multimedia Applications," in *Proceedings of the IEEE International Conference on Multimedia Computing and Systems (ICMCS)*, 1999.

[2] Richard West and Christian Poellabauer, "Analysis of a Window-Constrained Scheduler for Real-Time and Best-Effort Packet Streams," in *Proceedings of the 21st IEEE Real-Time Systems Symposium (RTSS)*, 2000.

[3] Richard West, Karsten Schwan and Christian Poellabauer, "Scalable Scheduling Support for Loss and Delay Constrained Media Streams", in *Proceedings of the 5th IEEE Real-Time Technology and Applications Symposium (RTAS)*, 1999.

[4] C. Liu and J. Layland. "Scheduling Algorithms for Multiprogramming in a Hard-Real-Time Environment," *Journal of ACM, 20(1)*, January 1973.

[5] P.Goyal, H.Vin, and H.Cheng, "Start-time fair queueing: A scheduling algorithm for integrated services packet switching networks," in *IEEE SIGCOMM'96*, IEEE,1996.

[6] K. Parekh. "A Generalized Processor Sharing Approach to Flow Control in Integrated Services Networks," *PhDthesis*, Department of Electrical Engineering and Computer Science, MIT, February 1992.

[7] "IXP 1200 Network Processor: Software Reference Manual", Part No. 278306-005. Sep. 2000.

[8] "IXP 1200 Network Processor: Programmer's Reference Manual", Part No. 278304-006. Sep. 2000.

[9] "IXP 1200 Network Processor: Development Tools User's Guide", Part No. 278302-005. Oct. 2000.

[10] P.Crowley, M.E.Fiuczynski, J.Baer, B.N.Bershad, "Characterizing processor architectures for Programmable Network Interfacess," *Proceedings of the 2000 International Conference on Supercomputing*, pp.54-65, May. 2000.

[11] Tammo Spalink, Scott Karlin, Larry Peterson, Yitzchak Gottliebln, "Building a Robust Software-Based Router Using Network Processors," *Proceedings of the 18th ACM Symposium on Operating Systems Principles (SOSP'01)* . pages 216--229, Chateau Lake Louise, Banff, Alberta, Canada, October 2001.

[12] Xiaohu Qie, Andy Bavier, Larry Peterson, Scott Karlin "Scheduling Computations on a Software-Based Router," *Proceedings of SIMETRICS 2001*, Jun 2001.

[13] D.C. Stephen, J.C.R.Bennett, H.Zhang, "Implementing scheduling algorithms in high-speed networks", *IEEE Selected Areas in Communications*, pp.1145-1158, Vol 17, No.6, Jun.1999

[14] A. Ioannou, M. Katevenis: "Pipelined Heap (Priority Queue) Management for Advanced Scheduling in High Speed Networks," *Proc. IEEE Int. Conf. on Communications (ICC'2001)*, Helsinki, Finland, June 2001, pp. 2043-2047.

[15] Jun Xu and Mukesh Singhal, "Cost-Effective Flow Table Designs for High-Speed Internet Routers: Architecture and Performance Evaluation," to appear in *IEEE Transactions on Computers*.

[16] Ranjita Bhagwan, Bill Lin "Fast and Scalable Priority Queue Architecture for High-Speed Network Switches," *IEEE INFOCOMM'00*, Tel Aviv, Vol. 2, pages 538-547, March 2000.

[17] R. Brown, "Calendar queues: a fast 0(1) priority queue implementation for the simulation event set problem," *Communications of the ACM*, vol. 31, pp. 1220--1227, October 1988.

[18] K. Bruce Erickson, Richard E. Ladner, Anthony LaMarca, "Optimizing Static Calendar Queues," *IEEE Symposium on* Foundations of Computer Science,1998.

[19] Rajamar Krishnamurthy, Karsten Schwan, and Marcel Rosu, "A Network Co-Processor-Based Approach to Scalable Media Streaming in Servers", *International Conference on Parallel Processing (ICPP)*, August 2000.

Distributed Dynamic Capacity Contracting: A Congestion Pricing Framework for Diff-Serv[*]

Murat Yuksel[1] and Shivkumar Kalyanaraman[2]

[1] CS Department, Rensselaer Polytechnic Institute,
110 8th Street, Troy, NY 12180, USA
yuksem@cs.rpi.edu
[2] ECSE Department, Rensselaer Polytechnic Institute,
110 8th Street, Troy, NY 12180, USA
shivkuma@ecse.rpi.edu

Abstract. In order to provide better Quality-of-Service (QoS) in large networks, several congestion pricing proposals have been made in the last decade. Usually, however, those proposals studied optimal strategies and did not focus on implementation issues. Our main contribution in this paper is to address implementation issues for congestion-sensitive pricing over a single domain of the differentiated-services (diff-serv) architecture of the Internet. We propose a new congestion-sensitive pricing framework Distributed Dynamic Capacity Contracting (Distributed-DCC), which is able to provide a range of fairness (e.g. max-min, proportional) in rate allocation by using pricing as a tool. Within the Distributed-DCC framework, we develop an Edge-to-Edge Pricing Scheme (EEP) and present simulation experiments of it.

1 Introduction

As multimedia applications with extensive traffic loads are becoming more common, better ways of managing network resources are necessary in order to provide sufficient QoS for those multimedia applications. Among several methods to improve QoS in multimedia networks and services, one particular method is to employ congestion pricing. The main idea is to increase service price when network congestion is more, and to decrease the price when congestion is less.

Implementation of congestion pricing still remains a challenge, although several proposals have been made, e.g. [1,2]. Among many others, two major implementation obstacles can be defined: need for *timely feedback* to users about price, determination of *congestion information* in an efficient, low-overhead manner.

The first problem, timely feedback, is relatively very hard to achieve in a large network such as the Internet. In [3], the authors showed that users do need feedback about charging of the network service (such as current price and prediction of service quality in near future). However, in our recent work [4], we illustrated that congestion control through pricing cannot be achieved if price changes are performed at a time-scale larger than roughly 40 round-trip-times (RTTs), which is not possible to implement for many cases. We believe that the

---

[*] This work is sponsored by NSF under contract number ANI9819112, and co-sponsored by Intel Corporation.

K.C. Almeroth and M. Hasan (Eds.): MMNS 2002, LNCS 2496, pp. 198–210, 2002.

problem of timely feedback can be solved by placing intelligent intermediaries (i.e. software or hardware agents) between users and service providers. In this paper, we do not focus on this particular issue and leave development of such intelligent agents for future research.

The second problem, congestion information, is also very hard to do in a way that does not need a major upgrade at network routers. However, in diff-serv [5], it is possible to determine congestion information via a good ingress-egress coordination. So, this flexible environment of diff-serv motivated us to develop a pricing scheme on it.

In our previous work [6], we presented a simple congestion-sensitive pricing "framework", *Dynamic Capacity Contracting (DCC)*, for a single diff-serv domain. DCC treats each edge router as a station of a service provider or a station of coordinating set of service providers. Users (i.e. individuals or other service providers) make *short-term contracts* with the stations for network service. During the contracts, the station receives congestion information about the network core at a time-scale smaller than contracts. The station, then, uses that congestion information to update the service price at the beginning of each contract. Several pricing "schemes" can be implemented in that framework.

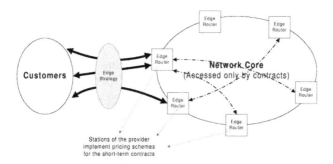

Fig. 1. DCC framework on diff-serv architecture.

DCC models a short-term contract for a given traffic class as a function of price per unit traffic volume P_v, maximum volume V_{max} (maximum number of bytes that can be sent during the contract) and the contract length T:

$$Contract = f(P_v, V_{max}, T) \tag{1}$$

Figure 1 illustrates the big picture of DCC framework. Customers can only access network core by making contracts with the provider stations placed at the edge routers. The stations offer contracts (i.e. V_{max} and T) to fellow users. Access to these available contracts can be done in different ways, what we call *edge strategy*. Two basic edge strategies are "bidding" (many users bids for an available contract) or "contracting" (users negotiate P_v with the provider for an available contract). So, edge strategy is the decision-making mechanism to identify which customer gets an available contract at the provider station.

However, in DCC, we assumed that all the provider stations advertise the same price value for the contracts, which is very costly to implement over a wide area network. This is simply because the price value cannot be communicated to all stations at the beginning of each contract. In this paper, we relax this assumption by letting the stations to calculate the prices locally and advertise different prices than the other stations. We call this new version of DCC as *Distributed-DCC*. We introduce ways of managing the overall coordination of the stations for the common purposes of fairness and stability. We then develop a pricing scheme Edge-to-Edge Pricing (EEP). We illustrate stability of EEP by simulation experiments. We address fairness problems related to pricing, and show that the framework can achieve max-min and proportional fairness by tuning a parameter, called as *fairness coefficient*.

The paper is organized as follows: In the next section, we position our work and briefly survey relevant work in the area. In Section 3 we describe Distributed-DCC framework, and investigate various issues, such as price calculation, fairness, scalability. Next in Section 4, we develop the pricing scheme EEP. In Section 5, we make experimental comparative evaluation of EEP. We finalize with summary and discussions.

2 Related Work

There has been several pricing proposals, which can be classified in many ways such as *static* vs. *dynamic*, *per-packet* charging vs. *per-contract* charging.

Although there are opponents to dynamic pricing in the area (e.g. [7,8]), most of the proposals have been for dynamic pricing (specifically congestion pricing) of networks. Examples of dynamic pricing proposals are MacKie-Mason and Varian's Smart Market [1], Gupta et al.'s Priority Pricing [9], Kelly et al.'s Proportional Fair Pricing (PFP) [10], Semret et al.'s Market Pricing [11], and Wang and Schulzrinne's Resource Negotiation and Pricing (RNAP) [12,2]. Odlyzko's Paris Metro Pricing (PMP) [13] is an example of static pricing proposal. Clark's Expected Capacity [14] and Cocchi et al.'s Edge Pricing [15] allow both static and dynamic pricing. In terms of charging granularity, Smart Market, Priority Pricing, PFP and Edge Pricing employ per-packet charging, whilst RNAP and Expected Capacity do not employ per-packet charging.

Smart Market is based primarily on imposing per-packet congestion prices. Since Smart Market performs pricing on per-packet basis, it operates on the finest possible pricing granularity. This makes Smart Market capable of making ideal congestion pricing. However, Smart Market is not deployable because of its per-packet granularity and its many requirements from routers. In [16], we studied Smart Market and difficulties of its implementation in more detail. While Smart Market holds one extreme in terms of granularity, Expected Capacity holds the other extreme. Expected Capacity proposes to use *long-term* contracts, which can give more clear performance expectation, for statistical capacity allocation and pricing. Prices are updated at the beginning of each long-term contract, which incorporates little dynamism to prices. Our work, Distributed-DCC, is a middle-ground between Smart Market and Expected Capacity in terms of granularity. Distributed-DCC performs congestion pricing at *short-term* contracts, which allows more dynamism in prices while keeping pricing overhead small.

Another close work to ours is RNAP, which also mainly focused on implementation issues of congestion pricing on diff-serv. Although RNAP provides a complete picture for incorporation of admission control and congestion pricing, it has excessive implementation overhead since it requires all network routers to participate in determination of congestion prices. This requires upgrades to all routers similar to the case of Smart Market. Our work solves this problem by requiring upgrades only at edge routers rather than at all routers.

3 Distributed-DCC: The Framework

Distributed-DCC is specifically designed for diff-serv architecture, because the edge routers can perform complex operations which is essential to several requirements for implementation of congestion pricing. Each edge router is treated as a station of the provider. Each station advertises locally computed prices with information received from other stations. The main framework basically describes how to preserve coordination among the stations such that stability and fairness of the overall network is preserved. A *Logical Pricing Server* (LPS) (which can be implemented in a centralized or distributed manner, see Section 3.6) plays a crucial role. Figure 2 illustrates basic functions (which will be better understood in the following sub-sections) of LPS. The following sub-sections investigate several issues regarding the framework.

3.1 How to Calculate p_{ij} ?

Each ingress station i keeps a "current" price vector p_i, where p_{ij} is the price for flow from ingress i to egress j. So, how do we calculate the price-per-flow, p_{ij}? The ingresses make estimation of budget for each edge-to-edge flow passing through themselves. Let $\hat{b}_{ij}$ be the currently *estimated budget* for flow f_{ij} (i.e the flow from ingress i to egress j). The ingresses send estimated budgets to the corresponding egresses (i.e. $\hat{b}_{ij}$ is sent from ingress i to egress j) at a deterministic time-scale. At the other side, the egresses receive budget estimations from all the ingresses, and also they make estimation of capacity $\hat{c}_{ij}$ for each particular flow. In other words, egress j calculates $\hat{c}_{ij}$ and is informed about $\hat{b}_{ij}$ by ingress i. Egress j, then, penalizes or favors f_{ij} by updating its estimated budget value, i.e. $b_{ij} = f(\hat{b}_{ij}, [parameters])$ where $[parameters]$ are optional parameters used for deciding whether to penalize or favor the flow. For example, if f_{ij} is passing through more congested areas than the other flows, egress j can penalize f_{ij} by reducing its budget estimation $\hat{b}_{ij}$.

At *another time-scale*[3], egresses keep sending information to LPS. More specifically, for a diff-serv domain with n edge routers, egress j sends the following information to LPS:

---

[3] Can be larger than ingress-egress time-scale, but should be less than contract length.

1. the *updated budget estimations* of all flows passing through itself, i.e. b_{ij} for $i = 1..n$ and $i \neq j$
2. the *estimated capacities* of all flows passing through itself, i.e. $\hat{c}_{ij}$ for $i = 1..n$ and $i \neq j$

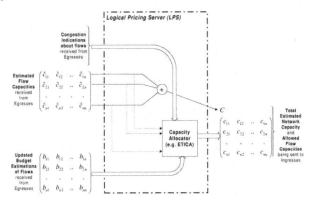

Fig. 2. Major functions of LPS.

LPS receives information from egresses and, for each f_{ij}, calculates *allowed capacity* c_{ij}. Calculation of c_{ij}s is a complicated task which depends on b_{ij}s. In general, the flows should share capacity of the same bottleneck in proportion to their budgets. We will later define a generic algorithm to do capacity allocation task. LPS, then, sends the following information to ingress i:

1. the *total estimated network capacity* C (i.e. $C = \sum_i \sum_j \hat{c}_{ij}$)
2. the allowed capacities to each edge-to-edge flow starting from ingress i, i.e. c_{ij} for $j = 1..n$ and $j \neq i$

Now, the pricing scheme at ingress i can calculate price for each flow by using c_{ij} and $\hat{b}_{ij}$. An example pricing scheme will be described in Section 4.

3.2 Budget Estimation at Ingresses

In order to determine user's real budget The ingress stations perform very trivial operation to estimate budgets of each flow, $\hat{b}_{ij}$. The ingress i basically knows its current price for each flow, p_{ij}. When it receives a packet it just needs to determine which egress station the packet is going to. Given that the ingress station has the addresses of all egress stations of the same diff-serv domain, it can find out which egress the packet is going to. So, by monitoring the packets transmitted for each flow, the ingress can estimate the budget of each flow. Let x_{ij} be the total number of packets transmitted for f_{ij} in unit time, then the budget estimate for f_{ij} is $\hat{b}_{ij} = x_{ij}p_{ij}$. Notice that this operation must be done at the ingress rather than egress, because some of the packets might be dropped before arriving at the egress. This causes x_{ij} to be measured less, and hence causes $\hat{b}_{ij}$ to be less than it is supposed to be.

3.3   Congestion-Based Capacity Estimation at Egresses

The essence of capacity estimation in Distributed-DCC is to decrease the capacity estimation when there is congestion indication(s) and to increase it when there is no congestion indication. This will make the prices *congestion-sensitive*, since the pricing scheme is going to adjust the price according to available capacity. In this sense, several capacity estimation algorithms can be used, e.g. Additive Increase Additive Decrease (AIAD), Additive Increase Multiplicative Decrease (AIMD). We now provide a full description of such an algorithm.

With a simple congestion detection mechanism (such as marking of packets at interior routers when congested), egress stations make a congestion-based estimation of the capacity for the flows passing through themselves. Egress stations divide time into deterministic *observation intervals* and identify each observation interval as *congested* or *non-congested*. Basically, an observation interval is congested if a congestion indication was received during that observation interval. At the end of each observation interval, the egresses update the estimated capacity. Then, egress j calculates the estimated capacity for f_{ij} at the end of observation interval t as follows:

$$\hat{c}_{ij}(t) = \begin{cases} \beta * \mu_{ij}(t), \ congested \\ \hat{c}_{ij}(t-1) + \triangle\hat{c}, \ non\text{-}congested \end{cases}$$

where β is in (0,1), $\mu_{ij}(t)$ is the measured output rate of f_{ij} during observation interval t, and $\triangle\hat{c}$ is a pre-defined increase parameter. This algorithm is a variant of well-known AIMD.

3.4   Capacity Allocation to Edge-to-Edge Flows

LPS is supposed to allocate the total estimated network capacity C to edge-to-edge flows in such a way that the flows passing through the same bottleneck should share the bottleneck capacity in proportion to their budgets, and also the flows that are not competing with other flows should get all the available capacity on their route. The complicated issue is to do this without knowledge of the topology for network core. We now propose a simple and generic algorithm to perform this centralized rate allocation within Distributed-DCC framework.

First, at LPS, we introduce a new information about each edge-to-edge flow f_{ij}. A flow f_{ij} is *congested*, if egress j has been receiving congestion indications from that flow recently (we will later define what "recent" is).

At LPS, let K_{ij} determine whether f_{ij} is congested or not. If $K_{ij} > 0$, LPS determines f_{ij} as congested. If not, it determines f_{ij} as non-congested. Let's call the time-scale at which LPS and egresses communicate as *LPS interval*. At every LPS interval t, LPS calculates K_{ij} as follows:

$$K_{ij}(t) = \begin{cases} \hat{k}, \ f_{ij} \ was \ congested \ at \ t-1 \\ max(0, K_{ij}(t-1) - 1), \ f_{ij} \ was \ non\text{-}congested \ at \ t-1 \end{cases} \quad (2)$$

where $\hat{k}$ is a positive integer. Notice that $\hat{k}$ parameter defines how long a flow will stay in "congested" state after the last congestion indication. So, $\hat{k}$ defines the time-line to determine if a congestion indication is "recent" or not. Note that instead of setting K_{ij} to $\hat{k}$ at every congestion indication, several different methods can be used for this purpose, but we proceed with the method in (2).

Given the above method to determine whether a flow is congested or not, we now describe the algorithm to allocate capacity to the flows. Let F be the set of all edge-to-edge flows in the diff-serv domain, and F_c be the set of *congested* edge-to-edge flows. Let C_c be the accumulation of $\hat{c}_{ij}$s where $f_{ij} \in F_c$. Further, let B_c be the accumulation of b_{ij}s where $f_{ij} \in F_c$. Then, LPS calculates the allowed capacity for f_{ij} as follows:

$$c_{ij} = \begin{cases} \frac{b_{ij}}{B_c}C_c, & K_{ij} > 0 \\ \hat{c}_{ij}, & otherwise \end{cases}$$

The intuition is that if a flow is congested, then it must be competing with other congested flows. So, a congested flow is allowed a capacity in proportion to its budget relative to budgets of all congested flows. Since we assume no knowledge about the interior topology, we *approximate* the situation by considering these congested flows as if they are traversing a single bottleneck. If knowledge about the interior topology is provided, one can easily develop better algorithms by sub-grouping the congested flows that are passing through the same bottleneck. If a flow is not congested, then it is allowed to use its own estimated capacity, which will give enough freedom to utilize capacity available to that flow.

3.5   Fairness

We examine the issues regarding fairness in two main cases:

- *Single-bottleneck case:* The pricing protocol should charge *same price to users of same bottleneck*. In this way, among users of same bottleneck, the ones with more budget will be given more capacity. The intuition behind this reasoning is that the cost of providing capacity to each customer is the same.
- *Multi-bottleneck case:* The pricing protocol should *charge more to users whose traffic traverses more bottlenecks* and causes more costs. So, other than proportionality to user budgets, we also want to allocate less capacity to users whose flows are traversing more bottlenecks than the others. For multi-bottleneck networks, two main types of fairness have been defined: max-min, proportional [10]. In max-min fairness, flows get equal share of bottlenecks, while in proportional fairness flows get penalized according to number of bottlenecks they traverse. Depending on cost structure and user utilities, provider may want to choose max-min or proportional fairness. So, we would like to have ability of tuning pricing protocol such that fairness of its rate allocation is in the way provider wants.

To achieve the above fairness objectives in Distributed-DCC, we introduce new parameters for tuning rate allocation to flows. In order to penalize f_{ij}, egress j can reduce $\hat{b}_{ij}$, which causes decrease in c_{ij}. It uses following function:

$$b_{ij} = f(\hat{b}_{ij}, r(t), \alpha, r_{min}) = \frac{\hat{b}_{ij}}{r_{min} + (r_{ij}(t) - r_{min}) * \alpha}$$

where $r_{ij}(t)$ is the estimated congestion cost caused by f_{ij}, r_{min} is the minimum possible congestion cost, and α is *fairness coefficient*. Instead of $\hat{b}_{ij}$, the egress j now sends b_{ij} to LPS. When α is 0, Distributed-DCC is employing max-min fairness. As it gets larger, the flow gets penalized more and rate allocation gets closer to proportional fairness. However, if it is too large, then the rate allocation will get away from proportional fairness. Let α^* be the α value where the rate allocation is proportionally fair. If the estimation $r_{ij}(t)$ is accurate, then $\alpha^* = 1$.

Assuming that severity of each bottleneck is the same, we can directly use the number of bottlenecks f_{ij} is traversing in order to calculate $r_{ij}(t)$ and r_{min}. In such a case, r_{min} will be 1 and $r_{ij}(t)$ should be number of bottlenecks the flow is passing through. If the interior nodes increment a header field of the packets at the time of congestion, then the egress station can estimate the number of bottlenecks the flow is traversing. We skip description of such an estimation algorithm to keep reader's focus on major issues.

3.6   Scalability

There are mainly two issues regarding scalability: LPS, the number of flows. First of all, the flows are not per-connection basis, i.e. all the traffic going from edge router i to j is counted as only one flow. This actually relieves the scaling of operations happening on per-flow basis. The number of flows in the system will be $n(n-1)$ where n is the number of edge routers in the diff-serv domain. So, indeed, scalability of the flows is not a problem for the current Internet since number of edge routers for a single diff-serv domain is very small.

LPS can be scaled in two ways. First idea is to implement LPS in a fully distributed manner. Edge stations exchange information with each other (like link-state routing). Basically, each station sends total of $n-1$ messages to other stations. So, this will increase overhead on network because of the extra messages, i.e. complexity will increase from $O(n)$ to $O(n^2)$ in terms of number of messages.

Alternatively, LPS can be divided into multiple local LPSs which synchronize among themselves to maintain consistency. This way the complexity of number of messages will reduce. However, this will be at a cost of some optimality again.

4   Edge-to-Edge Pricing Scheme (EEP)

For flow f_{ij}, Distributed-DCC framework provides an allowed capacity c_{ij} and an estimation of total user budget $\hat{b}_{ij}$ at ingress i. So, the provider station at ingress i can use these two information to calculate price. We propose a simple price formula to balance supply c_{ij} and demand $\hat{b}_{ij}$:

$$p_{ij} = \frac{\hat{b}_{ij}}{c_{ij}} \tag{3}$$

Also, the ingress i uses the total estimated network capacity C in calculating the V_{max} contract parameter defined in (1). A simple method for calculating

V_{max} is $V_{max} = C * T$ where T is the contract length. This allows all the available capacity to be contracted by a single flow, which is a loose admission control. More conservative admission control should be used to calculate V_{max}.

We now prove optimality of (3) for a single-bottleneck network. We skip the proof for a multi-bottleneck network for space considerations. We model user i's utility with the well-known [4] [10] function $u_i(x) = w_i log(x)$, where x is bandwidth given to the user and w_i is user i's budget (i.e. willingness-to-pay). Suppose p_i is the price advertised to user i. Then, user i will maximize his surplus S_i by contracting for $x_i = w_i/p_i$.

So, the provider can now figure out what price to advertise to each user by maximizing the social welfare $W = S + R$, where R is the provider revenue. Let $K(x) = kx$ be a linear function and be the cost of providing x amount of capacity to a user, where k is a positive constant. Then social welfare will be:

$$W = \sum_{i=1}^{n} [u_i(x_i) - kx_i]$$

We maximize W subject to $\sum_i x_i \leq C$, where C is the total available capacity. To maximize W, all the available capacity must be given to users since they have strictly increasing utility. Lagrangian and its solution for that system will be:

$$W = \sum_{i=1}^{n} u_i(x_i) - kx_i + \lambda(\sum_{i=1}^{n} x_i - C)$$
$$x_j = \frac{w_j}{\sum_{i=1}^{n} w_i} C, \quad j = 1..n \tag{4}$$

This result shows that welfare maximization of the described system can be done by allocating capacity to the users proportional to their budget, w_i, relative to total user budget. Since the user will contract for $x_i = w_i/p_i$ when advertised a price of p_i, then the optimum price for provider to advertise (i.e. p^*) can be calculated as follows:

$$p^* = p_i = \frac{\sum_{i=1}^{n} w_i}{C}$$

i.e. ratio of total budget to available capacity. So, provider should charge same price to users of same bottleneck route. EEP does that for an edge-to-edge route.

5   Simulation Experiments and Results

We present ns [17] simulation experiments of EEP on single-bottleneck and multi-bottleneck topology. Our goals are to illustrate fairness and stability properties of the framework. The single-bottleneck topology is shown in Figure 3-a and the multi-bottleneck topology is shown in Figure 3-b. The white nodes are edge nodes and the gray nodes are interior nodes. To ease understanding

---

[4] Wang and Schulzrinne introduced a more complex version in [12].

the experiments, each user sends its traffic to a separate egress. For the multi-bottleneck topology, one user sends through all the bottlenecks (i.e. long flow), crossed by the others. Bottleneck links have a capacity of 10Mb/s and all other links have 15Mb/s. Propagation delay on each link is 5ms, and users send UDP traffic with an average packet size of 1000B. Interior nodes mark the packets when local queue exceeds 30 packets. In the multi-bottleneck topology they increment a header field instead of just marking. Buffer size is assumed infinite.

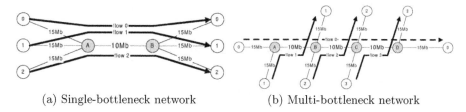

(a) Single-bottleneck network   (b) Multi-bottleneck network

Fig. 3. Topologies for Distributed-DCC experiments.

Each user flow maximizes its surplus by contracting for b/p amount of capacity, where b is its budget and p is price. b is randomized according to truncated-Normal distribution with mean b. We will refer to this mean b as flow's budget.

Ingresses send budget estimations to egresses at every *observation interval*. LPS sends information to ingresses at every *LPS interval*. Contracting takes place at every 4s, observation interval is 0.8s, and LPS interval is 0.16s. The parameter $\hat{k}$ is set to 25 (see Section 3.4). $\triangle\hat{c}$ is set to 1 packet (i.e. 1000B), the initial value of $\hat{c}_{ij}$ for each flow f_{ij} is set to 0.1Mb/s, and β is set to 0.95.

5.1   Experiment on Single-bottleneck Topology

We run a simulation experiment for EEP on the single-bottleneck topology, which is represented in Figure 3-a. There are 3 users with budgets of 10, 20, 30 respectively for users 1, 2, 3. Total simulation time is 15000s. Initially, only user 1 is active and after every 5000s one of the other users gets active.

Figure 4-a shows the flow rates averaged over 200 contract periods. We see the flows are sharing the bottleneck capacity almost in proportion to their budgets. The distortion in rate allocation is caused because of the assumptions that the generic edge-to-edge capacity allocation algorithm makes (see Section 3.4). Also, Figure 4-b shows the average prices charged to flows over 200 contract periods. As new users join in, EEP increases the price for balancing supply and demand.

Figure 4-c shows the bottleneck queue size. Notice that queue sizes make peaks transiently at the times when new users gets active. Otherwise, the queue size is controlled reasonably and the system is stable. The reason behind the transient peaks is that the parameter V_{max} is not restricted which causes the newly joining flow to contract for a lot more than the available capacity.

Also, average utilization of the bottleneck link was more than 90%.

5.2   Experiments on Multi-bottleneck Topology

On a multi-bottleneck network, we would like illustrate two properties:

– *Property 1:* provision of various fairness in rate allocation by changing the fairness coefficient α (see Section 3.5)
– *Property 2:* adaptiveness of capacity allocation algorithm (see Section 3.4)

In order to illustrate Property 1, we run a series of experiments for EEP with different α values. We use a larger version of the topology represented in Figure 3-b. In the multi-bottleneck topology there are 10 users and 9 bottleneck links. Total simulation time is 10,000s. Initially, the long flow is active. After each 1000s, one of the other cross flows gets active. So, as the time passes the number of bottlenecks in the system increases. We are interested in the long flow's rate, since it is the one that cause more congestion costs than the other flows.

Figure 4-d shows average rate of the long flow versus number of bottlenecks in the system. As expected, the long flow gets lesser capacity as α increases. When $\alpha = 0$, rate allocation to flows is max-min fair. Observe that when $\alpha = 1$, rate allocation follows the proportionally fair rate allocation. This variation in fairness is basically achieved by advertisement of different prices to the flows. Figure 4-e shows the average price that is advertised to the long flow as number of bottlenecks in the system increases. We can see that the price advertised to the long flow increases as number of bottlenecks increases. As α increases, framework becomes more responsive to the long flow by increasing its price more sharply.

Finally, to illustrate Property 2, we ran an experiment on the topology in Figure 3-b with small changes. We increased capacity of the bottleneck at node D from 10 Mb/s to 15Mb/s. Initially, all the flows have equal budget of 10 units. Total simulation time is 30000s. Between times 10000 and 20000, budget of flow 1 is temporarily increased to 20 units. α is set to 0. All the other parameters are exactly the same as in the single-bottleneck experiments of the previous section.

Figure 4-f shows the given volumes averaged over 200 contracting periods. Until time 10000s, flows 0, 1, and 2 share the bottleneck capacities equally presenting a max-min fair allocation because α is 0. However, flow 3's rate is larger, because bottleneck node D has extra capacity. This is achieved by the freedom given to individual flows by the capacity allocation algorithm (see Section 3.4).

Between times 10000 and 20000, flow 2 gets a step increase in its rate because of the step increase in its budget. In result of this, flow 0 gets a step decrease in its volume. Also, flows 2 and 3 adapt themselves to the new situation, trying to utilize the extra capacity leftover from the reduction in flow 0's rate. So, flows 2 and 3 get a step decrease in their rates. After time 20000, flows restore to their original rates, illustrating adaptiveness of the framework.

6   Summary

In this paper, we presented a new framework, Distributed-DCC, for congestion pricing in a single diff-serv domain. Distributed-DCC can provide a contracting framework based on *short-term* contracts between multimedia (or any other elastic, adaptive) application and the service provider. Contracting improves QoS if appropriate admission control and provisioning techniques are used. In this paper, we focused on pricing issues.

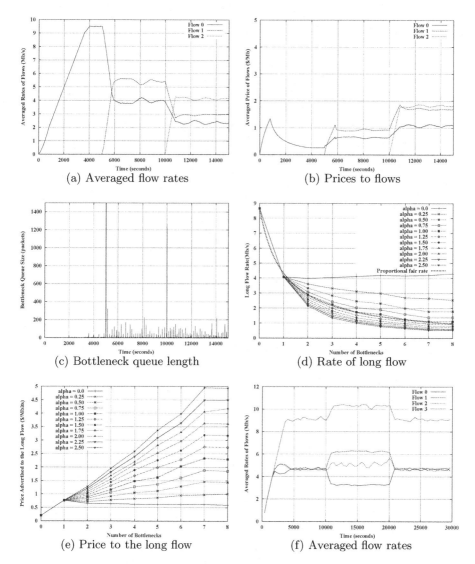

Fig. 4. (a)-(c): Results of single-bottleneck experiment for EEP. (d)-(f): Results of EEP experiments on multi-bottleneck topology.

Main contribution of the paper is to develop an *easy-to-implement* congestion pricing architecture which provides flexibility in rate allocation. We investigated fairness issues within Distributed-DCC and illustrated ways of achieving a *range of fairness types* (i.e. from max-min to proportional) through congestion pricing under certain conditions. The fact that it is possible to achieve various fairness types within a single framework is very encouraging. We also developed a pricing scheme, EEP, within the Distributed-DCC framework, and presented several simulation experiments. Future work should include investigation of issues related to Distributed-DCC on multiple diff-serv domains. Also, the framework should be supported by admission control techniques which will tune the contract parameter V_{max} and address minimum QoS settings in SLAs.

References

1. J. K. MacKie-Mason and H. R. Varian, *Pricing the Internet*, Kahin, Brian and Keller, James, 1993. 198, 200
2. X. Wang and H. Schulzrinne, "An integrated resource negotiation, pricing, and QoS adaptation framework for multimedia applications," *IEEE Journal of Selected Areas in Communications*, vol. 18, 2000. 198, 200
3. A. Bouch and M. A. Sasse, "Why value is everything?: A user-centered approach to Internet quality of service and pricing," in *Proceedings of IWQoS*, 2001. 198
4. M. Yuksel, S. Kalyanaraman, and B. Sikdar, "Effect of pricing intervals on congestion-sensitivity of network service prices," Tech. Rep. ECSE-NET-2002-1, Rensselaer Polytechnic Institute, ECSE Networks Lab, 2002. 198
5. S. Blake et. al, "An architecture for Differentiated Services," *RFC 2475*, 1998. 199
6. R. Singh, M. Yuksel, S. Kalyanaraman, and T. Ravichandran, "A comparative evaluation of Internet pricing models: Smart market and dynamic capacity contracting," in *Proceedings of Workshop on Information Technologies and Systems (WITS)*, 2000. 199
7. A. M. Odlyzko, "Internet pricing and history of communications," Tech. Rep., AT & T Labs, 2000. 200
8. I. Ch. Paschalidis and J. N. Tsitsiklis, "Congestion-dependent pricing of network services," *IEEE/ACM Transactions on Networking*, vol. 8, no. 2, 2000. 200
9. A. Gupta, D. O. Stahl, and A. B. Whinston, *Priority pricing of Integrated Services networks*, Eds McKnight and Bailey, MIT Press, 1997. 200
10. F. P. Kelly, A. K. Maulloo, and D. K. H. Tan, "Rate control in communication networks: Shadow prices, proportional fairness and stability," *Journal of Operations Research Society*, vol. 49, pp. 237–252, 1998. 200, 204, 206
11. N. Semret, R. R.-F. Liao, A. T. Campbell, and A. A. Lazar, "Market pricing of differentiated Internet services," in *Proceedings of IWQoS*, 1999, pp. 184–193. 200
12. X. Wang and H. Schulzrinne, "Pricing network resources for adaptive applications in a Differentiated Services network," in *Proceedings of INFOCOM*, 2001. 200, 206
13. A. M. Odlyzko, "A modest proposal for preventing Internet congestion," Tech. Rep., AT & T Labs, 1997. 200
14. D. Clark, *Internet cost allocation and pricing*, Eds McKnight and Bailey, MIT Press, 1997. 200
15. R. Cocchi, S. Shenker, D. Estrin, and L. Zhang, "Pricing in computer networks: Motivation, formulation and example," *IEEE/ACM Transactions on Networking*, vol. 1, December 1993. 200
16. M. Yuksel and S. Kalyanaraman, "Simulating the Smart Market pricing scheme on Differentiated Services architecture," in *Proceedings of CNDS part of SCS Western Multi-Conference*, 2001. 200
17. "UCB/LBLN/VINT network simulator - ns (version 2)," http://www-mash.cs.berkeley.edu/ns, 1997. 206

Fair Stateless Aggregate Traffic Marking Using Active Queue Management Techniques

A. Das, D. Dutta, and A. Helmy

University of Southern California
abhimand@usc.edu, ddutta@isi.edu, helmy@usc.edu

Abstract. The differentiated services architecture promises to provide QoS guarantees through scalable service differentiation among multimedia and best-effort flows in the Internet. Traffic marking is an important component of this Diffserv framework. In this paper, we propose two new stateless, scalable and fair aggregate markers for TCP aggregates and UDP multimedia aggregates. We leverage stateless Active Queue Management (AQM) algorithms to design markers that ensure fair and efficient token distribution among individual flows of an aggregate. We present the Probabilistic Aggregate Marker (*PAM*), that uses the token bucket burst size to probabilistically mark incoming packets to achieve TCP-friendly and fair marking, and the Stateless Aggregate Fair Marker (*F-SAM*) that approximates fair queueing techniques to isolate flows while marking packets of the aggregate. Our simulation results show that our marking strategies show upto 30% improvement over other commonly used markers while marking flow aggregates. When applied to aggregate TCP flows consisting of long-lived flows(elephants) and short lived web flows(mice), our F-SAM marker prevents any bias against short flows and helps the mice to win the war against elephants.

1 Introduction

The Differentiated Service architecture *(Diffserv)* [2] [16] aims to provide statistical QoS guarantees within IP. Unlike Intserv [22], Diffserv is stateless, and, hence, scalable. It uses fine grained, per-flow marking at the network edges to classify flows into the various classes, and, then, applies coarser per-class service differentiation (Per-Hop Behavior) at the network core. There are two main types of Per-hop Behaviors(PHB) currently defined, the Expedited Forwarding(EF) PHB, and the Assured Forwarding(AF) PHB.

In this paper, we design packet markers for an Assured Forwarding PHB domain [13]. Traffic is marked at the edge into different drop-priority classes, according to a traffic profile based on service level agreements (SLA) between two domains. The network core uses simple AQM techniques to provide preferential packet dropping among the classes. Since the SLA at an edge domain applies to the total egress traffic, we need to perform traffic marking on the aggregated traffic at the edge. Simple token-bucket based markers however cannot distinguish between flows within an aggregate. In particular, misbehaving,

K.C. Almeroth and M. Hasan (Eds.): MMNS 2002, LNCS 2496, pp. 211–223, 2002.
© Springer-Verlag Berlin Heidelberg 2002

non-responsive flows can get more tokens. Also there is no provision for preventing long TCP flows from squeezing out short duration web traffic. Token-bucket markers aggravate bursty behavior, encourage misbehaving flows, and increase packet drops; this can severely affect both TCP and multimedia performance.

Thus there is a need to mark a traffic aggregate fairly and efficiently according to a given traffic specification. We need to ensure that we protect the TCP traffic in an aggregate from misbehaving flows. Also, we need to ensure that within an aggregate of multimedia UDP flows, the congestion-controlled well-behaved flows do not suffer at the cost of the other non congestion-controlled UDP flows. Again, if we consider just TCP traffic, we do not want the short term TCP flows (mice) to lose out to the long lived TCP flows (elephants). Hence we need to look at traffic markers which can provide fairness among any aggregate without maintaining per-flow state, thus ensuring higher scalability.

Traffic belonging to a single aggregate is marked into conformant (IN) and non-conformant (OUT) packets. The issues in Diffserv traffic marking are also similar to those in Active Queue Management [7] schemes. Well established work in active queue management such as RED [9], CHOKE [17] and CSFQ [18] provide certain degrees of fairness to flows and/or better throughput for flows by probabilistic dropping of packets from the queue, without maintaining per-flow state. We leverage AQM techniques to design two novel stateless, fair, aggregate markers. We show through extensive simulations that our methods achieve fairness in token allocation between flows without maintaining per-flow state in a variety of scenarios containing UDP, TCP and mixed traffic. We are not aware of any other work that utilizes AQM techniques to mark aggregate traffic in a fair and stateless fashion. Our techniques hold promise to control well behaved multimedia traffic and TCP traffic from misbehaving traffic within the Diffserv framework.

The rest of this document is outlined as follows. Section 2 presents related work on markers. A brief background on traffic marking is given in Section 3 and our first scheme, PAM, is describes in Section 4. Section 5 details our second scheme, F-SAM. Our simulation results are discussed in Section 6. Section 7 outlines future work and concludes.

2   Related Work

Packet marking is a well visited topic. Many current markers perform sophisticated per-flow marking [1] [21]. Others mark packet aggregates without maintaining any per-flow states. Stateless markers are simpler to implement, and, hence, desirable. There has been some work in stateless, aggregate marking. They typically rely on metering the average rates and comparing them against a token traffic specification [11], [12]. However these markers do not address fairness issues within an aggregate.

A sophisticated aggregated marker can be found in Fang. et. al. [8]. It does probabilistic marking based on the average aggregate rates, and in this respect, is similar to PAM. However instead of a RED-like transfer function based on the average token-burst size, as in our case, they rely on the average incoming rate. Thus, their marker cannot handle bursty flows or the bias against short lived TCP flows while marking in a congested network.

Maintaining per-flow state can solve the problem of fair aggregate traffic marking. However, these schemes are not scalable when the number of flows entering a marker is varying and dynamic. Yeom and Reddy [21] address fair aggregate marking issues, but they assume that the individual flows within the aggregate have already been pre-allocated individual contract rate from the aggregate marker tokens. Also their algorithm is per flow based, and entails calculating individual flow throughput information using a TCP throughput model which requires Round Trip Time and packet size information for each flow. Unlike our markers, they only handle TCP flows.

In [19], the authors look specifically at the issue of sharing excess network bandwidth among traffic aggregates. However, they do not fairly marking individual flows within an aggregate, while we do. So their aggregate marker looks at inter-aggregate fairness as opposed to intra-aggregate fairness, as in our case.

In [1] the authors give preferential treatment to short-lived TCP flows in an aggregate, and perform a max-min fair allocation (of tokens) on the remaining TCP flows. But they assume that their marker has state about all the component TCP flows in the aggregate, which might not be practical or scalable. Also, their scheme works only for TCP.

In [14], Lloyd et. al. use the FRED algorithm to create a fair aggregate traffic marker. However this requires per-active flow computation at the marker, and is also more complex to implement than either of our markers. Also, they do not address the issues in fairness between long-lived and short-lived TCP flows.

Protection of TCP traffic and well-behaved multimedia traffic from each other and from misbehaving UDP traffic has been a great concern. In [3], the authors define thresholds for different classes of traffic. They use a dynamic threshold based scheme on top of RED to provide inter-class and intra class fairness between TCP and well behaved *tagged* multimedia traffic. Thus, they ensure that the well behaved UDP flows are not punished just due to their non-TCP friendly properties. However, their scheme does not use the Diffserv framework. Within a Diffserv framework, our markers will achieve the same goal if we mark TCP and UDP traffic with separate marker instances and decide to put the TCP and the UDP flows in different Diffserv classes. Also, unlike them, we present a class of fair markers that are based on AQM techniques.

We are not aware of any previous work in traffic marking that solves the problem of fair token distribution among flows within an aggregate without maintaining per-flow state, within the Diffserv framework. Besides, we are not aware of any marking techniques based on AQM techniques such as RED [9] and CSFQ [18].

3   Traffic Marking

Traffic marking is an essential component of the Diffserv architecture. The traffic marker looks at the incoming packets and compares it with a given traffic profile (for example, a token bucket(TB) characterization of a SLA between two domains). In-profile(IN) packets are marked with an identifier that indicates a higher priority. If packets are out of profile (OUT), it is *marked* with a lower priority.

The main challenge in marking is to efficiently and fairly distribute the allocated IN tokens (specified by the SLA) among individual flows of the edge network entering the marker. One solution is to maintain states of all flows and allocate IN-tokens according to the SLA. Clearly this is not scalable. The other alternative is to mark aggregates using a stateless algorithm. This is our approach.

The problem of aggregate marking is quite similar to the issue of queue management and scheduling. The queue receives packets from various flows and has to decide which packets from the incoming aggregate to buffer, which to drop, and how to allocated bandwidth fairly among flows. We can view a token bucket specification as a queue with the token bucket (TB) burst size as the queue size and the token arrival rate as the queue's link bandwidth. Marking an arriving packet as IN is same as queueing a packet for transmission, and marking it as OUT is equivalent to dropping an incoming packet from the queue. Both the average queue size and the average token bucket size give an indication of the congestion level at the queue/TB. However a small average queue size is equivalent to a large average token bucket size and vice versa. The problem of fair token distribution at a marker (using a Token Bucket traffic specification) among packets of various incoming flows, is equivalent to efficient buffer management and scheduling of incoming packets at a queue in a fair manner.

Active Queue Management techniques such as Random Early Detection(RED) [9] pro-actively drop packets before a queue overflow event, and allow for higher throughput and better fairness by reducing synchronization effects, bursty packet losses and biases against low bandwidth-bursty TCP flows. In addition, queue management techniques like Core Stateless Fair Queueing(CSFQ) [18], Flow Random Early Detection(FRED) [15], CHOKE [17] and Fair Queueing [6] try to distribute link bandwidth at the queue fairly among all flows of the aggregate.

We apply two algorithms from sample AQM techniques - CSFQ and RED, to aggregate Diffserv packet marking. We observe that the use of these techniques yields superior marker performance, in terms of throughput and fairness. In the next two section, we introduce our two stateless AQM based marking schemes. The first one, PAM, is based on RED and the second one, F-SAM, is based on CSFQ.

4   Probabilistic Aggregate Marker

Our Probabilistic Aggregate Marker (PAM) is based on *RED (Random Early Detection)* [9]. The aggregate traffic tries to consume tokens from the token bucket at a certain rate. We maintain an exponentially weighed moving average (EWMA) of the number of tokens in the token bucket. On every incoming packet, we look at this average token bucket size. If this bucket size falls below a certain threshold min_{th}, all packets are to be marked with a lower priority. If the bucket size varies between min_{th} and max_{th}, we mark the packet as OUT based on a probability function that depends on the size of the token bucket. If the token bucket size exceeds max_{th}, we mark the packet as IN. More formally, our probability function of marking as OUT $P(x)$ can be written as follows.

$$P(x) = \begin{cases} 1 & : & x < min_{th} \\ \frac{P_{max} - P_{min}}{max_{th} - min_{th}} \times (max_{th} - x) & : & min_{th} < x < max_{th} \\ 0 & : & x > max_{th} \end{cases} \quad (1)$$

where x is the average size of the token bucket. Our probability function for marking a packet as OUT, therefore a modification of the RED probability function for accepting a packet into the queue.

This marking scheme ensures that the ratio of IN packets to OUT packets is flow-independent. Hence, the flow that pushes more traffic into the edge will, on the average, have a greater number of OUT packets; hence it will have more of its packets will be dropped if the core is congested. We show in Section 6 show that this scheme will be fairer to TCP flows in the presence of a misbehaving non-responsive flow, than simple token bucket schemes. The main advantages of PAM include its simplicity in implementation and deployment, and its stateless property.

5   Fair Stateless Aggregate Marker

In this section, we propose a very efficient, stateless aggregate fair marker F-SAM that employs algorithms from Core Stateless Fair Queueing (CSFQ) [18] like algorithm. CSFQ provides approximate max-min fairness while buffering incoming packets at a queue, by using a probabilistic dropping function based on the average rate of the flow to which the packet belongs. This rate information, instead of being calculated at the queue using per-flow techniques is calculated near the source of the flow and inserted in every packet header. Similarly, we maintain the rate information of a flow in the packet header itself, and use this to calculate a token probability, on a per-packet basis in the edge marker. Packets which can get through the probabilistic dropping function based on their rate information to get tokens from the token bucket are marked as IN, while others are marked as OUT. The queue, the output link speed, and drop probability in [18] are replaced by the token bucket, token bucket rate and $(1 - P[in\ token])$.

In F-SAM, the rate information in each packet header is calculated and filled by the ingress node when the flow enters the edge domain. Since each ingress node is responsible for maintaining the rate of only the flows originating from it, this per-flow rate calculation is simple and scalable. At the egress edge router, the edge marker needs to calculate the fair rate, f, allocated to the flows, and then calculates the token allocation probability of a packet as $min(1, \frac{f}{r})$, where r is the rate of the corresponding flow. So the expected token allocation rate to a packet belonging to a flow of rate r, is then $min(r, f)$, which corresponds to the max-min fair rate of fair-queuing. As in [18], the fair-rate f, is calculated by an iterative method based on the average aggregate arrival rate of packets A, aggregate token allocation rate of packets R', and the token bucket rate C. Note that the fair-rate calculation algorithm does not need any per-flow measurements. Due to lack of space, we do not go into the specific algorithm details (see [18] or [4] for more details.)

Thus, F-SAM can distribute tokens among various flows in an approximate max-min fair manner like CSFQ. Note that fair token distribution among flow aggregates does not translate into a exactly fair division of throughput at the network core among TCP and UDP flows flows, if the core only implements simple RIO queueing. This is because the loss of any packet of a TCP flow would result in its halving its sending rate, while it does not affect the sending rate of the UDP flow. However, preventing large UDP flows from getting more IN tokens than TCP flows would significantly increase the throughput obtained by the TCP flows in presence of misbehaving traffic. Also, since this is a probabilistic marker, it will be not encourage bursty losses. Thus, even in the case of all-TCP aggregate traffic, the throughput and fairness obtained by individual TCP flows will be much higher than simple token bucket markers.

Note that even in case of aggregates of multimedia UDP flows, F-SAM will ensure fair token distribution to all the individual flows within the aggregate. Thus, given separate traffic specifications for UDP and TCP aggregates at a diffserv marker node, one could have two instances of the F-SAM marker operating on TCP and UDP aggregates separately, while maintaining fair token allocation within each aggregate.

Another interesting property of F-SAM is that it can eliminate bias against short TCP flows in aggregate traffic consisting of both long and short TCP flows. Short lived flows do not get enough time to ramp up their sending rate and RTT estimation, and any packet loss in short flows can be lethal. In [1] and [10], the authors look at ways to remove this bias against short TCP flows in the marking and queueing domains. However these papers use per-flow mechanisms to reduce this bias, while F-SAM is a completely stateless marker and reduces this bias by the very nature of its probabilistic marking based on average rate of each flow. To provide a theoretical explanation of how F-SAM preferentially treats short flows, one needs to keep in mind that in the CSFQ algorithm the dropping probability is inversely proportional to the flow rate specified in the packet header. Now, if we use an EWMA based rate estimation algorithm, then for short flows, the rate estimation calculation is lower than the actual sending rate of the flow, since the initial rate of the short flow is small and the EWMA does not have time to ramp up before the flow ends. Since packets belonging to short flows arriving at the F-SAM marker have a lower rate in their header than their actual sending rate, the short flows gets a slightly bigger proportion of IN packets than what they are actually entitled to in a fair queuing scheme. This translates into better throughput for the short flows, as we shall see in the next.

6   Experimental Results

Fig. 1. Simulation scenario: A simple core with two edges. The s_i inject traffic of different classes into the network while the d_is are the sinks.

In this section we evaluate our two AQM-strategy based markers, PAM and F-SAM in progressively complex scenarios, using packet level network simulation, and compare their performance with aggregate markers such as the Token-Bucket marker(TB) and the TSW2CM marker [8].

6.1   Experimental Setup

We have used the *ns-2* [20] network simulator. The topology used in our experiments is depicted in Figure 1. The source nodes are s_i and the destination or sink nodes are d_i. The source nodes are connected to the edge node $e1$ which inject traffic into the network core, c. The core is connected to the edge $2e$ which is further connected to the sink nodes d_is. The source node s_3 is used to generate background traffic in form of many TCP flows carrying bulk traffic. This background traffic is marked with a separate DSCP (e.g., 20) and is absorbed at d_2.

6.2   Validating the Marking Process

Marker	TCP Flow 1		TCP Flow 2		Misbehaving UDP Flow	
	IN pkts	OUT pkts	IN pkts	OUT pkts	IN pkts	OUT pkts
TokenBucket	67	1261	76	1267	2423	7215
PAM	236	935	378	1456	2011	7607
F-SAM	740	882	748	835	1042	8254

Fig. 2. Detailed Packet Marking results with 2 TCP flows and 1 misbehaving UDP flow. For every marker, we give the number of IN and OUT packets obtained by each flow at the marker. The UDP flow has a rate of 2Mb/s.

First, we evaluate our PAM and F-SAM markers and check the amount of tokens obtained by individual flows in an aggregate. We conduct simulations for

Marker	UDP Flow 1 (1Mb/s)		UDP Flow 2 (4Mb/s)		UDP Flow 3 (2Mb/s)	
	IN pkts	OUT pkts	IN pkts	OUT pkts	IN pkts	OUT pkts
TokenBucket	13	748	805	2869	387	1593
PAM	245	695	695	2883	387	1593
F-SAM	497	620	413	2952	456	1571

Fig. 3. Detailed Packet Marking Results with three UDP flows of varying bandwidths. For every marker, we give the number of IN and OUT packets obtained by each flow at the marker.

a mix of UDP and TCP flows and for a mix of UDP flows of varying bandwidth. We verify that the proportion of packets marked for each flow by our marker conforms to our claims. This result helps us to estimate the end-to-end performance results. Due to lack of space, we present a very brief summary. A detailed description can be found in [4].

Consider the table in Figure 2. This experiment had 2 TCP flows multiplexed with 1 misbehaving UDP flow(2Mb/s) injected into the core. For our markers, we use a committed information rate (CIR) of 500kb/s and a burst size of 100kb and ran the simulation for 40 seconds in virtual time. We also use background TCP traffic in the topology to prevent flow synchronization. We calculate the number of IN and OUT packets marked for each flow and we find that Token-Bucket markers allows the misbehaving UDP flow to squeeze the elastic TCP connections of IN tokens. However, in case of PAM, as we increase the sending rate, PAM marks IN packets proportionately i.e. the misbehaving flow gets penalized more (in terms of getting lesser IN packets than in the TB case). In other words, with PAM the ratio $\frac{IN\ packets}{total\ packets\ transmitted}$ is approximately the same for all flows. F-SAM demonstrates a fairer token allocation. We see that, in F-SAM, all the flows get approximately similar share of tokens from the marker, in spite of the large misbehaving UDP flow (which misappropriated most of the tokens from the TCP flows in the case of the TokenBucket marker). Thus we see, that the F-SAM marker effectively segregates flows from each other, and does not let misbehaving flows take away tokens from other well-behaved flows. In the next experiment, we consider only three UDP flows carrying CBR traffic, with varying transmission rates (1Mb/s, 4Mb/s, and 2Mb/s).

Looking at Figure 3, one can see a similar improvement of PAM and F-SAM over a TokenBucket Marker with respect to the fairness of token allocation among the three flows. With F-SAM, the number of tokens allocated to each flow is nearly the same, in spite of widely varying individual flows rates. Comparing with the token-bucket marker results , where the larger flows gather most of the tokens, we see that the F-SAM marker effectively isolates flows among the aggregates. It also evenly distributes tokens among the individual flows in a max-min fair manner, without maintaining any per-flow state.

6.3   End-to-End Performance

In this subsection, we compare the end-to-end performance of PAM and F-SAM with the TB (TokenBucket marker) and the sophisticated TSW2CM marker.

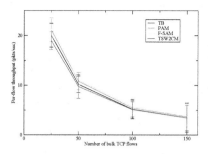

Fig. 4. Average throughput of flows, when only bulk TCP flows are used between $s1$ and $d1$

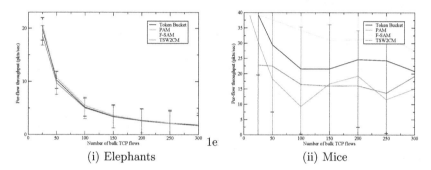

(i) Elephants   (ii) Mice

Fig. 5. Average throughput of flows when both bulk (elephants) as well as short lived TCP flows (mice) are used between $s1$ and $d1$

In all the experiments in this subsection, the CIR was 1Mb/s, the TB burst size was 500Kb/s and there was no separate background traffic as in the previous set of experiments. All the links except the one between *core* and $e2$(the bottleneck link) had a bandwidth of 10Mb/s, while the bottleneck had 5Mb/s. The delays in all the links were 5ms. We have used TCP Reno for all TCP agents and the short lived flows were generated by the HTTP 1.0 model in *ns-2*. The parameters for the RIO queues were the default ones in *ns-2*. We have got better results by tweaking the RIO parameters but we have not presented those results here.

First, we test our markers with long lived bulk TCP flows from $s1$ to $d1$ shown in Figure 4. We see that F-SAM is around 10% better than TB. PAM too performs better than TB (by 2-5%). It is interesting to note that both the throughputs due to PAM as well as F-SAM have a lesser standard deviation compared to TB, implying that our markers are more fair. The clear winner is F-SAM which has a much lesser standard deviation as it uses a max-min fairness criteria to distribute the token at the marker. Note that TSW2CM performs worse than TB in this scenario.

In the next experiment, we take several bulk TCP flows along with several short lived TCP flows (with an average arrival rate of 1 second and a payload size of 20KB) marked from the same token bucket. We illustrate the results for the long flow and short flows separately. Again, the average per-flow throughput for long flows with PAM and F-SAM yielded higher throughput and less standard deviation (Figure 5(i)). We must note that the F-SAM results have very low standard deviation (almost half of that of the TB marker), which demonstrates the fairness of F-SAM marking.

Figure 5(ii) depicts the bandwidth obtained by the short flow aggregates. Again, F-SAM beats the competition by a large margin. This is important as we can use F-SAM to win the war between mice and elephants[10] without maintaining per-flow state. Note that we do not need to detect which flows are short as our max-min fairness based F-SAM ensures fair token distribution. Also note that, the bandwidth obtained by mice is almost constant unlike the other markers. Surprisingly, for the short flows, we see that TB is better than PAM.

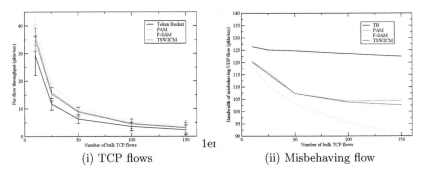

(i) TCP flows   (ii) Misbehaving flow

Fig. 6. Bandwidth obtained by flows when bulk TCP flows are present between $s1$ and $d1$ along with a single misbehaving UDP flow with a rate of 1Mb/s between $s2$ and $d1$

In the next set of experiments, we use a single misbehaving UDP flow generating CBR traffic at 1 Mb/s apart from many bulk TCP flows. The throughput results for the TCP flows are depicted in Figures 6(i), (ii). As a result of our marking, we see that the average bandwidth received by the bulk TCP flows in F-SAM is the highest among all the markers(around 50% more than TB). PAM too is higher than TB by around 30% and is marginally better than TSW2CM. We note that the performance of TSW2CM is closer to PAM since probabilistic rate based marking in TSW2CM too helps to check misbehaving UDP flows. The better TCP performance of F-SAM is clearly due to an evenly distributed out-profile packets (packets marked OUT) compared to bursty out-profile packets in the case of the TB marker in presence of misbehaving UDP flows. This is also demonstrated by Figure 6(i) which shows the bandwidth obtained by the misbehaving UDP flow in the previous scenario. Clearly this result correlates with

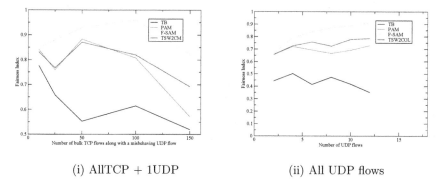

(i) AllTCP + 1UDP   (ii) All UDP flows

Fig. 7. Comparison of the Fairness Index of markers when only (i) many TCP flows and 1 misbehaving UDP flow is present and (ii) When only UDP flows are present.

Figure 6(ii), as we see F-SAM (and PAM to a lesser extent) penalizing the UDP flow much more than a TB marker. The fairer token distribution ensures that bandwidth is taken away from the misbehaving flow and is distributed among the TCP flows.

Figure 7(i) plots the fairness index for the previous experiment using the throughput of the TCP flows and the UDP flow. The fairness index [5] can be written as

$$FI = \frac{(\sum_i^N x_i)^2}{N \times \sum_i^N x_i^2} \qquad (2)$$

where x_i is the per-flow throughput. We see a marked increase in the fairness index of F-SAM over all the other markers. PAM too exhibits a much greater fairness index than TB. The performance improvement for both F-SAM and PAM continues as the bandwidth of the misbehaving flow is increased. This demonstrates the efficacy of our marking schemes. We should note that no special tuning of queue parameters were required to get our performance improvement. In fact, we have obtained better performance when we tuned the parameters of the PAM marker as well as the RIO queues.

Next, we consider a scenario with only UDP flows. This is important for multimedia transmission, where we want well behaved multimedia streams to be protected by misbehaving flows. In this experiment, we used an aggregate consisting of a varying number of UDP flows, each with a different bandwidth varying from 2Mb/s to 10Mb/s. Our results show that while TB shows a high degree of unfairness in the allocation of tokens to the different UDP flows, F-SAM allocates approximately the same number of tokens to all the UDP flows irrespective of their bandwidth. PAM (and TSW2CM) try and allocate tokens in proportion to the incoming rate and also show greater fairness than TB. Figure 7(ii) plots the fairness index among UDP flows within the aggregate. The figure clearly shows that F-SAM treats flows fairly irrespective of their bandwidth and hence protects well behaved multimedia flows from large misbehaving flows. We see that while TB performs the worst, PAM and TSW2CM perform better than TB and behave similar to each other.

Thus, we demonstrate that F-SAM does well to isolate misbehaving flows. We conjecture that techniques such as F-SAM perform close to the upper bound for fairness in aggregate marking, without per-flow calculations. PAM is a much less sophisticated marker, has less dramatic gains but its easier to implement than F-SAM. But they are both very easily deployable since they are stateless. Their performance shows a marked improvement over simplistic TokenBucket aggregate markers, and in fact come closer to that of many sophisticated per-flow marking schemes discussed in Section 2.

7   Conclusion and Future Work

In this paper, we have proposed two AQM based aggregate markers that ensure fairness among different flows in the aggregate without maintaining per-flow state. This makes our approach unique. Probabilistic Aggregate Marking (PAM) ensures fairness in a proportional fashion and allocates tokens to packets with a probability transfer function that looks similar to the transfer function of RED. We also presented a more sophisticated marker called Fair Stateless Aggregate Marker (F-SAM) which is based on fair queueing using *max-min* fairness criteria. The promising aspect of our work is F-SAM which can boost the performance of short lived flows and also ensure fairer bandwidth allocation between TCP and UDP flows of an aggregate, and within TCP aggregates and UDP aggregates separately.

The above markers are scalable and readily deployable. Our hope is that markers like PAM and F-SAM will enable a much more fairer and scalable solution to the problem of traffic marking in the differentiated services framework.

Future work in this area involves adapting other AQM techniques like CHOKe to develop fair aggregate markers. Additionally, for PAM, we plan to incorporate marking schemes based on PI controllers and try to dynamically auto-configure the RED-like parameters based on the traffic pattern. In F-SAM, we have not yet looked at the idea of weighted fair queueing while distributing tokens among the flows. Allowing for different weights to individual flows of the aggregate is the next logical step after approximating fair queueing. Finally, we want to explore how our markers can be used to implement good, fair pricing schemes in a diffserv QoS architecture.

References

1. A.Feroz, A. Rao, and S. Kalyanaraman. A tcp-friendly traffic marker for ip differentiated services. *Proc. of the IEEE/IFIP Eighth International Workshop on Quality of Service - IWQoS*, 2000. 212, 213, 216
2. S. Blake, D. Black, M. Carlson, E. Davies, Z. Wang, and W. Weiss. An architecture for differentiated services. *RFC 2475*, 1998. 211

3. Mark Claypool and Jae Chung. Dynamic-cbt and chips - router support for improved multimedia performance on the internet. *ACM Multimedia*, 2001. 213

4. A. Das, D. Dutta, and A. Helmy. Fair stateless aggregate marking techniques for differentiated services networks, university of southern california technical report usc-cs-tr-02-752, 2002. 216, 218

5. Bruce S. Davie and Larry L. Peterson. *Computer Networks: A Systems Approach.* Morgan Kauffmann, second edition, 2000. 221

6. A. Demers, S. Keshav, and S.J. Shenker. Analysis and simulation of a fair queueing algorithm. *Sigcomm*, 1989. 214

7. B. Braden et al. Recommendations on queue management and congestion avoidance in the internet. *RFC 2309*, 1998. 212

8. W. Fang, N. Seddigh, and B. Nandy. A time sliding window three colour marker (tswtcm), 2000. 212, 217

9. S. Floyd and V. Jacobson. Random early detection gateways for congestion avoidance. *IEEE/ACM Transactions on Networking, V.1 N.4*, 1993. 212, 213, 214, 214

10. L. Guo and I. Matta. The war between mice and elephants. *ICNP*, 2001. 216, 220

11. J. Heinanen and R. Guerin. A single rate three color marker. *RFC 2697*, 1999. 212

12. J. Heinanen and R. Guerin. A two rate three color marker. *RFC 2698*, 1999. 212

13. J. Heinehan, T. Finner, F. Baker, W. Weiss, and J. Wroclawski. Assured forwarding phb group. *RFC 2597*, 1999. 211

14. Lloyd Wood Ilias Andrikopoulos and George Pavlou. A fair traffic conditioner for the assured service in a differentiated services internet. *Proceedings of ICC 2000, vol. 2 pp. 806-810*, 2000. 213

15. Dong Lin and Robert Morris. Dynamics of random early detection. *SIGCOMM '97*, pages 127–137, september 1997. 214

16. K. Nichols, V. Jacobson, and L. Zhang. A twobit differentiated services architecture for the internet. *RFC 2638*, 1999. 211

17. R. Pan, B. Prabhakar, and K. Psounis. A stateless active queue management scheme for approximating fair bandwidth allocation. *IEEE INFOCOM 2000*, 2000. 212, 214

18. Ion Stoica, Scott Shenker, and Hui Zhang. Core-stateless fair queueing: Achieving approximately fair bandwidth allocations in high speed networks. *Sigcomm*, 1998. 212, 213, 214, 215, 215, 216, 216

19. H. Su and Mohammed Atiquzzaman. Itswtcm: A new aggregate marker to improve fairness in difserv. *Globecomm*, 2001. 213

20. UCB/LBNL/VINT. The NS2 network simulator, available at http://www.isi.edu/nsnam/ns/. 217

21. Ikjun Yeom and A. L. Narasimha Reddy. Adaptive marking for aggregated flows. *Globecomm*, 2001. 212, 213

22. Lixia Zhang, Steve Deering, Deborah Estrin, Scott Shenker, and Daniel Zappala. Rsvp: A new resource reservation protocol. *IEEE Network Magazine*, September 1993. 211

A Dynamic Marking Scheme of Assured Service for Alleviating Unfairness among Service Level Agreements

Seung-Joon Seok[1], Seok-Min Hong[1], Sung-Hyuck Lee[2], and Chul-Hee Kang[1]

[1] Department of Electronics Engineering, Korea University
1, 5-ga, Anam-dong, Sungbuk-gu, Seoul 136-701 Korea
{ssj, mickey, chkang}@widecomm.korea.ac.kr
http://widecomm.korea.ac.kr/~ssj
[2] Network Protocol T.G., i-Networking Lab., Samsung Advanced Institute of Technology
San 14-1, Nongseo-ri, Kiheung-eup, Yongin-shi, Kyungki-do, Korea
starsu@sait.samsung.co.kr

Abstract. Assured Service, which is a service model of the Internet Differentiated Services (DiffServ) architecture, is not currently well implemented on the Internet, mainly because TCP employs an AIMD (Additive Increase and Multiplicative Decrease) mechanism to control congestion. Many studies have shown that the current Assured Service model does not assure the target rate of high profile flows in the presence of numerous low profile flows, and does not equally distribute the reservation rate of an SLA among multiple flows included in the SLA. In this paper, the former problem is referred to as inter-SLA unfairness and the latter problem is referred to as intra-SLA unfairness. We propose a marking rule, called RAM (Rate Adaptive Marking) that simultaneously diminishes both of these unfairness problems. The RAM method marks sending packets, at a source node or at an edge router, in inverse proportion to throughput gain and in proportion to the reservation rate and throughput dynamics. Three experiments with the ns-2 simulator are performed to evaluate the RAM scheme. The simulation results show that the RAM scheme may significantly reduce inter-SLA unfairness and the intra-SLA unfairness.

1 Introduction

An Assured Service (AS), as first defined in [1], is an example of an end-to-end service that can be built from the proposed differentiated services enhancements to IP using a single PHB of Assured Forwarding PHB. The basic concept of the AS is that packets are forwarded with high probability as long as the traffic from the customer site does not exceed the subscribed rate (traffic profile). Thus, it is necessary for the Assured Service that the interior router allocates some bandwidth and a buffer for each AF class, and that a user or user group of an Assured Service establishes a contract with the provider, which defines the profile for the service expected to be obtained; SLA (Service Level Agreement). This contract can be made only for a TCP flow, aggregated TCP flows or a combination of multi-protocol flows. The building blocks of the AS include a traffic marker at the edge router of a domain and a differ-

K.C. Almeroth and M. Hasan (Eds.): MMNS 2002, LNCS 2496, pp. 224–236, 2002.

entiated dropping algorithm in the network interior router. The traffic marker ranks packets as IN or OUT depending upon the SLA. An example of a differentiated dropping algorithm is RIO (RED with IN and OUT). The RIO algorithm uses the same RED algorithm for the IN packets and OUT packets, albeit with a different set of parameters for each. In particular, the OUT packets are preferentially dropped, upon evidence of congestion at the bottleneck, before the IN packets.

In previous studies, it was reported that there are two types of unfairness in the case of an Assured Service. Firstly, let us suppose that TCP flows with an Assured Service path through the same bottleneck link. In particular, let us assume that the TCP flows have different traffic profile rates. Under these conditions, the flows expect to share the excess bandwidth of the bottleneck link so as to meet their target rates. The target rate is the sum of the traffic profile rate plus an equal share of the excess bandwidth of the bottleneck link for all flows. This is called the equal sharing target rate [3]. However, several studies [4][5][6] have shown that TCP flows with a high profile rate and/or long round trip time (RTT) barely meet their target rate in the presence of numerous flows with low profile rate. The reason for this problem is that current TCP additively increases its window size and multiplicatively decreases it when any packet is lost. This causes flows with a high profile rate to take a longer time to reach to their target rates following packet loss, or not to reach to. For convenience, this problem is herein referred to as "inter-SLA unfairness". Unfairness is defined as excess bandwidth of a bottleneck link not being distributed equably among flows that go through that link.

Next, the SLA may cover a set of flows. In this case, however, there exists unfair sharing of the reserved bandwidth or of the profile rate among the aggregated flows [7][8][9][10]. This unfairness between the aggregated flows is a serious problem in the Assured Service model. The unfairness can be caused by differences in RTTs, in link capacities, or in congestion levels experienced by flows within the network, though the total throughput of the aggregation still reaches the reservation rate. This type of unfairness is herein referred to as "*intra-SLA unfairness*". To balance or fix the unfairness, a sophisticated marking mechanism is required to distribute the profile rate fairly to the aggregated flows at the edge routers [7][8][9][10].

Most studies of Assured Service focus on TCP protocol extensions [3][11], shaping [12][13] and dropping policies [3][14]. However, few approaches propose to change the current general marking rule which is that the total IN marking rate is equal to the reservation rate. In this paper, we present a new marking rule to resolve the two unfairness problems. The rest of the paper is organized as follows. Section 2 describes TCP dynamics in a differentiated services network, previous approaches to changing the general marking rule in order to alleviate inter-SLA unfairness and the axiom of the approach set out in this paper, called the *Rate Adaptive Marking* (RAM) scheme, in order to reduce the dynamics. Section 3 details the architectures and algorithms of the RAM. Section 4 studies the performance of RAM using an ns-2 network simulator and compares it with that of normal marking schemes and section 5 discusses some unresolved issues and concludes this paper.

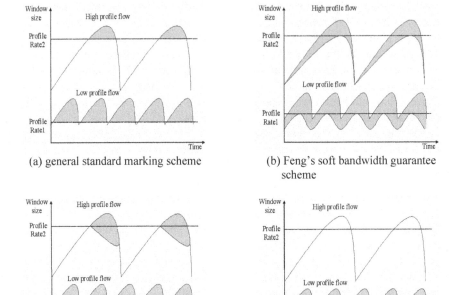

(a) general standard marking scheme

(b) Feng's soft bandwidth guarantee scheme

(c) Nam's proportional marking scheme

(d) proposed RAM scheme

Figure 1. Marking methods for two flows in the cases when a high profile flows and a low profile flows competes with each other at a bottleneck link, marking methods.

2   Two Previous Works and Rate Adaptive Marching Scheme

In the Assured Service architecture, it is generally assumed that sending packets are marked with IN as long as they do not exceed the reservation rate (traffic profile rate), otherwise marked OUT, since the marking rate is the same as the profile rate of the SLA. Figure 1(a) shows this general marking scheme for two flows having different reservation rates. In this figure, the shadowed region indicates the quantity of OUT marked packets. So far, there are few solutions that approach the problem from the point of view of changing this general marking rule. In this section, we describe the two approaches which do so, and then propose a new approach, called rate adaptive marking.

2.1 Previous Approaches

Wu Cheng Feng [15] proposed a "soft bandwidth guarantee" scheme that determines the marking rate adaptively according to a flow's throughput. In this scheme, by default, all packets are generated as low priority packets. If however, the observed throughput falls below the minimum requested rate, the marking mechanism starts prioritizing packets until the desired rate is reached. He considered that this scheme was carried out at the edge node or the source node. The first was referred to as source transparent marking and the second was referred to as source integrated marking. In particular, the second scheme considered the integration of the marking mechanism and the TCP control mechanism. Figure 4(b) shows marking method of Feng's scheme. Feng's scheme considers the reservation rate to be allocated to a flow as a target rate. Thus, it can not provide flows with equal share of excess bandwidth, in the case where network is lightly loaded.

Nam et al. [16] use a proportional marking method in which low profile flows have more OUT marked packets and, therefore, more dropped packets. In the proportional marking scheme, when a packet arrives, a meter calculates the average rate. If this average rate exceeds the flow's target rate, the proportional marking method marks the code point of the packet as OUT in proportion to the difference between the average rate and the target rate. Figure 4(c) shows the marking method of Nam's scheme. As figure 4(c) shows, the high profile flow has a marking rate which is lower than its reservation rate, following a situation in which temporary throughput is over the reservation rate. This can not help the fairness, though decreasing the marking rate of the low profile may help.

In this paper, another marking scheme, called Rate Adaptive Marking (RAM), is proposed. The two previous schemes considered only inter-SLA unfairness, while the RAM scheme can alleviate both inter-SLA unfairness and intra-SLA unfairness. The details of this scheme are described in the next two sections.

2.2 The Axiom of Rate Adaptive Marking

What is the Rate Adaptive Marking (RAM)? This subsection describes the conceptual and operational mechanisms of this scheme. A RAM marker determines a flow's marking rates periodically, depending on information about throughput rates collected during a previous period, and marks sending packets according to this rate during the next period. The basic principle of RAM strategy is marking packets as IN in inverse proportion to the throughput gain and in proportion to the reservation rate (equation1, 2). The gain denotes how much the throughput of a flow is over its reservation rate. Also, RAM makes a flow's IN marking rate to be proportional to the dynamics in that flow's throughput (equation 3). Unless otherwise stated, a simple marking rate denotes the IN marking rate.

$$\frac{1}{throughput\_gain} \propto marking\_rate \tag{1}$$

$$reservation\_rate \propto marking\_rate \tag{2}$$

$$throughput\_dynamics \propto marking\_rate \tag{3}$$

Let us assume that two flows with the same reservation rate have different throughputs. In the case of RAM, the flow that gets the higher throughput is given a lower marking rate than the flow with lower throughput. This marking strategy causes that one flow to experience packet loss earlier than the other, when next congestion arises. Therefore, the gap between the two throughputs is reduced. Whereas, in the normal marking strategy, the two flows are given identical marking rates, because the marking rate of a flow is generally the same as its reservation rate. Next, let us assume another case where there are two flows with different reservation rates: a high profile flow and a low profile flow. The difference in reservation rate is the most important reason leading to inter-SLA unfairness. The high profile flow takes a longer time to reach the temporal throughput just before a packet loss, because the congestion window size is reduced more in the high profile flow than in the low profile flow. In other words, the high profile flow has larger throughput dynamics, between the maximum temporal throughput and the average throughput (or minimum temporal throughput), than the low profile flow. Thus, in this case, RAM tries to render the marking rate proportional to the throughput dynamics.

The RAM marker maintains state information of all flows that pass through it, and periodically determines the marking rate for each flow according to the following RAM rule (equation 4). The RAM marker monitors two throughput levels for all flows; temporal throughput and long term average throughput. The temporal throughput is an average throughput for a short term interval such as an average RTT, while the long-term average throughput is based on a relative long period of time such as the congestion interval. The following equation is the RAM's rule for determining the marking rate.

$$marking\_rate = \frac{(Th\max - Thavg)}{(Th\max - RsvRate)} \times RsvRate \tag{4}$$

where *Thmax* is the maximum temporal throughput during the immediately preceding congestion interval and *Thavg* is the long term average throughput of the flow during the congestion interval. This equation connotes the basic principles of the RAM scheme. In the right-hand side of the equation, the "*Thmax-Thavg*" term denotes the flow's throughput dynamics and "*(Thmax-RsvRate)/(Thmax-Thavg)*" the flow's throughput gain. Finally "*RsvRate*" is the flow's reservation rate.

If a flow achieves an average throughput that is equal to its reservation rate (*RsvRate*) in the RAM scheme, the marking rate becomes the reservation rate. Also, if the average throughput is over the reservation rate, the marking rate will be lower than the reservation rate and proportional to the gap between the average throughput and the reservation rate. In contrast, if the average throughput is below the reservation rate, the marking rate will be higher than the reservation rate and also inversely proportional to the gap. However, it can happen that the result of equation 4 is negative or has an infinite value, when *Thmax* is below or equal to the *RsvRate*. This case denotes that the throughput does not reach its reservation rate as well as its target rate. The RAM scheme has an upper bound and a lower bound for the marking rate, in order to protect the marking rate and the throughput from experiencing heavy fluctuations. The upper bound is considered to be several times the reservation rate ("*α×RsvRate*") and the lower bound to be a half or less of the reservation rate (*"β×RsvRate"*). So the marking rate is set to the upper bound, if the result of equation 4 is over the upper bound or negative, and the lower bound, if the result is positive and under the lower bound. Thus, the equation 4 can be re-written as follows.

$$marking\_rate = \min\left(\alpha, \max\left(\beta, \left(\frac{Th\max - Thavg}{Th\max - RsvRate}\right)\right)\right) \times RsvRate \quad (5)$$

This RAM strategy supports various network environments and, in particular, various network congestion levels. If the network is over-subscribed or the flows are under-provisioned, the average throughputs of the flows or maximum temporal throughputs (*Thmax*) may be below their reservation rates and so the marking rates of the flows are much higher than the corresponding reservation rates. In this case, almost all packets are marked as IN (high precedence) and packet losses are proportional to the flow's marking rate. As a result, the flow's throughput is proportional to the reservation rate. On the other hand, if the flows are over-provisioned or the network is under-subscribed, all flows have an average throughput superior to their reservation rates and almost packets are marked as OUT (low precedence). This case is almost equal to the best-effort case, because the aggregation of the reservation rates is insignificant amount in comparison to the bottleneck link bandwidth. Therefore, all flows come to have similar excess bandwidth and so to have similar average throughputs.

Consider the case of a non-responsive flow using UDP or a flow with low dynamics in throughput, the gap between *Thmax* and *Thavg* is very small. Thus, the value of equation 4 approaches zero, if the flow is not in an under-provisioned state. Also, the marking rate becomes the lower bound, because the value is under the lower bound and positive. If the flow is over-provisioned, however, the marking rate is increased over its reservation rate because *Thmax* is less than *RsvRate*. This operation can reduce the impact of non-responsive flows (UDP) on responsive flow (TCP). Figure 1(d) shows the marking method of the RAM strategy, in which the high profile flow is marked more aggressively than in the other methods (shown in figure 1), but the low profile flow is marked less aggressively.

If a marker treats a single corresponding flow, then this marker can be located in a flow source or an edge router. The former case is referred to as source marking and the latter case as edge marking. An important feature of source marking is that the RAM marker can monitor the throughput accurately. This is because the ACK information can be provided to the marker. However, it is impossible for edge marking to estimate the throughput accurately, because of the absence of the ACK information. Thus, the edge marking RAM uses the sending rate of the flow source to measure the performance of the flow. In the source marking case, the marking rate is updated whenever packet loss is detected. The maximum temporal throughput can be derived from the congestion window size at that time, because the congestion window is maximized just before congestion control backs it off. The average throughput also denotes the average acknowledged traffic between the previous congestion point and this congestion point (congestion period). However, the RAM marker that is located in the edge router can not detect the flow's packet losses. Thus, the edge marker has two time intervals to implement for the RAM scheme. Every average round trip time, the edge marker calculates the temporal throughput as the average sending rate for the round trip time and compares this with previous ones, in order to determine the maximum value. Also, every average congestion interval, the average sending rate for the interval is calculated. Other behaviors of this marking scheme are the same as that of the source marking RAM scheme.

It is more general that an SLA includes multiple flows and a single traffic profile of aggregated flows. In this case, a marker must be located at the edge router to support multiple flows from different sources. The general marking scheme does not maintain each flow state and marks packets as IN, in proportion to the sending rates of the flows. The RAM scheme should also be carried out at the edge router. The RAM marker generates a RAM instance corresponding to each flow. This RAM instance determines the marking rate depending on RAM strategy (equation 5) and marks packets according to this marking rate. The Reservation rate of each flow is considered as the *traffic profile rate for aggregated flows / the number of flows*. The

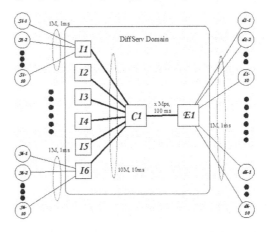

Figure 2. Experimental topology used to study inter-SLA
unfairness

Table 1. Simulation parameters for evaluation of inter-
SLA unfairness

Parameters	Value
S-I link bandwidth	1 Mbps
S-I link delay	1 ms
I-C link bandwidth	10 Mbps
I-C link delay	10 ms
C-E link bandwidth	5,6.3,7,8, and 9 Mbps
C-E link delay	100 ms
E-D link bandwidth	1 Mbps
E-D link delay	1 ms
Router buffer size	100 packets
Packet size	1000 byte
RIO parameter 1 (IN)	50/80/0.02
RIO parameter 2 (OUT)	10/40/0.5
Simulation time	200 s

marking algorithm for each flow is the same as the edge marking scheme of single flow. In particular, this scheme also uses the sending rate of each flow as information to determine the marking rate of the flow.

3 Performance Study

In order to confirm the performance effect of the RAM scheme as against previous approaches, two experiments have been performed, using ns-2 [20], on several simulation models. The first experiment is the evaluation of inter-SLA unfairness through the comparison of the RAM with Feng's soft bandwidth guarantee, Nam's proportional marking and the general marking scheme and the second experiment tests the intra-SLA unfairness using the RAM scheme, the general marking, and equally sharing scheme.

3.1 Evaluation of Inter-SLA Unfairness

We first examine the effectiveness of the RAM scheme to alleviate the inter-SLA unfairness when there are only TCP flows. Both RAM scheme types, source marking RAM and edge marking RAM, are considered in this experiment. Figure 2 depicts the

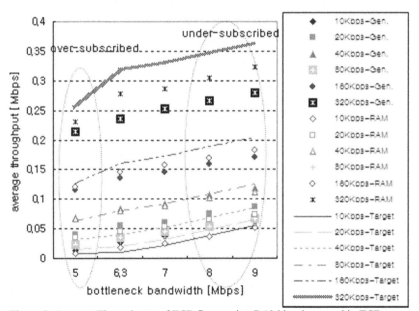

Figure 3. Average Throughputs of TCP flows using RAM implemented in TCP source and using normal marking
solid line : target rate (Target)
filled item : average throughput using general marking (Gen.)
empty item : average throughput using source marking RAM (RAM)

testbed topology for this experiment. In this topology, there are 60 TCP flows and each edge router is connected with 10 TCP sources. The profile rates for each TCP flow of s1-x, s2-x, s3-x, s4-x, s5-x and s6-x are 0.01Mbps, 0.02Mbps, 0.04Mbps, 0.08Mbps, 0.16Mbps and 0.32Mbps, respectively. All flows are routed through a common bottleneck link C1-E1 to model the competition for the excess bandwidth. In this way, the total reservation rate of the bottleneck link is 6.3Mbps. Also, this experiment considers several network environments in which different bottleneck link bandwidths, x = 5, 6.3, 7, 8, and 9Mbps, are used. Other parameters of the testbed are represented in table 1.

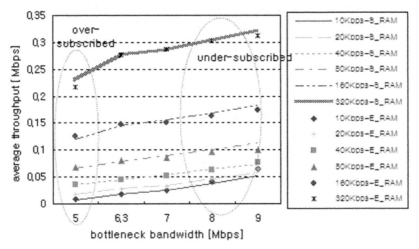

Figure 4. Average Throughputs of TCP flows using RAM implemented in TCP source and in edge router

solid line : RAM scheme in source (S_RAM)
item : RAM scheme in edge router (E_RAM)

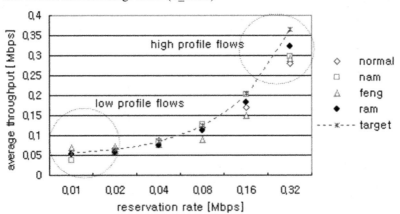

Figure 5. Comparison of effectiveness of marking schemes in the case when bottleneck link bandwidth is 9Mbps.

Figure 3 shows the average throughputs of the 10 TCP flows with the same reservation rate when the source marking RAM rule is applied and when the general marking rule is applied. These throughputs are compared with the ideal target rates. It is impossible for all average throughputs to be at the ideal target rates. It is required, however, for all average throughputs to be fairly near to their target rates. When the general marking rule is used, low profile (0.01, 0.02, 0.04, or 0.08 Mbps) flows achieve throughputs that are near or over their target rates, regardless of network load. Also, these throughputs are higher than those obtained when the source marking RAM rule is used. When the general marking is applied, however, the throughputs of the high profile (0.08, 0.16, or 0.32 Mbps) flows are less than those obtained when the source marking RAM rule is used, as well as being much less than the target rates. This problem can be ignored in the over-subscribed case, but is made worse as the network becomes under-loaded. However the RAM scheme can alleviate this problem. In figure 4, the source marking RAM rule is compared with the edge marking RAM rule. From this figure, we can see that the edge marking RAM technique can remedy the above problem as well as the source marking RAM technique does, because the result of the simulation using the edge marking RAM rule is similar to that of the source marking RAM rule, regardless of network load. Next, we compare the source marking RAM technique with Nam's scheme, Feng's scheme and the general marking scheme, when the bottleneck link is well-provisioned (9Mbps). Figure 5 shows that Nam's scheme gives the 40, 80, and 160Kbps profile flows the maximum throughput. For the 320Kbps profile flow, however, the RAM scheme is optimal. Because inter-SLA unfairness is mainly impacted by the degradation of the 320 Kbps flows (figure 3), improving the throughputs of these flows is the key factor for resolving this problem.

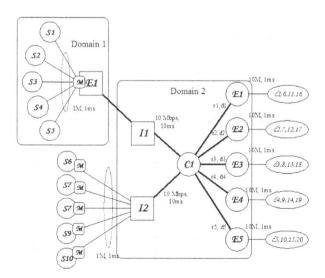

Figure 6. Experimental topology used to study the intra-SLA unfairness

Table 2. Simulation parameters for evaluation of intra-SLA unfairness

Parameters	Value
S-I or E-I link bandwidth	1 Mbps
S-I or E-I link delay	1 ms
I-C link bandwidth	10 Mbps
I-C link delay	10 ms
C-E link bandwidth (r1, r2, r3, r4, r5)	500/300 Kbps
C-E link delay (d1, d2, d3, d4, d5)	100 ms
E-D link bandwidth	10 Mbps
E-D link delay	1 ms
Router buffer size	100 packets
Packet size	1000 byte
RIO parameter 1 (IN)	50/80/0.02
RIO parameter 2 (OUT)	10/40/0.5
Simulation time	200 s

3.2 Evaluation of Intra-SLA Unfairness

In this experiment, we consider the case in which an SLA includes multiple flows. Figure 6 depicts the experimental topology used to test the intra-SLA unfairness. In this topology, domain 1 and domain 2 establish an SLA, in which 500Kbps is allocated as the traffic profile of the aggregated flows from sources (s1, s2, s3, s4 and s5). Thus, these flows should be remarked at the E1 according to the SLA. The other flows are used for background traffic and assumed to be coming into domain 2 from different domains, except for domain1. The background sources (s6, s7, s8, s9, and s10) have different marking rates (10, 100, 200, 300, and 400 Kbps respectively). In order that each flow included in the SLA experiences different network status, flows1, 2, 3, 4 and 5 are routed through different routes with different congestion levels within domain 2. The congestion levels are controlled by the background flows. Other simulation parameters are represented in table 2. In the ideal case, each flow included in an SLA has a throughput and Jain's fairness index becomes one. As unfairness among the flows increase, the fairness index value decreases.

In this experiment, we carried out two simulations. In the first simulation, CBR streams are considered as background traffic, and in the second simulation, TCP streams are considered. We monitored the average throughputs of TCP flows included in the SLA, in the case when general marking, RAM-edge marking, or equal sharing marking (Sharing) is used. The general marking scheme marks incoming packets in proportion to the incoming rate of each flow. In equal sharing marking, however, the SLA's reservation rate is distributed equally among aggregated TCP flows. Figure 7 shows the simulation results. In first simulation result (figure 7(a)), the fairness index value of the general, RAM, and Sharing scheme are about 0.88, 0.95, and 0.93, respectively. In the second simulation result (figure 7(b)), these values are 0.93, 0.98, and 0.97, respectively. From these results, we confirmed that the RAM scheme can reduce intra-SLA unfairness as well as inter-SLA unfairness.

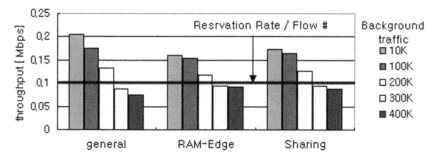

(a) In the environment in which background traffic is CBR stream, all core-egress link bandwidth is 0.5 Mbps.

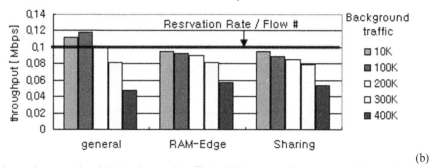

(b)

In the environment in which background traffic is TCP stream, all core-egress link bandwidth is 0.35 Mbps

Figure 7. Average Throughputs of TCP flows included in a SLA

4 Conclusion

In this paper, we described two serious problems, inter-SLA unfairness and intra-SLA unfairness, which arise when providing an Assured Service and we discussed previous reports on this topic. We proposed an approach which consists of a modified marking rule, called RAM (Rate Adaptive Marking), for the Assured Service, to alleviate both unfairness problems. The RAM scheme determines a flow's marking rate periodically, in inverse proportion to throughput gain, and in proportion to throughput dynamics and to the reservation rate during a previous time period. We described two scenarios to implement the RAM scheme, source marking RAM and edge marking RAM. The source marking RAM scheme cooperates with TCP congestion control to calculate throughputs accurately. The edge marking RAM scheme operates at an ingress edge router and exploits the sending rate of each flow, instead of the throughput. The edge marking RAM scheme can support the marking of aggregated flows, whereas the source marking RAM scheme can not. The effectiveness of RAM was evaluated through computer simulations. The simulation results showed that the RAM technique can alleviate both inter-SLA unfairness and intra-SLA unfairness simultaneously.

References

1. Heinanen, J., Baker, F., Weiss, W., and Wroclawski, J.: Assured Forwarding PHB Group. RFC2597, June (1999)
2. Blake, S., Black, D., Carlson, M., Davies, E., Wang, Z., Weiss, W.: An architecture for differentiated services. RFC 2598, June(1999)
3. Yeom, I., Reddy, A. L. N.: Realizing Throughput Guarantees in a Differentiated Service Network. In Proc. ICMCS'99, June (1999) 372-376
4. Rezende, J. F.: Assured Service Evaluation. In Proc. GLOBECOM'99, June (1999) 100-104
5. Seddigh, N., Nandy, B., Pieda, P.: Bandwidth Assurance Issues for TCP flows in a Differentiated Services Network. In Proc. GLOBECOM'99, June (1999) 1792-1798.
6. Ibanez, J. Nichols, K.: Preliminary Simulation Evaluation of an Assured Service. Internet Draft, Aug.(1998)
7. Yeom, I., Reddy, A. L. N.: Impact of marking strategy on aggregated flows in a differentiated services network. In Proc. IWQoS 1999 , May(1999)
8. Kim, H.: A Fair Marker. Internet Draft, April(1999)
9. Andrikopoulos, L., Pavlou, G.: A fair traffic conditioner for the assured service in a differentiated service Internet. In Proc. IEEE ICC 2000, June(2000)
10. Azeem, F., Rao, A., Kalyanaraman, S.: TCP-friendly traffic marker for IP differentiated services, In Proc. IWQoS'2000, June(2000) 35-48
11. Fang, W., Perterson, L.: TCP mechanisms for a diff-serv architecture, Tec. Rep
12. Cnodder, S. D., Elloumi, O., Pauwels, K.,: Rate adaptive shaping for the efficient transport of data traffic in diffserv networks. Computer Networks, Vol. 35(2001) 263-285
13. Li, N., Borrego, M., Li, S.: A rate regulating traffic conditioner for supporting TCP over Diffserv. Computer Commnications, Vol. 23(2000) 1349-1362
14. Park, W. H., Bahk, S., Kim, H.: A modified RIO algorithm that alleviates the bandwidth skew problem in Internet Differentiated Service. In Proc. ICC'00 (2000) 1599-1603
15. Feng, W., Kandlur, D., Saha, D., Shin, K.: Adaptive Packet Marking for Providing Differentiated Services in the Internet. In Proc. ICNP'98, Austin, TX, Oct. (1998) 108-117
16. Nam, D-H., Choi, Y-S. Kim, B-C., and Cho, Y-Z.: A traffic conditioning and buffer management scheme for fairness in differentiated services. in proc. ICATM 2001, April (2001)
17. Baines, M.: Using TCP Model To Understand Bandwidth Assurance in a Differentiated Services Network, In proc. IEEE Infocomm 2001 (2001)1800-1805
18. Padyhe, J., Firoiu, V., Townsley, D., Kurose, J.: Modeling TCP Throughput: A Simple Model and its Empirical Validation. CMPSCI Technical Report TR 98-008, University of Massachussetts, MA (1999)
19. Lee, S-H., Seok, S-J., Lee, S-J., Kang, C-H.: A Study of TCP and UDP flows in a Differentiated Services Network using Two Markers System. In proc. MMNS 2001, Oct. (2001) 198-203
20. Network Simulator – NS (version 2), http://www-mash.ca.berkely.edu/ns/

Minimizing Transmission Costs through Adaptive Marking in Differentiated Services Networks

Chen-Khong Tham and Yong Liu

Department of Electrical and Computer Engineering
National University of Singapore, Singapore 119260
{eletck,engp1130}@nus.edu.sg

Abstract. The issue of resource management in multi-domain Differentiated Services (DiffServ) networks has attracted a lot of attention from researchers who have proposed various provisioning, adaptive marking and admission control schemes. In this paper, we propose a Reinforcement Learning-based Adaptive Marking (RLAM) approach for providing end-to-end delay and throughput assurances, while minimizing packet transmission costs since 'expensive' Per Hop Behaviors (PHBs) like Expedited Forwarding (EF) are used only when necessary. The proposed scheme tries to satisfy per flow end-to-end QoS through control actions which act on flow aggregates in the core of the network. Using an ns2 simulation of a multi-domain DiffServ network with multimedia traffic, the RLAM scheme is shown to be effective in significantly lowering packet transmission costs without sacrificing end-to-end QoS when compared to static and random marking schemes.

Keywords: Multimedia network traffic engineering and optimization; QoS management; End-to-end IP multimedia network and service management

1 Introduction

Users of networked applications may be willing to pay a premium to enjoy network service that is better than the best effort service found in most networks and the Internet today. However, apart from specialized applications requiring a guaranteed service [1], such as a real-time control application, most users and their generally adaptive applications usually only have loose requirements such as "low delay" or "high throughput", perhaps with specified tolerable upper and lower limits.

The Differentiated Services (DiffServ or DS) framework [2] introduced the concept of Per Hop Behaviors (PHBs) such as Expedited Forwarding (EF) [3] and Assured Forwarding (AF) [4] at different routers in DS domains with the aim of providing quality of service (QoS) assurances for different kinds of traffic. DiffServ is itself a simplification of the per-flow-based Integrated Services (IntServ) model and deals with flow aggregates instead of individual flows in the core of the DS domain and in intermediate DS domains between source and

K.C. Almeroth and M. Hasan (Eds.): MMNS 2002, LNCS 2496, pp. 237–249, 2002.
© Springer-Verlag Berlin Heidelberg 2002

destination nodes. The question arises as to what is the appropriate PHB to use at each DS domain in order to achieve a certain level of end-to-end QoS[1]. Since PHBs are applied on packets based on their DiffServ Code Point (DSCP) value in the DS field of the IP packet header, the issue then becomes how to select the DSCP marking in packets belonging to flows with specific end-to-end QoS requirements. The common widely-accepted way of doing this is to mark packets from flows with stringent QoS requirements with the DSCP value corresponding to the EF PHB, packets from flows with less stringent QoS requirements with a DSCP value corresponding to a class of the AF PHB, and finally packets from flows with no specific QoS requirement with the DSCP value corresponding to the BE (best effort) PHB.

To achieve some level of QoS assurance, different DS domains have Service Level Agreements (SLAs) with their neighboring DS domains which specify performance parameters or limits for traffic carried between the domains - however, these are usually in terms of worst case values which may be significantly different from what is encountered during actual use. Furthermore, the actual QoS achieved between an ingress-egress router pair in different DS domains, for a particular PHB or Per Domain Behavior (PDB) selected based on the DSCP value, may be different.

In this paper, we propose a Reinforcement Learning-based Adaptive Marking (RLAM) scheme to mark packets of particular types of flows in different DS domains with the appropriate DSCP values to select specific PHBs so as to achieve the desired level of end-to-end QoS in a cost effective manner. The proposed method observes the effect on end-to-end QoS when different PHBs are selected in different DS domains in order to arrive at a PHB selection strategy at each domain for different types of flows, given the condition of the network traffic at that time. The RLAM scheme inter-operates with the underlying low-level QoS mechanisms such as scheduling and admission control, so long as they operate in a consistent and predictable manner. However, there is an implicit assumption that the desired end-to-end QoS can actually be achieved by using different PHBs in each DS domain. This assumption is not true when, for example, too much traffic has been allowed into the network which results in severe congestion and high delays and losses for all packets regardless of the selected PHB. Hence, buffer management and admission control mechanisms should also be deployed.

The organization of this paper is as follows. In the next section, we survey some existing work in adaptive marking. In Section 3, we describe the theory behind the feedback- and experience-based learning control method known as reinforcement learning (RL) or neuro-dynamic programming (NDP). In Section 4, we describe the design and implementation considerations of the proposed Reinforcement Learning-based Adaptive Marking (RLAM) scheme. This is followed by the description of an ns2 implemention of RLAM in Section 5 and the presentation of simulation results in Section 6. Finally, we conclude in Section 7.

---

[1] We simply use the term "QoS" to refer to the most common QoS parameters such as delay, jitter, throughput and loss.

2   Adaptive Marking in DiffServ Networks

There are two types of packet marking which take place concurrently in the Diff-Serv architecture: (1) marking of in- and out-of-profile packets within the traffic conditioner found in ingress or egress edge routers, and (2) marking packets with DSCP values in order to achieve the desired packet forwarding behavior at the routers in a DS domain.

In the first type of marking, a meter within the traffic conditioner measures packets belonging to a flow and compares them against a traffic profile. If the packets are found to be out-of-profile, they will be marked as such for subsequent handling by the shaper which delays the packets, or the dropper which discards the packets. Alternatively, these packets can also be remarked with another DSCP value corresponding to a lower PHB. In recent literature, an interesting example of this type of marking can be found in [5] in which a three-colour marking scheme in a Random Early Demotion and Promotion (REDP) marker allows EF or AF packets which have been demoted when the agreed bandwidth between certain domains have been exceeded, to be promoted again to their original marking so that they will be served ahead of BE packets in domains which have available bandwidth.

The second type of marking is the common mode of operation in DiffServ networks, in which either the source, a leaf router in the source domain, or the first ingress edge router encountered by the packet, provides the DSCP marking which usually remains unchanged all the way to the destination. In this paper, we focus on an adaptive form of this second type of marking which will be done even for in-profile packets.

An application of dynamic marking is described in [6] where a Packet Marking Engine (PME) marks with high priority packets from important TCP flows that will otherwise fall below their required throughput due to competition with other flows.

3   Reinforcement Learning

Reinforcement learning (RL) [7] (also known as neuro-dynamic programming (NDP) [8]) is a form of machine learning in which the learning agent has to formulate a *policy* which determines the appropriate action to take in each state in order to maximize the expected cumulative reward over time. An effective way to achieve reinforcement learning is to use the *Q-Learning* algorithm [9] in which the value of state-action pairs $Q(x, a)$ are maintained and updated over time in the manner shown in Equation 1:

$$Q_{t+1}(x, a) = \begin{cases} Q_t(x, a) + \eta_t[r_t + \gamma V_t(y_t) - Q_t(x, a)] \\ \qquad\qquad \text{if } x = x_t \text{ and } a = a_t, \\ Q_t(x, a) \qquad \text{otherwise.} \end{cases} \tag{1}$$

where y_t is the next state when action a_t is taken in state x_t, $V_t(y_t) = \max_{l \in A(y_t)} Q_t(y_t, l)$, $A(y_t)$ is the set of available actions in state y_t and r_t is the immediate reinforcement[2] that evaluates the last action and state transition. The γ term discounts the Q-value from the next state to give more weight to states which are near in time since they are more responsible for the observed outcome, while η_t is a learning rate parameter that affects the convergence rate of the Q-values in the face of stochastic state transitions and rewards.

A variation of Equation 1 is to use the Q-value associated with the actual action l_t selected in state y_t rather than the maximum Q-value across all actions in state y_t. In this case, the Q-value update equation becomes:

$$Q_{t+1}(x,a) = \begin{cases} Q_t(x,a) + \eta_t[r_t + \gamma Q_t(y_t, l_t) - Q_t(x,a)] \\ \qquad\qquad\qquad \text{if } x = x_t \text{ and } a = a_t, \\ Q_t(x,a) \qquad\qquad \text{otherwise.} \end{cases} \quad (2)$$

The action a in each state x_t is selected according to the Boltzmann probability distribution:

$$P(a|x_t) = \frac{e^{\beta Q_t(x_t,a)}}{\sum_{l \in A(x_t)} e^{\beta Q_t(x_t,l)}} \quad (3)$$

where $A(x_t)$ is the set of available actions at state x_t and β is a parameter which determines the probability of selecting non-greedy actions.

In the area of QoS control in communication networks, RL methods have been applied for single link admission control in ATM networks [10,11] and channel assignment in cellular networks [12]. To the best of our knowledge, the work reported in this paper is the first to use RL for resource management in a DiffServ network.

4   Reinforcement Learning-Based Adaptive Marking (RLAM)

4.1   Motivation

In the proposed RLAM scheme, a novel approach to provide assured end-to-end QoS to flows has been designed, i.e. through adaptive marking of DSCP values in IP packets to select different PHBs and PDBs in different DS domains. An example of how RLAM can be useful would be to consider packets from a session which requires low end-to-end delay, e.g. a Voice over IP session. Typically, packets in this session will be marked with the DSCP value corresponding to the EF or AF PHB. However, in lightly-loaded parts of the network, it may be possible for the BE PHB to satisfy the end-to-end delay requirement. Hence, if packets are marked with the DSCP value corresponding to the BE PHB in those parts of the network, cost savings can be realized since the user or service provider is usually charged a lower rate per bit transmitted for the BE PHB

---

[2] The reinforcement r_t is the net value of any positive reward that is awarded, e.g. when QoS is satisfied, less any cost or penalty, e.g. the cost of using the PHB over a particular link or DS domain, penalty from QoS violation etc.

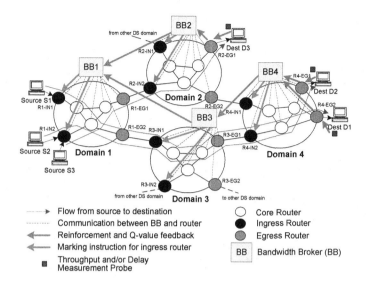

Fig. 1. Data forwarding and feedback paths in the RLAM scheme.

compared to the EF PHB. On the other hand, in medium to heavily-loaded parts of the network, the packet may need to be marked as requiring the EF PHB in order to satisfy the low end-to-end delay requirement.

4.2 Overview of Approach

The basic idea behind the proposed RLAM scheme is to (re)mark the DSCP value of packets arriving at each ingress edge router to a DS domain in such a way that the expected cumulative reinforcement achieved over the end-to-end connection is maximized. The cumulative reinforcement can take into account the extent to which the QoS requirements of the flow have been satisfied, less the costs arising from using different PHBs and PDBs in different DS domains and penalties from QoS violation and packet losses.

DSCP marking decisions are made by *RL agents* in each DS domain. From a logical point of view, there is an RL agent $RL_{d,ip}$ at each ingress interface p of every router i which can perform DSCP (re)marking in DS domain d, typically the ingress edge routers. For the rest of this paper, we shall assume that (re)marking does not take place in core or egress edge routers and the forwarding behavior at routers that are traversed by packets in the DS domain are based on the DSCP marking applied at the ingress edge router. The RL agent can either execute at the respective ingress edge router itself, or all the RL agents in the DS domain can be part of the Bandwidth Broker (BB) [13] for that DS domain.

To motivate our discussion, a multi-domain DiffServ network is shown in Figure 1 with details of the data forwarding and reinforcement feedback paths in the RLAM scheme for the case with three source-destination pairs.

Flows f are grouped into a finite number of *flow types ft* according to their QoS requirements, e.g. low end-to-end delay flow type for Voice over IP sessions, a high throughput flow type for bulk FTP sessions, and a combined low end-to-end delay and medium throughput flow type for video conferencing sessions. A source node informs the leaf router (the first router to which the source is connected) in the source domain about the end-to-end QoS requirement of a new flow using some signalling protocol such as RSVP. Subsequently, the leaf router assigns an appropriate flow type to that flow.

When a packet from the flow arrives at the leaf router, the flow type is tagged onto the packet. This can be done in a variety of ways, e.g. using the two currently unused (CU) bits in the DSCP field in the IP packet header or specific bit patterns in the codepoint space of the DSCP defined for experimental use, i.e. xxxx11 [14], EXP bits in the MPLS shim header or IP options field in the IP header. Other alternatives include using specific fields in UDP, TCP or RTP headers in higher layers of the protocol stack, but these would incur additional packet processing overhead. In our instantiation of this general design which will be described in Section 5, there are three flow types, hence the two CU bits in the DSCP field are sufficient to indicate the flow type that the packet belongs to.

At the ingress edge router of the first and subsequent DS domains, the RL agent corresponding to that router selects a DSCP marking for each flow type at the end of every interval of T seconds and sends the marking instruction to the marker at the ingress edge router. Subsequently, the marker marks all incoming packets of a particular flow type during the next interval with the selected DSCP value.

The ingress edge router then forwards the packets to the core routers in the DS domain using the underlying routing protocol. At this time, the packets become part of BAs which include packets from other source nodes coming from different ingress edge routers. Following the DiffServ convention that remarking is not done at the core routers and only packet forwarding using the PHB associated with the DSCP marking is carried out, the decision points in each DS domain for the proposed RLAM scheme are at the ingress edge routers only. The RLAM scheme can be readily extended to the case where remarking is done at core routers by implementing additional RL agents corresponding to these routers.

When the packets reach the egress edge router, the normal DS traffic conditioning is applied for traffic in BAs that leave the DS domain. At subsequent downstream DS domains, the operations at ingress edge routers, core routers and egress edge routers are performed in the same way described above until the packets reach their destination.

To facilitate clear discussion on the quantities involved in different steps of the RLAM approach, we introduce the (d, ip, jq, ft, k) notation which appears as the subscript of quantities like amount of traffic, loss, Q-value, states etc. The notation refers to a quantity in DS domain d which is relevant between ingress interface p of ingress edge router i and egress interface q of egress edge router j for a particular flow type ft at the kth time interval. If a certain element is not relevant, then that variable is omitted from the subscript. For brevity in descriptions, we shall refer to the ingress interface p of ingress edge router i in DS domain d as simply 'ingress dip router' and the egress interface q of egress edge router j in DS domain d as simply 'egress djq router'.

4.3   Measurements

A number of measurements are made at ingress edge routers and destinations, using either measurement probes or some built-in functionality at routers and host machines. The measurements at ingress edge routers that are required are: amount of traffic of each flow type arriving at the ingress dip router that is 'seen' by RL agent $RL_{d,ip}$, denoted by $t_{d,ip,ft,k}$[3]. These measurements are used to determine the state $x_{d,ip,k}$.

At a destination node, the measurements that are required are those related to the end-to-end QoS experienced by that flow such as end-to-end delay, throughput and loss [15]. End-to-end delay may be difficult to measure as it requires either a timestamp on each packet and clock synchronization between the source and the measurement probe, or a field within the packet which accumulates the actual delay experienced at each node. These measurements will be compared against the target QoS parameters for that flow type and the appropriate reward will be generated and sent to the BB of the last encountered DS domain.

In addition, the BB communicates with all the edge and core routers in the DS domain and can have a domain-wide view of aggregate traffic flows and packet losses between ingress-egress router pairs in the domain. We assume that the BB is able to provide information on the amount of traffic $t_{d,ip,jq,ft,k}$ (in unit of bps) and packet losses $l_{d,ip,jq,ft,k}$. Note that these quantities are for a flow aggregate which comprises a number of individual flows from multiple sources heading towards multiple destinations.

4.4   States and Actions

The state $x_{d,ip,k}$ at a particular RL agent $RL_{d,ip}$ comprises $[tt_{bg}][tt_{ft_1}][tt_{ft_2}]\ldots$ $[tt_{ft_{N_{ft}}}]$, where tt_{bg} is the traffic intensity of background traffic, tt_{ft_n} is the traffic intensity of flow type ft_n and N_{ft} is the total number of defined flow types. Note that RL agent $RL_{d,ip}$ is responsible for making marking decisions for each of the N_{ft} flow types based on the state information. Hence, the RL agent adds the context $[ft]$ to $x_{d,ip,k}$ whenever it accesses Q-values for a specific state and flow type.

The action $a_{d,ip,k}$ has several dimensions, one for each flow type ft. The DSCP marking for each ft is selected from the set of DSCP settings corresponding to available PHBs and PDBs such as EF, AF1 and BE. An example of $a_{d,ip,k}$ is [BE,AF1,EF] for flow types 01, 10 and 11 respectively.

---

[3] Note that $t_{d,ip,ft,k}$ is a local measurement and is different from the $t_{d,ip,jq,ft,k}$ value reported by the the the BB to $RL_{d,ip}$.

4.5   Aggregation of Reinforcement and Q-Value Feedback

In each domain d, per flow rewards are generated when end-to-end QoS parameters are satisfied for destination nodes in the domain; likewise, per flow penalties are generated for end-to-end QoS violations. The rewards and penalties for flows from the ingress dip router to the egress djq router d are aggregated together with the packet transmission costs and penalties for packet losses incurred for flows traversing the same ingress-egress pair in the same domain to produce the reinforcement signal $r_{d,ip,jq,ft,k}$. In addition, Q-value feedback messages are received from downstream DS domains.

All the reinforcement and Q-value feedback messages received by an RL agent $RL_{d,ip}$ are used to update its Q-value. Instead of forwarding all of these messages to upstream DS domains, only the $V(y)$ or $Q(y,l)$ value (see Equations 1 and 2) of that RL agent is fed back to the BB of the previous DS domain for dissemination to the RL agents at the ingress edge routers of that DS domain. Hence, the Q-value passed back by $RL_{d,ip}$ summarizes the 'goodness' of subsequent states and DS domains.

Traffic that enters the ingress dip router may be split into different proportions to multiple egress djq routers and subsequently to different destinations and downstream DS domains. When reinforcement and Q-value feedback messages from these downstream entities return to DS domain d, their influence on the Q-value update of RL agent $RL_{d,ip}$ are weighted by the equivalent number of flows from ingress dip to egress djq.

The prediction error $\varepsilon_{d,ip,jq,ft,k}$ determined from feedback messages from the egress djq router to RL agent $RL_{d,ip}$ for flow type ft is

$$
\begin{aligned}
\varepsilon_{d,ip,jq,ft,k} &= r_{d,ip,jq,ft,k} \\
&+ \gamma Q_{d\underline{jq},ip\underline{jq},ft,k}(y_{d\underline{jq},ip\underline{jq},k}, l_{d\underline{jq},ip\underline{jq},k}) \\
&- Q_{d,ip,jq,ft,k}(x_{d,ip,k}, a_{d,ip,k})
\end{aligned}
\tag{4}
$$

where $d\underline{jq}$ and $ip\underline{jq}$ terms refer to the downstream DS domain and the ingress router in that domain which are connected directly to the egress djq router of the current domain.

Finally, the Q-value at the ingress dip router for flow type ft is updated according to:

$$
\begin{aligned}
Q_{d,ip,ft,k+1}(x_{d,ip,k}, a_{d,ip,k}) &= \\
Q_{d,ip,ft,k}(x_{d,ip,k}, a_{d,ip,k}) & \\
+ \sum_{j} \sum_{q} \eta_k \frac{t_{d,ip,jq,ft,k}}{AR_{ft}} & \varepsilon_{d,ip,jq,ft,k}
\end{aligned}
\tag{5}
$$

where AR_{ft} is the average rate of flow type ft. In each interval, this procedure is repeated for the other flow types at the ingress dip router followed by the RL agents at other ingress ports in other ingress edge routers in domain d.

5   ns2 Implementation

5.1   Network Topology

The network shown in Figure 2 together with the RLAM scheme described above have been implemented using ns2 [16].

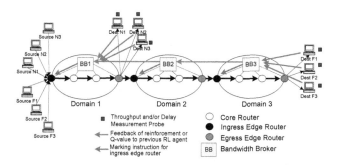

Fig. 2. ns2 implementation of network with three DS domains.

There are three flow types ($N_{ft} = 3$) with end-to-end QoS specifications:
1. High throughput required ($\geq$ 128 Kbps)
2. Low delay required ($<$ 100 ms end-to-end)
3. Moderate throughput ($\geq$ 64 Kbps) and low delay required ($<$ 200 ms end-to-end)

Note that these flow types represent the types of assured service offered by the network. These flow types are indicated in each packet using the CU bits in the DSCP field with values 01, 10 and 11 respectively, i.e. $ft \in \{01, 10, 11\}$. Packets from flows corresponding to background traffic which are not handled by the RLAM scheme will have the value 00 in their CU bits.

5.2   Traffic Characteristics

Traffic is generated by sources which represent user applications and their characteristics are shown in Table 1. We consider three types of traffic: (1) Bulk FTP with the average rate shown in the table and no delay requirement (sent using TCP); (2) Voice over IP (VoIP) sessions which are modelled as ON-OFF sources with the peak rate as shown and an end-to-end delay requirement of less than 150 ms (sent using UDP); and (3) video conferencing sessions also modelled as ON-OFF sources with a higher peak rate and end-to-end delay requirement of less than 200 ms (sent using UDP). VoIP and video conferencing traffic are ON/OFF sources with the same ON time (500 ms) and OFF time (500 ms); the holding time for all flows is 30 seconds. The appropriate flow types for these sessions would be 01, 10 and 11, respectively, which will be tagged onto packets by the leaf or edge router. In addition, different types of background traffic are generated and tagged with CU bits 00.

Table 1. Characteristics of the three traffic types.

Traffic Type	CU bit	Arrival Rate (s⁻¹)	Peak Rate (Kbps)	Average Rate (Kbps)	Packet Size (bytes)
Bulk FTP	01	1/10	/	128	1,000
VoIP	10	1/3	64	32	150
Video Conf	11	1/15	128	64	150
TCP bckgrd	00	1/15	/	128	1,000
VoIP bckgrd	00	1/15	64	32	150
Video bckgrd	00	1/15	128	64	150

6   Simulation Results

Simulations using the ns2 implementation described above have been carried out with the same traffic conditions for three marking schemes: (1) the proposed Reinforcement Learning Adaptive Marking (RLAM) scheme, (2) Static Marking (SM), in which all packets with flow types 01, 10 and 11 will be marked statically with the DSCP value corresponding to BE, AF1 and EF respectively, and (3) Random Marking (RM), in which the marking for these flow types will be selected randomly from the three DSCP values at the ingress router of each DS domain. Each simulation lasts for 6,000 seconds.

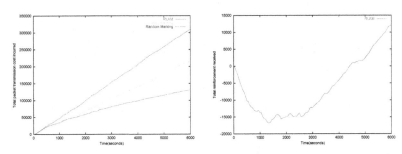

(a) Total cumulative packet transmission cost for the RLAM, SM and RM schemes.   (b) Total cumulative reinforcement received in RLAM scheme.

Fig. 3. Performance of the RLAM scheme.

Table 2. QoS achieved and transmission cost incurred using RLAM scheme

Traffic Type	Average Throughput (bps)	Average Delay (ms)	Total Loss (pkts)	Transm. Cost Incurred
Bulk FTP	125,935	59.9	39	8,137
VoIP	30,819	47.1	137	4,873
Video Conf	61,433	58.7	103	2,637

Table 3. QoS achieved and transmission cost incurred using SM scheme

Traffic Type	Average Throughput (bps)	Average Delay (ms)	Total Loss (pkts)	Transm. Cost Incurred
Bulk FTP	125,739	58.9	0	5,195
VoIP	30,679	45.7	1	14,363
Video Conf	63,053	57.2	1,131	17,527

Table 4. QoS achieved and transmission cost incurred using RM scheme

Traffic Type	Average Throughput (bps)	Average Delay (ms)	Total Loss (pkts)	Transm. Cost Incurred
Bulk FTP	125,665	58.8	4	26,054
VoIP	30,779	47.4	120	16,990
Video Conf	60,871	57.6	165	8,801

The simulation results for the three schemes will be presented in the following format. First, the total packet transmission cost for each of the three schemes will be presented. This will be followed by a discussion of the behavior of the proposed RLAM scheme. Lastly, the QoS achieved and the packet transmission cost over a defined period for each of the three schemes will be examined.

The total cumulative packet transmission cost for the six traffic sources of interest excluding the background traffic for each of the three schemes over the 6,000 seconds of simulation time can be seen in Figure 3(a). Throughout the whole period, it can be seen that the RM marking scheme incurs the highest cost. This is because a large number of packets from the bulk FTP sessions have used the higher PHBs such as EF and AF1 even when it is not necessary to do so in order to satisfy their QoS requirements.

In the early stages when $t < 400$ s, the cost incurred by RLAM is the same as that for the RM scheme, showing that marking action selection in RLAM is random at that time. When $t < 1,400$ s, the cost incurred by the RLAM scheme is slightly higher than that incurred by the SM scheme as the RL agents are still in their exploration and training phase. After 1,400 seconds, the total transmission cost for RLAM becomes lower than that for the SM and RM schemes, showing that RLAM has learnt to select cost-efficient PHBs. As time goes on, the difference in total transmission cost between the three schemes continues to increase, with RLAM incurring significantly lower cost compared to the other two schemes.

Next, we examine the variation in the total cumulative reinforcement received by the three RL agents in the RLAM scheme over the 6,000 second simulation period (Figure 3(b)). In the first 1,400 seconds, the RL agents encounter high costs and penalties due to QoS violations and selection of expensive PHBs and the net reinforcement received per unit time is negative. Between 2,000 to 2,700 seconds, the rewards received per unit time balance the costs and penalties incurred per unit time, hence the total reinforcement curve is flat during this period. After that, the total reinforcement curve increases almost linearly since the net reinforcement received per unit time is positive most of the time. This indicates that the QoS associated with each flow type are satisfied for most of the flows, i.e. the RL agents are selecting the appropriate PHBs for each flow type in each DS domain in order to provide the desired end-to-end QoS.

Since the objective of the RLAM scheme is to satisfy the QoS requirements associated with the flow types in a cost-effective way, we compare the QoS achieved and packet transmission cost incurred for the different traffic types from $t = 5,000$ to 6,000 s when the traffic conditions are stable and the RLAM scheme has converged. Tables 2, 3 and 4 show the average throughput and average delay per flow, and the total packet loss and transmission cost incurred for each of the three different traffic types.

As expected, the video conferencing sessions achieved significantly higher throughput when using the SM scheme compared to the other 2 schemes. This is due to the EF PHB, although some packet losses occurred since out-of-profile packets are discarded in the EF PHB. Other than that, since the network is moderately loaded, it can be seen that the average throughput and average delay of the corresponding traffic type under the three marking schemes are similar.

Most significantly, the total packet transmission cost incurred in this interval for the RLAM scheme is less than half that of the SM scheme and less than one-third that of the RM scheme, with most of the savings coming from being able to find a more cost effective way to carry VoIP and video conferencing traffic without severely violating the end-to-end QoS requirements.

The utilization of each of the provisions for the BE BA, AF1 BA and EF BA respectively, which includes the background traffic, in one of the links in Domain 2 for the three marking schemes are: (1) RLAM: 49.36%, 5.87%, 9.60% (2) SM: 26.74%, 17.51%, 16.53% (3) RM: 22.86%, 19.00%. 18.38%. Thus, the RLAM scheme has used more of the low cost BE PHB compared to the other two marking schemes to carry the traffic, thus enabling it to achieve significant cost savings. Note that RLAM has reached a balance and does not attempt to send all the traffic using the BE PHB since that would lead to penalties arising from QoS violations and packet losses.

7   Conclusion

In this paper, a Reinforcement Learning-based Adaptive Marking (RLAM) scheme has been proposed and its design and implementation considerations explained. Simulations done using ns2 show that the RLAM scheme is effective in providing end-to-end QoS to different user applications such as VoIP and video conferencing at a significantly lower total packet transmission cost compared to the commonly used static marking approach. In future work, we plan to improve the speed of convergence of the RLAM algorithm through the use of the TD(λ) temporal differences [17] algorithm as well as investigate the effectiveness of different ways of representing state information [18].

References

1. S. Shenker, C. Partridge and R. Guerin, Specification of Guaranteed Quality of Service, *IETF RFC 2212*, Sept 1997. 237
2. S. Blake, *et al*, An Architecture for Differentiated Services, *IETF RFC 2475*, Dec 1998. 237
3. V. Jacobson, et al, An Expedited Forwarding PHB, *IETF RFC 2598*, June 1999. 237
4. J. Heinanen, et al, Assured Forwarding PHB Group, *IETF RFC 2597*, June 1999. 237
5. F. Wang, P. Mohapatra and D. Bushmitch, A Random Early Demotion and Promotion Marker for Assured Services, *IEEE Jour. on Selected Areas in Communications*, vol. 18, no. 12, Dec 2000. 239
6. W. C. Feng, D. D. Kandlur, D. Saha and K. G. Shin, Adaptive Packet Marking for Maintaining End-to-End Throughput in a Differentiated-Services Internet, *IEEE/ACM Trans. on Networking*, vol. 7, no. 5, Oct 1999. 239
7. A. Barto, R. Sutton and C. Anderson, Neuron-like Elements That Can Solve Difficult Learning Control Problems, *IEEE Trans. on Systems, Man and Cybernetics*, vol. 13, pp. 835-846, 1983. 239
8. D. P. Bertsekas and J. N. Tsitsiklis, *Neuro-Dynamic Programming*, Athena Scientific, Belmont, MA, USA, 1996. 239
9. C. J. C. H. Watkins and P. Dayan, Q-Learning, *Machine Learning*, vol. 8, pp. 279-292, 1992. 239
10. H. Tong and T. X. Brown, Adaptive Call Admission Control Under Quality of Service Constraints: A Reinforcement Learning Solution, *IEEE Jour. on Selected Areas in Communications*, vol. 18, no. 2, Feb 2000. 240
11. P. Marbach, O. Mihatsch and J. N. Tsitsiklis, Call Admission Control and Routing in Integrated Services Networks using Neuro-Dynamic Programming, *IEEE Jour. on Selected Areas in Communications*, vol. 18, no. 2, Feb 2000. 240
12. J. Nie and S. Haykin, A Dynamic Channel Assignment Policy Through Q-Learning, *IEEE Trans. on Neural Networks*, vol. 10, no. 6, Nov 1999. 240
13. F. Reichmeyer, L. Ong, A. Terzis, L. Zhang and R. Yavatkar, A Two-Tier Resource Management Model for Differentiated Services Networks, *IETF Internet Draft 2-tier-draft*, Nov 1998. 241
14. K. Nichols, S. Blake, F. Baker and D. Black, Definition of the Differentiated Services Field (DS Field) in the IPv4 and IPv6 Headers, *IETF RFC 2474*, Dec 1998. 242
15. W. Jiang and H. Schulzrinne, QoS Measurement of Internet Real-Time Multimedia Services, *Technical Report CUCS-015-99*, Dept of Comp. Sc., Columbia University, 1999. 243
16. S. McCanne and S.Floyd, *ns2 - The Network Simulator*, available from http://www.isi.edu/nsnam/ns/. 245
17. R. S. Sutton, Learning To Predict by The Methods of Temporal Differences, *Machine Learning*, vol. 3, pp. 835-846, 1988. 249
18. C. K. Tham, Reinforcement Learning of Multiple Tasks using a Hierarchical CMAC Architecture, *Robotics and Autonomous Systems*, Special Issue on Reinforcement Learning and Robotics, vol. 15, pp. 247-274, Elsevier, July 1995. 249

Dynamic QoS Adaptation Using COPS and Network Monitoring Feedback

Toufik Ahmed[1,2], Ahmed Mehaoua[1], and Raouf Boutaba[2]

[1] University of Versailles, CNRS-PRiSM Lab.
45 av. des Etats-Unis, 78000, Versailles, France
{tad, mea}@prism.uvsq.fr
[2] University of Waterloo, Dept. of Computer Science
200 University Avenue West, Waterloo,
Ont. N2L 3G1, Canada
{tad, rboutaba}@bbcr.uwaterloo.ca

Abstract. This paper presents an approach to handle out of profile traffic using Common Open Policy Service and network monitoring feedback. The proposed approach is based on monitoring and reporting information sent by bandwidth monitors installed on each node of a Diffserv Domain. A monitor interacts with Policy Decision Point. This later, depending on the network state, pushes policy decision rules to the Policy Enforcement Point in order to accept, remark or drop out-of-profile traffic dynamically. This allows a dynamic reallocation and management of network resources based on current network state and applications QoS requirements. An implementation and a performance evaluation of the dynamic QoS adaptation framework using a Java COPS and a Linux-based network testbed are also presented.

Keywords: IP Diffserv, QoS Adaptation, COPS, Network Monitoring.

1 Introduction

Recent works on IP Quality of Service (**QoS**) Management led to the development and standardization of enhanced protocols and services. The IETF has defined the Policy-based Network Management (**PBNM**) architecture to configure network services. Currently most efforts are focused on Differentiated Services (Diffserv) in the Internet. The goal of the policy-based network management is to enable network control and management on a high abstraction level by defining configuration rules called policies. Policies specify how a network node must be configured in vendor-independent, interoperable and scalable manner.

Diffserv architecture defines, at a lower level, four types of data-path elements: traffic classifiers, actions elements, meters and queuing elements [1]. Combining these elements into higher-level blocks creates a Traffic Condition Block (**TCB**), which can be managed by policy-based network management tools. The configuration of Diffserv TCB using PBNM involves the use of administratively prescribed rules that specify actions in response to defined criteria. All the information needed to perform this task such as profiles, user information, network configuration data, and IP infrastructure data such as network addresses and name server information are

K.C. Almeroth and M. Hasan (Eds.): MMNS 2002, LNCS 2496, pp. 250–262, 2002.
© Springer-Verlag Berlin Heidelberg 2002

stored in a policy repository. These configurations do not change frequently because they are not associated with specific application or traffic but with the network management. The more difficult part in the configuration is to have the traffic entering the network appropriately marked (audio, video and other data). Since, the user is signed up for the service, edge devices could be configured to mark user's traffic with the appropriate PHB. With a known IP address and/or IP port number, the administrator can specify a policy that refers to user application IP address and marks traffic coming from that address appropriately.

In the actual configuration, when the user signs up for a particular service, he/she must specify his/her traffic profile and the action that must be taken when the traffic exceed this predefined profile (out of profile traffic). Generally, the out of profile traffic is dropped or marked as best effort traffic. This model is static and does neither respond to application needs nor favor an optimal utilization of network resources.

In this paper a Diffserv QoS management is explored with the objective to overcome the limitations of the static model. In addition to the techniques described above (i.e., PBNM, TCB, etc.), network monitors are used to make the system reactive by making automatic and real-time decisions concerning out of profile traffic. An architectural model allowing the configuration and dynamic management of the Diffserv domain will be presented, experimented and evaluated.

The reminder of this paper is as follows. In section 2, we compare static and dynamic policy decision approaches and present our proposal, which is based on dynamic QoS adaptation through network resource monitoring and feedback signaling. Section 3 is devoted to the implementation of the proposed QoS network management framework. Performance evaluation and results analysis are discussed in Section 4. Finally, we conclude in Section 5.

2   Dynamic QoS Adaptation

2.1   Static Policy Decision

In the Diffserv architecture, a particular traffic receives a predefined treatment based on predefined policies. This treatment is interpreted as a particular PHB [2], [3]. This task is done by the TC (Traffic Control) function, which assigns the correct DSCP [4] for the client's traffic according to it SLA (Service Level Agreement). Recall that each client defines it requirements and these are translated into SLAs. The allocation of resources (QoS) still static and can lead to bandwidth wasting and starving clients.

Some algorithms such as *Time Sliding Window Three Colour Marker* (TSWTCM) [5] and a *Two Rate Three Color Marker* (TRTCM) [6] can be used to mark IP packets treated by the edge router with a Diffserv PHB. These algorithms meter the traffic stream and marks packets based on measured throughput.

To receive a particular treatment, the user must specify it profile **TSpec** (Traffic Specification). TSpec specifies the temporal properties of a traffic stream selected by a classifier. It provides rules for determining whether a particular packet is in profile or out of profile. The Meter uses a Token Bucket to control user traffic. The following is a non-exhaustive list of potential profile parameters:

1. *Peak rate p* in bits per sec (bps)
2. *Token bucket rate r* (bps),
3. *Bucket depth b* (bytes),

An *Excess Treatment* parameter describes how the service provider will process excess traffic, i.e. out of profile traffic. The process takes place after Traffic Conformance Testing. Excess traffic may be dropped, shaped and/or remarked. Depending on the particular treatment, more parameters may be required, e.g. the DSCP value in case of re-marking or the shapers buffer size for shaping. All these actions are decided once the network element is configured and are not changed over the time. Fig. 1 gives an example of how out of profile traffic is treated using static configuration. In this Figure, user sends traffic not conforming to his Traffic Specification. Edge router control this traffic by a token bucket. Non-conforming traffic will be dropped always.

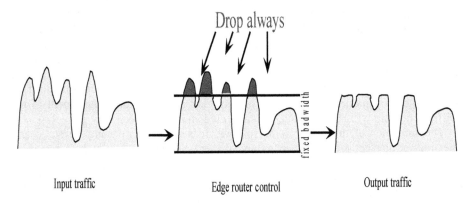

Fig. 1. Static Policy Decision

For this reason, there is a great need to control dynamically the action taken by the network element for more flexible resource allocation. For this, different conditioning actions may be performed on the in profile packets and out of profile packets or different accounting actions may be triggered dynamically according to current network state. Clearly, a more flexible resource allocation can be achieved by controlling dynamically network elements behavior.

2.2   Dynamic Policy Decision

In the static approach out of profile traffic is simply dropped, remarked or assigned a new profile. This decision is static and is taken once for all, i.e. when the network element is configured.

For example the *Policing Rule = drop out-of profile* packets can be applied to all the packets which are out of profile regardless of whether the network is capable or not to transmit this packet.

Fig. 2 shows where we can dynamically decide what actions must be applied to out of profile packets. In contrast to the static approach, these actions vary according to the network state (network link load, traffic behavior, etc.).

2.3   Automatic Diffserv Domain Configuration

When a network element is started, its local PEP requests the PDP for all policies concerning Diffserv traffic marking using COPS (Common Open Policy Service) [7], [8], [9]. The policies sent by the PDP to the PEP, may concern entire router QoS configuration or a portion of it, as an updating of a Diffserv marking filter. The PDP may proactively provision the PEP reacting to external events generated by some monitors such as a bandwidth monitor.

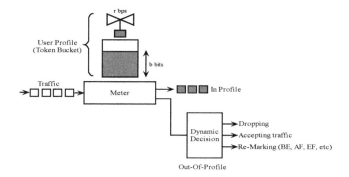

Fig. 2. Dynamic Decision

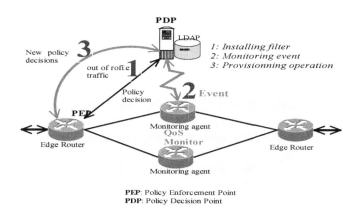

Fig. 3. COPS-PR with Monitoring Event

Fig. 3 shows the steps involved in the configuration of Diffserv domain. These steps are as follow:

- **Step 1**: When the edge router is started, the local PEP requests all policy decisions concerning Diffserv QoS Management (filtering, classes, queuing discipline, and actions for out of profile traffic). All incoming traffics are processed according to the pre-installed rules.

- **Step 2**: When the bandwidth monitor, installed on the core router, detects a significant change in the amount of available bandwidth, it triggers an external event reported to the PDP indicating the current bandwidth availability.
- **Step 3**: The PDP pushes to the edge router (PEP) an update of QoS Management decision.

These steps allow configuring correctly different policies related to the same traffic.

We introduce the following policy rule: let us **On event: If <profile> then <action>.**

A **Profile** is used to determine when a policy rule applies, for instance given pairs of source and destination addresses.

An **Action** is a performed by that the policy enforcement entity to traffic of a given profile. Examples of actions are marking, accepting or rejecting traffic.

Example of policy rules:

- Rule 1: Mark DSCP value EF on all packets with source addresses from 193.51.25.1 to 193.51.25.255 priority 0
- Rule 2: Mark DSCP value AF11 on all packets with destination address 200.200.200.100 priority 1

2.4   Example of Application

Assume, an audio application has subscribed to a particular Diffserv class (an Expedited Forwarding Class). Audio traffic is defined by a particular profile. In this example Diffserv class simply mean that the audio stream will be marked with the appropriate DSCP (EF PHB here). The Administrator of the Diffserv domain configures the environment to support the Gold, Silver, Bronze and other services. Such configuration can be done through a Bandwidth Broker.

Supporting different classes of service in the core network requires putting in place classifiers, which cause the devices to examine the Diffserv mark on the packet and then treat the traffic accordingly. These configurations do not change frequently because they are not associated with specific application or traffic but with the network management. Since, the application is signed up for the service, edge devices are configured to mark application's traffic with the appropriate PHB. Based on the IP address and/or the port number, the administrator can set a policy that marks traffic coming from that address with EF PHB.

In order for customized traffic going to audio application (e.g. feedback traffic, RTCP, client commands) to receive a Diffserv treatment, policy must be deployed to the opposite edge device of a Diffserv domain.

When the audio application starts sending the data, the edge router must ensure; (1) the data sent by the audio server does not exceed what the application has subscribe-to (SLA) and (2) marking conforming traffic (in profile traffic) with the appropriate PHB (EF PHB in our example). In case of receiving out of profile traffic, the edge router requests a decision from the PDP. Since the PDP knows the current network state - because it receives monitoring information from different monitors installed in the network, it decides a new policy rule, for example dropping, marking or accepting out of profile traffic. This decision varies according to current network state.

2.5   QoS Management Algorithm

We have configured 3 rules named Rule1, Rule2 and Rule3 to deal with out of profile traffic. The Policy Server can choose one rule among the several depending on information sent periodically by the monitors. The monitoring information concerns essentially the bandwidth usage of each link in the network. The calculation of shaped value of the bandwidth using *Exponentially Weighted Moving Average* (EWMA) is presented in section 2.6. Below in Fig. 4 our algorithm, which uses the predefined policy rules to make a decision depending on bandwidth usage in the network.

```
Initialization:
Start Bandwidth Monitor Mi for each Router i to
calculate the available bandwidth BW_i
Lambda ← 0.2      // Fixed value for historical data
X ←50% link capacity    // Initial value of EWMA
Min_th← 40% link capacity
Max_th← 70% link capacity
Loop:
BW ← max(BW_1, BW_2, ..., BW_i)    //EWMA available bandwidth X
X← (1-lambda) * BW + lambda * X
if  X < Min_th then
  Rule1: Accept out-of-profile traffic
else if Min_th<=X<Max_th then
  Rule2: Remark out-of-profile traffic with a new DSCP
else Rule3: Drop out-of-profile Traffic
End.
End loop
```

Fig. 4. Example of a simple algorithm using policies.

2.6   Calculating Bandwidth Usage in the Network Links

Our algorithm uses a low-pass filter to calculate the bandwidth usage. Bursty traffic can cause a transient congestion. The bandwidth usage is not affected by this transient congestion since we shape this value. The low-pass filter is an exponential weighted moving average.

The EWMA *(Exponentially Weighted Moving Average)* Chart is used when it is desirable to detect out-of-control situations very quickly. It is an Exponential Smoothing technique that employs one exponential smoothing parameter to give more weight to recent observations and less weight to older observations and vice-versa.

When choosing λ, it is recommended to use small values (such as 0.2) to detect small shifts and larger values (between 0.2 and 0.4) for larger shifts [10].

Policy decision depends on the EWMA statistic calculated by each network monitor and sent to the Policy Decision Point to be aggregated.

3   Implementation

Our prototype consists of three modules that perform Dynamic QoS adaptation in an administrative domain; these modules are Policy-based network management tool, Network Monitoring System, and Policy System (Policy Decision Point and Policy Enforcement Point). Fig. 5 shows the core components of our implementation.

3.1   Tool Manager

Our policy tool management is a Policy-based Web Bandwidth Broker. It consists essentially of a web interface installed in web application server. The administrator uses the web interface to configure the Diffserv domain and to enter new policy or to edit an old one. A Java Servlet engine is used to store all the information to a repository. We have used an OpenLDAP [11] server running on Linux. Other functions may be provided, such as validation, verification, conflict detection, etc. which are not yet available in our system.

In the top right of Fig. 5, a simple web-based interface of the bandwidth broker is shown. It illustrates the edge router configuration, specially the filter configuration and how setting PHB for the traffic entering the network.

3.2   Network Monitoring Agent

Network Monitoring provides a global network status in terms of resource availability and resource consumption, which is required for the management of the available bandwidth on the network. It is an application that tracks on live resources information in the network. A framework for supporting the traffic engineering of IP-based networks is presented in [12]. Different types monitoring measurements have been identified and are either **passive** or **active**. Passive measurement means that the statistics of the network element are maintained in the form of a Management Information Base (MIB), whereas in active measurement, test packets are injected into the network (like ping test) to gather information. Information collected about these packets are taken as representative of the behavior of the network. Metrics of this data are described in the framework presented in [13].

Our implementation consists of an agent written in Java which collects information on each interface of the router. The collected information consists of a real-time traffic flow measurement in input and output of each interface. This way, the agent augments the functionality of PEP by reporting monitoring information to the PDP in the form of COPS Report State Message. The PDP, when it detects a significant modification in the network state, delivers to the PEP a new policy decision in term of new policy rules. Decision-making is based on the algorithm described in Fig. 4.

3.3   Policy Management System

This system is composed of a PDP and a PEP communicating using COPS protocol. All system components are implemented in Java. The COPS-PR implementation is simplified to exchange policy rule between PDP and PEP.

Simplified COPS-PR implementation is used to exchange policy rules between the PDP and the PEP.

The PEP is associated with the interfaces to which the marking must be applied (edge router). It is notified when the policy changes (or is newly) by a COPS provisioning operation. The PEP receives the policy information and transforms it into a form suitable for the device, e.g. using a Linux Diffserv Traffic Control API. After this, all incoming packets to this device will be marked according to the new marking policy.

The PDP is responsible for decision making and uses for that the network monitoring agents. Our implementation is limited to one domain (there is no inter-domain communication).

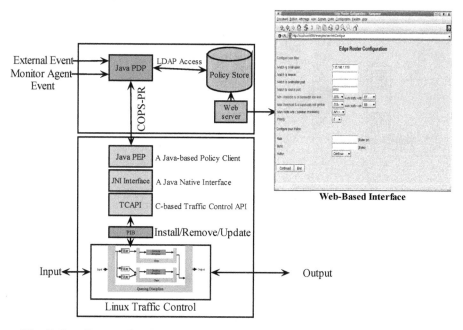

Fig. 5. Our System Implementation using Dynamic Policy-Based Management

4 Performance Evaluation and Results Analysis

The network administrator uses the PBNM tool (BB) to configure the edge and core routers according to a predefined set of policies. Suppose that the administrator's domain can handle EF, AF11 and BE class only. The administrator configures the filters using also PBNM tool. The task of the filter is to mark the traffic entering the network with the appropriate PHB according to user profile. At this step, the administrator chooses how to handle excess of traffic (out of profile traffic) by tuning two control thresholds (Min_th and Max_th).

4.1   Experimental Testbed

Fig. 6 depicts our experiments testbed. User transmits a customized traffic (audio traffic) across a Differentiated Services network. The network is composed of Diffserv capable routers. We use Linux-based IP routers with Diffserv implementation [14], [15]. The testbed is composed of two edge routers connecting by 10 Mb/s Ethernet links.

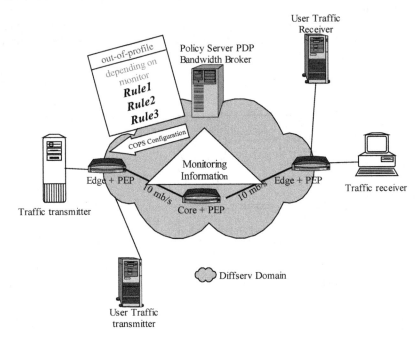

Fig. 6. Experimental Environment

By using our PBNM tool, we allocated 1.5Mbit/s for each AF class (i.e. AF1, 2, 3 and 4), all of which are bounded. We limit the amount of EF traffic to 15% of the bandwidth capacity rate, i.e. 1.5Mbit and we allocated 3.5Mbit for the best effort traffic that are allowed to borrow any available bandwidth. To get distinguish class of service, we used CBQ as our packet scheduler, which is an approach proposed in [16]. For CBQ a single set of mechanisms is proposed to implement link sharing and real-time services. In our implementation, CBQ is used to classify EF, AF, and BE traffic so that each user can get appropriate resources based on packet marking. The scheduler of the Diffserv core router employs GRED queuing discipline to support multiple drop priorities as required for the AF PHB group. One physical GRED queue is composed of multiple **VQs** (Virtual Queues). GRED can operate in **RIO** (RED with In/Out bit) *mode* [17], with coupled average queue estimates from the virtual queues, or in *standard mode* where each virtual queue has its own independent average queue estimate as required for RED [18]. In our testbed, we used GRED as the queuing discipline for AF classes, since our marking algorithm takes into account these properties to give different level of QoS.

4.2   Performance Analysis

We loaded the network using n IP traffic generator. One traffic generator is composed of a traffic transmitter and a traffic receiver. The traffic transmitter generates a UDP packet of 1024 bytes with IP and UDP headers according to a Poisson distribution with parameter $\lambda = 128$ packet/s that gives 1Mbit/s per traffic generator. In our test, and since our Ethernet links are 10 Mbit/s, we have taken $n=5$, $n=7$ and $n=10$ in order to load the network differently each time. Each source can be either on or off during exponentially distribution on/off period with an average of $\lambda_{on} = \lambda_{off} = 1s$.

We compare the different network and traffic scenario when activating the algorithm and not activating the algorithm with an IP Diffserv network model.

Policing is performed at the edge of the network for a particular traffic, which is identified by a couple <IP_adr, Port_number>. Policy is determined by the traffic specification **Tspec** (traffic profile). Tspec takes the form of a token bucket (r,b) and the following optional parameters : a peak rate (p), a minimum policed unit (m), and a maximum datagram size (M).

The token bucket and peak rate parameters require that traffic obeys the rule that over all time periods, the amount of data sent cannot exceed M+min[pT, rT+b-M] [19]. M is the maximum datagram size, and T is the length of time period. Datagrams which arrive at an element and cause a violation of the M+min[pT, rT+b-M] bound are considered out of profile (non-conformant) and require a decision from the PDP.

In our experiment, we set the parameters for the token bucket to $r=1Mbit/s$ and $b=2K$, for user traffic. This means that this traffic must not exceed 1Mbit/s.

For testing purposes, we transmit an out of profile traffic (not conform to TSpec). This traffic is at a constant bit rate of 1.5 Mbit/s. The token buckets accept only 1Mbit/s, therefore, the 0.5 Mbit/s are considered out of profile. The in profile traffic will be marked with EF PHB whereas the out of profile traffic will be marked either by EF or AF11 or dropped (according to our predefined policy).

Fig. 7 (a) shows the bottleneck link load during the period of the experiment (180s). This load represents the traffic sent from the n traffic generators to the receivers. This measure has been taken from the ingress interface of the core router. During to first 60 seconds there are only n=5 traffic generators that can be either on or off. From time 60s to 120s there are n=7 traffic generators. In the last 60 second (from 120s to 180s) the number of the traffic generators are $n=10$.

The PDP makes the decision according to the smoothing value of the bandwidth usage (i.e., EWMA). This decision is a policy rule sent directly to the edge router of the Diffserv network.

In our experiments, we set the value of Min_th=4Mbit and the value of Max_th=7Mbit. The read time of the bandwidth usage performed by the bandwidth agent is set to 1 second.

The events sent by the PDP are listed below with the corresponding timestamps (see Table 1).

Table 1: List of policies sent by the PDP

TIME (SECOND)	ACTION TAKEN BY THE EDGE ROUTER (POLICY)
0	Rule1: Accept out of profile traffic (EF traffic)
12	Rule2: Remark out of profile traffic with AF11
37	Rule1: Accept out of profile traffic (EF traffic)
38	Rule2: Remark out of profile traffic with AF11
40	Rule1: Accept out of profile traffic (EF traffic)
47	Rule1: Accept out of profile traffic (EF traffic)
103	Rule3: Drop out of profile Traffic
105	Rule2: Remark out of profile traffic with AF11
107	Rule3: Drop out of profile Traffic
109	Rule2: Remark out of profile traffic with AF11
110	Rule3: Drop out of profile Traffic
111	Rule2: Remark out of profile traffic with AF11
112	Rule3: Drop out of profile Traffic
116	Rule2: Remark out of profile traffic with AF11
117	Rule3: Drop out of profile Traffic
141	Rule2: Remark out of profile traffic with AF11
144	Rule3: Drop out of profile Traffic
177	Rule2: Remark out of profile traffic with AF11
179	Rule1: Accept out of profile traffic (EF traffic)

These events show how traffic is subject to a dynamic behavior in the network. This is an interesting function, since it allows an Internet Service Provider making new strategies of traffic engineering easily.

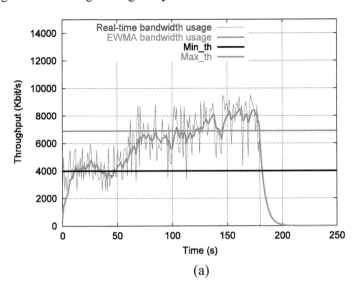

(a)

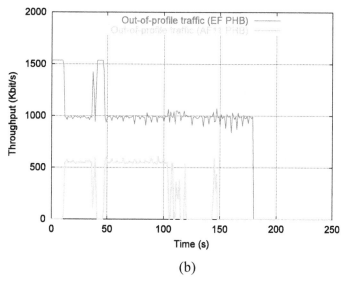

(b)

Fig. 7.   **(a) Bottleneck Link Usage**

(b) Received Audio Traffic with different PHB Color

Fig. 7 (b) shows the received audio traffic with the different PHB colors. In-profile traffic (1Mbits) is always marked as EF whereas out-of-profile traffic (0,5 Mbits) is dynamically accepted as EF, as AF11, or dropped.

The events shown in the Table represent the time at which the policy is sent from the PDP to the edge router. This later updates traffic policing to reflect this change. For example in the first 60 second, bottleneck link is under load (X <Min_th), so the edge router can accept out of profile traffic as shown in Fig. 7 (b). In the next 60 second (from time 60 to 120 s), load is between Min_th and Max_th, so we accept out of profile but with remarking policy. From time 120 to 180 s, bottleneck link is congestionned, in this case, out of profile traffic is dropped. See Fig. 7 (b) for more details.

5   Conclusion

This paper address the issue of out-of-profile traffic in a Diffserv network. It describes our proposal of using network monitoring feedback and policy decision point. The collected monitoring information is used to manage and to adapt dynamically QoS parameters for user traffic. The example configuration rules described in our testbed clearly demonstrate the advantage of using our proposed resource network management framework. Our system involves a policy-based management system to achieve a more dynamic network behavior in handling user traffic.

Several issues arise when using dynamic control decisions to handle out-of-profile traffic. One problem is the pricing and charging schemes in use: Who pays for the service (out-of-profile traffic), the sender or the receiver ? More work has to be done in order to define accurately the amount of traffic that excesses the profile in order to establish a payment scheme. Also, time-scale measurement of the PDP response is important and should be evaluated in future work.

References

1. S. Blake, D. Black M. Carlson,E. Davies, Z. Wang, W. Weiss "RFC 2475: An Architecture for Differentiated Services", December 1998.
2. V. Jacobson, K. Nichols, K.Poduri "RFC 2598 An Expedited Forwarding PHB", June 1999.
3. J.Heinanen, , F.Baker , W. Weiss, J. Wroclawsk "RFC 2597 : Assured Forwarding PHB Group", June 1999.
4. K. Nichols, S. Blake, F. Baker, D. Black "RFC 2474: Definition of the Differentiated Services Field (DS Field) in the IPv4 and IPv6 Headers", December 1998.
5. W. Fang, Seddigh, B. Nandy "RFC2859 - A Time Sliding Window Three Colour Marker (TSWTCM)", June 2000.
6. J. Heinanen, R. Guerin "RFC2698 - A Two Rate Three Color Marker (TRTCM)", September 1999.
7. D. Durham, Ed, J. Boyle, R. Cohen, S. Herzog, R. Rajan,w, A. Sastry "RFC 2748: The COPS (Common Open Policy Service) Protocol", January 2000.
8. S. Herzog, Ed., J. Boyle, R. Cohen, D. Durham, R. Rajan, A. Sastry "RFC 2749: COPS usage for RSVP", January 2000.
9. K. Chan, J. Seligson, D. Durham, S. Gai, K. McCloghrie, S. Herzog, F. Reichmeyer, R. Yavatkar, A. Smith "RFC 3084: COPS Usage for Policy Provisioning (COPS-PR)", March 2001.
10. J. Stuart Hunter. "The Exponentially Weighted Moving Average" J Quality Technology, Vol. 18, No. 4, pp. 203-207, 1986.
11. "OpenLDAP software" available at http://www.openldap.org/
12. W.Lai, B.Christian, R.Tibbs, S.Berghe "Framework for Internet Traffic Engineering Measurement" Internet draft, Work in progress, November 2001.
13. V. Paxson, G. Almes, J. Mahdavi, M. Mathis "RFC2330: Framework for IP Performance Metrics", May 1998.
14. Werner   Almesberger   "Differentiated   Services   on   Linux"   Home   Page http://diffserv.sourceforge.net/
15. Werner Almesberger, Jamal Hadi Salim, Alexey Kuznetsov "Differentiated Services on Linux", Work in progress, June 1999.
16. S. Floyd et al. "Link-sharing and Resource Management Models for Packet Networks" IEEE/ACM Transactions on Networking, Vol. 3, No. 4, pp. 365-386, August 1995.
17. David D. Clark and Wenjia Fang "Explicit Allocation of Best Effort Packet Delivery Service" ACM Transactions on Networking, pp. 362-373, August 1998.
18. Sally Floyd and Van Jacobson "Random early detection gateways for congestion avoidance", IEEE/ACM Transactions on Networking. Vol. 1, no. 4, pp. 397-413, August 1993.
19. L. Georgiadis, R. Gu_erin, V. Peris and R. Rajan "Efficient Support of Delay and Rate Guarantees in an Internet" in ACM SIGCOMM, volume 26, number 4, October 1996.

Design and Implementation of an Application Layer Protocol for Reducing UDP Traffic Based on User Hints and Policies

William Kulju[1] and Hanan Lutfiyya[2]

[1] DB2 CLI/ODBC Application Enablement
IBM Toronto Laboratory
Toronto, Ontario, Canada
wkulju@ca.ibm.com

[2] Department of Computer Science
The University of Western Ontario
London, Ontario, Canada N6A 5B7
hanan@csd.uwo.ca

Abstract. This paper presents an application-layer protocol for UDP that makes use of user hints (e.g., a screen saver being invoked or covering a window with another) to reduce network traffic, which in turn may help reduce congestion. The architectural components used to implement the application-layer protocol can generally be applied to a reduction in resource (e.g., CPU) consumption. We present an architecture and experimental results.

Keywords. Policies, User hints, UDP, management

1   Introduction

Interactive applications (e.g., video conferencing) do not react well to TCP's congestion control mechanisms. As a result, many developers use UDP for multimedia applications. UDP provides little functionality beyond basic data transfer. Additional functionality is to be implemented at the application layer by the developer. This has the effect of the developer creating their own 'tailor-made' application-layer protocol with UDP as the underlying data transfer mechanism. These application-layer protocols have included congestion control schemes (e.g., [4]). These protocols augment UDP to provide a particular class of multimedia applications (e.g., video conferencing tools, shared whiteboards) with services they would likely find useful (e.g., time-stamping for video applications).

One approach to reducing UDP traffic is based on the use of user *hints*. For example, if a video-on-demand client is running in a window that is minimized then this is a strong 'hint' that the user's interest has changed. If the source of the video source is made aware of this fact, it could reduce its output to audio feed, pause the video feed or slow down the rate that it sends the video feed. Basically, the source can alter its transmission behaviour in a fashion that

K.C. Almeroth and M. Hasan (Eds.): MMNS 2002, LNCS 2496, pp. 263–275, 2002.

minimises unwanted network traffic. These user actions are referred to as *hints*. Hints such as minimising and restoring windows, the covering and uncovering of windows, and the activation and deactivation of screen savers and locks are all excellent indicators of the interest users have in their applications.

This paper presents an application-layer protocol for UDP that makes use of *hints*. The design of the architectural components that are used to implement the protocol can also be used for not only reducing UDP traffic but also reducing consumption of host computing resources. The paper is organized as follows. Section 2 describes considerations to take into account when contemplating the design. Section 3 describes the architecture and the interactions among the components of the architecture. Section 4 describes the prototype implementation and initial experimental results. Section 5 describes related work. Section 6 has a detailed discussion that analyzes the protocol and the architecture. Section 7 states the conclusions and some of the future work.

2   Consideration in Design

A protocol can be informally defined as a set of well-known rules and formats needed for communication between two processes. Protocols enforce policies. A policy specifies actions that are to be undertaken by a protocol end-point when an event occurs. For example, a TCP source re-transmits data packets that have not been acknowledged (an action) before a time-out period expires (an event). The action ensures data 'lost' in the network is re-transmitted, which is necessary to effect TCP's guaranteed data delivery. Similarly, a TCP source throttles its transmission rate by half (an action) when the same event described earlier occurs in order to resolve network congestion.

There are a number of application-layer protocols (used to augment UDP), each incorporating a congestion control scheme, that have been proposed for various types of multimedia applications Application-layer protocols used to augment UDP with a congestion control scheme (e.g.,[4]) provide a particular class of multimedia applications (e.g., video conferencing tools, shared whiteboards) with services they would likely find useful (e.g., time-stamping for video applications). Therefore, a developer creating an application that fits into one of these classes could benefit by using the available protocol associated with that class rather than trying to make their own.

A shortcoming of these protocols is that the enforced policies for congestion control are static. In other words, once the protocol source code has been compiled, the congestion control algorithm of the resultant protocol executable is immutable. Thus, protocol designers usually decide on a single set of congestion control policies to be enforced. This often leads to a design of protocols based on worst-case requirements (e.g., 'computationally challenged' client and server machines connected by a 'slow' wireless link) since protocol developers cannot possibly anticipate in advance all the scenarios under which the protocol will be deployed. Therefore, developers are encouraged to design protocols that over-compensate rather than under-compensate [7] (e.g., a protocol might statically reserve more memory for input/output buffering than is realistically required as protection for the rare situations — perhaps when it is used on a 'slow' machine — where buffer overflow might otherwise occur). This often means that protocols do not always effectively manage resources.

The design of the application-layer protocol in this work allows for dynamic policies in the following sense: Policies can be dynamically negotiated between client(s) and server(s) both at the beginning of, and throughout a multimedia session. Once negotiated, these policies are then enforced for the duration of the ensuing session (or until they are re-negotiated) in a manner that is transparent to the applications relying on it.

3 Architecture

The management architecture is graphically depicted in Figure 1. The following example is used to help describe the architectural components. Assume that there is a video-on-demand session in progress between a client video application and a streaming server application connected by the Internet. We further assume that the client video display is presently a top-level window being viewed by an end-user. Now suppose that the end-user decides to check his e-mail. To do so, he opens a separate e-mail window. Let us also suppose he immediately positions this new window on his desktop in such a way that it covers the entire video display. This suggests that the end-user is less interested in the video display since he cannot even see it. A reasonable policy to enforce under these circumstances is the following: *'When the video display window area is at least 75% covered by other windows then the streaming video service provider should pause the stream of video from the server to the client. This video stream is continued when the video display window area is less covered with other windows'.*

3.1 End-User Interaction Monitors

An end-user typically interacts with a video display window, keyboard, a mouse and a chair. These entities can be characterized by attributes that change in response to an end-user's behaviour. For example, a video display window has an attribute that represents its obscurity level (i.e., extent to which the end-user has covered the video display window with other windows). Another example is that of a workstation monitor. It has an attribute that represents whether or not the screen saver is activated as a result of end-user activity. When the value of these attributes changes, it may be a 'hint' that an end-user's interest in a multimedia application has also changed. Detecting 'hints' is the responsibility of *end-user interaction monitors.*

Each interaction monitor monitors an attribute within the client-side multi-media environment for changes in the value of that attribute. Upon detecting an attribute change, the monitor then determines if a particular condition on this attribute has become 'satisfied' or 'unsatisfied'. If so, the end-user interaction monitor notifies interested objects (e.g., client coordinator, which is discussed

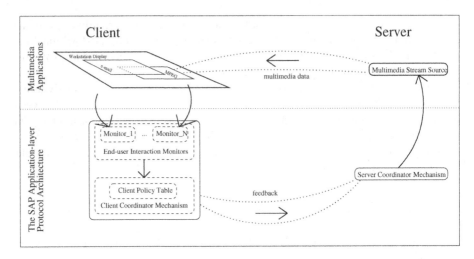

Fig. 1. The protocol used to (re)allocate streaming video server resources
labelfig:client-server

in the next section) about the changed attribute condition. There may be more
than one attribute condition that is evaluated.

Definition 1.

An *attribute condition* is defined as follows:

$$attribute\ condition = (anAttribute, (comparisonOperator, aThreshold))$$

where *anAttribute* denotes the attribute being monitored for value changes by the
interaction monitor, *aThreshold* denotes a threshold that the value of *anAttribute*
is being compared to, and *comparisonOperator* denotes the comparison operator
by which the value of *anAttribute* and *aThreshold* are to be compared. □

Example 1.

Suppose a 'window obscurity' monitor detects changes in the attribute representing how much of the video display window has been covered by other windows.
Let x denote this attribute. The monitor could evaluate the attribute condition $(x, (>=, 75))$ (i.e., "At least 75% of the total video display window area is
covered by other windows") whenever a change in the value of x is detected. □

An end-user interaction monitor maintains a list of attribute conditions and
provides methods that includes initializing and creating an attribute condition,
changing parameters in an attribute condition, and allowing an external object
to register with the end-user interaction monitor to receive notification when
a previously 'unsatisfied' attribute condition has become 'satisfied' and when a
previously 'satisfied' attribute condition has become 'unsatisfied'.

3.2   Client Coordinator

The client coordinator maintains a table that maps attribute conditions to actions. This table is referred to as the *client policy table* and it represents the policies to be enforced. Whenever an end-user interaction monitor determines that a previously 'true' attribute condition has become false (or vice versa), it notifies the client coordinator. The client coordinator updates the client policy table that a particular attribute condition has changed from unsatisfied to satisfied or from satisfied to unsatisfied. Based on this information, it is then determined what actions the client coordinator should execute.

Definition 2.

A *policy* is defined as follows:[1]

> $policy$ = ($attributeConditon_1$, ..., $attributeCondition_n$, $actionList_1$, $actionList_2$)

$attributeCondition_j$ denotes an attribute condition that is either 'true' or 'false', $actionList_1$ denotes actions the client coordinator is to execute if the conjunction of $attributeCondition_1$ through $attributeCondition_n$ has just become 'true' (i.e., it has gone from 'unsatisfied' to 'satisfied'). In contrast, $actionList_2$ denotes actions the client coordinator is to execute if the conjunction of $attributeCondition_1$ through $attributeCondition_n$ has just become 'false' (i.e., it has gone from 'satisfied' to 'unsatisfied'). □
An **action** that is found in either $actionList_1$ or $actionList_2$ of the policy definition is defined as follows:

Definition 3.

An **action** is defined as follows:

> $action$ = *(targetObject, (actionMethod, actionMethodParameter))*

targetObject denotes an object and *actionMethod* denotes a method to be executed on *targetObject*. *targetObject* may be either local to or remote from the client multimedia application process space. Finally, *actionMethodParameter* denotes zero or more parameters to be included with the *actionMethod* call (e.g., a command message, another action). Note that *actionMethodParameter* is optional in any particular *action*. □

Example 2.

Suppose a streaming video service provider would like to 'pause' all transmitted bandwidth to a client video application end-user whenever more than 75% of the total video display play window area is covered by other windows.
  ((*"percentage of the total video display window area covered by other windows"*,

---

[1]   This definition of policy is based on that found in IETF standards at http://www.ietf.org.

('greater than', 75)),
(serverCoordinator, Update(), (streamSource, Pause())),
(serverCoordinator, Update(), (streamSource, Continue()))))

This policy can be interpreted as follows: When the video display window area is 75% covered by other windows then the streaming video service provider should pause the stream of video from the server to the client. This video stream is continued when the video display window area is less covered with other windows. □

3.3   Server Coordinator

The server coordinator is a server-side mechanism that performs two tasks. The first of these tasks results in providing entries for the client policy table. When the client initiates a multimedia session, the client coordinator sends the server coordinator a list of attributes that is referred to as the **attribute profile**. This list specifies all client-side attributes the client coordinator is able to have monitored for value changes by end-user interaction monitors. When the server coordinator receives the attribute profile, it examines its list of policies. If the attribute condition of the policy has a corresponding match in the attribute profile, the server coordinator places that policy on a list that is sent to the client coordinator. Each policy on the list is added to the client coordinator's policy table.

The second task is that of dynamic adjustment of the service transmitted to a client in response to feedback from the client. Feedback is information is provided by the client coordinator. The feedback is used by the server coordinator to adjust the quality of the multimedia stream transmitted to the client application associated with that particular client coordinator.

The server coordinator maintains a list of handles to client coordinators. Furthermore, the server coordinator is able to differentiate between client coordinators via these handles, thus implying that different dynamic adjustments to the quality of the multimedia stream can be done based on the client.

3.4   Interactions

This section describes the relationship between the management and application components.

The architecture assumes that the client coordinator is implemented as a thread of the process executing the application. This thread is initiated through instrumentation code (code which is inserted into an application at strategic locations). Each application has one client coordinator. A similar assumption is made for the server coordinator. It sometimes makes sense for an end-user interaction monitor to interact with more than one client coordinator (e.g., an end-user interaction monitor that detects the presence or absence of a screen saver). End-user interaction monitors provide a set of methods. One of these methods includes a registration method that allows client coordinators to receive notification when a previously 'unsatisfied' attribute condition has become 'satisfied' (or vice-versa). The registration method allows for the specification of the attribute condition (i.e., the comparison operator and a threshold to compare values of the attribute). Thus, it is possible for an end-user interaction monitor to maintain a list of entries where each entry is an attribute condition and handles for client coordinators. When the value of the attribute changes then each attribute condition is evaluated. If there is a change from 'satisfied' to 'unsatisfied' (or vice-versa) then a notification is sent to the client coordinators that registered to receive a notification when the result of an attribute condition evaluation changes.

As described earlier, the server coordinator receives a list called the attribute profile from the client coordinator. This list specifies all client-side attributes that the client coordinator is able to have monitor through end-user interaction monitors. The client coordinator creates this list from its profile file or from a profile list received from a management agent. The profile file(list) contains entries that are a pair, with the first element being the attribute name and the second element being the location of a client-side executable or dynamic link library to an interaction monitor that monitors the attribute. It should be noted that when the client coordinator is initialised it is given the handle of a server coordinator.

Upon receiving an attribute profile from a client coordinator, the server coordinator examines its *server policy list*. Each entry of this list is a policy. Upon receiving an attribute profile from a client coordinator, the server coordinator examines each attribute condition of each policy in the server policy list. If the attribute component of the attribute condition of a policy can be found in the attribute profile of the client coordinator, then the server coordinator places that policy in a list. This list is sent to the client coordinator. The client coordinator uses this to add entries to the client policy table and instantiates end-user interaction monitors as needed.

This allows for a server policy list to be created in advance that specifies an arbitrarily large number of policies and attribute conditions within those policies. Moreover, it can be assumed that any particular client coordinator will only be able to have an arbitrary fraction of the attribute conditions in the list monitored by end-user interaction monitors. The server coordinator dynamically chooses the policies it wants an arbitrary client coordinator to enforce in a multimedia session, given the capabilities of that client coordinator.

This approach also allows a server policy list to provide differentiated services by providing different policies for different client processes.

Policies can be re-negotiated as needed during an ensuing session. Examples of why this may be necessary include a change in the number of multimedia session participants, changed resource conditions at the client or server, or changes in congestion within the network. This is the result of the client coordinator being designed so that it provides methods that allow for the policies of the client policy table to be modified. If the change in policy involves a change in the threshold value used in an attribute condition, then the method of the end-user interaction monitor that changes the threshold is called by the client coordinator.

4   Implementation

This section describes the implementation of a prototype based on the architecture described in the previous section.

4.1   Client and Server Coordinators, Policy Table and Interaction Monitors

The client coordinator, server coordinator and policy table were implemented as objects in Java 2.0 [1] Remote communication between the client coordinator and server coordinator objects is achieved through use of the Java Media Framework 2.0 (JMF) version of the Real-time Transfer Protocol (RTP) [1]. RTCP (Real-time Transfer Control Protocol) [12,2] is used for client and server coordinator communication.

We implemented the following end-user interaction monitors for incorporation within our prototype. The window obscurity monitor detects when a specified window on the end-user's monitor has become obscured after being unobscured (based on some threshold value) or has become unobscured after being obscured. It was implemented using X11 [8]. The second interaction monitor implemented is a video frame rate monitor that detects when the rate of video frames rendered to the end-user's workstation screen has fallen below a certain threshold rate for a specified duration. The third interaction monitor detects when the screen saver has been activated.

The attribute profile (which is sent to the server coordinator) of the client and the server's list of policies are found in files.

4.2   Applications and Policies Used in Experimentation

We constructed a video receiver application and modified an existing streaming video server to use our protocol. The video receiver application was written entirely in Java using Java 1.2 and JMF 1.2. Video data transmitted by a remote streaming video server is forwarded to the receiver by an RTP channel. In JMF, the local RTP end-point within the client that receives this data is referred to as the client's 'session manager'. In JMF, the local RTP end-point within the client that receives this data is referred to as the client's 'session manager'. A session manager also maintains a RTCP channel for communication of application-specific control information between end-points. End-points communicate via RTCP. This allows us to leverage the channel already made available by the session manager rather than implement a second RTCP (and hence a second RTP) channel. The server application is a modified version of the JMStudio multimedia application. The policies used are informally stated as follows: (1) If the video display is obscured by 75% or more, the server co-ordinator is to pause transmission to the client. This was more formally stated in Example 2. (2) If the screen saver is on, the server coordinator is to pause transmission to the client.

4.3   Testing and Experiments

We will now briefly summarize some of the experimental results. The following discussion is based on the first policy, but similar results were achieved for the other policy. After the policy agreed upon by the client and the server coordinators, we took measurements from our testing tools. The UNIX 'top' utility on the server machine revealed that roughly 45% of server machine CPU utilisation was devoted to transmitting the video data and that 39 megabytes of RAM was reserved by the source application. Furthermore, the cumulative number of packets sent by the server was increasing steadily. These observations were largely identical to those measured with the unmodified JMStudio video server. Similarly, a 'top' utility on the client machine revealed that approximately 7% of client machine CPU effort was devoted to decoding and rendering the received video data, while 32 megabytes of RAM was reserved by the receiver application. These observations closely paralleled those made with an otherwise equivalent receiver application that did not use our prototype. This suggests that our protocol does not have much overhead.

When portions of the 'actual' video display window were obscured such that the total was less than 75% of the total video display window area, there was no visible reaction. However, once more than 75% of the total video display window area had become obscured, video transmission was paused at the source within at most 5 seconds (in all of our trials). Then, almost instantly, the rendering of video to the client workstation monitor halted as well. In this state, the CPU utilisation of both source and receiver applications quickly fell to 0% (although reserved RAM remained unchanged on both client and server machines). The packets sent also fell to zero. These results suggest that our prototype had significantly reduced the amount of 'unwanted' data traffic entering the network and that it was highly reactive since full traffic reduction was achieved within seconds of the source video data becoming 'unwanted'.

Generally, the prototype was extensively tested under different circumstances including the following: (i) A client may have no interaction monitors, which basically implies that no policies may apply and hence there is no opportunity to reduce resource consumption; (ii) The client's attribute profile has attributes that do not match with any policies that the server has; (iii) The server policy file may be empty. In all cases, the prototype worked.

5   Related Work

The work closest to ours is that found in [4] which describes a dynamic video conferencing model called SCUBA. SCUBA is a scalable control protocol that employs 'hints' about end-user interest that occur at the workstation display to adapt the transmission rate of media sources to the receivers that are part of the multicast session. Our work differs in that it provides more flexibility in the types and number of user hints (SCUBA only takes into account window placement). We provision for incorporating additional end-user hints. Second, the SCUBA policies are hardcoded. A change requires re-compilation.

There are a number of other works that address network congestion control. Receiver-driven protocols (e.g., [10]) are where receivers are given control over the transmission behaviour of sources by the protocol. Sender-driven protocols (e.g., [5]) are where senders determine their own bandwidth transmission rate (usually on the basis of receiver feedback). Receivers may be best equipped to make decisions regarding issues local to them (e.g., network congestion). But in a multicast session, it is generally not a good idea to let individual receivers adjust source transmission behaviour since the receiver will likely have no regard for the effects of these changes on other receivers. Hence the logic behind sender-driven protocols is to have receivers submit feedback to the source so that the source can then make decisions that will best benefit the entire group.

In both types of protocols there is a notion of policies, but the policies are static. Thus, the congestion control achieved through these policies can be ineffective when used under the precise conditions for which the protocol was defined.

There has been relatively little research (e.g., [3,9,13]) and industrial effort investigating how to effectively make use of hints of user activity to guide resource management. The work is domain-specific and limited in scope. While these issues were raised in [3], no design or implementation work was ever completed. [9] also examines these issues, but only in the context of their own 3D landscape environment, and not generally available production environments. From industrial research, Microsoft Windows 95, 98, and NT [11] can capture some user hints to adjust application priorities and time quanta slightly as applications are foregrounded and backgrounded. Some flavours of UNIX have limited support for user hints, by adjusting scheduling according to I/O activity.

6   Discussion

This section describes the requirements that the proposed protocol satisfies and provides a broader context for this work.

Use of Multiple Interaction Monitors. It is possible for our protocol to receive input from a potentially arbitrary set of end-user interaction monitors. In our implementation client coordinators have access to a file (i.e., the attribute profile) that specifies both the available end-user interaction monitors and details on how to instantiate each of those monitors. The addition of new end-user interaction monitors means an additional entry in the policy file for the client. If the server specifies polices in its policy file that have attributes in the attribute condition that cannot be monitored by the client then that policy is not applied to the client. This allows the server process to enforce policies for different client processes even though the different client processes monitor different attributes.

Development Issues. On the surface, it would seem that the development of client and server coordinators as well as monitors is difficult and time-consuming. It should be noted that the client and server coordinators were designed to be independent of the specific applications. It should be noted that Definitions 1, 2 and 3 can easily map to Java classes (as well as C++ classes). The methods defined are relatively simple in that they are primarily being used to manipulate the structures found in Definitions 1, 2 and 3. We found that these classes could be applied to any of the policies and applications used. The coordinators are implemented as Java classes and can be reused by different applications.

The interaction monitors are more difficult. The 'window obscurity' monitor is rather difficult to implement, but it can be used by multiple applications. It should be noted that there would have to be a 'window obscurity' monitor class for each platform. The monitoring of the frame rate can be encapsulated as a class and used by multiple applications. It is this reuse aspect that reduces the amount of development work.

The window obscurity and frame rate monitors execute outside of an application. However, the frame rate monitor are part of an application's instrumentation. The application developer needs to know the methods of the class encapsulating the monitoring, but is not concerned with the details on how the frame rate is actually calculated.

Flexibility. Example 2 states that if the video display window area is 75% covered by other windows then the streaming video service provider should pause the stream of video from the server to the client. However, it may be desirable to pause the video but not the audio. This can be done by having a policy that states that the action to be taken is to only pause the video.

Specification and Distribution of Policies. There already exists formalisms for specifying policies. One example can be found in [6]. Our policies can easily be specified using this formalism.

Dynamically Changing Policies. Assume that it is decided that a server process changes the policy about window obscurity. For example, the server is to be notified when video display window area is 60% covered as opposed to 75% covered. The server coordinator process informs the client coordinator, which then notifies the end-user interaction monitor to change the threshold associated with the attribute condition and the specific client coordinator.

7   Conclusions and Future Work

The main significance of our work is that it permits both the monitors that detect end-user activity, and the policies specifying actions to undertake when that activity occurs, to be dynamically negotiated between client(s) and server(s) at run-time. This is an important consideration because receivers in a multimedia session might not all have the same capacity for detecting end-user activity or responding to that activity. For example, detecting whether or not an application end-user is seated in the chair before their workstation first requires some sort of sensory device especially geared to the task. If a particular receiver does not possess this device, then our work permits the source to decide upon an alternative action (e.g., substitution of hints from the 'seat monitor' with hints detected by another sensory device).

Our work allows for dynamic modification of policies. As discussed in the previous section, it may be decided that a server is to be notified when the video display window area is 60% covered as opposed to 75% covered. This may be done if high network congestion is detected. This change permits the server to reduce the number of packets it is sending based on user interest. Thus, our approach permits congestion control policies to be finely tuned at run-time so that they are as aggressive as possible.

There are a number of issues to be addressed in the future and are briefly described as follows.

- This work relies on the assumption that the attribute profile and the server policy list have an agreement on attribute names. Thus, two syntactically identical attribute names are assumed to be semantically equal. We will closely examine how to ensure this assumption. We will examine the use of XML to specify universal attribute semantics, but let the client and server coordinators apply their own syntax to those semantics. This can be accomplished by having end-user interaction monitor developers associate an external document type definition (DTD) with each new interaction monitor release. That DTD would specify the semantics of the attribute condition that monitor was designed to detect. All DTDs constructed could be deposited in special Internet DTD repositories, which would make them 'universal'. A server coordinator uses the DTD to reconstruct the attribute in a syntax the server coordinator understands. This facilitates the use of user hints and policies for application components in different administrative domains.
- We are especially interested in applying our work to a production environment involving machines of faculty, staff and graduate students in our department as well as using at least one application such as video-conferencing for further validation. We will install the prototype software on these machines (of course, with permission) and evaluate different policies.
- We will apply our protocol to SCUBA and other protocols (both send and receiver oriented) and evaluate their performance.
- Policies may conflict. To make this protocol truly successful, we must find a heuristic for detecting this type of conflict.

Copyright Information

States, other countries, or both. UNIX is a registered trademark of The Open Group in the United States and other countries. Other company, product, or service names may be trademarks or service marks of others.

Acknowledgements

This work is supported by the National Sciences and Engineering Research Council (NSERC) of Canada, and the Canadian Institute of Telecommunications Research (CITR).

References

1. Sun Microsystems Inc. Internet site, www.java.sun.com/products. 270, 270
2. *Java Media Framework API Guide.* Sun Microsystems Inc, JMF 2.0 FCS, November 1999. 270
3. M. Alfano. Design and Implementation of a Cooperative Multimedia Environment with QoS Control. *Computer Communications (21), Elsevier Science,* Fall 1997. 272, 272
4. E. Amir, S. McCanne, and R. Katz. Receiver-driven bandwidth adaptation for light-weight sessions. *ACM Multimedia,* November 1997. 263, 264, 271
5. M. Barcellos and P. Ezhilchelvan. An end-to-end reliable multicast protocol using polling for scaleability. *Proceedings of the Conference on Computer Communications (IEEE Infocom), (San Francisco, California),* page 1180, March 1998. 272
6. N. Damianou, N. Dalay, E. Lupu, and M. Sloman. Ponder: A language for specifying security and management policies for distributed systems: The language specification (version 2.1). Technical Report Imperial College Research Report DOC 2000/01, Imperial College of Science, Technology and Medicine, London, England, April 2000. 273
7. S. Floyd. Internet research: Comments on formulating the problem. an open letter prompting discussion. *Unpublished paper,* January 1998. www.aciri.org/floyd/. 264
8. A. Nye. *Xlib Programming Manual for Version 1.1.* O'reilly & Associates Inc., 1995. 270
9. M. Ott, G. Michelitsch, D. Reininger, and G. Welling. An Architecture for Adaptive QoS and its Application to Multimedia Systems Design. *Computer Communications Special Issue on Guiding Quality of Service into Distributed Systems,* August 1997. 272, 272
10. S. Raman and S. McCanne. Scaleable data naming for application level framing in reliable multicast. *In ACM Multimedia '98 (Bristol, England),* September 1998. 272
11. J. Richter. *Advanced Windows, Third Edition.* Microsoft Press, 1997. 272
12. H. Schulzrinne. RFC 1889, RTP: A Transport Protocol for Real-Time Applications. November 1995. Available from: www.cs.columbia.edu/ hgs/rtp/. 270
13. J. Walpole, R. Koster, S. Cen, C. Cowan, D. Maier, D. McNamee, C. Pu, D. Steere, and L. Yu. A Player for Adaptive MPEG Video Streaming Over The Internet. *Proceedings of the 26th Applied Imagery Pattern Recognition Workshop,* Washington DC, October 1997. 272

A Management Framework for Service Personalization

Govindan Ravindran[1, 2], Muhammad Jaseemudin[2] and Abdallah Rayhan[2]

[1] SOMA Networks, Inc, 312 Adelaide St W, Toronto, ON M5V 1R2, Canada
[2] Dept. of Electrical and Computer Engineering, Ryerson University, Toronto, Canada
gravin@somanetworks.com, jaseem@ee.ryerson.ca,
rayhan@ee.ryerson.ca

Abstract. Content Network, also referred to as Content Distribution Network or Content Delivery Network, is an overlay network of caches and web servers between content providers' origin servers and end users. It allows content providers to move content closer to end users thereby improving content availability and user access latencies. Recently, value-added content delivery has become both economically and technologically feasible with the advent of last-mile broadband access. Of particular interest is *Service Personalization* that refers to the process of delivering personalized services, that operate on and provide value addition to the basic content based on end-user service and device profile information. Examples of personalized services include virus scanning, content adaptation based on subscriber bandwidth and device capability, request and content filtering, and localization services. In this paper, we propose a framework for managing service personalization in a content network. We believe such a service management framework is essential in increasing the scale and reachability of service personalization and in improving the reliability and availability of content services. The framework builds on the IETF-proposed OPES (Open Pluggable Edge Services) model by adding two components, namely, a Service Manager and an Authorization Server, to automate the service personalization process. The service manager is involved in all phases of service personalization management including subscriber management, authorization of content service requests, service layer fault management, and service layer accounting. The authorization server, on the other hand, collects and maintains subscriber profile, generates accounting records and performs service authorization for end-users.

Keywords. Service Management, Content Network, Service Personalization, Subscriber Management, Open Pluggable Edge Services, Content Services Network.

1 Introduction

Content Network (CN), also referred to as Content Distribution Network or Content Delivery Network (CDN), is an overlay network of caches and web servers between content providers' origin servers and content consumers or end-users. The content network allows content providers to move content closer to end-users by replicating content in intermediate cache servers [7]. This results in i) improved content availability, ii) decreased user perceived latencies during content access, and iii) reduced bandwidth demands and web processing loads on origin servers. Traditionally,

K.C. Almeroth and M. Hasan (Eds.): MMNS 2002, LNCS 2496, pp. 276-288, 2002.
© Springer-Verlag Berlin Heidelberg 2002

web-caching proxies [6] are used to cache content closer to end-users. The introduction of content networks, however, helped content providers to meet the growing demands without placing cache management and distribution burden on them. This is achieved by delegating the authority to content networks to act on behalf of and in close co-operation with content providers.

The content network is traditionally associated with caching and delivery of raw content to end-users without any modification or adaptation [7], [10]. Considering the potential limit on the revenue of basic content delivery, the content network operators look for ways to value add services (on behalf of content providers), such as adapting content to suit end-user device capability, in an efficient and scalable manner. With recent technological advances in last-mile broadband access, the delivery of enriched and value-added content has become both economically and technologically feasible. An overlay network on top of a traditional content network infrastructure can realize the delivery of enriched content, by content adaptation and modification. Such a content services overlay has been referred to previously as *Content Services Network* (CSN) and *Open Pluggable Edge Services Network* (OPES). In a CSN, a set of Application Proxy Servers collaborate among themselves and with content providers' origin servers and user agents to deliver enriched content [8]. In an OPES network, *surrogates* interact with external *call-out servers* to provide value-added services to end-users[1] [3]. With content services overlay the content provider is no longer directly involved in managing content services and delegates the authority to deliver enriched content to the content networks.

One emerging content service is *Service Personalization* that refers to the process of delivering personalized services to end users based on individual service and device profile information [1]. Examples of such personalized services include virus scanning, content adaptation based on subscriber bandwidth and device profiles, request and content filtering and localization services.

In this paper, we build on the proposed OPES model by adding a *Service Manager* and an *Authorization Server* components to automate the process of delivering personalized services to end users. The service manager and authorization server interact with OPES intermediaries and content provider origin servers to perform service layer fault, performance and accounting management.

The rest of the paper is organized as follows. In Section 2, we discuss related work in general and the OPES model and its components in particular. In Section 3, we discuss the service personalization process. In Section 4, we present and discuss management framework for service personalization and present scenarios for subscriber management, service authorization, service layer fault, performance, and accounting management. In sections 5, we discuss scalability and performance of the service personalization network in general, and a broadcast notification mechanism to improve the scalability in our management framework in particular. We conclude in Section 6.

---

[1] *Surrogate* and *call-out servers* are explained in Section 2.

2   Related Work

2.1   Content Service Network

Content Services Network (CSN) [8] was proposed to allow content transformation and processing as an infrastructure service accessible to end-users. A CSN layer can be considered as an overlay built around CNs that interacts collaboratively with user-agents (end-users), content origin servers, and other network intermediaries in the content delivery process to provide value-added services. Both the pre-distribution and post-distribution services in the CSN model are static in nature and lacks dynamic content adaptation and service delivery based on subscriber and content profiles as in the service personalization model. Furthermore, the CSN model does not describe service layer management in general, and service layer fault, performance, and accounting management in particular.

2.2   Open Pluggable Edge Services Network

The Open Pluggable Edge Services (OPES) model, proposed by the IETF OPES Working Group is a form of content services overlay network [3]. The OPES model defines the surrogate and the call-out server intermediaries in the content path. The OPES also defines an *Admin Server* whose primary purpose is to authenticate and authorize policy rule authors and service module authors. Once the authors are authenticated and authorized, policy rules and service modules can be downloaded into admin server and then into surrogates and/or call-out servers. To prevent unauthorized content processing and service delivery, OPES is constrained to provide services that are only authorized either by a content provider or an end-user.

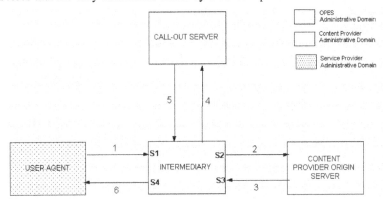

Figure 1: Service execution points in an OPES network

Figure 1 illustrates a typical data flow for an HTTP content service request:
1. The request for content from a user agent arrives at a surrogate through a requesting routing mechanism[2] (1).

---

[2] The user request is routed to a surrogate that most likely has the requested content and/or is located closer to the end-user. Sometimes content requests are routed to a surrogate based on additional factors such as surrogate load factor, surrogate administrative state, etc.

2. The surrogate retrieves content from its local store if it has the valid copy of the requested content. Otherwise, the surrogate establishes a session with content provider's origin server to retrieve the content (2), (3).
3. The retrieved content is then vectored to an external call-out server for processing (4), (5).
4. The enriched content is delivered to the user agent (6).

Figure 1 also shows the four common processing points in the OPES surrogate. The processing points 'S1' to 'S4' represent locations in the round trip message flow where policy rules can be evaluated against content request and response messages that trigger service module executions [4]. Depending on the service type, rules can be evaluated at any of these processing points. For example, for a pre-distribution service[3], rules are evaluated at 'S3' to add value-added services to content before it is stored in the cache. For a post-distribution service[4], rules are evaluated at 'S4' to add value-add services just before the content is delivered to end-users. Though content provider rule modules can be evaluated at any of the processing points, there are constraints placed on which service execution points end-user rule modules can be evaluated [3].

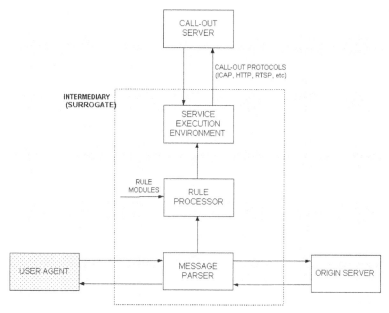

Figure 2: Rule-based service execution in an OPES surrogate

Figure 2 presents the core components of an OPES surrogate. The surrogate vectors content flow to service modules through a message parser and rule processor. The message parser traps content for processing and sends it to the rule processor,

---

[3] A pre-distribution service is performed on content before it is cached in the surrogate and distributed to end-user.

[4] A post-distribution service is performed on content just before it is delivered to end-user.

which evaluates parsed content against policy rule modules[5] and invokes execution of service module(s) when certain rules are fired. The service modules run either in surrogate's local service execution environment (referred to as *proxylets*) or in a remote service execution environment in an external call-out server. In the latter, the content requests and/or responses are encapsulated in an HTTP or ICAP (Internet Content Adaptation Protocol) PDU and forwarded to the call-out server for processing [4], [5].

The admin server, on the other hand, primarily provides authentication and authorization services for policy rule authors. The admin server is not located in the content path and therefore is not involved in any real-time service delivery management. The policy rule authors, once authenticated and authorized, download policy rule modules in the admin server from where they are distributed to surrogates and/or call-out servers.

3   Service Personalization

The goal of service personalization is to provide the means for retrieving the optimal variant of content (as response to content requests) based primarily on (i) subscriber profile including service preferences and end-device capabilities, (ii) content profile, and (iii) content provider policies.

There are several advantages in delivering personalized services from a content services overlay infrastructure such as the OPES network:

1. It mitigates the reach and scalability concerns of providing service personalization from centralized servers since the content provider has to collect and maintain subscriber and device profiles for potentially a very large number of subscribers.
2. The content provider can delegate certain functions such as collection and maintenance of subscriber information, service authorization, and generation of service detailed records to content network operators.
3. The content provider can simply act as a policy decision point for service execution. For instance, the content provider, through content and service policies, can place constraints on the processing of content. The content services network such as OPES can act as a policy execution point for content provider's content and service policies.
4. Because surrogates are delegated to operate on behalf of and often in close co-operation with one or more content providers, they provide an ideal platform for content aggregation from a select set of content sources. This allows for generation of rich variety of dynamic content in a distributed and scalable fashion.
5. Surrogates provide the widest possible audience of subscribers for a given set of content when compared to caching proxies that are often located at ISP domains.

A subscriber profile may include description of device capabilities, access rate, accounting information, and service subscriptions such as content filtering service, translation and localization services. Content profile, on the other hand, describes content type information and policies for acceptable content manipulation. For

---

[5] The rule modules are written in a standard policy rule language such as the proposed Intermediary Rule Mark-up Language.

instance, a content profile may dictate policies on what type of services that can be applied on the content. Content provider service policy help to choose optimal transformation for a given content. Subscriber and content profile together with content provider service policies contain all information needed to make any personalization decision.

There are two ways of generating optimal or the most appropriate content variant for a subscriber:

1. Modifying or transforming content (retrieved from a content source) to completely or most closely fit subscriber's profile given the content profile and content provider's service policy. Service modules (in call-out servers) and/or proxylets (in surrogates) carry out the transformation of content. The service modules and proxylets take base content as input and generate transformed content suitable for delivery.

2. The content source may have multiple versions of the same content and therefore generating a content variant for a subscriber reduces to the process of selecting the most appropriate content version. For instance, in HTTP Web sites, authors are allowed to store multiple versions of the same information under a single URL. *Transparent Content Negotiation* (TCN), a proposed mechanism to select the best appropriate variant of the content, is layered on top of HTTP and provides a mechanism for automatically selecting the best content variant when the URL is accessed [11].

4   Management Framework for Service Personalization

We present in this section a management framework for the service personalization model described earlier. The management framework enables and automates the service personalization process thereby increasing its reach and scalability. The main functions of the proposed framework include:

1. *Subscriber Management* involving collection and maintenance of subscriber service and device profile information, authentication and authorization services for end-users, and communicating with AAA servers in other administrative domains for end-user authentication and accounting purposes.

2. *Fault Management* involving anticipating and reacting to call-out servers failure in real-time.

3. *Performance Management* involving real-time collection of load and usage statistics from call-out servers and using the data to decide primary and alternate servers for service delivery mainly for load balancing and for resource optimization of call-out servers.

4. *Service Accounting* involving generation of service detailed records that are forwarded to the content provider's billing server for processing and invoice generation.

The service personalization network we describe builds on the OPES model by adding service manager and authorization server components. Figure 3 describes various components and data flow (for a content adaptation service) in a service personalization network:

1. A user agent request for a personalized content is routed through a request-routing mechanism and arrives at a surrogate at the service execution point S1 (1).
2. The surrogate evaluates the content request against policy rule modules authored by the content provider to determine whether the content service requested requires authorization. If an authorization is required, the content is forwarded to the service manager for authorization (2). For instance, the surrogate could send an HTTP GET or POST request to the service manager with the original content request passed in either on the URL string or as an HTTP payload.
3. The service manager in turn sends an authorization request to the authorization server (3). The authorization server consults subscriber profile repository to determine services the end-user is subscribed to and authorized to receive. Optionally, the authorization server can contact the AAA server in end-user's access network for user authentication. It then sends an authorization response back to the service manager along with user's service and device profiles (4).
4. The service manager combines user's service preferences, content profile information, content provider's service policy, along with call-out servers' load and usage statistics to generate a policy rule module for service execution in call-out server(s). The service manger then uploads the policy rule module as part of the authorization response (5).

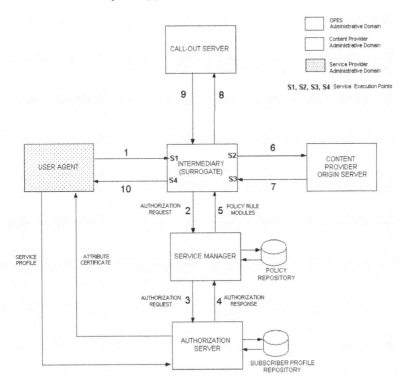

Figure 3: Components of a service personalization network

5. The surrogate after receiving service manager's authorization response retrieves content either from the local store or from the content provider's origin server (6), (7). The content will then be evaluated against the uploaded policy rule module at the service execution point 'S4'. The policy rule module will trigger service module executions at one or more call-out servers for content processing before it is delivered to the user agent (8), (9), and (10).

4.1   Policy Rule Modules

A rule processor on the surrogate matches rules by evaluating rule conditions against content properties and system and environment variables. A service module or proxylet is invoked based on the specified rule actions in all matching rules. The rule modules can be written using a policy specification language such as the proposed *Intermediary Rule Mark-up Language* (IRML) [2]. The policy rule modules processed in our framework include the *per-user* and *request-authorization* rule modules.

The per-user rule module is generated at the service manager and authorized by the end-user and/or the content provider whereas the request-authorization rule module is generated and authorized by the content provider. The per-user policy rules specify services that reflect the intent of the end-user and content provider. The content provider, through content profile and service policies, identifies conditions under which content is transformed. In addition, the content provider specifies optimal content transformation processes for various services. The end user, on the other hand, specifies preferred services through service subscriptions. Figure 4 shows an example per-user policy module written in IRML [2].

```
<?xml version="1.0"?>
  <rulemodule xmlns="http://www.rfc-editor.org/rfc/rfcxxxx.txt">
    <author type="delegate">
      <name>service-personaliztion</name>
      <contact>rule-info@cdn.com</contact>
      <id>www.cdn.com</id>
    </author>
    <ruleset>
    <authorized-by class="content-consumer" type="group">
      <name>GR</name>
      <id>www.comcast.com/irml-groups/vs-subscribers</id>
    </authorized-by>
    <protocol>HTTP</protocol>
    <rule processing-point="4">
      <execute>
        <service name="McAfee Virus Scanning Service"  type="primary" >
          <uri>icap:://mcafee.spn.com/vscan</uri>
        </service>
      </execute>
    </rule>
    </ruleset>
  </rulemodule>
```

Figure 4: Service Manager generated per-user policy module.

The rule module shown in Figure 4 is authored by the delegate on behalf of an end-user. It has a single rule-set authorized by the end-user. It specifies content request/response protocol, service execution point (on the surrogate), and the service module(s) to run. In this example, invoking a service module at the call-out server 'mcafee.spn.com' provides a virus scanning service. We can see that a second rule-set (authorized by the content provider) can be easily added to our example that overrules the service module specified in the end-user ruleset by specifying another service module in a different call-out server.

The request-authorization rule-set is processed at the service execution point 'S1'. It contains the property 'name' attribute that specifies the message property to match and the 'matches' attribute that specifies the message property value to match against. The content request URI that matches the specified property value is forwarded to the service manager for authorization.

4.2   Service Manager Interaction

In order to perform service layer management, the service manager interacts with several server components located both within and outside its administrative domain. Figure 5 illustrates service manager interaction with various server components located both in its local administrative domain and in other administrative domains:

1. The service manager generates per user policy rule modules based on the subscriber profile information it receives from the authorization server and the content and service policy from content provider's administrative/policy server. The service manager responds to authorization requests from surrogates by uploading per-user policy rule modules. The per-user policy rule module specifies service module invocations for content processing to meet end-user's service profile.

2. The service manager receives load and usage statistics, and administrative state information from call-out servers. The data is used in computing the primary and alternate call-out servers for service module executions.

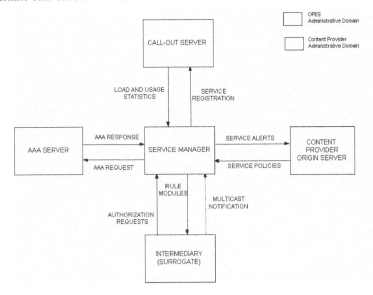

Figure 5: Service manager interaction in a service personalization network

3. Call-out servers send 'registration' messages to the service manager when they come up for the first time and when new service modules are loaded from the admin server.

4.3   Content Access and Interaction with AAA Services

The end-user is initially authenticated and authorized for network usage by the AAA server in his ISP's access network before his content requests are forwarded to the service personalization network. For instance, in dial-up Internet access, the end-user provides AAA credential (e.g. user NAI, key, etc) to the Network Access Server (NAS) during the login process. The NAS acting as the AAA attendant communicates with the AAA server located in the access network to perform user authentication and authorization. Due to static trust relationship between the ISP and the service personalization network, content request from an end user arriving at a surrogate is not usually authenticated. Exception to this occurs when a content request arrives from a roaming user in which case the authorization server authenticates the user with the AAA server of the User Home Organization [12].

Content request identifies content by its URN embedded in the URL [9]. The users may subscribe to content services by using protocols such as the AAA protocol or the proposed ISDP protocol [8]. In the former, the user directly connects to a service personalization network's authorization server to input his service profile. As a token of subscription the user obtains *Attribute Certificate* (AC), which he includes in his subsequent requests. The AC is used in part to authorize the user for services.

Another level of interaction may happen between the authorization server and the ISP's AAA server to retrieve relevant network information, which may be necessary

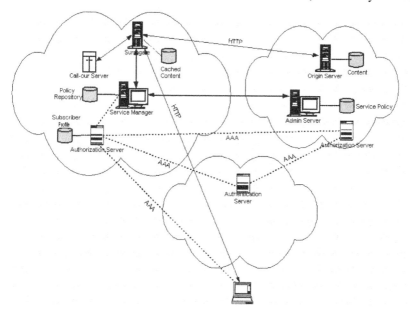

Figure 6: Service personalization network interaction

for providing some services. For instance, to deliver location-based services the service manager may need user location information. Alternatively, if the host itself is equipped with GPS, the location information can be embedded in the request.

Figure 6 illustrates the interaction of the service manager with surrogates, the authorization server in the OPES administrative domain, and the policy/admin server in the content provider's administrative domain. The authorization server communicates with AAA server in the access network to authenticate user and to retrieve access network profile. The authorization server also communicates with the AAA server in the content provider domain to retrieve user service authorization information. Figure 6 also illustrates the end-user interaction with the authorization server to subscribe to various content services.

4.4   Subscriber Management

The authorization server primarily carries out subscriber management. The user before initiating requests for content services for the first time typically goes through a service registration process with the content provider. During this process he will be redirected to the authorization server of a service personalization network. The authorization server collects user's service preference, subscription, and accounting information on behalf of the content provider and stores them locally in the subscriber profile repository. For every subsequent change in user's profile he will be directed to the same authorization server to update his profile.

After the initial registration process, the user's content request arriving at a surrogate will be redirected to the service manager. The service manager acting as an attendant issues the authorization request. The authorization server responds by sending user's service, network, and device profile information to the service manager. The service manager uses this profile information along with content provider's service policy to generate per-user policy rule module(s). Optionally, the authorization server communicates with the AAA server of user's access network for user authentication and with content provider's AAA server for user service authorization. Refer to Figure 3 for the subscriber management data flow.

4.5   Fault Management

For each service, the per-user rule module specifies a primary call-out server (for the service module execution) and optionally one or more alternate call-out servers. There are two failure scenarios of the primary call-out server:

1. The primary server fails to execute the service application and returns an error code to the surrogate. The surrogate then invokes a similar service application on one of the alternate call-out server.
2. The primary server is down. In this case the surrogate times out waiting for the service module response and automatically invokes another service module in an alternate call-out server.

The service manager determines the primary and alternate call-out servers to optimize server resource usage and to balance the processing load across multiple call-out servers. The decision takes into account real-time data such as call-out servers' load and usage statistics, and their administrative state information.

4.6   Service Accounting and Content Provider Interaction

The authorization server is a natural place to log service accounting records as it has access to subscribers' service subscription and billing information as well as it is aware of subscriber content requests. This enables the authorization server to generate a *Service Detailed Record* (SDR) for each content request. The SDRs are then sent to content provider's billing server to generate invoices. The content provider also receives service alerts notifying any exceptions during service delivery.

5   Service Management Scalability and Performance

The OPES framework provides value added content services but adds call-out processing to the content response. In the proposed service management framework, the service manager is involved in all content requests that require authorization. This adds another processing step in the content request path. The latency introduced by the call-out processing and the service management framework amortizes over the content delivery time, but could add significant overhead to content delivery depending upon factors such as content size, available bandwidth, etc. One way to reduce the management overhead, especially for a large subscriber base, is to use a broadcast surrogate notification mechanism that prevents the involvement of service manager in most (if not all) content requests.

Figure 7 illustrates the broadcast notification mechanism. When a content request arrives first time from a user it is directed to the service manager for authorization and for downloading the per-user rule module. The authorization issued by the service manager is valid for a certain amount of time. Subsequent content requests that arrive within this time period do not require service manager's authorization and uses previously cached per-user policy module. Any future change in the user's service profile will be notified to all surrogates. Once notified, surrogates will retrieve the new rule module from the service manager. Since user profiles change infrequently, notifications are handled less often than content requests. Hence, a simple broadcast mechanism for notifications will work well. The service manager in this case merely acts as a dispatcher: it receives notification from the authorization server when a user profile is changed and broadcasts it to all surrogates. The surrogates having stale copy of the rule modules subsequently download them from the service manager.

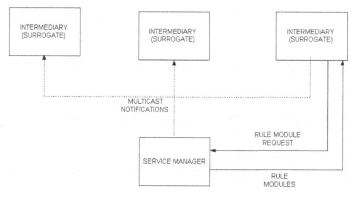

Figure 7: Multicast notifications in a service personalization network

6   Conclusion

We presented in this paper a management framework for enabling and automating the delivery of personalized services. The management framework builds on the proposed OPES framework by adding service manager and authorization server components. The service manager generates per-user policy rule modules while the authorization server collects and maintains subscriber service and device profile information. The service manager interacts with content provider's admin server to retrieve content and service policies and with the authorization server to retrieve user profile information. The service manager then combines user profile with content and service profile to generate per-user rule modules that are evaluated against content response to deliver personalized services. We discussed the scalability and performance issues of the service management framework, and proposed a simple broadcast notification mechanism that avoids processing at the service manager for every content request. We believe such a service management framework is essential in increasing the scale and reach of service personalization and in improving the reliability and availability of content services.

In future, we would like to implement our framework to understand the applicability and viability of this approach. Another important issue worth investigating is the content delivery to mobile users, which we would like to pursue next.

References

[1] A. Barbir, N. Bennett, R. Penno, R.Menon, J. Mysore, and S. Sengodan, "A Framework for Service Personalization", draft-barbir-opes-fsp-00.txt, http://www.ietf-opes.org/

[2] A. Beck and A. Hoffman, "IRML: A Rule Specification Language for Intermediary Services", draft-beck-opes-irml-02.txt, http://www.ietf-opes.org/

[3] G. Tomlinson, R. Chen, M. Hoffman, R. Penno, and A.Barbir, "A Model for Open Pluggable Edge Services", draft-tomlinson-opes-model-00.txt, http://www.ietf-opes.org/

[4] L. Yang and M. Hoffman, "OPES Architecture for Rule Processing and Service Execution", draft-yang-opes-rule-processing-service-execution-00.txt, http://www.ietf-opes.org/

[5] "ICAP the Internet Content Adaptation Protocol", draft-elson-opes-icap-02.txt, http://www.ietf-opes.org/

[6] J. Wang, "A survey of web caching schemes for the Internet", ACM Computer Communication Review, no. 5, vol. 29, pp. 36--46, October 1999.

[7] M. Green, B. Cain, G. Tomlinson, S. Thomas, P. Rzewski, "Content Internetworking Architectural Overview", draft-ietf-cdi-architecture-01.txt, http://www.ietf.org/

[8] W. Ma, B. Shen, and J. Brassil, "Content Services Network: the Architecture and Protocols", In Proceedings of the 6th Int'l Web Caching Workshop and Content Delivery Workshop, June 2001.

[9] R. Fielding, J. Gettys, J. Mogul, H. Frystyk and T. Berners-Lee, "Hypertext Transfer Protocol -- HTTP/1.1", RFC 2068, http://www.ietf.org/

[10] B. Krishnamurthy, C. Wills, and Y. Zhang, "On the Use and Performance of Content Distribution Networks", ACM SIGCOMM Internet Measurement Workshop, 2001.

[11] K. Holtman and A. Mutz, "Transparent Content Negotiation in HTTP", RFC 2295, http://www.ietf.org/

[12] J. Vollbrecht, P. Calhoun, S. Farrell, L. Gommans, G. Gross, B. de Bruijn, C. de Laat, M. Holdrege, D. Spence, "AAA Authorization Framework", RFC 2904, http://www.ietf.org/

Efficient Access Using Hierarchical WML Decks for Multimedia Services under Wireless and Mobile Networks

Dae-gun Kim[1], Seung-Jin Lee[2], Lynn Choi[3], Chul-Hee Kang[3]

[1]Korea Telecom
Woomyeong-dong 17, Seocho-gu, Seoul, Korea
dkim@kt.co.kr
[2]LG Electronic Inc
Emerald BD, 1042 Hogye-Dong, Dongan-Gu, Anyang-City,
Kyongki-Do, 431-080, Korea
linuz@lge.com
[3]Electronics and Computer Engineering, Korea University
1,5-ka, Anam-Dong, Sungbuk-ku, Seoul, 136-701, Korea
{lchoi,chkang@korea.ac.kr}

Abstract. In this paper, we introduce the design and implementation of a new efficient HTML filter that can optimize the amount of data transmitted in a wireless environment. This can be accomplished by creating hierarchical WML Decks from existing HTML pages and by performing the Web access on demand on a per-WML-Deck basis. The intelligent and automatic creation of structured WML decks also allows the efficient display of wired Internet contents on a mobile device with limited resources such as small display and limited memory. We demonstrate the effectiveness of the proposed HTML filter by showing the translation results on several commercial Web sites. We also analyze and evaluate the performance of the proposed HTML filter by comparing its results to those of the baseline HTML filter that generates WML Decks without hierarchy.

1 Introduction

To facilitate Internet access via wireless mobile devices, the Wireless Application Protocol (WAP) and Wireless Markup Language (WML) were first released in April 1998. Recently WAP 2.0 was released in August 2001 [11]. However, existing HTML documents are designed to work with the standard Internet communication protocols such as TCP/IP and HTTP. Therefore, for the adaptation of access to various Internet based information services in WAP environment, HTML filter is required to automatically convert those HTML documents into corresponding WML ones.

The conversion of HTML documents into WML Decks requires the modification of not only the markup tags but also the document structure. The WAP forum and a number of external parties have proposed the following three solutions to the conversion process:

K.C. Almeroth and M. Hasan (Eds.): MMNS 2002, LNCS 2496, pp. 289-301, 2002.
© Springer-Verlag Berlin Heidelberg 2002

1) *HTML reformatting* converts the HTML content into a new format and layout so that the content may appear on a wireless mobile device entirely different from the original HTML format. This process involves the separation of the header, tags and data from a HTML document, the analysis of the format and layout of the data, and the generation of new WML documents [2,4,5,7]. To reduce information transmitted in a wireless environment, the reformatting often involves filtering out irrelevant data according to a particular user interest [2,5].

2) *Tag conversion* can simply convert each HTML tag into a corresponding WML tag. Because each HTML tag is mapped one-on-one onto the WML tag, this approach is capable of converting only simple HTML documents. Thus, the layout of the HTML content is ignored in the conversion process. Moreover, some of the content may be lost or may not display properly if there is no appropriate WML tag for a HTML tag. This tag conversion can be accomplished by using a manual tag editor or an automated rule-based tag conversion [6].

3) *Web clipping* searches and filters WML documents from Internet sites with mixed HTML and WML documents. This process usually involves clipping and sometimes the conversion of the selected parts of Web documents [10,11]. The conversion process is usually done manually or by the automatic tag conversion.

Among these three techniques, the tag conversion and Web clipping approaches are already in common use because they are relatively easy to develop. On the contrary, the HTML reformatting research is still in early development stage since this reformatting usually involves complex procedures of information reshaping required by the limitations of the target mobile clients [3,8,9]. A number of problems are discovered with the conversion process. First, the poor resolution and the small screen size of existing wireless portable devices prevent the effective display of wired Internet contents [1]. Second, the size of the WML Decks after the conversion is often larger than the memory capacity that can be stored in hand-held devices.[1]

In this paper we propose a new HTML filter that creates WML decks of hierarchical structure in order to provide a mobile client with a global view and easy navigation of the wired Internet contents. The hierarchically structured WML decks can be transmitted in stages as demands occur. This can address such problems of small display size and small memory capacity of wireless mobile devices. In addition, it can also minimize the bandwidth and latency of Internet access in a low bandwidth wireless environment. This is different from the traditional HTML filter approach, which transmits the entire content of HTML-to-WML conversion results all at once [11].

We have implemented the proposed HTML filter and demonstrate the effectiveness and the performance of the HTML filter by performing the conversion on several existing commercial websites. The results show that the additional processing overhead due to the hierarchical structure is minimal and the demand-driven transmission can decrease the bandwidth and the latency in a low-bandwidth wireless environment.

This paper is structured as follows. Section 2 discusses our motivation for the hierarchical structure for the HTML reformatting and how we analyze and build hierarchical index structure from a complex HTML document. The section also covers the

---

[1] The conversion usually creates a number of WML Decks since the size of most HTML documents usually exceeds the limit of a WML Deck, i.e. 1.5kbytes.

motivation and the concepts of the demand-driven transmission that selectively transmits WML Decks in a low-bandwidth wireless environment. Section 3 defines the structural components of the actual HTML filter and discusses our implementation philosophy on those structural components. Section 4 shows the actual conversion results on several commercial websites. Then it analyzes and discusses the conversion and transmission performance of the proposed HTML filter by comparing to the traditional HTML filter approach. Section 5 discusses our direction for future research and concludes the paper.

2 HTML Filter with Hierarchical Decks

2.1 Creation of Hierarchical Decks

Due to the size limitation (less than 1.5KB) of a WML Deck, existing HTML filters often create a number of WML Decks in succession without any index. However, this linear structure with forward and backward links exhibits several limitations. First, navigation and searching in a HTML page can take time proportional to the number of Decks created. Second, a user is given only a limited view of the HTML page referenced since there is neither index nor any global information in the converted Decks. Third, even though a user may want to access only a small part of the HTML page, the entire Decks created must be sent and viewed, which might increase the transmission overhead as well as the latency of the communication.

To address the above issues, we propose a new HTML reformatting scheme that creates WML Decks with hierarchical indexes. The hierarchical structure has the following advantages:

1) Hierarchical indexes provide a user with a more efficient web searching, i.e. a logarithmic search rather than the linear search available in the traditional approach. In addition, this enables an easy and effective navigation of the referenced HTML page in a mobile device.

2) The hierarchical structure can give a wider view of a Web site than linear structure. For example, the top-level index can provide a global view of the source HTML page.

3) Hierarchical indexes can be used to reduce the bandwidth and latency requirements of the data transmission since it can transmit only the Decks referenced instead of the entire Decks created.

There are different ways of creating hierarchical indexes. Creating an ideal index would require the analysis of not only the syntax but also the semantics of a source HTML document as performed by a human. However, in this paper we limit our discussion to the syntactic analysis, i.e. the analysis of tags and the structure of the document, and the conversion that can be obtained from such analysis. From the syntactic point of view, today's HTML documents are usually quite large and include many types of complex structures such as frames, tables, scripts, and multimedia objects. Many of these complex structures cannot be easily presented on a portable wireless device such as smart phones. Again, in this paper we focus on the conversion of textual information including tables to simplify our discussion.

In the transcoding of textual information, the number of <table> tags, the size of textual data, the layout of both textual data and tables, and the size limit of a WML Deck are the parameters we consider in creating hierarchical indexes. Without a <table> tag, a HTML document is said to have a simple format and can be converted easily. We therefore primarily focus on the <table> tag for the creation of hierarchical indexes. The other issue is how higher index Decks can represent lower Decks so that we can use the index to navigate and search lower Deck contents. In general, the large and bold characters in a HTML web page represent the context of the page. We therefore implement this index scheme by using the <index>, <font>, <bold> tags of a HTML page.

We now summarize how we build higher Decks indexes. First, we separate information inside a <table> tag into an independent Deck. If there are several tables at the same level of a hierarchy, each table is converted into an independent Deck, or possibly an independent hierarchy of Decks depending on the amount of the data inside the table. Second, a nested table can create a nested hierarchy of Decks. However, when a table includes a table without much data, the creation of a new Deck at each level may not be necessary and the Decks in different levels can be integrated into a single Deck. We call this *level aggregation*. Third, if a textual data is over 1.5KB, we need to create multiple Decks at the same level of a hierarchy. In such case, instead of separating a Deck by the size limit, our scheme finds a natural boundary of textual data by checking tags such as <p>, <center>, <div> etc. Finally, we use <index>, <bold> tags to decide the index for lower decks. In this way the proposed HTML filter automatically analyzes the syntactic structure in a source HTML document and creates hierarchical Decks adaptively.

2.2 Transmission of Hierarchical Decks in a Low Bandwidth Wireless Environment

2.2.1 Demand Driven Transmission (DDT)

In general, on today's wired Internet people often experience a delay due to the display of unwanted information such as moving images, videos or scripts. The situation is even worse in a wireless environment. If the delay increases too much, the user may disconnect the wireless Internet services. Accordingly, a clever scheme is to transmit only the information referenced by the user on demand, thus minimizing the amount of unnecessary transmission. For a low bandwidth wireless environment, we introduce a new scheme so called *demand driven transmission* (DDT), which uses the hierarchical indexes. In the following, we assume that our HTML filter is located in a WAP Gateway.[2]

Fig. 1 shows the information flow of a wireless Internet access in a WAP environment with the proposed HTML filter. After the HTML filter converts a source HTML document into WML Decks, it automatically creates and stores hierarchical Decks and provides the top-level index Deck to the WAP client. When the client

---

[2] Generally a HTML filter can be located in any place between a mobile client and a web server including the WAP gateway.

requests a lower Deck, a response can be given from the Gateway's database without accessing the Web server. The appropriate record for the lower Deck can be found from the gateway's database, and there is no need to access the Web server's database except synchronization of the whole data update. We call this demand driven transmission.

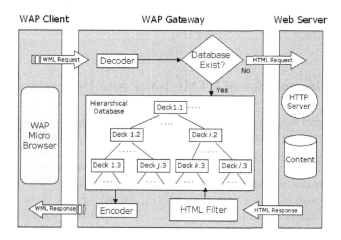

Fig. 1. The new HTML filter model to support *demand driven transmission*

With the demand driven transmission, the user receives only the requested information. Thus, the amount of transmitted data can be minimized. Because the wireless hand-held device needs to process a smaller amount of data, the performance of wireless mobile devices can be increased under limited resources such as small display size and small memory capacity. On the other side, the signaling delay may increase since the transmission of each deck will incur an entire roundtrip delay between the client and the gateway. However, we can reduce this delay by transmitting several Decks at once. Besides, the retransmission due to the unstable wireless connection will be decreased since the amount of data retransmitted is small and the retransmission may be covered by the WAP gateway rather than the Web server. Therefore, there is certainly a tradeoff between the delay and the bandwidth. However in a low bandwidth environment as common in today's wireless services, the proposed demand driven transmission may turn out to be quite effective as demonstrated in Section 4.

2.2.2 WAP Protocol to Support the Demand Driven Transmission (DDT)

To implement the demand driven transmission, we can use the cache-directive in WSP (Wireless Session Protocol) without modifying the underlying WAP protocol. The cache-directive is defined in the well-known-field-name of a WSP message header. We can use the cache-control-value of No-cache and Only-if-cached to control the access of hierarchical database in a WAP gateway. If there is no related hierarchical database, No-cache value is used. Otherwise, Only-if-cached value is used. Therefore, HTML filter constructs the indexes of lower decks with Only-if-cached value while the client requests lower decks by using Only-if-cached value.

Also the HTML filter should have a function to periodically administrate the hierarchical database. If a Web site hasn't been accessed for a while, the related contents of the database expires and may need to be deleted and replaced with another content. And if a related Web site has been updated, the associated hierarchical Decks have to be automatically updated. In the future we will further investigate both issues. The WAP values related to the administration are last-modified-value and if-modified-since-value, if-unmodified-since-value [11].

3   The Implementation of HTML Filter with Hierarchical Decks

When we observe carefully the existing researches on the design of the HTML filter, even though there are references to the design of an HTML filter, there is usually no definition of the basic elements involved in its detailed design. In this section, we discuss the definition and implementation of the basic components of an HTML filter.

Fig. 2 shows the architecture of our proposed HTML filter, which consists of the following function blocks: Parsing Engine (PE) to analyze the syntax of a source document, Markup Language Translator (MLT) to convert and create the hierarchical Decks, and RuleSet Database to designate language conversion rules. In the following, we will examine the design principles of each functional block in detail.

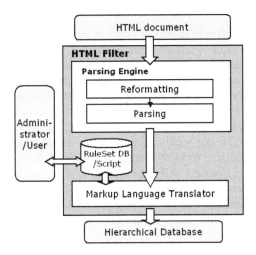

Fig. 2. The architecture of the proposed HTML filter

3.1   RuleSet Database and Scripts

The RuleSet database defines the rules related with the translation of a source language into a target language. In our implementation, each rule states the conversion of an HTML tag into a set of WML tags and associated attributes. The RuleSet database also includes the rules and scripts to create the hierarchical indexes as described in Section 2. These rules and scripts are added or removed by the administrator and stored in the RuleSet database. The Mark Language Translator module performs the conversion by referring to this RuleSet database.

There are about 90 different HTML tags and it is difficult to define a conversion rule for each and every type of tag. Some HTML tags are simply converted into the corresponding WML tags. Other HTML tags need the conversion of not only the tag itself but also its attributes. In general we classify the conversion rules into five different tag types and apply different conversion procedures to each type of tags for a faster and more efficient conversion. Table 1 shows the five different tag types, their conversion process and examples.

Table 1. The conversion process and examples for each tag type

TagType	Conversion process	Example
valid	Convert only HTML tag one to one	`  ¡æ  `, `<b> ¡æ <b/>`
validAttributes	Convert tag and some of its Attributes	`<a href=x target==y> ¡æ <a href=x>`
validAttributes_Data	Like validAttributes, convert tag and some of its Attributes. In addition, the conversion involves the data of the WML document.	`<img alt=xxx> ¡æ "[IMG]xxx" as data`
validall	Delete HTML tag itself, but perceive all internal tag and data inside the HTML tag without conversion	`<pre><htmltag>xxx</pre> ¡æ "<html tag>xxx" as data`
discard	Delete impracticable tag, but execute the conversion process again for internal tag and data	`<font color=black>xxx </font>¡æ "xxx" as data`
discardall	Delete Tag and all of its data including its internal tags, because the conversion is not possible	`<script>xxx</script> ¡æ discard all`

3.2 Parsing Engine (PE)

The major functionality of the Parsing Engine is to analyze the lexical content of an HTML document, to reformat for the deletion of tags not supported such as image and scripts, and to construct a parse tree from the stream data. Specifically, the lexical analysis recognizes HTML tags. Reformatting discards the character set not supported in WML and deletes annotated notes, multimedia data and scripts. And, parsing separates the HTML contents into header, tags and data.

3.3 Markup Language Translator (MLT)

The Markup Language Translator consists of two function blocks: language translator and hierarchical Deck creator. Generally the language translator can perform a conversion of any source Markup language into any destination Markup language as illustrated in Fig. 3. By separating the RuleSet database from the MLT, the same

MLT can be used independent of source and destination Markup languages (XML, WML, HTML, HDML etc.) without any change or modification if the conversion rule is provided. Fig. 4 shows the conversion process of tag conversion and Deck creation in relation to the RuleSet database.

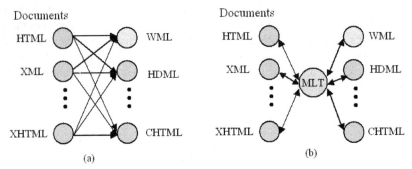

Fig. 3. The functionality of Markup Language Translator (MLT). (a) A traditional implementation requires different translators for each source and destination language pair. (b) In contrast, by separating the translator and RuleSet databases, our MLT can perform any type of translation by simply adding the rules for each pair

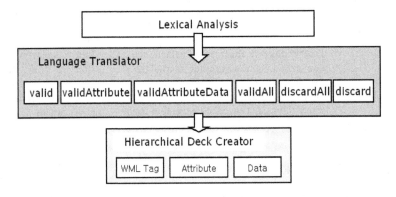

Fig. 4. The conversion process in relation to the RuleSet database

4   Experimental Results

To evaluate the effectiveness of our proposed HTML reformatting scheme, we have fully implemented both a baseline HTML filter and the HTML filter that creates WML Decks with hierarchical indexes. The purpose of our experimentation is two-fold. First, we want to test the functional performance of proposed HTML filter, i.e. the effectiveness of hierarchical indexes on a small display. Second, we want to evaluate the delay and bandwidth properties of a demand driven transmission in a low bandwidth wireless environment.

In order to perform a test on the functions of the HTML filter, several commercial WWW (World Wide Web) HTML documents are converted using the HTML filter we implemented. The WAP browser used in the test is WAP Emulator from M3Gate. Thus, WML documents through the HTML filter are displayed on a general PC screen using the emulator. We display the translated results of higher and lower levels and the linkage between them on a popular web site.

To evaluate the delay and bandwidth properties of the proposed HTML filter, we assume that the user of wireless mobile terminal wants to receive only a selected part of HTML documents because most of the users tend to receive only the requested information, minimizing the bandwidth and thus minimizing the communication expenses. The performance data presented include the processing delay of HTML to WML conversion as well as the bandwidth and latency under demand driven transmission from WAP Gateway to a mobile client.

4.1 Functional Evaluation

The evaluation of the proposed HTML filter is divided into three categories: the analysis of Web document layout, the creation process of hierarchical Decks, and the navigation process among Decks

Fig. 5 shows the conversion results from *YAHOO* website. The figure displays the WML Decks at three different levels and the links between the upper layer indexes and lower Decks. Each level has one or more Decks and each Deck has many detailed lower Decks and links to navigate between higher and lower Decks. The top level Deck has its contents and three links to navigate to its lower decks; Shop, Make a connection with Yahoo Personals and Local Yahoos. In this experiment each link is implemented by simple *anchor tag* of WML language. However, other methods such as *Template* function of WML language can be used to link lower levels. Similarly, two decks in level 2 include links for their lower decks arrowed by tree lines. As seen in the figure, the hierarchical structure can give a simple and global layout of the site. In addition, since only a small deck needs to be displayed in the screen of WAP browser, it is more suitable to be displayed on wireless terminals with small display and small memory.

4.2 Performance Evaluation

In order to evaluate the performance of HTML filter with hierarchical Decks, average processing time of conversion from HTML to WML, average bandwidth for transmission from WAP Gateway to wireless terminal, and mean transmission delay are measured. For simplicity, we assume that the retransmission between a mobile client and WAP gateway will occur more frequently as the loss rate of the wireless network increases. The WSP header length used in the experiment is 19 bytes.

Table 2 shows the processing time of the conversion, the average size of the input and output documents, and the depth of hierarchical decks. As shown in Table 2, both our proposed HTML filter and the baseline filter show similar processing time for the translation, which shows the additional overhead due to hierarchical Deck creation is negligible. On average the processing delay is about 2.5 seconds, and the average depth of the hierarchy is about 5, which is relatively large considering the number of Decks created. However, with more optimization technique such as level aggregation, which we have not implemented yet, we can decrease the average depth of the hierarchy. Also the processing time can be reduced considerably by using several simple optimizations we are considering.

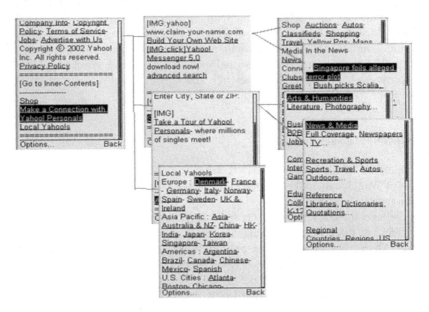

Fig. 5. The conversion example on the yahoo site: http://www.yahoo.com.

Concerning the performance of the demand driven transmission (DDT), Figure 6 shows the amount of traffic generated by the DDT compared to traditional WAP approach assuming wireless channel rate of 19.2kbps and different channel loss rate ranging from 0% to 30%. The traffic generated by the proposed HTML filter depends on the number of Decks accessed on each session. We performed several experiments to investigate the average number of Decks retrieved by the user for each session, which ranges from 4 to 6 depending on the depth of Deck hierarchy and how long the user spends on the Web site. We use these data to compute the traffic generated by the DDT.

We can make two main observations from Fig. 6. First, the traffic generated by the DDT is generally lower compared to traditional approach. This is expected since the DDT only transmits the data referenced instead of the entire Decks created. The situation is more pronounced in CNN and NY Times Web sites, which inherently has significantly more textual data compared to WAP Forum site as evidenced by the number of Decks created in Table 2. Second, as the channel loss rate increases, the traditional transmission results in increased retransmission. Thus, the DDT can get higher performance in the presence of higher channel loss rates.

Table 2. The translation results of our HTML filter on several commercial Web sites

	Yahoo!	CNN	NY Times	WapForum	Average Length
Input Document Size (bytes)	41601	187985	169457	160167	139802
Output Deck size (bytes) (proposed/traditional)	1085/ 9491	1207/ 14449	1473/ 22107	1252/ 5229	1254.25/ 12819
The number of Decks in proposed filter	14	18	21	6	14.75
Conversion Time (sec) (proposed/traditional)	3.0/3.0	3.0/3.1	3.0/3.2	1.0/1.0	2.5/2.6
Hierarchical Depths	6	4	5	4	4.75

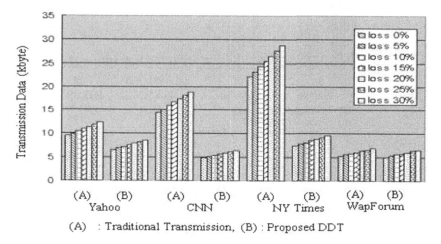

(A) : Traditional Transmission, (B) : Proposed DDT

Fig. 6. The amount of traffic generated by the demand driven transmission compared to traditional approach for several commercial Web sites

Fig. 7 shows the network transmission delay of the proposed HTML filter with DDT compared with traditional HTML filter approach. Because the channel rates of the current IS-95A, IS-95B, IS-95C and IMT2000(cdma2000 3x) are 14.4, 64, 144, 384kbps respectively, we assume that realistic transmission speed is about half of each speed in realistic wireless environment. The transmission delay of the proposed HTML filter with DDT is much shorter than that of traditional HTML filter in the low to medium bandwidth networks such as IS-95A, IS-95B, and IS-95C. Therefore, the demand driven transmission scheme may turn out to be quite effective in current wireless network generation. However, in the next-generation network such as cdma2000 3x (IMT-2000), the proposed DDT may be no longer attractive since the total delay is dominated by the signaling delay in the underlying network rather than the bandwidth required by different transmission schemes. To further reduce the delay, we are considering a group transmission scheme which transmits a group of Decks frequently referenced instead of transmitting a single Deck at a time, thus increasing the traffic but reducing the signaling delay incurred by frequent transmission in DDT. Based on the cache history in the WAP gateway, we can selectively choose the group of Decks transmitted, we can even lower the network delay both in low and high bandwidth network environments. Fig. 7 shows the delay of an ideal group transmission scheme that can perfectly predict the group of Decks to be referenced by the user.

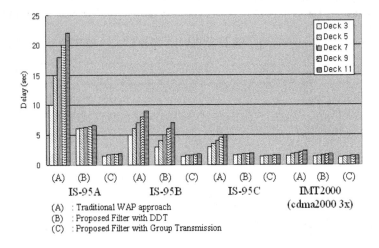

Fig. 7. The network delay of three transmission schemes in different network bandwidth

5   Conclusions

This paper addresses one of the fundamental issues in a wireless internet, the transcoding of large complex wired Internet contents on a mobile wireless device with limited resources such as small display and small memory. This transcoding problem is known as one of the most key technical barriers in enabling a widespread use of wireless Internet on WAP-enabled terminals. As a first step in addressing the issue, we propose the HTML filter that creates WML Decks with hierarchical indexes. The hierarchical structure not only allows a more efficient display on the small display of such devices but also enables an easy and more efficient navigation of the wired Internet contents. In addition, the hierarchical indexes can lead to demand driven transmission of converted WML Decks, which can be quite useful in a low bandwidth wireless environment.

We have fully implemented the proposed HTML filter and showed the effectiveness of our approach by showing the conversion results on several commercial websites. The experimentation results suggest that the additional overhead due to the creation of hierarchical indexes is negligible. And, the demand driven transmission can lead to a more effective use of the network bandwidth in a low bandwidth environment.

Several issues still remain to be addressed. In the near term, we will investigate how we can build better indexes by analyzing the syntactical information alone. Then, we will address several other constructs of a HTML document that we ignored in the current HTML filter implementation, such as frames, scripts, and multimedia objects. For the long term, we also want to tackle a much harder problem, the semantic analysis of the source documents to enable a human-like transcoding in the HTML filter of the future.

Acknowledgment

This work was supported by a Korea University Grant in 2001.

References

1. Bill N. Schilit, et al: m-links: An infrastructure for very small internet devices. SIGMOBILE (2001) 122 – 131
2. Carsten Lanquillon, Ingrid Renz: Adaptive information filtering. Proceedings of the eighth international conference on Information knowledge management (1999) 538-544
3. IBM Transcoding Publisher, http://www-4.ibm.com/software/webservers/transcoding/
4. Jonathan Hodgson: Do HTML Tags Flag Semantic Content? IEEE Internet Computing, Vol. 5, Issue 1 (2001) 20-25
5. Jussi Myllymaki: Effective Web data extraction with standard XML technologies. The tenth international World Wide Web conference on World Wide Web (2001) 689-696
6. Lee Sun-jin, Kim Dae-gun, Lynn Choi, Kang Chul-hee: Design of HTML Filter Based on Wireless Application Protocol for Expandable Web Service. Korean Information Science Association, Presentation Paper for Spring Symposium, Vol. 28, No. 1 (2001) 391-393
7. Marcin Metter, Dr Robert Colomb: Wap Enabling Existing HTML Applications. User Interface Conference, (2000) 49-57
8. Mario Canataro, Domenico Pascuzzi: An Object-Based Architecture for WAP-Compliant Applications. Proceedings of the 11th International Workshop on Database and Expert Systems Applications (2000) 178-185
9. Oracle 9i AS WE, http://otn.oracle.com/software/products/iaswe/
10. Subhasis Saha Mark Jamtgaard, John Villasensor: Bringing the Wireless Internet to Mobile Devices. IEEE Computer, Vol. 34, Issue 6, (2001) 54-58
11. WAP Forum: Wireless Application Protocol: WAP 2.0. Technical White Paper. http://www.wapforum.org (2001)

Roaming Scenarios Based on SIP

Andrea Floris[1] and Luca Veltri[1]

[1] CoRiTeL – Research Consortium on Telecommunication,
Via Anagnina 203, 00040 Roma, Italy
{floris, veltri}@coritel.it

Abstract. This work deals with the problem of IP mobility amongst different access domains. In particular the problem of the integration of the SIP (Session Initiation Protocol) signaling within a roaming environment is considered. Although SIP natively supports only user mobility, it can be also used to manage full terminal mobility. In this work different SIP registration scenarios for the so-called Pre-call terminal mobility are identified and described in detail. The general aim is allowing mobile users to remain reachable under the same application-layer identifier as terminals change IP address and thus while roaming. In the proposed scenarios the problem of service control from both home and foreign domains has been also considered.

1 Introduction

The rapid growth of the Internet and the increasing demand for ubiquitous mobile wireless services are the driving forces behind intense activities towards the design of all IP wireless networks in the main international standardization groups. The aim is the definition of an all IP wireless environment that allows roaming users to access integrated data, voice and multimedia services of the Internet via their wireless IP terminals or appliances.

The Session Initiation Protocol (SIP) [1] has been selected, within the IETF, as signalling protocol to set-up, maintain and teardown user calls, to perform complete session management, and to provide user and/or service portability/mobility.

As far as terminal mobility support is concerned, different protocols/mechanisms can be used in combination with specific access network procedures. For instance, a possible solution could be to implement mobility support at network layer, by using the Mobile IP architecture/protocol [2][3]. The primary advantage of using a network layer protocol for terminal mobility is that it can support efficiently applications that are not "mobility aware" (e.g. normal TCP-based applications). However, some disadvantages of this approach are:

- increased terminal complexity because of the use of multiple protocols for terminal, service and personal mobility;

- use of different protocols and network entities to perform similar functions; for instance, in case of a Mobile IP and SIP combination [4], wireless users use Mobile IP registration and Home Agent or Foreign Agent [2], while wireline users

K.C. Almeroth and M. Hasan (Eds.): MMNS 2002, LNCS 2496, pp. 302-314, 2002.
© Springer-Verlag Berlin Heidelberg 2002

utilize SIP REGISTER messages and SIP Registrar servers [1] for similar functions;

- Mobile IP suffers of the well-known problem of triangular routing, i.e. a packet to a mobile host always passes via the home agent, before reaching the terminal [2]; in general, no direct route is used between the mobile node and the corresponding node.

An application layer mobility support may overcome some of the Mobile IP disadvantages. In particular SIP could be used to support terminal, service as well as personal mobility [5][4][6]. In this way, in addition to the overcoming of the triangular routing and IP encapsulation associated with Mobile IP, some other important advantages arise. First, the minor complexity of terminals, which could use only one protocol for all kinds of mobility; second, SIP mobility easily interacts with preexisting IETF protocols for host configuration, authentication, etc (such as AAA, DHCP or DRCP, SDP, RTP/UDP). Moreover, it might reduce the time required for the registration process.

This work analyses the SIP mobility support for wireless network architectures. We only refer to the so-called "pre-call mobility" [7], i.e. the case in which the user moves before starting new calls. Different user's registration cases are here analyzed and illustrated. The proposed SIP-based roaming model is also compliant with the 3GPP signaling architecture [8].

This paper is structured as follows. In section 2 a brief description of the Session Initiation Protocol is given, with particular attention to mobility aspects. In section 3 a general architecture with SIP mobility support is presented. In section 4 several different SIP registration scenarios for a roaming user are proposed and described in detail. Finally some conclusions are given in section 5.

2   The Session Initiation Protocol

In this section we introduce the Session Initiation Protocol. Particular attention is given to functionalities that are concerned with mobility and location update procedures.

2.1 SIP Overview

The Session Initiation Protocol (SIP) [1] is an application-layer control protocol that can establish, modify, and terminate multimedia sessions in an IP-based environment. In particular, SIP provides different capabilities such as: i) *User location*: determination of the end system to be used for communication; ii) *User availability*: determination of the willingness of the called party to engage in communications; iii) *User capabilities*: determination of the media and related parameters to be used; iv) *Session set-up*: "ringing", establishment of session parameters at both called and calling party; v) *Session management*: including transfer and termination of sessions, modifying session parameters and invoking services.

Moreover, SIP transparently supports name mapping and redirection services, which allows personal mobility; i.e. users can maintain a single externally visible identifier (SIP URI) and be reachable, regardless of their network location.

2.2 SIP Registration Mechanism

SIP is a protocol that offers discovery capability. Each time a SIP user starts a session, SIP discovers the current host(s) on which the called user is reachable. This discovery process is accomplished by the use of SIP proxy, redirect and registrar servers, which are responsible for receiving a request, determining where to send it based on knowledge of the location of the user, and then relay the request. The user location is performed by consulting a location service, which provides address bindings for a particular domain. These address bindings map an incoming SIP URL, in the form of sip:user@domain, to one or more SIP URLs which refer to the current location of the user.

There are many ways by which the content of the location service can be established. SIP also provides its own mechanism that allows a user agent to explicitly create a binding in the location service. This mechanism is known as registration.

The process of registration entails sending a REGISTER message [1] to a special type of SIP server known as a Registrar. The registrar acts as a front end to the location service for a domain, creating, modifying and deleting URLs mappings based on user registration requests.

Generally, a SIP registrar is expected to resolve URLs for its local domain. When a registrar server receives a request for a user registered within its domain, it relays the request to the contact addresses registered for that specified user.

2.3 Mobility Support with SIP

The SIP REGISTER request is the core mechanism for supporting personal, service and pre-call mobility [1][5][4][6]. In particular:

i)   *Personal mobility* is the ability for a user to be reachable under the same identifier while using different terminals and independently of its current location, thus while roaming.

ii) *Service mobility* refers to the ability to obtain the same services regardless of where a user may be roaming. A related aspect of service mobility is the ability to maintain the same set of services when changing providers or proxies.

iii) *Pre-call terminal mobility* describes the ability of a terminal to dynamically acquire IP addresses, but remain reachable under the same application-layer identifier.

In the following we focus on the *Pre-call terminal mobility* since it could be the basis for roaming scenarios entirely based on SIP. The registration procedure is still the basic mechanism for supporting such kind of mobility.

3 SIP Roaming Model

In this section a general architecture for mobility support with SIP, for next generation wireless networks, is introduced and described. We will mainly focus on the
components involved for supporting the so-called *Pre-call terminal mobility*.

3.1 Reference Architecture and Logical Entities

Let us consider a network architecture composed by several administrative domains,
and let us consider the case of a mobile user that moves with his/her terminal between
two different domains (Fig. 1).

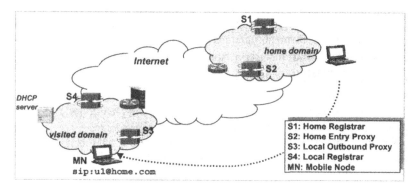

Fig. 1. SIP Roaming: reference architecture

The following entities are considered:

Mobile Node (MN): it is the user mobile terminal that allows users to communicate,
and also provides means of interactions and control between users and the network.
The MN updates its IP address as it roams between subnets, either within the same
administrative domain or in different domains. As a MN moves (i.e., it changes point
of attachment to the network), it needs to acquire a new IP address, possibly a new
default gateway/router, subnet mask, other network parameters and information.
All MNs have SIP user agents that provide means of interactions with the SIP servers
within the network. We assume that a MN has been permanently assigned a constant
identifier by its own domain and is allowed to maintain it regardless of its point of
attachment to the network (e.g., while changing its IP address). A user maintains a
universal SIP URL anywhere he is roaming. Such identifier may be, for example,
embedded by configuration into the communications device (e.g., for an Ethernet
phone, personal laptop or workstation) or associated temporarily with a device by
some token carried by the user (examples of such tokens include SIMs – Subscriber
Identifier Module, and smart-cards).
This address implies a home domain and thus at least an Entry Proxy, derived by the
DNS SRV lookup of the *host address* field of the SIP URI. In addition, each device
has at least a temporary IP address, which can be used to identify it during a session.

In some cases, the temporary address might not be directly reachable, for example due to the presence of firewalls and/or network address translators.

Home Registrar: it is a SIP server in the home network that behaves as a registrar for the mobile user: it accepts registration requests and performs request message redirection and/or forwarding. Moreover, it carries out the session control service for the mobile user: it maintains a session state as needed by the network operator for supporting of the user services. In order to carry out its functionalities, the Home Registrar maintains a database with information concerning users' profiles and details, needed to support mobility management and service control.

Home Entry Proxy: it is the first contact point within the home network for all SIP request messages destined to a subscriber of that domain (operator), or a roaming subscriber currently located within that network operator's service area. There may be multiple entry proxies within an operator's network. As far as the SIP registration procedure is concerned, the main functions performed by the Entry Proxy are:

- assigning a SIP registrar to a user performing SIP registration;
- forwarding a SIP Register request, received from another network, towards the selected registrar.

The Entry Proxy is mostly a load-balancing node and can also be used to hide configuration, capacity, and topology of the network from the outside.

Moreover, the Entry Proxy may solve the problem of how a MN discovers its home registrar as it is roaming in a visited network. In this way a user cannot be tied to any particular SIP server.

Local Outbound Proxy: it is the first point of contact (at SIP signalling level) for the mobile user that is roaming within a foreign domain. All SIP messages, sent and received by the roaming user, should cross the proxy. As far as the SIP registration procedure is concerned, the main functions performed by the Outbound Proxy are:

- forwarding the SIP *REGISTER* request received from the mobile user to the Entry Proxy of the mobile user's home network (determined using the home domain name);
- optionally starting the registration of the mobile user with the local domain (in this case, it has to select the right SIP local registrar).

Local Registrar: it is a SIP server in the local visited domain that can behave as a registrar for the roaming mobile users: it accepts *REGISTER* request messages. Moreover, it could optionally perform session control service for the mobile user, according to roaming agreements with the home domain. In other words, it may act as a local serving SIP proxy for the roaming users. The registration within the currently visited domain may improve the control of ongoing/incoming sessions.

DHCP Server: it's the entity that provides the means for the terminal configuration. A MN should receive a new IP address and other network information (default router, DNS, outbound proxy, etc.) as soon as it roams into a new network (intra-domain roaming) or a new administrative domain (inter-domain roaming). A DHCP server provides such information [3][10]. The MN configuration process follows the basic operation of DHCP [3]. There are also some proposals for dynamic host configuration that are more tied for mobile scenarios than DHCP. A proposal appeared as internet draft is DRCP [11]. DRCP offers functionality to configure a MN on a foreign domain and to provide basic roaming service. DRCP, with respect to DHCP, does not perform address collision resolution process, and it tries to reduce the configuration delay.

4 Registration Scenarios for Roaming Users

In this section different SIP registration scenarios are identified and described. Let us consider a mobile user that attaches for the first time to a new visited domain and starts a SIP registration procedure in order to register with his/her Home Registrar updating his/her point of presence (local URL or IP address).

The home network should always maintain the control of end users' sessions and services regardless of whether the user is at home or in a visited network. In order to support user/service/terminal mobility, mobile users always register with their home networks.

Local registration within the current visited domain can be also performed, in order to deal with some issues as firewall filtering, AAA, etc., and to improve service and network's performances.

It's worth to notice that in the considered roaming environment (Fig. 1) where the user moves into a visited network different from its own home domain, AAA (Authentication, Authorization and Accounting) functionalities are expected. The local domain should perform an access control procedure in order to restrict the usage of network resources and services only to authorize users, according to roaming agreements. Thus there is the need to tie the SIP architecture to a general AAA infrastructure and to carry out the SIP registration together with the AAA procedure [12].

However, the SIP-AAA interworking does not change the basic SIP registration signalling, but only introduces some extra steps. Therefore, for simplicity, in the following we will not refer to AAA functionalities.

Now let us consider five roaming scenarios:

4.1 Basic Home Registration

In this case (see Fig. 2), the mobile user simply acquires a local IP address in the visited network (for instance from a DHCP server) and sends a SIP *REGISTER* message towards its home domain, with a SIP Contact header indicating that address. This message has the following main fields:

```
REGISTER sip:home.com SIP/2.0
  Via: A2
  To: <sip:u1@home.com>
  From: <sip:u1@home.com>
  Contact: <sip:u1@A2>
```

where *home.com* is mapped to s2.*home.com* that is the Home Entry Proxy for *home.com*, and *A2* is the local IP address in the foreign domain.

The request reaches the Home Entry Proxy that dynamically selects the right SIP Registrar for the mobile user and forwards the registration to it. The Entry Proxy does not maintain any state information about the user.

The *REGISTER* message that arrives to the selected Home Registrar is of the form of:

```
REGISTER sip:s1.home.com SIP/2.0
  Via: s2.home.com
  Via: A2
  To: <sip:u1@home.com>
  From: <sip:u1@home.com>
  Contact: <sip:u1@A2>
```

This scenario is very simple and involves only few SIP entities. It follows the basic SIP registration rules [1].

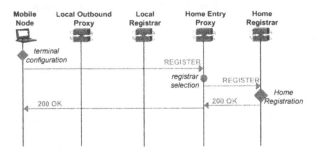

Fig. 2. Basic Home Registration

It makes no difference whether the visited network provides SIP services or not. A Local Outbound Proxy (S3 in Fig. 1) can be used, but it simply forwards the *REGISTER* request to the home domain.

This approach only works if the visited network does not use any firewall or policy to restrict the access service. Moreover, each movement inside the same visited domain (that implies IP address's change) requires a new SIP registration message to be sent towards the home domain, for location update at the home registrar. It's evident that, in order to overcome these drawbacks, a local registration should be expected/required. This approach will be considered in the following scenarios.

4.2 Third-Party Local Registration

A third-party registration occurs when the party sending the registration request is not the party that is being registered. In this case, the *From* header will contain the URL of the party submitting the registration on behalf of the party identified in the *To* header. In other words, an entity, different from the registering user, acts as User Agent for the latter.

a) Proxy Initiated

In this case (see Fig. 3) the Local Outbound Proxy intercepts the *REGISTER* request and any other outgoing SIP messages of the mobile user and changes the address in the *Contact* field into a SIP identifier, assigned to the mobile user within the visited domain.

The Local Proxy first forces the registration of the roaming user with the local domain. For this aim it creates a new SIP *REGISTER* message and sends it to a local registrar, properly selected (for example s4.visited.com). Moreover, it has to create a new temporary user identifier (for example "u2@s4.visited.com") that allows the identification of the user in the local domain. It's worth to note that the *From* header of the local *REGISTER* message contains the URL of the party submitting the registration request on behalf of the party identified in the *To* header and thus it must contain the Local Outbound Proxy's address (it is a third-party registration).

It's important that the Local Proxy generates itself the SIP *REGISTER* message for the registration in the local domain, without any explicit intention from the user, which is therefore completely unaware of the local registration procedure.

The user sends a SIP *REGISTER* message to its own home domain, as in the Basic Home Registration case.

The Outbound Proxy builds the following SIP message, for local registration:

```
REGISTER sip:s4.visited.com SIP/2.0
 Via: s3.visited.com
 To: <sip:u2@s4.visited.com>
 From: <sip:s3.visited.com>
 Contact: <sip:u1@A2>
```

In the simplest case the local identifier for the mobile user can be built as:

u2=u1#home.com (i.e. u2@s4.visited.com=u1#home.com@s4.visited.com).

After the reception of the *200 OK* for the local registration, the proxy forwards the original SIP *REGISTER* message towards the home domain. This message has the following main fields:

```
REGISTER sip:home.com SIP/2.0
 Via: s3.visited.com
 Via: A2
 To: <sip:u1@home.com>
 From: <sip:u1@home.com>
 Contact: <sip:u1#home.com@s4.visited.com>
```

The *Contact* header has been modified and contains the address of the local registrar (*s4.visited.com*), according to the local registration.

As in the previous scenario, this message reaches the Home Entry Proxy (*s2.home.com*) that dynamically selects the right SIP Registrar and forwards the registration to it.

This approach has the advantage that it forces incoming requests to use the local registrar in the foreign domain. Such procedure should be required in network scenarios that implement firewall between access domain and the rest of Internet. In this cases, a local registration can be used to open an entry in the firewall for both the signalling and voice/audio flows. In the considered scenario, all successive movements of the MS within the visited domain requiring new registrations for the mobile user (new IP addresses), are managed locally, without participation of the home domain. In this way there is an improvement of the location-update procedure and better use of network resources; registration with the home domain is only required for expiration prevent or for inter-domain roaming. Besides that, local registration allows the control of multimedia services to be transferred into the current visited domain.

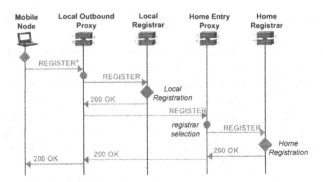

Fig. 3. Proxy-initiated Local Registration

A problem however can arise if some authentication mechanisms are used between the mobile user and its home domain. In fact, in this case, the *Contact* field can be protected and thus it cannot be modified by the Outbound Proxy, otherwise authentication would be lost. Moreover, if any cryptographic algorithm is used, between the mobile user and its home domain to protect the signalling, the local proxy cannot even read the message.

b) User Initiated

This scenario is similar to the previous one and the message flow chart is the same (Fig. 3). The only difference is the fact that, this time, the user implicitly asks the Outbound Proxy to execute the local registration for itself.

This implies that the user has to:

- know which new identifier should be used locally (e.g. u2@visited.com);
- know which local registrar he is going to be registered to;
- indicate both these pieces of information in the SIP REGISTER message.

The easiest way to allow the user to get the above information is placing them within ad-hoc DHCP options [10]. During the terminal's configuration procedure, the user, besides the IP address and other local network's parameters, receives the information for the SIP registration procedure.

The *REGISTER* message sent by the mobile user is therefore in the form of:

```
REGISTER sip:home.com SIP/2.0
  Via: A2
  To: <sip:u1@home.com>
  From: <sip:u1@home.com>
  Contact: <sip:u1#home.com@s4.visited.com>
```

The local proxy, upon reception of the registration request from the mobile user, creates a new SIP *REGISTER* message and sends it to the local registrar (s4.visited.com), in order to execute the registration in the visited domain. Afterwards, it simply forwards the original *REGISTER* message to the home domain, without any modification.

The local registration is again a third-party procedure as the *REGISTER* message is generated by the outbound proxy, which has also to know the user's local IP address in order to build the right *Contact* header.

The main fields of the local registration message are:

```
REGISTER sip:s4.visited.com SIP/2.0
  Via: s3.visited.com
  To: <sip:u1#home.com@s4.visited.com>
  From: <sip:s3.visited.com>
  Contact: <sip:u1@A2>
```

This approach has the advantage that it does not interfere with cryptographically signed registration requests, as the *Contact* field of the original *REGISTER* message is not modified by the local proxy. In this way, authentication between the mobile user and its home domain is not violated. However, modifications of the SIP User Agent and of the local DHCP server [3][10] are required to allow the mobile user to build ad-hoc *REGISTER* requests.

c) Home Initiated

This scenario (see Fig. 4) is another case of third-party local registration. This time, the home registrar, upon reception of the SIP *REGISTER* message of the mobile user, registers the user in the visited domain supplying its own credential. This approach has the fundament characteristic that the home registrar should act also as registering user agent, and thus both registered and registering parties belong to the same administrative domain. This scenario can be used in those cases where the home domain wants to have more control of its mobile users that are roaming.

The *REGISTER* message received by the home domain is in the form of:

```
REGISTER sip:home.com SIP/2.0
  Via: s3.visited.com
  Via: A2
  To: <sip:u1@home.com>
  From: <sip:u1@home.com>
  Contact: <sip:u1@local-host-name>
```

As usual, the Home Entry Proxy, once received the message, selects the registrar for the mobile user and forwards the following SIP message to it:

```
REGISTER sip:s1.home.com SIP/2.0
  Via: s2.home.com
  Via: s3.visited.com
  Via: A2
  To: <sip:u1@home.com>
  From: <sip:u1@home.com>
  Contact: <sip:u1@local-host-name>
```

The Home Registrar uses the domain name supplied by the user in the *Contact* header in order to create the *Register* message for the registration in the visited domain. This can obviously work only if the mobile user supplies a domain name of the local access point rather than the relative IP address. The home registrar has to extrapolate the visited domain name from the "local-host-name" provided by the *Contact* header in the home registration message. Moreover, it has to create an identifier (u2) for the identification of the mobile user in the visited domain

The message for the registration in the visited domain is in the form of:

```
REGISTER sip:visited.com SIP/2.0
  Via: s1.home.com
  To: <sip:u2@visited.com>
  From: <sip:s1.home.com>
  Contact: <sip:u1@local-host-name>
```

It is worth to notice that the home registrar can perform the Home Registration procedure only after the reception of the *200 OK* of the Local Registration, as the former depends on the successful of the latter.

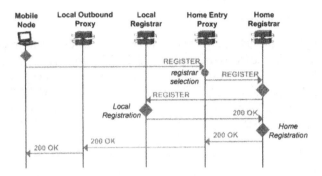

Fig. 4. Home-initiated Local Registration

4.3 Dual Registration

In this case (see Fig. 5), the mobile user sends two SIP *REGISTER* messages:
1) One to the local registrar, via multicast or the DHCP-configured outbound proxy, in order to execute the Local registration
2) The second one to the home domain in order to execute the Home registration
The first message (local registration) has the following main fields:

```
REGISTER sip:s4.visited.com SIP/2.0
  Via: A2
  To: <sip:u2@s4.visited.com>
  From: <sip:u2@s4.visited.com>
  Contact: <sip:u1@A2>
```

The local registration uses the canonical visitor name to avoid collisions (e.g. u2=u1#home.com).
The second message (home registration) has the following main fields:

```
REGISTER sip:home.com SIP/2.0
  Via: A2
  To: <sip:u1@home.com>
  From: <sip:u1@home.com>
  Contact: <sip:u2@s4.visited.com>
```

The home registration uses the local identifier and the name of the chosen local registrar.
This approach has the advantage that error handling is simplified, as both local and home registrations are fully separated. However the user should first execute the local registration and, only after the reception of the *200 OK*, begin the home registration (Fig. 5). In order to reduce the time required for the registration, the *REGISTER* messages could be sent at the same time. The outbound proxy only forwards the outgoing messages, without modifying any fields.

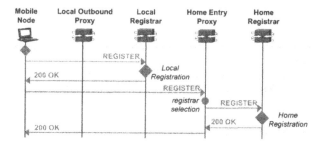

Fig. 5. Dual Registration

This approach requires two messages to be sent by the mobile user and this fact implies:

- inefficient use of the radio interface: the exchange of signalling messages between the user and the network is not minimized. This is strongly undesirable, particularly for bandwidth-constrained environments.

- changes in current SIP User Agent are required, as the mobile user must know the address of the local registrar and the new identifier (u2) that should be used in the Contact header of the message sent to the home registrar

Moreover, the mobile user must know all the information required to both registration procedures. Extensions [3][10] are thus required at DHCP servers as well.

5 Conclusions

In this paper the problem of roaming within an all-IP wireless environment has been focused. The SIP architecture has been considered as control platform for the management of both user and terminal mobility. In particular we focused on the so-called *SIP pre-call terminal mobility*, that is the capacity for a user to be reachable when moving with its terminal amongst different administrative domains (or ISPs). Different SIP registration scenarios have been identified and described. For each scenario the message flow has been detailed, and the main advantages and drawbacks have been outlined. The proposed registration mechanisms can fit different call handling approaches and can be used to implement various service models. For example, different scenarios can refer to service models in which the service is controlled by the home domain, by the visited domain, or by both networks, according to user and/or service profile. We are currently working on the development of such roaming scenario in a real testbed. An interesting point for further works, is the performance evaluation of both signaling load and MS handover latency, by means of ad-hoc simulation studies or through a real implementation.

References

1. J. Rosenberg, H. Schulzrinne et al. - "SIP: Session Initiation Protocol", IETF Request For Comments, RFC 3261, June 2002.
2. Charles E. Perkins – "IP Mobility Support", IETF Request For Comments, RFC 2002, October 1996.
3. M. Cappiello, A. Floris, L. Veltri, " IP Roaming Scenarios with AAA Support", IEEE International Communication Conference 2002 (ICC2002, New York, April/May 2002).
4. Elin Wedlund, Henning Schulzrinne - "Mobility Support Using SIP" ACM/IEEE, Internationl Conference on Wireless and Multimedia, WOWMOM, August 1999
5. H. Schulzrinne, E. Wedlund - "Application-Layer Mobility Using SIP", Mobile Computing and Communication Review, Volume 1, Number 2.
6. Dutta, F. Vakil, J.C Chen, Miriam Tauil, S. Baba, N. Nakajima, and Henning Schulzrinne - "Application Layer Mobility Management Scheme for Wireless Internet " 3G Wireless 2001
7. Vakil, A. Dutta, J-C. Chen, M. Tauil, S. Baba, N. Nakajima, Y. Shobatake, H. Schulzrinne - "Supporting Mobility for Multimedia with SIP", IETF Internet Draft, draft-itsumo-sipping-mobility-multimedia-01.txt, July 2001 [expired].
8. 3GPP TS 23.228 - "IP Multimedia Subsystem (IMS); Stage 2 (Release 5)", 3rd Generation Partnership Project, Technical Specification Group Services and System Aspects (work in progress)
9. R. Droms - "Dynamic Host Configuration Protocol", IETF Request For Comments, RFC 2131, March 1997.
10. H. Schulzrinne - "DHCPv4 Option for SIP Servers", IETF Internet Draft, draft-ietf-sip-dhcp-06.txt, March 2002.
11. McAuley, S. Madhani, S. Baba, Y. Shobatake - "Dynamic Registration and Configuration Protocol (DRCP)", IETF Internet Draft, draft-itsumo-drcp-01.txt, July 2000 [expired].
12. H. Basilier, P. R. Calhoun, et al. "AAA Requirements for IP Telephony/Multimedia", IETF Internet Draft, draft-calhoun –sip-aaa-reqs-04.txt, March 2002.

Low-Weight Congestion Control for Multi-sender Applications

Jeremiah Scholl and Peter Parnes

Department of Computer Science/Centre for Distance-spanning Technology
Luleå University of Technology, 971 87 Luleå, Sweden
{jeremiah, peppar}@cdt.luth.se

Abstract. This paper presents a prototype for single-rate reliable multicast congestion control, which has been built into an existing commercial whiteboard. The prototype was developed using a novel scheme that was engineered around conflicting industry provided requirements for collaborative workspaces. This required the scheme to be both low-weight when used with many senders and compatible with NAT, firewalls and reflectors. The key to overcome this conflict was to combine congestion control and recovery feedback. This differs from many current solutions in that they are often designed for use with a wide variety of protocols and thus operate independent of the recovery mechanism. This paper does not go into the detail required to specify a protocol but instead discusses a few important design requirements for multi-sender applications, which are generally not considered by current research, and describes an approach towards meeting these requirements.

1 Introduction

Over the past several years there has been an increase in the demand for scaleable real-time media applications. This demand combined with the popularity of IP-networks has lead to an increase in the number of applications that take advantage of IP-multicast. Currently, for many reasons, there remain reservations about the wide deployment of the current generation of these applications. One such reason is that they lack effective mechanisms for fair bandwidth sharing with TCP, which could lead to massive congestion problems if they are deployed on a large scale.

For many to many applications the traditional congestion control approach has been to keep the aggregate bandwidth for the session below a static level [1]. This method can provide good performance if network conditions are constant and the administrator of the session selects the correct bandwidth limit. However, the amount of bandwidth available in IP-networks is dynamic by nature causing this static approach to perform very unreliably in practice. As the network becomes congested this becomes a serious issue because the applications will use bandwidth in an over aggressive manner and can severely impact the performance of other multicast applications as well as traditional TCP applications (for instance email and the web) running over the same network.

K.C. Almeroth and M. Hasan (Eds.): MMNS 2002, LNCS 2496, pp. 315-327, 2002.

It has been generally recognized that in order for multicast applications to become popular, effective congestion control schemes must be implemented that allow them to adjust their bandwidth to current network conditions. Because these applications must coexist with TCP, a large number of researchers now share the conservative viewpoint that a flow is acceptable only if it has a long or medium term throughput to any receiver that does not exceed the rate that would be achieved by TCP between the multicast sender and that receiver [2], [3], [4], a state often referred to as TCP-friendly. This viewpoint is especially strong regarding reliable multicast because there is a general view that reliable multicast transport protocols are more likely to cause severe congestion problems than best-effort protocols [5]. So, achieving TCP-friendliness has become the target of the majority of reliable multicast congestion control research.

Up to this point there has been a lot of theoretical research in congestion control but much of this research is not applicable to many current applications. The primary reason for this is that many of these applications have requirements that have not been considered by the designers of existing schemes. For example, much research has focused specifically on single-sender applications based on the assumption that as long as each sender can act independently these schemes could be used effectively by multi-sender applications. However this is not always the case as multi-sender applications must scale in terms of the number of senders as well as the number of receivers. The reality is that multicast protocols are complex and much of this complexity is extended to the design of congestion control schemes. So, the fact that existing schemes are not appropriate for some applications in no way suggests design flaws in these schemes but rather shows that just like there is no "one-size-fits-all" reliable multicast protocol there will also not be a "one-size-fits-all" reliable multicast congestion control scheme.

Therefore, as part of the SIRAM project [6] at Luleå University of Technology we are exploring congestion control for specific use with multimedia collaborative workspaces with an emphasis on creating real world solutions and a highly deployable implementation. In the long term this demands the creation of dynamic schemes for all common media used by collaborative workspaces (whiteboard, audio, video and other) as well as effective bandwidth sharing mechanisms that allow the media to interact in a way that provides the best user experience. Because congestion control for reliable multicast is seen as a priority by standardizing bodies [5], we view the first step to be the implementation of a reliable multicast congestion control scheme for whiteboard traffic and similar reliable media. This paper describes both the requirements for such a scheme as well as an implementation based on those requirements.

Using a real-world approach has encouraged the utilization of a close existing partnership between the University and Marratech AB [7]; a Swedish software company that creates multicast based e-meetings products. The main benefit of this partnership is that it has enabled the design requirements and the general assumptions for the scheme to be based on Marratech's experience deploying IP-multicast-based applications in the general market. In addition, in order to demonstrate compatibility with existing applications the prototype discussed in this paper has been added to the whiteboard that is part of Marratech's e-meetings product suite.

Although the scheme has been designed specifically to intertwine with Marratech's existing reliable multicast implementation this paper should still be of value to many developers of other interactive, time-critical applications that require delivery guarantees. This is because Marratech has implemented well-known and widely used protocols, (SRM and RTP) thus making the methods described applicable to applications of a similar structure.

The next section of the paper gives a discussion of the requirements, which were the result of placing real-world demands on the scheme. In section 3 we go on to discuss existing schemes in the context of these requirements and in section 4 we describe the prototype. A summary and future work then conclude the paper.

2 Requirements and General Assumptions

In order to create a scheme that is useful for today's applications it is critical to keep a real-world perspective. For example, while the definition for TCP-friendliness given in the introduction is gaining general acceptance, the reality is that collaborative workspaces are sometimes run over private networks where the old static approach is attractive because it can give the session priority bandwidth usage over other traffic. In the near future this scenario is likely to be common as the availability of intra-domain multicast (i.e. between the customers of an Internet Service Provider (ISP)) increases while the availability of inter-domain multicast (i.e. from one ISP to another) is expected to remain scarce. Therefore, in order to handle both "friendly" and "non-friendly" deployments the scheme was designed with the intent of providing TCP-friendliness but also to allow for some non-friendly configuration of bandwidth usage. The following requirements and assumptions were used throughout the design process and were developed during meetings with Marratech in order to ensure the practical view necessary for use with real applications.

1. The scheme must not harm the ability of the group to communicate. This means that the scheme cannot destroy interactivity among users nor the reliability of data delivery.
2. All hosts are potential senders and many sessions may run within the same multicast domain. Therefore, special consideration is necessary for keeping the scheme as low-weight as possible both in the amount of bandwidth consumed and in the number of multicast addresses used.
3. The scheme must be end-to-end in nature because router assistance is not currently available.
4. The scheme must be compatible with the use of reflectors, Network Address Translators (NATs) and firewalls. This implies that unicast connections between all hosts in the session will not always be available.

2.1 Sender-Based or Receiver-Based

Because the scheme must preserve interactivity and remain low-weight a single-rate rather than a multi-rate scheme seems to be appropriate.   Multi-rate congestion control can be attractive because it allows receivers to be more independent, and does not penalize faster receivers for operating in a session with a few slow receivers. This receiver independence is achieved by having the sender layer the data across several channels making each receiver responsible for subscribing to the channel(s) that have an aggregate send rate within its acceptable reception range [8].

However, when used in conjuncture with reliable media, layered congestion control schemes have high overhead and can make it difficult for receivers with dissimilar reception rates to communicate. The problem is that unlike in a best effort setting, reliable media cannot be layered in a way that allows increasing quality of reception with each layer. Each receiver must receive the entire data set, so redundant data must be passed in the layers [1]. This results in a different reception rate for each receiver rather than a different quality of reception for each receiver. The overhead created by this redundant data can be large and the different reception rates between receivers can create severe interactivity problems over the long term.   For these reasons we have focused specifically on a single-rate rather than multi-rate scheme.

2.2 A Potential Conflict

The fourth requirement (pure multicast) is not intuitive and can be seen as inconsistent with keeping the scheme low-weight because unicast traffic is sometimes used to reduce overhead by keeping packets from reaching uninterested receivers [3]. However, pure multicast often becomes the only solution for multi-sender distributed applications due to the lack of a single access point (server) which can be opened up for all clients. The difficulty that pure multicast imposes on designers is that in order to keep the scheme low-weight control traffic must be kept to an absolute minimum.

One could make attempts to avoid this entirely because a unicast connection can be emulated perfectly by creating a multicast session with two members. However, this has its own drawbacks in that, depending on the type of unicast traffic desired it could potentially require one multicast address to be reserved for each sender-receiver pair, leading to the reservation of an unacceptable number of multicast addresses for each session. For n hosts the number of addresses needed would be:

$$n(n-1)/2 \ . \tag{1}$$

It should be possible to reduce the number of addresses needed for many situations by creating some sort of address sharing mechanism. But the number of addresses needed should still be least n. This has the potential to significantly reduce the number of concurrent sessions that can run within a multicast domain as it might require each session to reserve addresses for the maximum allowable session size in order to guarantee available address space for each new host. In any case, as shown in section 4, by maximizing cooperation between the congestion control scheme and the underlying delivery mechanism it is possible to create a pure multicast scheme that is lightweight enough to make such address hogging unnecessary.

3   Related Work

The available TCP send rate of a host is directly related to the way that TCP varies the number of packets sent per round trip time (rtt) based on loss-events [9]. This behavior can be summarized as incrementing the send-rate for each rtt where a loss-event does not occur, and cutting the send rate in half when a loss-event does occur.

In order to calculate the proper TCP-friendly send-rate for a multicast session, the sender must identify the slowest receiver, which can change over time, and obtain rtt and loss-event information about this receiver. Therefore, the primary design issues for single-rate schemes revolve around obtaining and processing feedback to make this possible. This must be done in a scalable way and must be robust when facing feedback suppression. In general, modern single-rate congestion control schemes follow the same basic architecture in that they identify the worst receiver in the session, and then calculate the send rate based on loss events by this receiver. Three schemes that follow this model are LE-SBCC [10], PGMCC [3] and TFMCC [4].

LE-SBCC is an extreme attempt at low-weight congestion control in that it attempts to provide TCP friendliness without creating any additional feedback and instead relies entirely on feedback provided by the recovery mechanism. The only assumption made by LE-SBCC regarding the nature of recovery feedback used is that time stamps are included in loss-indications (NACKs or ACKs) giving the sender the ability to calculate each receiver's rtt. The sender uses this rtt information along with the arrival times of loss-indications in order to identify loss-events by each receiver. It then adjusts its send rate in a similar way to TCP for each loss-event by the receiver with the highest loss-event rate.

The advantage of LE-SBCC is that it can be deployed with existing single-sender applications rather easily because it is completely source based, requiring only the multicast sender to be updated. Thus, it can be quite useful if updating the receivers presents logistical problems. However, the fact that it does not take measures to handle feedback suppression causes it to perform unreliably. It has clearly shown to act aggressively when NACKs from the worst-receiver are suppressed causing the sender to misidentify the worst-receiver and/or calculate its available data rate as too high. For this reason it is considered unpractical for general use.

A more complete single-rate reliable multicast congestion control scheme is PGMCC, which has demonstrated the robustness that LE-SBCC lacks. It includes two mechanisms for overcoming feedback suppression, one to help the sender correctly identify the worst-receiver and one to make sure it can identify loss-events by this receiver when facing feedback suppression.

The process of selecting the worst-receiver is aided by having each receiver include loss-rate as well as time stamp information in NACKs. The sender can then compare the available send rate of the receivers using the formula,

$$1/RTT\sqrt{r} \, , \tag{2}$$

where r is a receiver's loss rate and RTT is its round trip time. The formula serves as a simple model of the additive increase and multiplicative decrease aspect of TCP and is adequate for comparative purposes. The advantage of have receivers include loss-rate information in NACKs is that feedback suppression can cause a delay in identifying the worst-receiver, but not long term problems, because only one NACK by the worst-receiver needs to reach the sender in order for it to be identified.

Once the worst-receiver (referred to as "the acker") is selected it is required to unicast acknowledgments of each packet received back to the sender. As only one receiver at a time can be the worst-receiver, this provides very robust TCP-like feedback without impacting the scalability of the application. However, if unicast connections are not available between the worst-receiver and sender then ACKs must be multicasted and the overhead incurred by the congestion control scheme becomes considerable. With n senders sending m packets each the number of unwanted acknowledgments received by each host is:

$$m(n-1) \, . \tag{3}$$

Due to its effectiveness and simplicity PGMCC has been well received by the research community for use with one to many applications. However, in the context of the requirements discussed in section 2, giving such generous feedback to the sender can be viewed as undesirable for multi-sender applications.

TFMCC is a complex and well-designed scheme intended for best-effort media. One primary difference in creating a single-rate scheme for best-effort traffic is that the underlying recovery mechanisms used by reliable multicast protocols create feedback that congestion control schemes can take advantage of. Since this feedback is not available with best-effort traffic much of the design work in TFMCC focused on creating scaleable "extreme feedback" mechanisms for identifying the slowest receiver where only important receivers are required to pass feedback to the sender. This has shown to be effective while scaling to potentially thousands of receivers. TFMCC also introduced a scaleable way for "important" receivers to calculate their round-trip-times from the sender allowing receivers to report loss-event rates back to the sender. This allows the sender to select the worst-receiver based on more precise loss-event information than the estimations given with formula (2).

The feedback methods employed by TFMCC are clearly effective but could be considered overkill when used with reliable multicast if sufficient information for congestion control can be obtained from the underlying protocols. PGMCC demonstrates in part how to accomplish this by relying on information added to NACKs, which are used by many reliable multicast protocols, for selecting the worst-receiver. If this idea is extended so that adequate loss-event feedback is also available from the recovery mechanism then very low-weight schemes should be possible.

4   Description of the Prototype

In this section we describe a scheme that was designed using a different approach than the schemes above in that it was specifically designed around the requirements given in section two, and for use with SRM or similar protocols that use random-timer based NACK suppression. Previous schemes do not make assumptions about how the underlying recovery mechanism operates and can be used with protocols of an entirely different nature, for example those based on router aggregation. The advantage in taking a streamlined approach is that by merging congestion control and other control data it is possible to reduce the overheard required for calculating the proper send-rate. This idea by itself is not new, but the closeness by which the scheme works with SRM-like suppression timers is a novel idea and allows the scheme to avoid expensive loss-event feedback.

4.1 Quick NACK Feedback from the Worst Receiver

SRM [1] provides a framework based on random timers, which has become the most widely used method for providing scalability in NACK-oriented protocols. Random timer feedback suppression provides scalability by effectively choosing at random the host to send a NACK when many hosts loose the same packet. This NACK suppression can make it difficult for the sender to identify loss-events by the worst receiver, as it must compete against all other hosts for the right to NACK.

This competition can be removed if the timer mechanism for the worst receiver is altered so that it acts like a "quick nacker", sending a NACK as soon as it realizes it has lost a packet. This will result in a behavior identical to that as if the worst case receiver is always given a value of 0 for its random timer and will preserve scalability of the recovery mechanism because just like there is only one acker in PGMCC, there should also only be one quick nacker. This feedback method is advantageous because it will incur no overhead beyond that of SRM unless the NACK created by the worst-case receiver results in a redundancy that would not have occurred otherwise. This will occur on a per-packet basis if the following three conditions are met.

1. There is at least one receiver that looses the same packet as the worst receiver.
2. The random timer for one of these receivers expires before it receives the quick NACK from the worst receiver.
3. This NACK reaches the worst receiver before its "normal" random timer would have expired.

In practice this should be uncommon for two reasons. The first is that this situation becomes more likely when there are receivers behind the same bottleneck as the quick nacker that are much closer to the sender than the worst-receiver, which will not happen in every topology. The second is that even if there are such receivers, the use of exponentially distributed timers [11] causes each of these receivers to likely have long rather than short random timer values, so the quick NACK will most often reach them in time to suppress their NACKs. Further more, the exponential distribution of random timers is now the norm because it has been shown that NACK suppression is improved when there are a few "early NACKers" to fulfill the repair needs of the remainder of the group. The quick nacker helps to fulfill this principle and in some situations will reduce NACK redundancies from receivers farther away from the sender than the worst receiver.

We leave the investigation of the "true" overhead of this feedback mechanism up to future work. For now we only mention that inevitably this will depend on the topology used, so we plan on resolving this by performing tests of our prototype deployed in practice over real networks.

4.2 Selection of the Worst-Receiver

The Marratech whiteboard runs in an RTP-based multimedia environment, which supplies the sender with rtt and loss-rate information about all receivers from RTP receiver reports. This information can be used with formula (2) in order for a sender to identify its worst receiver. The information provided by RTP receiver reports is used by the prototype because it does not require additional overhead in terms of bandwidth in order to identify the slowest receiver. The periodic nature of receiver reports will inevitably cause some delay in identifying a necessary switch in the worst receiver. However, we take the pragmatic stance that over the long term this will not affect the ability of the scheme to clear up congestion. In fact, in some situations this is beneficial because constant switching between receivers can cause single-rate schemes to perform unreliably and is something that needs to be avoided [3].

When a report arrives the sender identifies the current worst-receiver in the following way.

a. The first receiver sending a report becomes the initial worst-receiver and this receiver's throughput is stored. Each time a report comes in from the worst receiver its throughput is updated.

b. If a receiver other than the current worst-receiver reports a throughput that is worse than this stored value it becomes the new worst receiver.

Because these receiver reports are multicasted to the group all hosts should be aware of the current worst-receiver. However, there could be a problem if some hosts loose these reports. This can be avoided by having the sender include the location of the current worst receiver in each data packet. A receiver then sends out quick loss-event feedback only if the last data packet it received identified it as the worst receiver.

An Alternative to Receiver Reports

Receiver reports are not used by every application and the above method of selecting the worst receiver will not be available in this case. In this situation it is possible to have receivers add rtt and loss-rate information to NACKS for use with formula (2), in similar fashion to PGMCC. This slightly increases the size of a NACK but has the advantage that it facilitates switches in the worst receiver as soon as NACKs arrive, rather than requiring the sender to wait for the next report that comes in.

Quick NACK feedback will cause any NACK-based selection process to naturally favor the current worst receiver over receivers behind the same bottleneck because it will suppress NACKs from other receivers that have a similar loss pattern. However, it will not interfere with the ability of the congestion control scheme to identify a new worst-receiver that is not behind the same bottleneck because in order to have a higher loss rate than the worst case receiver, this receiver will have to loose some packets that were not lost by the worst receiver, and these packets are unaffected by the quick NACK mechanism.

4.3 Configurablity

The main drawback of using single-rate congestion control is that single-rate schemes inevitably suffer from the "crying baby" problem where one receiver drastically reduces performance for the entire group. A commonly suggested solution is to set a bandwidth floor and force a host to leave the session if its reception rate falls below this limit [4]. This allows the session to remain TCP-friendly for the entire group without dropping bandwidth usage to unusable levels.

However, for group communication applications it can be necessary to take a softer stance where these receivers can stay in the session even though they will sometimes operate in a congested state. Congested receivers will have difficulty communicating with the rest of the group but this may be considered "the lesser of two evils" as they will still be able to participate in some aspects of the session. In order to keep one receiver from pushing bandwidth usage to unacceptable levels for the rest of the group we have included a mechanism to allow the owner of the session to configure bandwidth usage so that there is a floor and ceiling on the send rate. When this is enabled the mechanism will calculate the rate in normal fashion but the actual send thread will not respond to requests for a rate beyond these limits.

This is realistically just a compromise between the old static approach, which some users of collaborative workspaces prefer, and the new dynamic approach, and will obviously cause problems if configured incorrectly. However, this will allow at least some reaction by the application to congestion, which will be an improvement. We admit at this point that we have taken the simplest solution possible to deal with this problem and in the future more sophisticated and statistical methods of dealing with the crying baby may become a new research topic.

4.4 Initial Testing

Initial testing of the prototype has focused on demonstrating effective bandwidth sharing with TCP on a congested link as well as some simple tests to determine if the application could correctly identify the worst receiver. We have also conducted some preliminary tests with multiple senders in a session in order to demonstrate that effective congestion control for multi-sender applications can be obtained by having each sender react independently.

TCP flows were created using a common windows application (the simple cut and paste of a file onto a remote host) and Dummynet [12] was used as a bandwidth limiter along with EtherPeek [13] as a packet sniffer in order to monitor actual use of network bandwidth by the applications under precisely controlled conditions. Figures 1 – 3 each contain two graphs representing bandwidth usage by two competing flows with a 400 Kb/s bottleneck with a 50-slot buffer as well as 50ms delay time placed on the outgoing link.

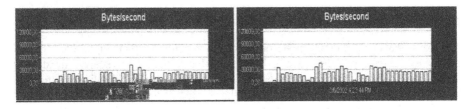

Fig. 1. Bandwidth usage by two competing TCP flows. Each bar represents the mean bandwidth usage of a flow over a 5 second time period

The first figure is included as a reference point and shows two TCP flows in competition. Each "bar" shows the average bandwidth consumption of a flow and as expected both of the flows were able to transfer data without being denied a portion of the bandwidth.

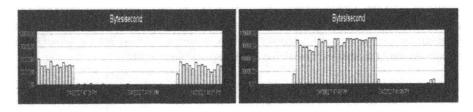

Fig. 2. A TCP transfer (*left graph*) being interrupted by an overaggressive whiteboard transfer (*right graph*). Each bar represents the mean bandwidth usage of a flow over a 1 second time period

However, this is not the case with Figure 2 which shows a severe example of a TCP flow being "dropped to zero" by an overaggressive whiteboard transfer using UDP with a static bandwidth limit that is higher than the available bandwidth. The graphs demonstrate that once the whiteboard transfer starts, the TCP flow is forced to delay all transfer of data until the whiteboard transfer is finished.

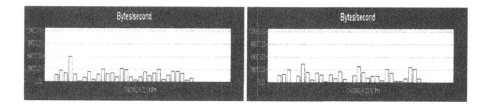

Fig. 3. The graphs show the concurrent transfer of an identical file by TCP (*right graph*) and the whiteboard with congestion control (*left graph*). Each bar represents the mean bandwidth usage of a flow over a 5 second interval.

Figure 3 shows how with congestion control enabled, the whiteboard and a TCP application can coexist while neither of the flows is dropped to zero. As long as each sender uses effective end-to-end congestion control then this idea can be extended for use with multi-sender applications.

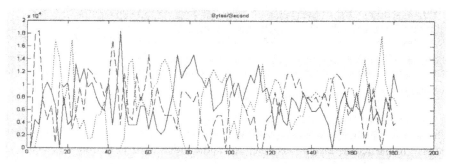

Fig. 4. A plot of bandwidth usage between 3 senders in a whiteboard session. Each host transferred an identical 1.05 MB file and a 200 Kb/s, 50-slot bottleneck with 100 ms of delay was placed between the senders. The first sender (*dashed line*) averaged a throughput of 7301 bytes/second. The second sender (*solid line*) started its transfer 96 ms after the first sender and had an average bandwidth consumption of 7619 bytes/second. The third sender (*dotted line*) started its transfer 1.07 seconds after the second sender and had an average bandwidth consumption of 7485 bytes/second.

A brief demonstration of this behavior is given in figure 4, which shows three members of a congestion control enabled whiteboard session transferring an identical file. While controlling their send-rates' independently, the difference between their bandwidth usages was less than 5% for the life of the transfer (app. 180 seconds).

4.5 Quality of Feedback

While initial tests have shown a flow using the scheme to compete fairly with a TCP flow they also demonstrate one drawback of using NACK rather than ACK based feedback in congestion control. Schemes using NACK based feedback react slower to congestion and cannot take advantage of many of the sophisticated congestion avoidance mechanisms used by TCP. A glimpse into the effects of this is given by figures 1 and 3. Due to the use of congestion avoidance the two TCP flows in figure 1 seem to "level out" after a certain period of time and have very similar send rates over the 5 second time scale thereafter and this behavior in not observed by the flows in figure 3. However, because effective TCP-friendly congestion control can be achieved without using ACK feedback and while reacting much slower to congestion than TCP [9] this does not keep the scheme from achieving its goal of TCP-friendliness.

5   Summary and Future Work

We have discussed why current single-rate congestion control schemes have trouble fulfilling industry provided requirements for multiple sender applications. In particular, these schemes either do not handle feedback suppression well, or take such a liberal approach towards providing feedback that they can reduce the number of effective senders that can participate in a session. We have explored a possible solution for reducing this feedback that alters timer-based NACK suppression used by SRM-like protocols so that the slowest receiver sends immediate NACKs. We have implemented a prototype based on this idea into an existing commercial whiteboard that runs in an RTP and SRM environment and have conducted initial testing of this prototype.

In the future we will continue our work towards creating a complete rate control scheme for collaborative workspaces but will shift our focus towards best effort media. In particular, layered schemes for audio/video need to be implemented and effective methods for bandwidth management need to be developed that can delegate available resources to the separate media in the optimal way. We will also conduct further analysis of the "true" overhead of quick NACK feedback over real networks, as this was the essential feature that enabled for low-weight feedback. This could lead to an attempt at standardizing a quick NACK based feedback mechanism with the IETF, as this is the only part of existing schemes that conflicts with our design requirements.

References

1. S. Floyd, V. Jacobson, C. Liu, S. McCanne: A Reliable Multicast Framework for Light-weight Sessions and Application Level Framing. IEEE/ACM Transactions on Networking. December 1997
2. S. Floyd, K. Fall, Promoting the Use of End-to-End Congestion Control in the Internet. IEEE/ACM Transactions on Networking, August 1999.
3. L. Rizzo: PGMCC: a TCP-Friendly single rate multicast congestion control scheme. ACM SIGCOMM 2000.
4. J. Widmer, M. Handley. Extending Equation-based Congestion Control to Multicast Applications. ACM SIGCOMM 2001.

5. A. Manking, A. Romanow, S. Bradner, V. Paxon. RFC2357: IETF Criteria for Evaluating Reliable Multicast Transport and Application Protocols. The Internet Society (1998)
6. The SIRAM project, http://www.cdt.luth.se/projects/siram
7. Marratech AB, http://www.marratech.com
8. S. McCanne, V. Jacobson, M. Vetterli. Receiver-driven Layered Multicast. ACM SIGCOMM 1996.
9. S. Floyd, M. Handley, J. Padhye, J. Widmer: Equation Based Congestion Control for Unicast Applications. ACM SIGCOMM 2000.
10. P. Thapliyal, Sidhartha, J. Li, S. Kalyanaraman. LE-SBCC: Loss Event Oriented Source-based Multicast Congestion Control. Multimedia Tools and Applications, 2002, to appear. Available from:
http://www.ecse.rpi.edu/Homepages/shivkuma/research/papers-rpi.html
11. J. Nonnenmacher, E. Biersack: Optimal Multicast Feedback. Technical report, Institute EURECOM, BP 193, 06904 Sophia Antipolis cedex, FRANCE, July 1998
12. L. Rizzo. Dummynet: a simple approach to the evaluation of network protocols. ACM Computer Communication Review, Vol. 27, N.1, Jan 1997.
13. EtherPeek http://www.wildpackets.com/products/etherpeek

Routing-Based Video Multicast Congestion Control

Jun Peng and Biplab Sikdar

Electrical, Computer and Systems Engineering Department
Rensselaer Polytechnic Institute
110 8th St., Troy, NY 12180, USA

Abstract. Congestion control is critical for a multicast transport protocol to be deployed and coexist fairly with current unicast transport protocols, such as TCP. We present a new congestion control protocol for video multicast: Routing-based Video Multicast Congestion Control (RVMCC), which combats congestion from a new direction: enriching abstractions of the routing layer. RVMCC overcomes most of the disadvantages of current end-to-end multi-layer video multicast congestion control schemes, such as unstable throughput and unfair sharing of bandwidth with other sessions [9] [10]. These disadvantages are inherent for end-to-end multi-layer video multicast congestion control schemes and extremely hard for them to deal with [10]. RVMCC not only achieves good stability of throughput but also approaches Max-Min fairness closely at bottlenecks. The former is necessary for ensuring the viewing quality of transmitted video, while the latter is necessary for the deployment of multicast in the current Internet. Furthermore, unlike existing network-assisted video multicast congestion control schemes, RVMCC does not require the change of the queuing, scheduling, or forwarding structure of the current Internet. RVMCC can be integrated with minimum assistance from network by enriching the abstractions of the routing layer.

1 Introduction and Previous Work

When a video source needs to transport a piece of video to multiple receivers, it can set up a unicast session with each receiver and send one copy of each packet to each of them at each transmission. A more economic way to accomplish this is to set up one multicast session with all receivers and send a single copy of each packet to the first hop router at each transmission, and then multicast routers on the multicast tree duplicate each packet when the packet reaches forks of the multicast tree. Although the advantages of multicast are obvious, the deployment of multicast lags far behind. One hurdle for the deployment is the lack of a mature multicast congestion control scheme. Congestion must be avoided at any branch of the multicast tree, but at the same time each receiver should receive data at the highest rate affordable to the path leading to it. This goal is hard to achieve because of the heterogeneity of receivers and of links leading to them. For example, if a video multicast source needs to serve three receivers at the same time, and the bandwidth of the access links of the three receivers is 64Kb/s, 128Kb/ and 256Kb/s, respectively, which rate should the video source choose to serve these receivers?

K.C. Almeroth and M. Hasan (Eds.): MMNS 2002, LNCS 2496, pp. 328–340, 2002.
© Springer-Verlag Berlin Heidelberg 2002

One smart way to solve this heterogeneity problem was first suggested in [1] [13] and elaborated on or reported in [2] [3] [4] [5] [6]. The basic idea is to encode video into several number of layers and multicast each layer to a different multicast group. The receivers then adapt to congestion by adding and dropping layers (i.e. joining and leaving multicast groups). In the last example, the video source can be encoded into 4 layers with a rate of 64Kb/s per layer. So the three receivers in our example can subscribe to 1, 2 and 4 layers, respectively, and then every receiver is satisfied. When available bandwidth changes, they just need to add or drop layers to adapt to it. A transport protocol based on this idea was proposed in [7]: Receiver-driven Layered Multicast (RLM). Another similar protocol that shows more potential for inter-session fairness is Receiver driven Layered Congestion control (RLC) [8].

Although these protocols represent an indisputable advance in congestion control for video multicast, they have several inherent shortcomings [9] [10]. Three main ones are slow convergence, inter-session unfairness and unstable layers and throughput. As pointed out in [10], without changing the foundations of these protocols, these problems are hard to solve. One of the most important foundations of these protocols is the join experiment: adding layers to explore for available bandwidth. Because of the delay of multicast grafting and pruning, failed experiments come with a high price to pay: a period of congestion. But if they are too conservative in adding a layer, bandwidth will be underutilized or grabbed by other sessions. So it is very hard for them to achieve a balance among bandwidth utilization, stability of layers and fairness between sessions. Although the scheme in [11] solves the join-experiment problem partly, it has some serious disadvantages. Dynamic layering is hard, if not impossible, to realize for video source. Routing overhead is heavy because of continuous joining-group and leaving-group actions of receivers. Furthermore, it still has fairness problem with TCP.

With all of these disadvantages of end-to-end video multicast congestion control schemes, some researchers are exploring another direction to deal with this problem: requesting assistance from the network by changing queuing, scheduling or forwarding structures of the network [12] [14]. Although the approach in [14] can improve the stability of video quality, it still has problems in achieving fairness with TCP sessions, since it does not touch the foundation of RLM. Although the scheme in [12] could get good results, there are several disadvantages, as pointed out by the author. First, routers need states of downstream neighboring routers. Second, it requires class-based network service. The last is that the scheduling policy is complex.

In this paper we present a new video multicast congestion control protocol: Routing-based Video Multicast Congestion Control (RVMCC), which deals with the video multicast congestion control problem from a new perspective. Instead of changing the queuing, scheduling or forwarding structure of the current Internet, RVMCC enriches the abstractions of the routing layer to deal with congestion. Since routing protocols reside in routers, it is easy for them to obtain the states of the network and the traffic. They also can respond fast if necessary. In addition, since routing decisions directly apply to flows, the control response is quick. So RVMCC converges quickly. Furthermore, RVMCC achieves not only good stability of throughput but also approaches Max-Min fairness closely. This is because RVMCC can get much more knowledge about the states of the network (such as queue status) and about the going-on traffic (such as the number of sessions competing for the bandwidth at a bottleneck) than end-to-end schemes do.

The rest of the paper is organized as follows. We introduce RVMCC in details in Section 2. In Section 3, we show detailed simulation results of the protocol. Summary appears in Section 4.

2   The RVMCC Protocol

Let us consider the transmission of a piece of video to some receivers across the Internet with the RVMCC protocol active in routers. The source encodes the video data into several layers and strips them across several multicast groups (we call all layers from the same source a Video Multicast (VM) session). Receivers of the VM session subscribe to some of these layers to receive video data at appropriate rate. Meanwhile, if congestion occurs at a link where VM sessions are passing through, RVMCC starts to observe that link. Specifically, RVMCC samples the traffic to get the knowledge about the number of VM and TCP sessions passing through the link; the rate of each VM session is also estimated. RVMCC decides whether or not to block a layer of a VM session passing through the link according to the total bandwidth that all VM sessions passing through the link are using. If the VM sessions are using unfair share of bandwidth, RVMCC blocks a layer of the VM session that is using the most bandwidth among the VM sessions. At the same time, RVMCC keeps observing the queue status of the link. When the free-bandwidth state of the link is observed, RVMCC channels a layer of the VM session that is using the least bandwidth among the VM sessions. In this process, receivers add and drop layers to cooperate.

Before we discuss the details of the RVMCC protocol below, we give some definitions to facilitate our description. We base our definition on a link that VM and TCP sessions are passing through.

- C: the bandwidth of the link
- M: the number of VM sessions passing through the link
- N: the number of TCP sessions passing through the link
- B: the total bandwidth used by all VM sessions passing through the link
- *link-equal-share*: $C / (M+N)$
- *VM-equal-share*: B / M
- *VM-share-ratio*: VM-equal-share / link-equal-share = $(B / M) * ((M+N) / C)$
- *VM-total-link-equal-share*: M * link-equal-share = $M * C / (M+N)$

2.1   Layer Definition and Layer Priority in RVMCC

In a video multicast session, layers usually have different significances. The lower the layer, the higher its priority. In RVMCC, this priority information is embedded in the multicast address that a layer of a session uses. The lower the address, the higher its priority. But this rule only applies to layers of the same VM session, not to layers of different VM sessions.

Each time a VM session applies for multicast addresses, it should be assigned a block of continuous addresses. Then the VM session assigns lower addresses to its lower layers and higher addresses to its higher layers. Furthermore, each VM session is assigned a VM session number by the source host. This session number is used to distinguish two different sessions initiated from the same host. The session number needs only to be unique in the source host but not globally unique. The layers with the same source address and VM session number are assigned different priorities according to their multicast addresses when RVMCC needs to block or channel a layer.

2.2 Solving Congestion and Claiming Bandwidth

Instead of using layer-add and layer-drop as in end-to-end video multicast congestion control schemes, RVMCC uses layer-block and layer-channel to solve congestion and to claim bandwidth, respectively. Layer-block is the modification of the multicast routing table to prevent a layer from entering a congested link, while layer-channel is the modification of the routing table to allow a layer to enter a link. In layer-block, routing states such as the source address of the layer, the multicast address of the layer and the link at which the layer is blocked, are saved and are used later for layer-channel. Those routing states can only be deleted by unsubscription actions of receivers.

In fact, for efficient network resource utilization, the router that just blocked a layer should forward the blocking information upstream. So the upstream routers that do not need to forward that layer to other branches except the congested one may also block that layer. In this way, no layer will reach a router where no downstream receiver will receive the layer. When the router that blocked layers just now needs to channel a layer, it also has to send channeling information upstream to graft the multicast branch leading to it. With this mechanism, although bandwidth will be efficiently used in data transmission, a considerable amount of communication and cooperation will be required among routers.

In RVMCC, blocking information is not forwarded upstream. Instead, receivers actively participate in the adjustment of session rate to simplify the network assistance and to relieve routers of excessive communication and processing burden. Every receiver unsubscribes to all but the lowest empty layer of its session. An empty layer is a layer subscribed to by a receiver but receiving no data because of being blocked somewhere in the network. At the same time, when the empty layer is channeled and data arrives at the empty layer, receivers must subscribe to another layer to prepare for a new empty layer, if more layers are available for subscription.

With this simplified mechanism, although one redundant layer may arrive at some upstream routers above a bottleneck, network and processing overhead is considerably lowered. Furthermore, with this mechanism, data will arrive at receivers faster when congestion disappears, since grafting above the bottleneck is not needed anymore. Especially for video multicast, this is a great advantage.

2.3 Achieving Fairness and Stability

Intra-session fairness is successfully achieved in a VM session. The number of layers that a receiver can receive is not decided by its own actions or by other receivers' actions but only by the bottleneck on the path leading to it from the multicast source. This is not true for most current end-to-end multi-layer multicast congestion control schemes, although they adopt different methods trying to achieve this goal.

Inter-session fairness is a tough topic for all transport protocol design. Even for mature unicast transport protocols, such as TCP, fairness is not always achieved between their own sessions. When two TCP sessions sharing the same bottleneck have quite different RTTs, their shares of the bottleneck bandwidth can be far from equal. RVMCC approaches the Max-Min fairness closely and shows the following characteristics in inter-session fairness: (1) With best effort, every session is assigned the link-equal-share bandwidth; (2) With best effort, spare bandwidth from any session is shared by all other sessions; (3) No session is starved for bandwidth. The design details for achieving these goals are described below.

First, RVMCC ensures that VM sessions get the instantaneous VM-total-link-equal-share. When congestion occurs at a link, if the total bandwidth currently used by all VM sessions passing through the link is less than the VM-total-link-equal-share, RVMCC will not block layers. This has some meaning of class-based service. But for variable bit rate (VBR) video sources, this does not ensure the long-run VM-total-link-equal-share because layers may be blocked during their peak-rate period.

Second, when blocking is necessary, the VM session with the highest share of bandwidth among all VM sessions passing through the link is selected to block a layer. On the other hand, when channeling is necessary, the VM session with the lowest share of bandwidth among all VM sessions passing through the link is selected to channel a layer.

Third, when a new VM session arrives and congestion occurs, the link-equal-share is recalculated. If VM sessions are using more bandwidth than the new VM-total-link-equal-share, some layers of these sessions are blocked.

Fourth, when a new TCP session arrives, RVMCC blocks layers of VM sessions only if the VM-share-ratio is larger than a threshold or there is no TCP session passing through the link. When the VM-share-ratio is less than the threshold, the new TCP session has to grab bandwidth from other current TCP sessions. But when a new TCP session arrives and the threshold is reached, the VM-total-link-equal-share is recalculated and some bandwidth is released if VM sessions are using more bandwidth than the VM-total-link-equal-share. This procedure can stabilize VM traffic while not starve TCP sessions at any time. Since TCP sessions may come and go frequently, to respond to every new TCP session may cause unstable VM traffic.

Fifth, when a VM session leaves, the remaining VM sessions claim some bandwidth from it to achieve the new VM-total-link-equal-share. In this process, TCP sessions also get some bandwidth. This is necessary for fairness, since a departing VM session usually releases a significant amount of bandwidth.

The last, when a TCP session leaves, RVMCC only claims some bandwidth from it if the VM-share-ratio is less than a threshold. Otherwise, the bandwidth spared by the departing TCP session is claimed by other TCP sessions. The consideration is also for the stability of VM traffic, since TCP sessions may come and go frequently.

2.4 Further Design for Stability

When losses are observed at a link, RVMCC does not block layers instantly if there is no new session, even if the total bandwidth being used by all VM sessions is greater than the VM-total-link-equal-share. Only if the losses persist for some time longer than a threshold, does RVMCC start to block layers. This procedure further stabilizes VM traffic.

Because of the Additive Increase and Multiplicative Decrease (AIMD) flow control scheme implemented with TCP, TCP traffic usually shows saw-tooth like fluctuation and may cause temporary light congestion. So the above procedure can filter out this kind of temporary but possibly frequent light congestion.

One important point is that, unlike end-to-end video multicast congestion control schemes, RVMCC can afford the time to judge temporary congestion because it can solve the congestion quickly if the congestion turns out to be serious. For end-to-end schemes, delayed response to serious congestion comes with a high price to pay.

2.5 Network Cost

Although the RVMCC protocol does not require any change of the structure of the current Internet, there is some network cost in its operation, mainly the estimation of the number of sessions and the rates of VM sessions passing through a congested link. But because the estimation is only started at a link when congestion occurs at that link during a multicast session, the total cost for a multicast session may not be high. Furthermore, we believe the cost is worthwhile. First, it has not been shown that an end-to-end multi-layer video multicast congestion control scheme can coexist with TCP with some kind of fairness, although research has been going on for some time. Second, other existing network-assisted schemes need considerable change of the current Internet. Finally, the rate estimation of multicast sessions at congested links can prevent the abuse of current Internet resources, intentionally or accidently, by multicast applications. If the cost does become a concern for backbone routers, they can ignore the rate estimation of each multicast session. Instead, they select sessions to block or channel a layer only according to the total number of layers that each session has. Then backbone routers are relieved of excessive burden. This will not affect the scheme significantly because it has been shown that losses in MBone mainly occur on local networks [15].

3 Simulation Results

In this section we present the simulation results. We are mainly interested in observing the convergence, fairness and stability characteristics of RVMCC. Two kinds of VM sources are used: Constant Bit Rate (CBR) sources and Variable Bit Rate (VBR) sources. The VBR sources have exponentially distributed burst-times and idle-times. One source (VBR1) has an average burst time of 200ms and an average idle time of 100ms, while both the average burst time and the average idle time of the other source (VBR2) are 200ms. Each source has 5 layers and the average rate of each layer is 200Kb/s. The throughput shown in our figures is averaged over one second, so it does not represent the instantaneous rate of a session.

3.1   Network Topology and Parameters in Our Simulations

The topology used in our simulations is shown in Fig. 1. There are two concatenated bottlenecks in this topology. The first one has a bandwidth of 2.4Mb/s, a capacity of 12 layers, while the second one has a bandwidth of 1.2Mb/s, a capacity of 6 layers. Receivers Rm1 and Rm2 are with the VM session 1. Rm1 is under the first bottleneck, while Rm2 is under the second bottleneck. VM session 2 also has two receivers, Rm3 and Rm4. Rm3 is under the first bottleneck, while Rm4 is under the second bottleneck. Rt is the receiver of the TCP session and located under the second bottleneck. So all three sessions will compete for bandwidth at both bottlenecks if all of them are alive. But Rm1 and Rm3 are only affected by the first bottleneck, while Rm2, Rm4 and Rt are under the influence of both bottlenecks.

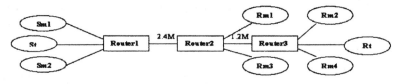

Sml: source of VM1   Sm2: source of VM2   St: source of TCP
Rm1, Rm2: receivers of Sm1   Rm3, Rm4: receivers of Sm2   Rt: receiver of TCP
Delay for each link: 100ms   Bandwidth of other links not marked: 10Mb/s
Queue type and limit: drop-tail with 15 packets limit
Simulation tool: NS2

Fig. 1. Simulation Topology

3.2   Simulation Scenarios

Scenario One: Two Competing VM Sessions In this scenario, the interaction between two VM sessions is tested. The first VM session starts at time 0 and stops at the 1200th second, while the second VM session starts at the 100th second and stops at the 1100th second. The results are shown in Fig. 2, Fig. 3 and Fig. 4

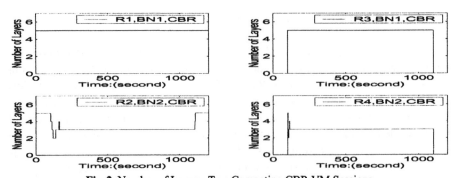

Fig. 2. Number of Layers: Two Competing CBR VM Sessions

The first thing we can see in these figures is that fairness is good at both bottlenecks, even if the two VM sessions start at different times. In the CBR case, R1 and R3 sharing the first bottleneck get 5 layers each, while R2 and R4 sharing the second bottleneck get 3 layers each. Although the first bottleneck can sustain 12 CBR layers (2.4M / 200k = 12), each VM source has only 5 layers, so R1 and R3 only get 5 layers each. At the second bottleneck, 1.2Mb/s is shared equally by two VM sessions, so R2 and R4 get 3 layers each. In the VBR case, the situation is a little complicated. With the VBR1 source, the bandwidth-sharing pattern is almost the same as that with CBR source, except that R2 and R4 only get 2 instead of 3 layers each. With the VBR2 source, both R1 and R3 get 4 layers, but R2 and R4 get different numbers of layers: 1 layer and 2 layers, respectively.

The reason that in the VBR2 case there is one layer difference between the two VM sessions at the second bottleneck is that the second bottleneck can only sustain 3 VBR2 layers (we will discuss why bottlenecks sustain a different number of layers with different VBR sources later). The 3-layer capacity can not be shared equally between the two VM sessions, so one VM session gets 2 layers while the other gets 1 layer. Generally, the granularity of the fairness in multi-layer multicast congestion control is one layer. When a bottleneck can only sustain a number of layers that can not be assigned equally among the sessions passing through it, one layer difference between some sessions is inevitable. We know end-to-end multi-layer video multicast congestion control schemes show serious unfairness between competing multicast sessions [9] [10]. Usually, late arrivals cannot grab a right share of bandwidth. In the RVMCC case, although VM session 1 and VM session 2 start at different times, they get a right share of the bandwidth at both bottlenecks.

The second thing we observed is that the number of layers at each bottleneck has good stability in all cases. The number of layers is almost constant in the CBR case, except the layer adjustment for the incoming or the outgoing VM session. In the VBR case, although there is some layer adjustment at each bottleneck, the layer adjustment only occurs in one VM session at each bottleneck. The other session still has a stable number of layers. Furthermore, in the session with layer adjustment the adjustment is rare and only goes in one direction from a basic level. At R1 in Fig. reffig:vs1alay, the adjustment is from the basic level of 5 layers to 4 layers and then goes back to the basic level of 5, while at R4, the adjustment is from the basic level of 2 layers to 3 layers and then goes back. In RVMCC, higher variance of traffic only causes a less number of layers sustained by the bottleneck but not an unstable number of layers. This can be observed in Fig. 4.

The third thing we can conclude from these figures is that higher variance of VM sources usually renders lower throughput at bottlenecks. With the VBR1 source, only 4 layers are sustained by the second bottleneck, but it sustains 6 CBR layers. With the VBR2 source, which has a higher variance than the VBR1 source, only 3 layers are sustained at the second bottleneck and the first bottleneck also only sustains 8 layers. This is due to the varying-rate characteristic of VBR sources. Without enough bandwidth reserved for a VBR source at a bottleneck, at its peak rate the VBR source may cause heavy losses and consequent layer-blocking at the bottleneck. The higher the variance, the more the bandwidth needed to be reserved for the peak rate. So higher variance usually causes lower throughput. A lower number of layers for VBR sources with higher rate variance is also necessary for maintaining fairness with TCP sessions, since frequent losses may throttle TCP traffic.

Lastly, the convergence is clear in all cases. With an incoming session or an outgoing session, other sessions respond appropriately to release or claim bandwidth. This can be observed in all figures.

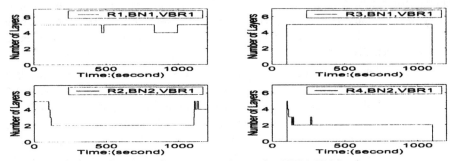

Fig. 3. Number of Layers: Two Competing VBR1 VM Sessions

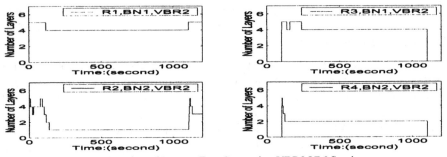

Fig. 4. Number of Layers: Two Competing VBR2 VM Sessions

Scenario Two: A TCP Session Joining Existing VM Sessions In this scenario, how VM sessions respond to a new TCP session is observed. The TCP session starts 100 seconds later after two VM sessions have started. The simulation results are shown in Fig. 5, Fig. 6, Fig. 7 and Fig. 8. In these figures, we can see that the good stability and convergence characteristics observed in scenario 1 are still preserved in this scenario. We will focus on the fairness issue in the following text.

In the CBR case, in Fig. 5 we can see that R1 and R3 get 5 layers each at the first bottleneck, but the link-equal-share at the first bottleneck is 800Kb/s (2.4Mb/s among 3 sessions), which means less than 5 layers for each session. This can be explained if we have a look at the second bottleneck. Still in Fig. 5, we see that R2 and R4 get 2 layers each at the second bottleneck, which is just the link-equal-share there (6-layer capacity

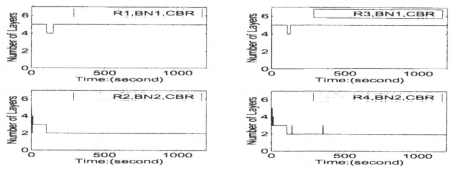

Fig. 5. Number of Layers: TCP Session Joining CBR VM Sessions

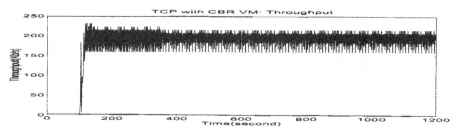

Fig. 6. TCP Throughput: TCP Session Joining CBR VM Sessions

for 3 sessions). So the TCP session also gets a share of 2 layers (400Kb/s) at the second bottleneck. Because of the restriction at the second bottleneck, the TCP session can only consume at most 400Kb/s at the first bottleneck. This means that 2Mb/s out of 2.4Mb/s is left for the two VM sessions at the first bottleneck. If Max-Min fairness is approached, the two VM sessions should get 1Mb/s each at the first bottleneck. This is just what shown in Fig. 5. But in Fig. 6 we can find that the TCP session only achieves an average throughput much less than 400Kb/s. The reason is that TCP uses the AIMD flow control scheme that limits its efficiency in bandwidth utilization.

In the VBR case, in Fig. 7 we see that at the second bottleneck the two VM sessions have a one-layer difference. This is because the VM-total-link-equal-share there (400Kb/s x 2 = 800Kb/s) can only sustain 3 VBR1 layers due to the varying rate of the layers. In Fig. 8, the TCP session achieves an average throughput almost the same as that in Fig. 6. So there is still about 2Mb/s bandwidth left for the two VM sessions at the first bottleneck because of the restriction at the second bottleneck for the TCP session. Because the two VM sessions have VBR1 sources, each of them only achieves a throughput of 4 layers there.

In summary, in this scenario of TCP joining VM sessions, VM sessions still have stable numbers of layers and the convergence is still stable and clear. Furthermore, Max-Min fairness is closely approached at bottlenecks.

Scenario Three: VM Sessions Joining the Existing TCP Session In this scenario, the behavior of VM sessions joining an existing TCP session is tested. VM session 1 and VM session 2 start 100 seconds later after the TCP session has started. The simulation results are shown in Fig. 9, Fig. 10, Fig. 11 and Fig. 12.

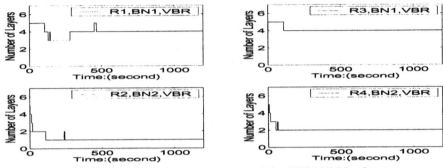

Fig. 7. Number of Layers: TCP Session Joining VBR1 VM Sessions

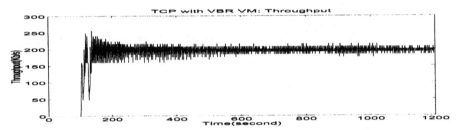

Fig. 8. TCP Throughput: TCP Session Joining VBR1 VM Sessions

In fact, this scenario is very similar to the last one, except that the VM sessions start later instead of earlier than the TCP session. If we compare figures from 9 through 12 with figures from 5 through 8, respectively, we can find that when all three sessions are alive the bandwidth-sharing patterns are almost the same in each pair of figures. For example, we can have a look at Fig. 5 and Fig. 9. In Fig. 5, both VM sessions get 5 layers at the first bottleneck almost all the time. At the second bottleneck, they get 3 layers each before the TCP session arrives at the 100th second. After that they both get 2 layers each. In Fig. 9, after the two VM sessions become alive at the 100th second, they get 5 layers each at the first bottleneck and get 2 layers each at the second bottleneck. So after the 100th second, which is the point that all 3 sessions become alive, the bandwidth-sharing pattern in Fig. 5 is almost the same as that in Fig. 9. The same thing happens for other pairs of figures.

In summary, in this scenario Max-Min fairness is still closely approached at both bottlenecks, although the two VM sessions become alive later than the TCP session. Both VM sessions still have good stability in number of layers. Furthermore, convergence is still steady and clear.

4 Summary

The RVMCC protocol attacks the multi-layer video multicast congestion control problem from a new direction: enriching the abstractions of the routing layer. It overcomes most of the inherent disadvantages of end-to-end multi-layer video multicast congestion control schemes, such as unfairness in sharing bandwidth and instability in throughput.

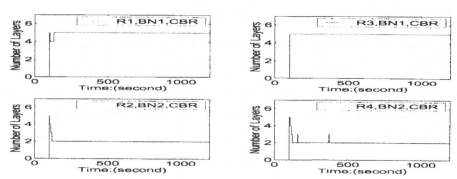

Fig. 9. Number of Layers: CBR VM Sessions Joining a TCP Session

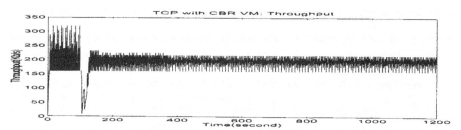

Fig. 10. TCP Throughput: CBR VM Sessions Joining a TCP Session

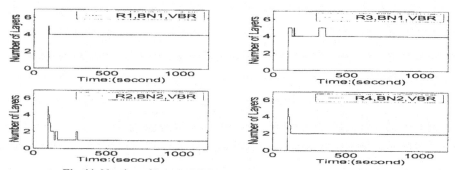

Fig. 11. Number of Layers: VBR1 VM Sessions Joining a TCP Session

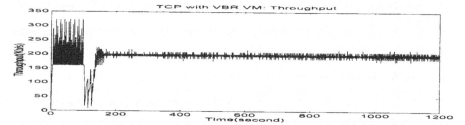

Fig. 12. TCP Throughput: VBR1 VM Sessions Joining a TCP Session

It also avoids the complexity of most network-assisted congestion control schemes. No structural change of queuing, scheduling or forwarding of the current Internet is necessary for implementing this protocol. RVMCC is also scalable because there is no communication overhead for RVMCC protocol. Control actions in a router or receiver are independent of those in other routers and receivers. In end-to-end multicast congestion control schemes, communication overhead or necessary dependence of actions among receivers usually restricts their scalability. All of these characteristics give the RVMCC protocol the strength to be a good candidate for a standardized multi-layer video multicast congestion control protocol.

References

1. S. Deering "Internet multicast routing: State of the art and open research issues," Multimedia Integrated Conferencing for Europe (MICE) Seminar at the Swedish Institute of Computer Science, Stockholm, Oct. 1993.
2. N. Chaddha and A. Gupta "A frame-work for live multicast of video streams over the Internet," Proceedings of the IEEE International Conference on Image Processing , Lausanne, Switzerland, Sept. 1996.
3. L. Delgrossi, C. Halstrick, D. Hehmann, G. Her-rtwich, O. Krone, J. Sandvoss and C. Vogt "Media scaling for audiovisual communication with the Heidelberg transport system," Proceedings of ACM Multi-media ' 93 Aug. 1993
4. D. Hoffman and M. Speer "Hierarchical video distribution over Internet-style networks," Proceedings of the IEEE International Conference on Image Processing Lausanne, Switzerland, Sept. 1996.
5. Mccanne, S. and Vetterli, M. "Joint source/channel coding for multicast packet video," Proceedings of the IEEE International Conference on Image Processing Washington, DC, Oct. 1995.
6. T. Turletti and J.-C. Bolot "Issues with multicast video distribution in heterogeneous packet networks," Proceedings of the Sixth International Workshop on Packet Video Portland, OR, Sept. 1994.
7. S. McCanne, V. Jacobson and M. Vetterli, "Receiver-driven Layered Multicast," Proceedings ACM SIGCOMM 96, August 1996.
8. L. Vicisano, L. Rizzo and J. Crowcrof, "TCP-like Congestion Control for Layered Multicast Data Transfer," Proceedings of IEEE INFOCOM, San Franciso, March 1998.
9. R. Gopalakrishnan, J. Griffioen, G. Hjalmtysson and C. Sreenan. "Stability and Fairness Issues in Layered Multicast," Proceedings of the NOSSDAV '99, June 1999.
10. A. Legout and E. W. Biersack, "Pathological Behaviors for RLM and RLC," Proc. of NOSS-DAV'00, pp. 164–172, Chapel Hill, North Carolina, USA, June 2000.
11. J. Byers, M. Frumin, G. Horn, M. Luby, M. Mitzenmacher, A. Roetter and W. Shaver. "FLID-DL: Congestion Control for Layered Multicast," Proceedings of NGC 2000, pages 71–81, November 2000.
12. S. Sarkar and L. Tassiulas, "Back Pressure Based Multicast Scheduling for Fair Bandwidth Allocation;" Proceedings of IEEE Infocom April, 2001
13. N. Shacham, "Multipoint communication by hierarchically encoded data," Proc. IEEE IN-FOCOM'92, pp. 2107-2114, May 1992.
14. R. Gopalakrishnan, J. Griffoen, G. Hjalmtysson, C. Sreenan, and S. Wen, "A Simple Loss Differentiation Approach to Layered Multicast," Proc. IEEE INFOCOM'00, Mar 2000.
15. M. Yajnik, J. Kuros and D. Towslcy, "Packet Loss Correlation in the MBone Multicast Network," In Proceedings of IEEE Global Internet, November 1996.

Random Early Detection Assisted Layered Multicast

Yung-Sze Gan and Chen-Khong Tham

Department of Electrical and Computer Engineering
National University of Singapore, Singapore 119260
{engp0515, eletck}@nus.edu.sg

Abstract. The deployment of the Random Early Detection (RED) algorithm in multicast routers can improve the performance of layered multicast congestion control schemes. In this paper, a new layered multicast protocol called RED Assisted Layered Multicast (RALM) is proposed to realise the integration of RED and layered multicast. It utilises the packet marking feature and two-level drop prioritisation capability in the Differentiated Services (DiffServ) architecture to differentiate losses in the layers of an RALM session. By marking the layers' packets appropriately and dropping them differently during congestion, the RALM protocol guides all receivers to a stable optimal subscription level that satisfies their common bandwidth requirement within a short period of time. Moreover, the DiffServ architecture permits the network administrator to control the amount of bandwidth consumed by RALM sessions through the deployment of suitable queue schedulers in the routers.

1 Introduction

The widespread employment of congestion control protocols like TCP in unicast IP networks has helped them to perform well in the face of ever increasing amount of traffic. Similarly, the success of multicast networks is dependent on the implementation of equivalent congestion control schemes. Possible candidates can be drawn from layered multicast protocols like Receiver-driven Layered Multicast (RLM) [1], Receiver-driven Layered Congestion Control (RLC) [2] and Packet Pair RLM (PLM) [3].

In layered multicast, a server encodes data into cumulative layers (i.e. a layer is decoded only if its lower layers are present) that are multicasted through separate addresses/ports. The clients adapt to their bottleneck bandwidths by subscribing to the maximum number of layers that can traverse the bottleneck links. A receiver discovers this subscription level by periodically simulating the addition of a layer to its current subscription. If the addition induces losses in its reception, it indicates that the receiver should not raise its current subscription level, and it has reached its optimal subscription level which fully utilises its bottleneck bandwidth. In current networks where droptail queues are deployed in the routers, losses occur because the queues are full and subsequent incoming packets are dropped. Thus, by the time the receivers detect and react to the

K.C. Almeroth and M. Hasan (Eds.): MMNS 2002, LNCS 2496, pp. 341–353, 2002.
© Springer-Verlag Berlin Heidelberg 2002

losses, congestion would have occurred for some time. The resulting loss rate is unnecessarily high. It would be ideal if the routers can signal to the receivers that congestion is approaching by dropping some packets before their queues are full, thus permitting the receivers to lower their subscription levels to avoid the congestion. This can be accomplished by using the Random Early Detection (RED) [4] algorithm to manage the queues in the routers.

A RED queue provides early congestion indications by randomly dropping packets when a certain proportion of the queue is filled. Thus, traffic sources can reduce their transmission rates before actual congestion occurs. The packet dropping probability is calculated based on the average queue length and not on the current queue length. Hence, a RED queue can tolerate some traffic bursts due to fluctuations in the transmission rates without dropping any packets. Moreover, the random packet drops are performed across all sessions passing through the router which helps to ensure that burst losses do not occur within any session. As RED queues are implemented in routers and are transparent to all congestion control schemes, they can work with any layered multicast protocol without requiring any modification.

The focus of this paper is on exploring the possibilities of realising layered multicast congestion control with the help of intermediate routers that implement RED queues. However, simply running the RLM protocol over a RED enabled network does not improve the protocol's performance. In section 2, we will look at why the RED algorithm by itself does not help the RLM protocol. In addition, the idea of using the RED algorithm to provide loss differentiation in a layered multicast scheme to improve its performance will be introduced. In section 3, a new layered multicast protocol, RED Assisted Layered Multicast (RALM) that uses loss differentiation in its operations will be presented. Finally, some simulation results on the RALM protocol will be presented and implications raised by the simulations will be discussed before this paper is concluded.

2   Loss Differentiation and Layered Multicast

The RLM protocol is known to exhibit some pathological behaviours [5] and the mechanisms underlying these behaviours would also interfere with the RED algorithm. They are described in the following list:

1. A receiver probes for spare bandwidth to consume by adding a new layer to its current subscription level in a join experiment. The experiment fails when a packet loss is detected by the receiver and the newly subscribed layer is dropped immediately. Obviously, deploying a RED queue in the bottleneck router benefits the RLM protocol by providing early congestion indication before the queue is saturated. However, the router does not immediately stop forwarding the dropped layer when it receives an IGMP [6] leave request from the receiver. The router must first ensure that the layer is not subscribed by other receivers through a query/timeout mechanism before executing the leave request. The resulting multicast leave latency can be long. As a result, the benefit of providing early congestion signals is lost.

2. A layered multicast session's transmission rate is adjusted by adding or dropping a layer. Normally, a layer carries a significant portion of the total traffic generated by the server. An increase in the subscription level can result in rapid depletion of the bottleneck router's RED queue due to a rapid increase in the traversing traffic. Coupled with the problem of long multicast leave latency, the probability of a RED queue degenerating into a droptail queue during join experiments is very high. Thus, operating the RLM protocol over a RED enabled network only improves its loss rate marginally.

3. An RLM receiver is said to have reached a stable state when its join timer is sufficiently long compared to the duration of a join experiment. In this state, the receiver transits to a hysteresis state when it detects a packet drop, and waits for a detection timer's period before measuring the loss rate. This unresponsive period may be long enough that the RED queue overflows. The loss rate sampled will thus be similar to that produced by a droptail queue. Moreover, the receiver does not react to early congestion signals. As a result, a new RLM session cannot grab sufficient bandwidth from a pre-existing session by conducting join experiments to achieve max-min fairness [7] in the bandwidth share. Therefore, enhancing the bottleneck router with a RED queue does not improve the inter-session fairness of the RLM protocol.

To ensure that the RLM protocol works well with the RED algorithm, it is essential to replace the concepts of join experiments and a high loss tolerant stable state with an alternative spare bandwidth probing method that reacts fast to early congestion indications through fine-grained layer transmission rate adjustments without jeopardising the stability of the protocol.

The basic idea of the RALM protocol is to group the layers within the session's optimal subscription level together and mark their packets with a high forwarding priority. Other layers that are beyond the optimal subscription level will have their packets marked with a low forwarding priority. As the bottleneck router forwards the high priority layers, called protected layers, at the expense of the low priority layers, the layers that constitute the optimal subscription level will be protected from losses induced by oversubscription or traffic fluctuations. These losses are absorbed by the low priority layers, known also as sacrificial layers. Since low priority packets received by the RALM receiver can be decoded, the loss absorption capability of sacrificial layers can be seen as a form of fine-grained layer transmission rate adjustment.

A receiver increases its subscription level based on two different loss rates sampled in its current subscription. These rates vary as RED queues drop packets to indicate looming congestion in the bottleneck router, making the RALM protocol highly sensitive to early congestion indications. The highest current subscribed layer is used to probe for new bandwidth by comparing its loss rate against a loss threshold for the receiver to decide whether to add a higher layer. On the otherhand, the aggregated loss rate sampled in all the lower subscribed layers is used by the receiver to decide whether to reduce its subscription level.

At startup, a receiver samples both loss rates from high priority layers as it has not reached the optimal subscription level yet. Thus, the loss rates are

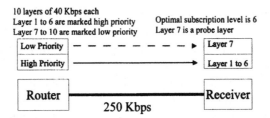

Fig. 1. The basic idea behind the RALM protocol

low and the receiver will increase its subscription level. The receiver raises its subscription level repeatedly until it subscribes a low priority layer. At this point, it has reached the optimal subscription level, excluding the low priority layer, as shown in Figure 1. The losses induced by the oversubscription of one layer will be concentrated in the low priority layer. Correspondingly, the loss rate in the layers that compose the optimal subscription level is very low, stabilising the subscription level by preventing any further layer addition or drop. If new bandwidth is available, the loss rate sampled in the subscribed low priority layer will drop below a loss threshold and the subscription level can be increased. No timer is set to probe for spare bandwidth as in join experiments. Due to the role of the highest current subscribed layer in the discovery of new bandwidth, it is called the probe layer in the RALM protocol.

The idea of applying two-level loss differentiation on layered multicast is not new. A similar concept is suggested by Gopalakrishnan et al. [8] in their Receiver-Selectable Loss Priorities (RSLP) and Receiver-driven Layered Multicast with Priorities (RLMP) protocols. In these protocols, the multicast routers are modified to support two-level drop priority in their forwarding path and the IGMP protocol is extended to permit the receiver to indicate the drop priority for each layer it subscribes. These modifications are not required in the RALM protocol. Instead, the drop priority is set by the server based on feedbacks provided by the receivers. The multicast routers simply forward the layers based on their packet markings. No intelligence is needed in the routers to determine the forwarding priority of the layers. The loss rate in the RLMP protocol is smoothed through the use of an exponential weighted moving average (EWMA). In contrast, the loss rate is used directly in the RALM protocol as it has already been smoothed by the RED algorithm operating in the routers. Finally, the loss thresholds used by receivers to decide subscription level adjustments are determined differently in the RLMP and RALM protocols.

3 RED Assisted Layered Mutlicast

In the RALM protocol, an algorithm that provides loss differentiated congestion control functionality is implemented in every receiver. This algorithm requires the cooperation of the server and routers in providing layer differentiation through the use of two-level priority packet marking and dropping mechanisms. A separate protocol that defines how the session sets the proper layer marking is required to permit the receivers to reach a fair and stable optimal subscription level. In this paper, the focus is on the receiver driven congestion control algorithm and not on the layer marking discovery protocol, which will be investigated in a later work.

3.1 Two-Level Drop Priority Support in IP Networks

The IETF has defined the Differentiated Services (DiffServ) architecture [9] and two per-hop forwarding behaviours (PHB) to provide packet service differentiation in current IP networks. Of the two defined PHBs, the assured forwarding (AF) PHB groups [10] provide 3 drop priority levels within 4 AF PHB classes. The AF PHB classes are implemented as four separate physical queues in a DiffServ router in addition to the best-effort droptail queue. The drop priorities in each AF class are in turn implemented as virtual queues in each AF queue through the use of a 3-level RED algorithm. By using a single AF PHB class (e.g. AF1x) and restricting the number of drop priority used to just two (e.g. AF11 and AF12), two-level loss differentiation can be realised in routers.

In an RALM session, the server generates and marks the layers' packets with either an AF11 or AF12 DiffServ codepoints (DSCP) before transmitting them into the network. RFC 2597 defines AF11 to have a higher forwarding priority than AF12. In other words, packets marked with AF12 DSCP are dropped in preference to packets marked with AF11 DSCP when congestion occurs. As stated earlier, how the server decides which layer to mark with which DSCP will not be discussed here. The DiffServ routers in the multicast tree simply forward the packets in each layer based on their DSCP.

Ideally, the layers within the optimal subscription level should be marked with AF11 while other layers are marked with AF12. However, the server may occasionally mark the layers improperly due to under- or over-estimation of the session's optimal subscription level. Improper layer markings also exist when there are multiple bottlenecks in the multicast tree through which different numbers of layers can traverse. In other words, different branches of the multicast tree have different optimal subscription levels and so require different layer markings. The inability of the layer marking to match the optimal subscription level would result in instability and unfairness in the RALM protocol's performance.

In the RALM protocol, all multicast packets are marked with an AF DSCP while the best-effort traffic is not marked at all (i.e. DSCP is zero). Therefore, the multicast traffic in the DiffServ network is segregated from best-effort traffic as they are served from different physical queues in the routers. Traffic segregation ensures that TCP flows which form part of the best-effort traffic are not buffered in the RED queues. Thus, it is not necessary to consider how the TCP flows will be affected by the RED parameters which are configured solely for the RALM protocol in the AF queues (it has been shown that setting proper RED parameters to allow TCP flows to work with different bandwidth adaptive flows is difficult [11]). The DiffServ router can partition the link bandwidth between the multicast and unicast traffic fairly through the use of a fair queuing scheduler.

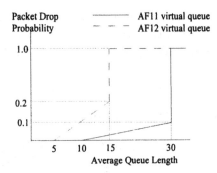

Fig. 2. The different RED parameter values used in the AF virtual queues

The RED parameters of the AF virtual queues are not configured based on any strict criterion. The only two requirements that must be kept in mind when choosing their values are that they must be close to the values recommended by the network community [4] [12] and that the AF12 queue must be penalised way before the AF11 queue when congestion occurs. In the RALM protocol, it is decided that the AF12 queue's drop thresholds must be shorter than that of the AF11 queue and its maximum drop probability must be higher than the corresponding parameter in the AF11 queue. The net result is that AF12 packets are dropped sooner and faster than AF11 packets when the router starts to experience queue buildup due to congestion. Figure 2 shows the queue thresholds and maximum drop probability that may be configured in the AF virtual queues.

3.2 Receiver-Driven Congestion Control Algorithm

The optimal subscription level of an RALM session is reached when two conditions are satisfied: 1. There are no excessive losses in the AF11 marked protected layers such that there is a need to decrease the current subscription level; 2. There are enough losses in the AF12 marked sacrificial layers to avoid subscribing more than one sacrificial layer. For a given bottleneck link shared by multiple sessions, the optimal subscription level of each session is achieved when they share the bandwidth in a max-min fair manner. Once the layer markings in an RALM session match its optimal subscription level, the receivers will be able to reach this level by adding layers until they receive the first sacrificial layer.

Basically, the receiver joins an RALM session by subscribing the minimal two layers and increases its subscription level by using its current highest subscribed layer as a probe layer. The loss rate sampled in the probe layer is compared to the layer add loss threshold

$$T_{add} = max_{add} - \delta_{add} \times l \tag{1}$$

where max_{add} is the maximum loss rate beyond which no new layer is added, δ_{add} is the separation between adjacent subscription levels' T_{add}, and l is the receiver's current subscription level. If the sampled loss rate is lower than this threshold, a new layer is added unless all layers in the session have been subscribed. The

aggregated loss rate sampled in the lower layers is compared to the layer drop
loss threshold

$$T_{drop} = max_{drop} - \delta_{drop} \times l \qquad (2)$$

where max_{drop} is the maximum loss rate beyond which all layers are dropped,
δ_{drop} is the separation between adjacent subscription levels' T_{drop}, and l is the
receiver's current subscription level. If the sampled loss rate is higher than this
threshold, the probe layer will be dropped unless the minimum subscription level
of two has been reached. The receiver samples the loss rates in current subscribed
layers using a 10 secs measurement window, which is sufficiently long to negate
the effect of the long IGMP leave latency.

When a receiver's subcription level is below the optimal level, all its subscribed layers are protected from congestion due to their AF11 marking. The
loss rate sampled in its probe layer will be lower than the current level's T_{add},
which is a good indication that there is sufficient bandwidth for the receiver
to increase its subscription level. To avoid a contradicting layer drop indication
by the aggregated loss rate in the lower layers, T_{add} is set below T_{drop} of each
subscription level as shown in Figure 3. Thus, the receiver adds a new layer to
its current subscription. This is continuously done until the receiver subscribes
a sacrificial layer. Since the optimal subscription level is near the bottleneck
bandwidth, adding the sacrificial layer causes the probe layer's loss rate to rise
drastically beyond the current level's T_{add}. However, the subscribed protected
layers' aggregated loss rate is still below the current level's T_{drop}. Now, the receiver has converged on the optimal subscription level, and will neither increase
nor decrease its subscription level. Conversely, if the receiver's subscription level
is above the optimal subscription level, part of the aggregated loss rate will be
sampled from sacrificial layers. Thus, the excessive losses in these layers will cause
the receiver to drop them as its current subscription level's T_{drop} is exceeded.

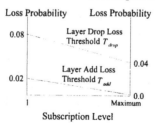

Fig. 3. The range of values that T_{add} and T_{drop} in an RALM session can take

Note that an RALM receiver converges on the optimal subscription level
by oversubscribing a sacrificial layer. The condition of convergence requires the
probe layer to suffer excessive losses while layers within the optimal subscription
level are protected from the ongoing congestion. Thus, the loss rate performance
of the RALM protocol is measured from the layers constituting the optimal
subscription level and excluding the probe layer. Whether to utilise the data
received in the probe layer is decided by individual receiver.

The degree of congestion in a bottleneck router is matched in the loss rate
curves sampled by all downstream receivers. The implicit sharing of loss rate

knowledge can help receivers in different RALM sessions to cooperate in the discovery of their optimal subscription levels that share the bottleneck bandwidth fairly. This cooperation is realised by scaling the T_{drop} and T_{add} with the subscription level. Thus, for two RALM sessions that stream the same number of layers, the session at a lower subscription level has a higher loss tolerance than the other session at a higher subscription level. Through the judicious use of layer markings, a new session can force an incumbent session to drop its subscription level by causing a lowering of the optimal subscription level that the competing session should converge on. This new optimal subscription level should represent the fair share of the network bandwidth between the RALM sessions.

4 Evaluations

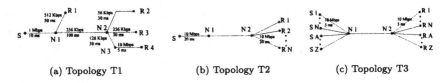

| (a) Topology T1 | (b) Topology T2 | (c) Topology T3 |

Fig. 4. Simulation topologies

Three scenarios are simulated using the three topologies shown in Figure 4 to study the performance of the RALM protocol. The sources and receivers are RALM nodes unless otherwise specified. N1, N2 and N3 are the DiffServ routers in the network. The bottleneck bandwidth is varied according to simulation scenarios but their transmission delays are fixed at 100 millisecs and 20 millisecs in topology T2 and T3 respectively. In all simulations, the RALM sources generate 10 equal size layers of 40 Kbps constant bit rate (CBR) traffic each. The simulation time is fixed at 1000 secs.

The congestion control algorithm in the RALM protocol is implemented in the *ns* simulator [13] that supports DiffServ mechanisms. The server generates a fixed number of layers for a multicast session and marks them with the appropriate DSCP before transmission. The optimal subscription level of the RALM session is assumed to be known before the start of the simulations. The server marks all layers within the optimal subscription level with AF11 DSCP and all higher layers with AF12 DSCP right from the start of the simulations. The layer markings are not changed for the duration of the simulations.

Protocol Independent Multicast Dense Mode (PIM-DM) [14] is used in the simulations. A two-level drop priority RED queue with its queue thresholds and max_p configured as in Figure 2 is implemented in the DiffServ routers alongside a 20 packets droptail queue for best-effort traffic. Their queue burst sensitivity weights are set to 0.02 and average packet size expected is 500 bytes. Since the layers in the RALM protocol are marked by the server and the routers forward packets based on their DSCP, the routers do not implement profile meters and policers. In the simulations, unicast traffic is not marked and thus is served through the droptail queues as best-effort traffic. A simple round robin scheduler serves the RED and droptail queues.

4.1 Accuracy and Stability

In Scenario 1, there is no single optimal subscription level that satisfies the bandwidth requirements of the receivers. Looking at the connecting bandwidth in topology T1, receiver R1 and R2 have extremely high and low bandwidth requirements respectively as R1's optimal subscription level is 10 (maximum possible level) and R2's optimal subscription level is 2 (minimum possible level). Receiver R3 and R4 have intermediate bandwidth requirements. As the layer markings are determined before the start of the simulations, two optimal subscription levels are picked separately (3 layers: 120 Kbps; and 6 layers: 240 Kbps) to meet the bandwidth requirement of receiver R4 (128 Kbps) and R3 (256 Kbps).

From the layer transition graphs of Figure 5, it can be seen that receiver R1 and R2 converge on their respective optimal subscription levels of 10 and 2 reasonably quickly and are able to maintain them during the session. Receiver R3 and R4 also converge on their respective optimal subscription levels of 6 and 3 reasonably quickly. But the subscription level is only stable if the source marks the layers correctly to match the optimal subscription level. Thus, receiver R4 has a stable subscription level in Figure 5(a) but finds that its subscription level fluctuates between layer 2 and 4 in Figure 5(b). Likewise, stable subscription level of receiver R3 is found only in Figure 5(b) but fluctuates between layer 6 and 7 in Figure 5(a). In both cases, the simulations illustrate the impossibility of having a session-wide optimal subscription level that satisfies the bandwidth requirements of all receivers in a heterogeneous network.

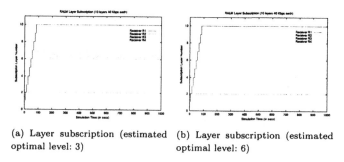

(a) Layer subscription (estimated optimal level: 3)   (b) Layer subscription (estimated optimal level: 6)

Fig. 5. Accuracy and stability of layer subscriptions in an RALM session

4.2 Intra-session Interactions

From Figure 6(c), it can be seen that 30 RALM receivers converge on the session-wide optimal subscription level of 5 (for bottleneck link bandwidth of 220 Kbps) rapidly regardless of their start time and number if the layer markings match this level accurately. The extra layer 6 that the receivers subscribed is the sacrificial layer that stabilises their subscription levels by absorbing most of the losses induced in the network as shown in Figure 6(d). This is a good example of the role of loss differentiation in guiding new receivers to the session-wide optimal subscription level. When a new receiver joins an RALM session, the low loss rates in the protected layers within the optimal subscription level encourages it to subscribe towards the level that has already been reached by earlier receivers. Once it reaches this level, the high loss rate in the sacrificial layer discourages it from further subscription.

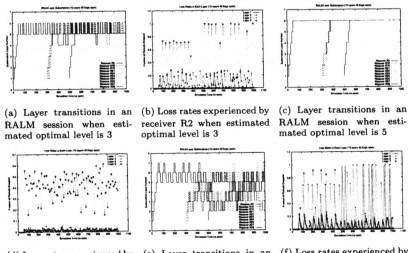

(a) Layer transitions in an RALM session when estimated optimal level is 3

(b) Loss rates experienced by receiver R2 when estimated optimal level is 3

(c) Layer transitions in an RALM session when estimated optimal level is 5

(d) Loss rates experienced by receiver R2 when estimated optimal level is 5

(e) Layer transitions in an RALM session when estimated optimal level is 7

(f) Loss rates experienced by receiver R2 when estimated optimal level is 7

Fig. 6. Effect of layer markings on an RALM session

Figure 6(a) shows that the receivers cannot maintain stable subscription levels when the layer markings underestimate the session-wide optimal subscription level. The subscription levels fluctuate between layer 5 and 6 with occasional dips to layer 4 but never drops to layer 3. This is expected as the lower 3 layers are protected by their high priority marking. Thus, the layers higher than the estimated subscription level of 3 suffer burst losses as shown in Figure 6(b) when a receiver oversubscribes. The losses induced are shared by sacrificial layers 4, 5 and 6 with no losses in the protected layers. As a result, no receiver is forced to drop its subscription level below the level estimated by the layer markings.

In contrast, the subscription levels of the receivers in an RALM session whose layer markings overestimate the bottleneck bandwidth fluctuate wildly as shown in Figure 6(e). This is because all layers that are subscribed by the receivers have the same forwarding priority. In other words, no loss differentiation exists to protect the lower layers from the effect of oversubscribing layer 6 and 7. Therefore, losses induced by the oversubscribed layers are shared by all layers as shown in Figure 6(f).

Comparing the simulation results, it can be concluded that it is preferable to underestimate than to overestimate the session-wide optimal subscription level. Underestimation does not provide the RALM receivers with a stable subscription level. But it at least protects the base layers from losses when oversubscription occurs. This is a desirable property when the base layers are significantly more important than higher layers as is the case in layered video applications.

4.3   Inter-session Interactions

In Scenario 3, 2 sets of simulations are conducted on topology T3 to investigate the RALM protocol's behaviour in the presence of other traffic types. In the first set of simulations, 3 RALM sessions simulated across a 700 Kbps bottleneck link are squeezed by a 400 Kbps CBR source from simulation time 500 secs to 600 secs. In the second set of simulations, one RALM session shares a 400 Kbps bottleneck link with two TCP sources that generate FTP packet streams.

When multiple RALM sessions operate within a network, they share the bottleneck bandwidth fairly by adopting a network-wide optimal subscription level. However, the layer markings of an individual session might underestimate or overestimate the network-wide optimal subscription level. To investigate these possibilities, 3 layer markings (optimal: 5, underestimate: 3, overestimate: 7) are configured in the first set of simulations. Likewise, a layer marking of 3 is configured in the RALM session for the second set of simulations, assuming that the RALM session is able to discover the subscription level for fair bandwidth share with the TCP sessions.

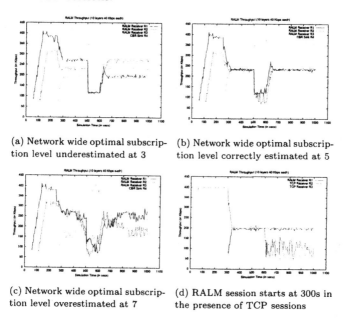

(a) Network wide optimal subscription level underestimated at 3

(b) Network wide optimal subscription level correctly estimated at 5

(c) Network wide optimal subscription level overestimated at 7

(d) RALM session starts at 300s in the presence of TCP sessions

Fig. 7. Throughput in RALM sessions in the presence of CBR traffic (7(a), 7(b) and 7(c)) and TCP traffic (7(d))

The throughput curves of RALM receivers shown in Figure 7 represent the individual session-wide optimal subscription levels achieved with the indicated layer markings in the presence of CBR or TCP traffic. Figure 7(b) shows that when the layer markings match the network-wide optimal subscription level, the RALM sessions are able to share the bottleneck bandwidth fairly regardless of the presence of the CBR traffic. In contrast, Figure 7(a) and 7(c) show that the RALM sessions do not receive their fair bandwidth share when the layer markings do not match this subscription level.

Underestimating layer markings discourage fair bandwidth share among competing RALM sessions. In fact, new sessions are disadvantaged in their ability to compete because they are prevented from increasing their subscription levels due to losses induced in their sacrificial layers by the actions of pre-existing sessions. On the other hand, overestimating layer markings cause all layers carried by the bottleneck link to be marked with the same priority. Thus, the base layers are not protected from losses induced by either the CBR traffic or an RALM session oversubscribing its fair bandwidth share. By not having a sacrificial layer in their subscriptions, the RALM sessions cannot enter a stable state.

In Figure 7, it is observed that the best-effort CBR traffic cannot reach its configured 400 Kbps rate. This is because the CBR traffic is served through a separate physical queue from the multicast traffic. The simple round robin scheduler that serves the queues partitions the bottleneck bandwidth equally between the AF marked multicast traffic and the best-effort unicast traffic. Thus, a traffic type has a minimum bandwidth of 350 Kbps that is protected from congestion caused by the other traffic type. This phenomenon is also observed in Figure 7(d) where the RALM session is able to grab its fair bandwidth share and is protected from any change in the TCP traffic.

The segregation of RALM traffic from other traffic types offers the network administrator the ability to limit multicast bandwidth consumption by configuring a weighted queue scheduler appropriately. Thus, a rogue multicast session that does not implement any congestion control scheme will not be able to congest competing best-effort traffic sharing the same router. An additional advantage of traffic segregation is that the network administrator can configure the AF queue's RED parameters without affecting TCP performance. This should make it easier to deploy the RALM protocol in current IP networks.

5   Conclusion

The RALM protocol that provides layered multicast congestion control through the use of loss differentiation is presented in this paper. A series of simulations have shown that receivers in an RALM session converge accurately, rapidly and stably on the session-wide optimal subscription level when the layer markings match this level in a homogeneous network. And the RALM protocol scales with the session size and provides excellent inter-session bandwidth fairness when all sessions mark their layers to match the network-wide subscription level. Unfortunately, in a heterogeneous network where a single optimal subscription level cannot be found to satisfy varied receivers' bandwidth requirements, some receivers will not be able to maintain stable subscription levels even though they may receive a throughput close to their bandwidth requirements. In such cases, it is preferable for the layer markings to underestimate the bandwidth requirements so that the base layers received by the mismatched receivers are protected from any losses induced by their frequent oversubscriptions. Finally, the proportion of network bandwidth consumed by RALM traffic with respect to best-effort traffic can be adjusted by deploying weighted schedulers to serve the queues. Since the RALM traffic is segregated from the best-effort traffic, the AF queues' RED parameters in the RALM protocol can be configured without affecting the TCP performance of a best-effort session.

To actually deploy the RALM protocol in a DiffServ network, the servers in the sessions must discover the layer markings that will provide the network-wide optimal subscription level. Therefore, a layer marking discovery protocol that receivers can use to estimate their optimal subscription levels and communicate these estimates back to the servers for actual layer markings is required. The actual scheme to be used in this protocol will be investigated in the future.

References

1. S. McCanne, V. Jabcobson, and M. Vetterli, "Receiver-driven Layered Multicast", in Proc. ACM SIGCOMM '96, Stanford, CA, Aug. 1996, pp. 117-130
2. L. Vicisano, L. Rizzo, and J. Crowcroft, "TCP-like Congestion Control for Layered Multicast Data Transfer", in Proc. IEEE INFOCOM '98, San Francisco, CA, Mar. 1998, pp. 996-1003
3. A. Legout and E. W. Biersack, "PLM: Fast Convergence for Cumulative Layered Multicast Transmission Schemes", in Proc. ACM SIGMETRICS '00, Santa Clara, CA, June 2000
4. S. Floyd and V. Jacobson, "Random Early Detection Gateways for Congestion Avoidance", IEEE/ACM Transactions on Networking, V.1 N.4, Aug. 1993, pp. 397-413
5. A. Legout and E. W. Biersack, "Pathological Behaviors for RLM and RLC", in Proc. NOSSDAV '00, Chapel Hill, NC, June 2000
6. W. Fenner, "Internet Group Management Protocol, Version 2", RFC 2236, IETF, Nov. 1997
7. D. Rubenstein, J. Kurose, and D. Towsley, "The Impact of Multicast Layering on Network Fairness", in Proc. ACM SIGCOMM '99, Sept. 1999, pp 27-38
8. R. Gopalakrishnan, J. Griffioen, G. Hjalmtysson, C. Sreenan and S. Wen, "A Simple Loss Differentiation Approach to Layered Multicast", in Proc. IEEE INFOCOM '00, Tel Aviv, Israel, Mar. 2000
9. S. Blake, D. Black, M. Carlson, E. Davies, Z. Wang and W. Weiss, "An Architecture for Differentiated Services", RFC 2475, IETF, Dec. 1998
10. J. Heinanen, F. Baker, W. Weiss and J. Wroclawski, "Assured Forwarding PHB Group", RFC 2597, IETF, June 1999
11. D. Lin and R. Morris, "Dynamics of Random Early Detection", in Proc. ACM SIGCOMM '97, Cannes, France, Oct. 1997, pp. 127-137
12. S. Floyd, various notes on RED, http://www.aciri.org/floyd/red.html
13. NS2, Network Simulator - ns-allinone-2.1b8a, LBL / Xerox PARC / UCB / ISI, http://www.isi.edu/nsnam/ns
14. S. Deering, D. Estrin, D. Farinacci, V. Jacobson, A. Helmy, D. Meyer, and L. Wei, "Protocol Independent Multicast Version 2 Dense Mode Specification (PIM-DM)", work in progress, IETF, Nov. 1998

Author Index

Lecture Notes in Computer Science

For information about Vols. 1–2404
please contact your bookseller or Springer-Verlag

Vol. 2439: J.J. Merelo Guervós, P. Adamidis, H.-G. Beyer, J.-L. Fernández-Villacañas, H.-P. Schwefel (Eds.), Parallel Problem Solving from Nature – PPSN VII. Proceedings, 2002. XXII, 947 pages. 2002.

Vol. 2440: J.M. Haake, J.A. Pino (Eds.), Groupware: Design, Implementation and Use. Proceedings, 2002. XII, 285 pages. 2002.

Vol. 2441: Z. Hu, M. Rodríguez-Artalejo (Eds.), Functional and Logic Programming. Proceedings, 2002. X, 305 pages. 2002.

Vol. 2442: M. Yung (Ed.), Advances in Cryptology – CRYPTO 2002. Proceedings, 2002. XIV, 627 pages. 2002.

Vol. 2443: D. Scott (Ed.), Artificial Intelligence: Methodology, Systems, and Applications. Proceedings, 2002. X, 279 pages. 2002. (Subseries LNAI).

Vol. 2444: A. Buchmann, F. Casati, L. Fiege, M.-C. Hsu, M.-C. Shan (Eds.), Technologies for E-Services. Proceedings, 2002. X, 171 pages. 2002.

Vol. 2445: C. Anagnostopoulou, M. Ferrand, A. Smaill (Eds.), Music and Artificial Intelligence. Proceedings, 2002. VIII, 207 pages. 2002. (Subseries LNAI).

Vol. 2446: M. Klusch, S. Ossowski, O. Shehory (Eds.), Cooperative Information Agents VI. Proceedings, 2002. XI, 321 pages. 2002. (Subseries LNAI).

Vol. 2447: D.J. Hand, N.M. Adams, R.J. Bolton (Eds.), Pattern Detection and Discovery. Proceedings, 2002. XII, 227 pages. 2002. (Subseries LNAI).

Vol. 2448: P. Sojka, I. Kopeček, K. Pala (Eds.), Text, Speech and Dialogue. Proceedings, 2002. XII, 481 pages. 2002. (Subseries LNAI).

Vol. 2449: L. Van Gool (Ed.), Pattern Recognotion. Proceedings, 2002. XVI, 628 pages. 2002.

Vol. 2451: B. Hochet, A.J. Acosta, M.J. Bellido (Eds.), Integrated Circuit Design. Proceedings, 2002. XVI, 496 pages. 2002.

Vol. 2452: R. Guigó, D. Gusfield (Eds.), Algorithms in Bioinformatics. Proceedings, 2002. X, 554 pages. 2002.

Vol. 2453: A. Hameurlain, R. Cicchetti, R. Traunmüller (Eds.), Database and Expert Systems Applications. Proceedings, 2002. XVIII, 951 pages. 2002.

Vol. 2454: Y. Kambayashi, W. Winiwarter, M. Arikawa (Eds.), Data Warehousing and Knowledge Discovery. Proceedings, 2002. XIII, 339 pages. 2002.

Vol. 2455: K. Bauknecht, A M. Tjoa, G. Quirchmayr (Eds.), E-Commerce and Web Technologies. Proceedings, 2002. XIV, 414 pages. 2002.

Vol. 2456: R. Traunmüller, K. Lenk (Eds.), Electronic Government. Proceedings, 2002. XIII, 486 pages. 2002.

Vol. 2458: M. Agosti, C. Thanos (Eds.), Research and Advanced Technology for Digital Libraries. Proceedings, 2002. XVI, 664 pages. 2002.

Vol. 2459: M.C. Calzarossa, S. Tucci (Eds.), Performance Evaluation of Complex Systems: Techniques and Tools. Proceedings, 2002. VIII, 501 pages. 2002.

Vol. 2460: J.-M. Jézéquel, H. Hussmann, S. Cook (Eds.), «UML» 2002 – The Unified Modeling Language. Proceedings, 2002. XII, 449 pages. 2002.

Vol. 2461: R. Möhring, R. Raman (Eds.), Algorithms – ESA 2002. Proceedings, 2002. XIV, 917 pages. 2002.

Vol. 2462: K. Jansen, S. Leonardi, V. Vazirani (Eds.), Approximation Algorithms for Combinatorial Optimization. Proceedings, 2002. VIII, 271 pages. 2002.

Vol. 2463: M. Dorigo, G. Di Caro, M. Sampels (Eds.), Ant Algorithms. Proceedings, 2002. XIII, 305 pages. 2002.

Vol. 2464: M. O'Neill, R.F.E. Sutcliffe, C. Ryan, M. Eaton, N. Griffith (Eds.), Artificial Intelligence and Cognitive Science. Proceedings, 2002. XI, 247 pages. 2002. (Subseries LNAI).

Vol. 2465: H. Arisawa, Y. Kambayashi (Eds.), Conceptual Modeling for New Information Systems Technologies. Proceedings, 2001. XVII, 500 pages. 2002.

Vol. 2469: W. Damm, E.-R. Olderog (Eds.), Formal Techniques in Real-Time and Fault-Tolerant Systems. Proceedings, 2002. X, 455 pages. 2002.

Vol. 2470: P. Van Hentenryck (Ed.), Principles and Practice of Constraint Programming – CP 2002. Proceedings, 2002. XVI, 794 pages. 2002.

Vol. 2471: J. Bradfield (Ed.), Computer Science Logic. Proceedings, 2002. XII, 613 pages. 2002.

Vol. 2475: J.J. Alpigini, J.F. Peters, A. Skowron, N. Zhong (Eds.), Rough Sets and Current Trends in Computing. Proceedings, 2002. XV, 640 pages. 2002. (Subseries LNAI).

Vol. 2476: A.H.F. Laender, A.L. Oliveira (Eds.), String Processing and Information Retrieval. Proceedings, 2002. XI, 337 pages. 2002.

Vol. 2477: M.V. Hermenegildo, G. Puebla (Eds.), Static Analysis. Proceedings, 2002. XI, 527 pages. 2002.

Vol. 2478: M.J. Egenhofer, D.M. Mark (Eds.), Geographic Information Science. Proceedings, 2002. X, 363 pages. 2002.

Vol. 2479: M. Jarke, J. Koehler, G. Lakemeyer (Eds.), KI 2002: Advances in Artificial Intelligence. Proceedings, 2002. XIII, 327 pages. (Subseries LNAI).

Vol. 2480: Y. Han, S. Tai, D. Wikarski (Eds.), Engineering and Deployment of Cooperative Information Systems. Proceedings, 2002. XIII, 564 pages. 2002.

Vol. 2483: J.D.P. Rolim, S. Vadhan (Eds.), Randomization and Approximation Techniques in Computer Science. Proceedings, 2002. VIII, 275 pages. 2002.

Vol. 2484: P. Adriaans, H. Fernau, M. van Zaanen (Eds.), Grammatical Inference: Algorithms and Applications. Proceedings, 2002. IX, 315 pages. 2002. (Subseries LNAI).

Vol. 2488: T. Dohi, R. Kikinis (Eds), Medical Image Computing and Computer-Assisted Intervention – MICCAI 2002. Proceedings, Part I. XXIX, 807 pages. 2002.

Vol. 2489: T. Dohi, R. Kikinis (Eds), Medical Image Computing and Computer-Assisted Intervention – MICCAI 2002. Proceedings, Part II. XXIX, 693 pages. 2002.

Vol. 2496: K.C. Almeroth, M. Hasan (Eds.), Management of Multimedia in the Internet. Proceedings, 2002. XI, 355 pages. 2002.

Vol. 2498: G. Borriello, L.E. Holmquist (Eds.), UbiComp 2002: Ubiquitous Computing. Proceedings, 2002. XV, 380 pages. 2002.